# For Reference

Do Not Take From the Library

# Mental Health Disorders

## Disorders

# SOURCEBOOK

*Sixth Edition*

## Health Reference Series

*Sixth Edition*

# Mental Health Disorders
## SOURCEBOOK

*Basic Consumer Health Information about Healthy Brain Functioning and Mental Illnesses, Including Depression, Bipolar Disorder, Anxiety Disorders, Posttraumatic Stress Disorder, Obsessive-Compulsive Disorder, Psychotic and Personality Disorders, Eating Disorders, Compulsive Hoarding Disorder, and More*

*Along with Information about Medications and Treatments, Mental Health Concerns in Specific Groups, Such as Children, Adolescents, Older Adults, Minority Populations, and LGBT Community, a Glossary of Related Terms, and Directories of Resources for Additional Help and Information*

## OMNIGRAPHICS

615 Griswold, Ste. 901, Detroit, MI 48226

Bibliographic Note
Because this page cannot legibly accommodate all the copyright notices, the Bibliographic
Note portion of the Preface constitutes an extension of the copyright notice.

\* \* \*

Omnigraphics, Inc.
Editorial Services provided by Omnigraphics, Inc.,
a division of Relevant Information, LLC

Keith Jones, *Managing Editor*

\* \* \*

Library of Congress Cataloging-in-Publication Data

Names: Omnigraphics, Inc., issuing body.

Title: Mental health disorders sourcebook : basic consumer health information
about healthy brain functioning and mental illnesses, including depression, bipolar
disorder, anxiety disorders, posttraumatic stress disorder, obsessive-compulsive
disorder, psychotic and personality disorders, eating disorders, impulse control
disorders, and more; along with information about medications and treatments,
mental health concerns in specific groups, such as children, adolescents, older
adults, minority populations, and people in poverty, a glossary of related terms,
and directories of resources for additional help and information.

Description: Sixth edition. | Detroit, MI : Omnigraphics, Inc., [2016] | Series:
Health reference series | Includes bibliographical references and index.

Identifiers: LCCN 2016007846| ISBN 9780780814844 (hardcover : alk. paper) |
ISBN 9780780814837 (ebook)

Subjects: LCSH: Mental illness. | Psychiatry.

Classification: LCC RC454.4 .M458 2016 | DDC 616.89--dc23

LC record available at http://lccn.loc.gov/2016007846

This book is printed on acid-free paper meeting the ANSI Z39.48 Standard. The infinity
symbol that appears above indicates that the paper in this book meets that standard.

Printed in the United States

# Table of Contents

## Part II: Mental Illnesses

## Part III: Mental Health Treatments

## Part IV: Pediatric Mental Health Concerns

## Part V: Other Populations with Distinctive Mental Health Concerns

## Part VII: Living with Mental Health Disorders

## Part VIII: Additional Help and Information

# *Preface*

## *About This Book*

Mental health encompasses thoughts, actions, and feelings. Mentally healthy individuals are able to cope with life's challenges, handle stressful situations, deal with anger, maintain meaningful relationships with others, and enjoy life. Despite the benefits, maintaining a healthy mind is not always possible, and mental disorders are common. According to statistics compiled by the Substance Abuse and Mental Health Services Administration, an estimated 43.6 million (18.1%) Americans ages 18 and up experienced some form of mental illness.

*Mental Health Sourcebook*, Sixth Edition, discusses how the brain works, the components of mental wellness, and the processes that lead to illness. It offers information about the major types of mental illness and their treatments, including affective disorders, anxiety disorders, psychotic disorders, personality disorders, and disorders that impact behavior, including impulse control disorders, addictions, and eating disorders. A special section looks at pediatric issues in mental health and another examines the distinctive concerns of other specific populations. Information is also included about the relationship between mental health and chronic illnesses, such as cancer, epilepsy, heart disease, pain, and sleep disorders. The book concludes with a glossary of mental health terms, a list of crisis hotlines, and a directory of mental health organizations.

## How to Use This Book

This book is divided into parts and chapters. Parts focus on broad areas of interest. Chapters are devoted to single topics within a part.

*Part One: The Brain and Mental Health* explains the components of healthy brain functioning and the processes that can go awry leading to mental illness. It also discusses lifestyle and other factors that can help develop and reinforce mental wellness.

*Part Two: Mental Illnesses* begins with information about the link between suicide and mental illness and facts about suicide risks and prevention. It goes on to describe the various classifications of mental health disorders, including depressive and other affective disorders, anxiety disorders, psychotic disorders, personality disorders, and other disorders that impact behavior.

*Part Three: Mental Health Treatments* addresses the different ways mental health disorders are diagnosed and treated. It offers guidelines for identifying mental health emergencies, explains the services available from different types of mental health professionals, and discusses medications used to help control symptoms of mental illness. The part concludes with a chapter about complementary and alternative medicine for mental health care, which includes facts about dietary, physical, and spiritual therapies.

*Part Four: Pediatric Mental Health Concerns* describes the special issues that arise when children and teens have psychiatric needs. It offers specific details about some of the most commonly occurring mental health issues among young people, including attention deficit hyperactivity disorder, autism spectrum disorder, bipolar disorder, depression, and learning disabilities.

*Part Five: Other Populations with Distinctive Mental Health Concerns* addresses concerns among men, women, older adults, and other groups for whom special considerations may impact mental wellness. These include people dealing with the psychological impact of prejudice and discrimination, trauma or disaster, cultural isolation, and poverty.

*Part Six: Mental Illness Co-Occurring with Other Disorders* explains the ways physical conditions can sometimes affect psychological well-being. It discusses specific disorders commonly associated with changes in mental health status, including cancer, diabetes, epilepsy, AIDS, heart disease, and stroke. It also addresses issues related to sleep disorders and mental functioning, and it examines the complex relationship between mental health and the experience of pain.

*Part Seven: Living with Mental Health Disorders* discusses practices that people with mental health problems can follow for their well-being. It also discusses the role educators and community and faith leaders can play in assisting those with mental health disorders. The part concludes with information on Medicare and the health care benefits available to those suffering from mental illness.

*Part Eight: Additional Help and Information* provides a glossary of mental health terms, a list of toll-free helplines and hotlines for people in crisis, and a directory of mental health organizations.

## Bibliographic Note

This volume contains documents and excerpts from publications issued by the following U.S. government agencies: Administration on Aging (AOA); Agency for Healthcare Research and Quality (AHRQ); Centers for Disease Control and Prevention (CDC); Defense Health Agency (DHA); National Cancer Institute (NCI); National Center for Complementary and Integrative Health (NCCIH); National Heart, Lung, and Blood Institute (NHLBI); National Institute of Child Health and Human Development (NICHD); National Institute of Diabetes and Digestive and Kidney Diseases (NIDDK); National Institute of Mental Health (NIMH); National Institute of Neurological Disorders and Stroke (NINDS); National Institute on Drug Abuse (NIDA); National Institutes of Health (NIH); National Park Service (NPS); Office on Women's Health (OWH); Substance Abuse and Mental Health Services Administration (SAMHSA); The Nemours Foundation, U.S. Department of Health and Human Services (HHS); U.S. Department of Veterans Affairs (VA); U.S. Office of Personnel Management (OPM); and U.S. Public Health Service (USPHS).

In addition, this volume contains copyrighted documents from the following organization: The Nemours Foundation.

## About the Health Reference Series

The *Health Reference Series* is designed to provide basic medical information for patients, families, caregivers, and the general public. Each volume takes a particular topic and provides comprehensive coverage. This is especially important for people who may be dealing with a newly diagnosed disease or a chronic disorder in themselves or in a family member. People looking for preventive guidance, information about disease warning signs, medical statistics, and risk factors for health problems will also find answers to their questions in the *Health Reference Series*. The *Series*, however, is not intended to serve as a tool for diagnosing illness, in prescribing treatments, or as a substitute for the physician/patient relationship. All people concerned about medical symptoms or the possibility of disease are encouraged to seek professional care from an appropriate health care provider.

## A Note about Spelling and Style

*Health Reference Series* editors use *Stedman's Medical Dictionary* as an authority for questions related to the spelling of medical terms and the *Chicago Manual of Style* for questions related to grammatical structures, punctuation, and other editorial concerns. Consistent adherence is not always possible, however, because the individual volumes within the *Series* include many documents from a wide variety of different producers, and the editor's primary goal is to present material from each source as accurately as is possible. This sometimes means that information in different chapters or sections may follow other guidelines and alternate spelling authorities.

## Medical Review

Omnigraphics contracts with a team of qualified, senior medical professionals who serve as medical consultants for the *Health Reference Series*. As necessary, medical consultants review reprinted and originally written material for currency and accuracy. Citations including the phrase, "Reviewed (month, year)" indicate material reviewed by this team. Medical consultation services are provided to the *Health Reference Series* editors by:

Dr. Vijayalakshmi, MBBS, DGO, MD
Dr. Senthil Selvan, MBBS, DCH, MD

## Our Advisory Board

We would like to thank the following board members for providing initial guidance on the development of this series:

- Dr. Lynda Baker, Associate Professor of Library and Information Science, Wayne State University, Detroit, MI

- Nancy Bulgarelli, William Beaumont Hospital Library, Royal Oak, MI

- Karen Imarisio, Bloomfield Township Public Library, Bloomfield Township, MI

- Karen Morgan, Mardigian Library, University of Michigan-Dearborn, Dearborn, MI

- Rosemary Orlando, St. Clair Shores Public Library, St. Clair Shores, MI

## Health Reference Series *Update Policy*

The inaugural book in the *Health Reference Series* was the first edition of *Cancer Sourcebook* published in 1989. Since then, the *Series* has been enthusiastically received by librarians and in the medical community. In order to maintain the standard of providing high-quality health information for the layperson the editorial staff at Omnigraphics felt it was necessary to implement a policy of updating volumes when warranted.

Medical researchers have been making tremendous strides, and it is the purpose of the *Health Reference Series* to stay current with the most recent advances. Each decision to update a volume is made on an individual basis. Some of the considerations include how much new information is available and the feedback we receive from people who use the books. If there is a topic you would like to see added to the update list, or an area of medical concern you feel has not been adequately addressed, please write to:

Managing Editor
*Health Reference Series*
Omnigraphics, Inc.
615 Griswold, Ste. 901
Detroit, MI 48226

# Part One

# The Brain and Mental Health

# Chapter 1

# *Mental Health Begins with Healthy Brain Functions*

## *Chapter Contents*

Section 1.1

# Brain Basics

This section includes excerpts from "Brain Basics,"
National Institute of Mental Health (NIMH), May 6, 2011.
Reviewed March 2016; and text from "Brain Basics:
Know Your Brain," National Institute of Neurological
Disorders and Stroke (NINDS), April 17, 2015.

## Introduction

Mental disorders are common. You may have a friend, colleague, or relative with a mental disorder, or perhaps you have experienced one yourself at some point. Such disorders include depression, anxiety disorders, bipolar disorder, attention deficit hyperactivity disorder (ADHD), and many others.

Some people who develop a mental illness may recover completely; others may have repeated episodes of illness with relatively stable periods in between. Still others live with symptoms of mental illness every day. They can be moderate, or serious and cause severe disability.

Through research, we know that mental disorders are brain disorders. Evidence shows that they can be related to changes in the anatomy, physiology, and chemistry of the nervous system. When the brain cannot effectively coordinate the billions of cells in the body, the results can affect many aspects of life.

Scientists are continually learning more about how the brain grows and works in healthy people, and how normal brain development and function can go awry, leading to mental illnesses.

## The Growing Brain

### Inside the Brain: Neurons and Neural Circuits

Neurons are the basic working unit of the brain and nervous system. These cells are highly specialized for the function of conducting messages.

A neuron has three basic parts:

1. Cell body, which includes the nucleus, cytoplasm, and cell organelles. The nucleus contains DNA and information that the cell needs for growth, metabolism, and repair. Cytoplasm is the substance that fills a cell, including all the chemicals and parts needed for the cell to work properly including small structures called cell organelles.

2. Dendrites branch off from the cell body and act as a neuron's point of contact for receiving chemical and electrical signals called impulses from neighboring neurons.

3. Axon, which sends impulses and extends from cell bodies to meet and deliver impulses to another nerve cell. Axons can range in length from a fraction of an inch to several feet.

Each neuron is enclosed by a cell membrane, which separates the inside contents of the cell from its surrounding environment and controls what enters and leaves the cell, and responds to signals from the environment; this all helps the cell maintain its balance with the environment.

Synapses are tiny gaps between neurons, where messages move from one neuron to another as chemical or electrical signals.

The brain begins as a small group of cells in the outer layer of a developing embryo. As the cells grow and differentiate, neurons travel from a central "birthplace" to their final destination. Chemical signals from other cells guide neurons in forming various brain structures. Neighboring neurons make connections with each other and with distant nerve cells (via axons) to form brain circuits. These circuits control specific body functions such as sleep and speech.

The brain continues maturing well into a person's early 20s. Knowing how the brain is wired and how the normal brain's structure develops and matures helps scientists understand what goes wrong in mental illnesses.

Scientists have already begun to chart how the brain develops over time in healthy people and are working to compare that with brain development in people mental disorders. Genes and environmental cues both help to direct this growth.

## The Changing Brain—Effects of Genes and the Environment

There are many different types of cells in the body. We say that cells differentiate as the embryo develops, becoming more specialized

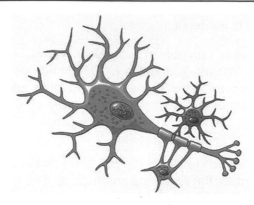

**Figure 1.1.** *Neuron*

for specific functions. Skin cells protect, muscle cells contract, and neurons, the most highly specialized cells of all, conduct messages.

Every cell in our bodies contains a complete set of DNA. DNA, the "recipe of life," contains all the information inherited from our parents that helps to define who we are, such as our looks and certain abilities, such as a good singing voice. A gene is a segment of DNA that contains codes to make proteins and other important body chemicals. DNA also includes information to control which genes are expressed and when, in all the cells of the body.

As we grow, we create new cells, each with a copy of our original set of DNA. Sometimes this copying process is imperfect, leading to a gene mutation that causes the gene to code for a slightly different protein. Some mutations are harmless, some can be helpful, and others give rise to disabilities or diseases.

Genes aren't the only determinants of how our bodies function. Throughout our lives, our genes can be affected by the environment. In medicine, the term environment includes not only our physical surroundings but also factors that can affect our bodies, such as sleep, diet, or stress. These factors may act alone or together in complex ways, to change the way a gene is expressed or the way messages are conducted in the body.

Epigenetics is the study of how environmental factors can affect how a given gene operates. But unlike gene mutations, epigenetic changes do not change the code for a gene. Rather, they effect when a gene turns on or off to produce a specific protein. Scientists believe epigenetics play a major role in mental disorders and the effects of medications. Some, but not all mutations and epigenetic changes can be passed on to future generations.

Further understanding of genes and epigenetics may one day lead to genetic testing for people at risk for mental disorders. This could greatly help in early detection, more tailored treatments, and possibly prevention of such illnesses.

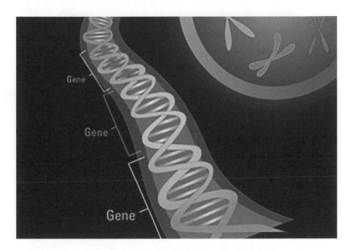

**Figure 1.2.** *Effects of Genes and the Environment*

## The Working Brain

### Neurotransmitters

Everything we do relies on neurons communicating with one another. Electrical impulses and chemical signals carrying messages across different parts of the brain and between the brain and the rest of the nervous system. When a neuron is activated a small difference in electrical charge occurs. This unbalanced charge is called an action potential and is caused by the concentration of ions (atoms or molecules with unbalanced charges) across the cell membrane. The action potential travels very quickly along the axon, like when a line of dominoes falls.

When the action potential reaches the end of an axon, most neurons release a chemical message (a neurotransmitter) which crosses the synapse and binds to receptors on the receiving neuron's dendrites and starts the process over again. At the end of the line, a neurotransmitter may stimulate a different kind of cell (like a gland cell), or may trigger a new chain of messages.

Neurotransmitters send chemical messages between neurons. Mental illnesses, such as depression, can occur when this process does not work correctly. Communication between neurons can also be electrical, such as in areas of the brain that control movement. When electrical signals are abnormal, they can cause tremors or symptoms found in Parkinson disease.

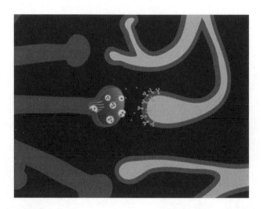

**Figure 1.3.** *Neurotransmitters*

*The following are some of the common neurotransmitters:*

- Serotonin—helps control many functions, such as mood, appetite, and sleep. Research shows that people with depression often have lower than normal levels of serotonin. The types of medications most commonly prescribed to treat depression act by blocking the recycling, or reuptake, of serotonin by the sending neuron. As a result, more serotonin stays in the synapse for the receiving neuron to bind onto, leading to more normal mood functioning.

- Dopamine—mainly involved in controlling movement and aiding the flow of information to the front of the brain, which is linked to thought and emotion. It is also linked to reward systems in the brain. Problems in producing dopamine can result in Parkinson disease, a disorder that affects a person's ability to move as they want to, resulting in stiffness, tremors or shaking, and other symptoms. Some studies suggest that having too little dopamine or problems using dopamine in the thinking and feeling regions of the brain may play a role in disorders like schizophrenia or attention deficit hyperactivity disorder (ADHD).

- Glutamate—the most common neurotransmitter, glutamate has many roles throughout the brain and nervous system. Glutamate is an excitatory transmitter: when it is released it

8

increases the chance that the neuron will fire. This enhances the electrical flow among brain cells required for normal function and plays an important role during early brain development. It may also assist in learning and memory. Problems in making or using glutamate have been linked to many mental disorders, including autism, obsessive compulsive disorder (OCD), schizophrenia, and depression.

## Brain Regions

Just as many neurons working together form a circuit, many circuits working together form specialized brain systems. We have many specialized brain systems that work across specific brain regions to help us talk, help us make sense of what we see, and help us to solve a problem. Some of the regions most commonly studied in mental health research are listed below.

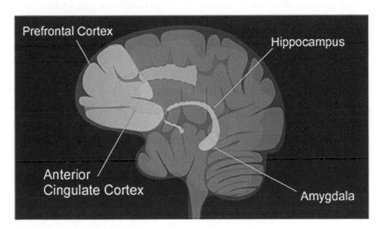

**Figure 1.4.** *Brain Regions*

- **Amygdala**—The brain's "fear hub," which activates our natural "fight-or-flight" response to confront or escape from a dangerous situation. The amygdala also appears to be involved in learning to fear an event, such as touching a hot stove, and learning not to fear, such as overcoming a fear of spiders. Studying how the amygdala helps create memories of fear and safety may help improve treatments for anxiety disorders like phobias or post-traumatic stress disorder (PTSD).

- **Prefrontal cortex (PFC)**—Seat of the brain's executive functions, such as judgment, decision making, and problem solving.

9

Different parts of the PFC are involved in using short-term or "working" memory and in retrieving long-term memories. This area of the brain also helps to control the amygdala during stressful events. Some research shows that people who have PTSD or ADHD have reduced activity in their PFCs.

- **Anterior Cingulate Cortex (ACC)**— the ACC has many different roles, from controlling blood pressure and heart rate to responding when we sense a mistake, helping us feel motivated and stay focused on a task, and managing proper emotional reactions. Reduced ACC activity or damage to this brain area has been linked to disorders such as ADHD, schizophrenia, and depression.

- **Hippocampus**—Helps create and file new memories. When the hippocampus is damaged, a person can't create new memories, but can still remember past events and learned skills, and carry on a conversation, all which rely on different parts of the brain. The hippocampus may be involved in mood disorders through its control of a major mood circuit called the hypothalamic-pituitary-adrenal (HPA) axis.

## The Architecture of the Brain

The brain is like a committee of experts. All the parts of the brain work together, but each part has its own special properties. The brain can be divided into three basic units: the forebrain, the midbrain, and the hindbrain.

The hindbrain includes the upper part of the spinal cord, the brain stem, and a wrinkled ball of tissue called the cerebellum. The hindbrain controls the body's vital functions such as respiration and heart rate. The cerebellum coordinates movement and is involved in learned rote movements. When you play the piano or hit a tennis ball you are activating the cerebellum. The uppermost part of the brainstem is the midbrain, which controls some reflex actions and is part of the circuit involved in the control of eye movements and other voluntary movements. The forebrain is the largest and most highly developed part of the human brain: it consists primarily of the cerebrum and the structures hidden beneath it. When people see pictures of the brain it is usually the cerebrum that they notice. The cerebrum sits at the top most part of the brain and is the source of intellectual activities. It holds your memories, allows you to plan, enables you to imagine and think. It allows you to recognize friends, read books, and play games.

The cerebrum is split into two halves (hemispheres) by a deep fissure. Despite the split, the two cerebral hemispheres communicate with each other through a thick tract of nerve fibers that lies at the base of this fissure. Although the two hemispheres seem to be mirror images of each other, they are different. For instance, the ability to form words seems to lie primarily in the left hemisphere, while the right hemisphere seems to control many abstract reasoning skills.

For some as-yet-unknown reason, nearly all of the signals from the brain to the body and vice-versa crossover on their way to and from the brain. This means that the right cerebral hemisphere primarily controls the left side of the body and the left hemisphere primarily controls the right side. When one side of the brain is damaged, the opposite side of the body is affected. For example, a stroke in the right hemisphere of the brain can leave the left arm and leg paralyzed.

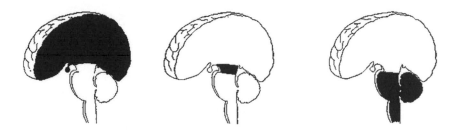

**Figure 1.5.** *The Forebrain, Midbrain, and Hindbrain*

## Neurological Disorders

When the brain is healthy it functions quickly and automatically. But when problems occur, the results can be devastating. Some 50 million people in this country—one in five—suffer from damage to the nervous system. The NINDS supports research on more than 600 neurological diseases. Some of the major types of disorders include: neurogenetic diseases (such as Huntington disease and muscular dystrophy), developmental disorders (such as cerebral palsy), degenerative diseases of adult life (such as Parkinson disease and Alzheimer disease), metabolic diseases (such as Gaucher disease), cerebrovascular diseases (such as stroke and vascular dementia), trauma (such as spinal cord and head injury), convulsive disorders (such as epilepsy), infectious diseases (such as AIDS dementia), and brain tumors.

## Section 1.2

# *Keep Your Brain Healthy*

Text in this section is excerpted from "Staying Sharp,"
Administration for Community Living (ACL), September 5, 2015.

Thinking clearly about brain health means knowing how to keep you on top of your game. It also means being able to discern between scientific principles of brain health—and popular myths and legends.

## *Things to You Can Do to Keep Your Brain Sharp*

### *Supporting Your Brain Health*

Every day, scientists are discovering how closely our minds and bodies are connected. It turns out the things you do to help keep your body and heart healthy may be good for your brain. Learn what healthy activities you should incorporate into your daily life.

### *Get Moving*

Nightly walks, playing with the grandkids—it doesn't matter what physical activities as long as you're getting your heart pumping for 30 minutes most days.

Being active is associated with lower risk of brain issues.

### *Eat Up*

Try eating a healthy, low solid fat diet with lots of veggies and fruits, like strawberries, blueberries and broccoli.

### *Drink Moderately, If at All*

Alcohol may act differently in older adults than in younger people. Some older adults can feel "high" without increasing the amount of alcohol they drink. This can make them more likely to be confused or have accidents.

### *Get Some Shuteye*

Poor sleep, or inadequate sleep due to issues such as insomnia or sleep apnea, can not only have serious physical effects, but can affect memory and thinking, too. Get comfy and go to bed. Seven to eight hours is a good night's rest.

### *Discover a New Talent*

When you learn new things, you engage your brain. Pick up a new hobby like dancing, learn to speak French or just do something you haven't done before. Challenging your brain on a regular basis is fun and beneficial.

### *Pick Up the Phone*

Stay connected with your family and friends. Invite them over for a healthy meal, go on a hike together or just hang out. Science has shown having regular engagement in social activities can help reduce some risks to your brain.

Chapter 2

# The Components of
# Mental Health

## Chapter Contents

## Section 2.1

# *Myths about Mental Health*

Text in this section is excerpted from "Mental Health
Myths and Facts," U.S. Department of Health and
Human Services (HHS), May 31, 2013.

## *Mental Health Problems Affect Everyone*

### *Myth: Mental Health Problems Don't Affect Me.*

Fact: Mental health problems are actually very common. In 2014,
about:

- One in five American adults experienced a mental health issue

- One in 10 young people experienced a period of major
depression

- One in 25 Americans lived with a serious mental illness, such as
schizophrenia, bipolar disorder, or major depression

Suicide is the 10th leading cause of death in the United States.
It accounts for the loss of more than 41,000 American lives each
year

### *Myth: Children Don't Experience Mental Health Problems.*

Fact: Even very young children may show early warning signs of
mental health concerns. These mental health problems are often clinically diagnosable, and can be a product of the interaction of biological,
psychological, and social factors.

Half of all mental health disorders show first signs before a person
turns 14 years old, and three quarters of mental health disorders begin
before age 24.

Unfortunately, less than 20% of children and adolescents with diagnosable mental health problems receive the treatment they need. Early
mental health support can help a child before problems interfere with
other developmental needs.

*Myth: People with Mental Health Problems Are Violent and Unpredictable.*

Fact: The vast majority of people with mental health problems are no more likely to be violent than anyone else. Most people with mental illness are not violent and only 3%-5% of violent acts can be attributed to individuals living with a serious mental illness. In fact, people with severe mental illnesses are over 10 times more likely to be victims of violent crime than the general population. You probably know someone with a mental health problem and don't even realize it, because many people with mental health problems are highly active and productive members of our communities.

*Myth: People with Mental Health Needs, Even Those Who Are Managing Their Mental Illness, Cannot Tolerate the Stress of Holding down a Job.*

Fact: People with mental health problems are just as productive as other employees. Employers who hire people with mental health problems report good attendance and punctuality as well as motivation, good work, and job tenure on par with or greater than other employees.

When employees with mental health problems receive effective treatment, it can result in:

- Lower total medical costs
- Increased productivity
- Lower absenteeism
- Decreased disability costs

*Myth: Personality Weakness or Character Flaws Cause Mental Health Problems. People with Mental Health Problems Can Snap out of It If They Try Hard Enough.*

Fact: Mental health problems have nothing to do with being lazy or weak and many people need help to get better. Many factors contribute to mental health problems, including:

- Biological factors, such as genes, physical illness, injury, or brain chemistry
- Life experiences, such as trauma or a history of abuse
- Family history of mental health problems

17

People with mental health problems can get better and many recover completely.

## Helping Individuals with Mental Health Problems

*Myth: There Is No Hope for People with Mental Health Problems. Once a Friend or Family Member Develops Mental Health Problems, He or She Will Never Recover.*

Fact: Studies show that people with mental health problems get better and many recover completely. Recovery refers to the process in which people are able to live, work, learn, and participate fully in their communities. There are more treatments, services, and community support systems than ever before, and they work.

*Myth: Therapy and Self-Help Are a Waste of Time. Why Bother When You Can Just Take a Pill?*

Fact: Treatment for mental health problems varies depending on the individual and could include medication, therapy, or both. Many individuals work with a support system during the healing and recovery process.

*Myth: I Can't Do Anything for a Person with a Mental Health Problem.*

Fact: Friends and loved ones can make a big difference. Only 44% of adults with diagnosable mental health problems and less than 20% of children and adolescents receive needed treatment. Friends and family can be important influences to help someone get the treatment and services they need by:

- Reaching out and letting them know you are available to help

- Helping them access mental health services

- Learning and sharing the facts about mental health, especially if you hear something that isn't true

- Treating them with respect, just as you would anyone else

- Refusing to define them by their diagnosis or using labels such as "crazy"

*Myth: Prevention Doesn't Work. It Is Impossible to Prevent Mental Illnesses.*

Fact: Prevention of mental, emotional, and behavioral disorders focuses on addressing known risk factors such as exposure to trauma that can affect the chances that children, youth, and young adults will develop mental health problems. Promoting the social-emotional well-being of children and youth leads to:

- Higher overall productivity
- Better educational outcomes
- Lower crime rates
- Stronger economies
- Lower healthcare costs
- Improved quality of life
- Increased lifespan
- Improved family life

# Section 2.2

# *Mental and Emotional Well-Being*

This section includes excerpts from "Mental and Emotional Well-Being," U.S. Department of Health and Human Services (HHS), May 2014; text from "Well-Being Concepts," Centers for Disease Control and Prevention (CDC), March 6, 2013; and text from "Good Mental Health Is Ageless," Substance Abuse and Mental Health Services Administration (SAMHSA), 2015.

## *Mental and Emotional Well-Being*

Mental and emotional well-being is essential to overall health. Positive mental health allows people to realize their full potential, cope with the stresses of life, work productively, and make meaningful contributions to their communities. Early childhood experiences have lasting, measurable consequences later in life; therefore, fostering emotional well-being from the earliest stages of life helps build a foundation for overall health. Anxiety, mood (e.g., depression), and impulse control disorders are associated with a higher probability of risk behaviors (e.g., tobacco, alcohol, and other drug use; risky sexual behavior), intimate partner and family violence, many other chronic and acute conditions (e.g., obesity, diabetes, cardiovascular disease, HIV/STIs), and premature death.

## Individuals and Families

- Build strong, positive relationships with family and friends.

- Become more involved in the community (e.g., mentor or tutor youth, join a faith or spiritual community).

- Encourage children and adolescents to participate in extracurricular and out-of-school activities.

- Work to make sure children feel comfortable talking about problems, such as bullying, and seek appropriate assistance as needed.

*What are some correlates and determinants of individual-level well-being?*

There is no sole determinant of individual well-being, but in general, well-being is dependent upon good health, positive social relationships, and availability and access to basic resources (e.g., shelter, income).

Numerous studies have examined the associations between determinants of individual and national levels of well-being. Many of these studies have used different measures of well-being (e.g., life satisfaction, positive affect, psychological well-being), and different methodologies resulting in occasional inconsistent findings related to well-being and its predictors. In general, life satisfaction is dependent more closely on the availability of basic needs being met (food, shelter, income) as well as access to modern conveniences (e.g., electricity). Pleasant emotions are more closely associated with having supportive relationships.

Some general findings on associations between well-being and its associations with other factors are as follows:

### Genes and Personality

At the individual level, genetic factors, personality, and demographic factors are related to well-being. For example, positive emotions are heritable to some degree, suggesting that there may be a genetically determined set-point for emotions such as happiness and sadness. However, the expression of genetic effects are often influenced by factors in the environment implying that circumstances and social conditions do matter and are actionable from a public policy perspective. Longitudinal studies have found that well-being is sensitive to life events (e.g., unemployment, marriage). Additionally, genetic factors alone cannot explain differences in well-being between nations or trends within nations.

Some personality factors that are strongly associated with well-being include optimism, extroversion, and self-esteem. Genetic factors and personality factors are closely related and can interact in influencing individual well-being.

While genetic factors and personality factors are important determinants of well-being, they are beyond the realm of public policy goals.

### Age and Gender

Depending on which types of measures are used (e.g., life satisfaction vs. positive affect), age and gender also have been shown to be related to well-being. In general, men and women have similar levels of well-being, but this pattern changes with age, and has changed over time. There is a U-shaped distribution of well-being by age—younger and older adults tend to have more well-being compared to middle-aged adults.

### Income and Work

The relationship between income and well-being is complex. Depending on which types of measures are used and which comparisons are made, income correlates only modestly with well-being. In general, associations between income and well-being (usually measured in terms of life satisfaction) are stronger for those at lower economic levels, but studies also have found effects for those at higher income levels. Paid employment is critical to the well-being of individuals by conferring direct access to resources, as well as fostering satisfaction, meaning and purpose for some. Unemployment negatively affects well-being, both in the short- and long-term.

### Relationships

Having supportive relationships is one of the strongest predictors of well-being, having a notably positive effect.

### *Community, Nonprofit, and Faith-Based Organizations*

- Provide space and organized activities (e.g., opportunities for volunteering) that encourage social participation and inclusion for all people, including older people and persons with disabilities.

- Support child and youth development programs (e.g., peer mentoring programs, volunteering programs) and promote inclusion of youth with mental, emotional, and behavioral problems.

- Train key community members (e.g., adults who work with the older adults, youth, and armed services personnel) to identify the signs of depression and suicide and refer people to resources.

- Expand access to mental health services (e.g., patient navigation, support groups) and enhance linkages between mental health, substance abuse, disability, and other social services.

## *Early Learning Centers, Schools, Colleges, and Universities*

- Implement programs and policies to prevent abuse, bullying, violence, and social exclusion; build social connectedness; and promote positive mental and emotional health.

- Implement programs to identify risks and early indicators of mental, emotional, and behavioral problems among youth and ensure that youth with such problems are referred to appropriate services.

- Ensure students have access to comprehensive health services, including mental health and counseling services.

## *Health Care Systems, Insurers, and Clinicians*

- Educate parents on normal child development and conduct early childhood interventions to enhance mental and emotional well-being and provide support (e.g., home visits for pregnant women and new parents).

- Screen for mental health needs among children and adults, especially those with disabilities and chronic conditions, and refer people to treatment and community resources as needed.

- Develop integrated care programs to address mental health, substance abuse, and other needs within primary care settings.

- Enhance communication and data sharing (with patient consent) with social services networks to identify and treat those in need of mental health services.

### Businesses and Employers

- Implement organizational changes to reduce employee stress (e.g., develop clearly defined roles and responsibilities), and provide reasonable accommodations (e.g., flexible work schedules, assistive technology, adapted work stations).

- Ensure that mental health services are included as a benefit on health plans and encourage employees to use these services as needed.

- Provide education, outreach, and training to address mental health parity in employment-based health insurance coverage and group health plans.

### State, Tribal, Local, and Territorial Governments

- Enhance data collection systems to better identify and address mental and emotional health needs.

- Include safe shared spaces for people to interact (e.g., parks, community centers) in community development plans, which can foster healthy relationships and positive mental health among community residents.

- Ensure that those in need, especially potentially vulnerable groups, are identified and referred to mental health services.

- Pilot and evaluate models of integrated mental and physical health in primary care, with particular attention to underserved populations and areas, such as rural communities.

## Good Mental Health Is Ageless

### Good Mental Health Can Help You:

- Enjoy life more.
- Handle difficult situations.
- Stay better connected to your family, your friends, and your community.
- Keep your body strong.

Being in good mental health doesn't mean that you'll never feel sad, lonely, or "down." But when these feelings disrupt your life or go on too long, there may be a bigger problem.

## *Unusual Feelings of Sadness or Depression Can Happen When:*

- You have to move from your home.

- People you love get sick or die.

- You have to depend on others to get around, or even to do the simple things you used to do yourself.

- Physical health problems seem overwhelming.

## *In Addition to Feelings of Depression, Some of the following Changes in Behavior May Suggest Other Emotional Problems:*

- Being easily upset

- Not having the energy to do the things you want to do, or used to do

- Changing sleep habits

- Increasing forgetfulness

- Being afraid of things

- Changes in eating habits

- Neglecting housework

- Crying a lot

- Having trouble managing money

- Believing that you can't do anything worthwhile

- Being confused

- Getting lost a lot

- Staying alone a lot of the time

- Spending little or no time with friends

- Feeling hopeless or overwhelmed

- Thinking life isn't worth living

- Thinking about hurting yourself

*Here Are Some Things You Can Do If Depression or Other Changes in Your Behavior Last Longer than Two Weeks:*

• Talk with your doctor or other health care professional. Tell them exactly how you're feeling, and let them know how this is different from the way you used to feel. They can check for any problems you may be having, and can discuss treatment options with you.

• Share your feelings with a friend, family member or spiritual advisor. These people can sometimes notice changes that you might not see.

• Ask for advice from a staff member at a senior center or other program you participate in.

• Call for information from the National Eldercare Locator at 1-800-677-1116, or speak with the Federal Center for Mental Health Services (CMHS) by calling 240-276-1310 or visiting its Web site at http://beta.samhsa.gov/about-us/who-we-are/offices-centers/cmhs. These organizations can help you find a program or provider near you.

• Check your local yellow pages for organizations that can help.

# Chapter 3

# *Lifestyles and Mental Health*

## *Chapter Contents*

## Section 3.1

# *Sleep and Mental Health*

Text in this section is excerpted from "Get Enough
Sleep," U.S. Department of Health and Human
Services (HHS), December 30, 2015.

## *The Basics: Overview*

Everyone needs to get enough sleep. Sleep helps keep your mind and body healthy.

### *How Much Sleep Do I Need?*

Most adults need 7 to 8 hours of good quality sleep on a regular schedule each night. Make changes to your routine if you can't find enough time to sleep. Getting enough sleep isn't only about total hours of sleep. It's also important to get good quality sleep so you feel rested when you wake up. If you often have trouble sleeping–or if you don't feel well rested after sleeping–talk with your doctor.

### *How Much Sleep Do Children Need?*

- Kids need even more sleep than adults.
- Teens need at least 9 hours of sleep each night.
- School-aged children need at least 10 hours of sleep each night.
- Preschoolers need to sleep between 11 and 12 hours a day.
- Newborns need to sleep between 16 and 18 hours a day.

### *Why Is Getting Enough Sleep Important?*

Getting enough sleep has many benefits. It can help you:
- Get sick less often
- Stay at a healthy weight
- Lower your risk of high blood pressure and diabetes

- Reduce stress and improve your mood
- Think more clearly and do better in school and at work
- Get along better with people
- Make good decisions and avoid injuries (For example, sleepy drivers cause thousands of car crashes every year.)

### Does It Matter When I Sleep?

Yes. Your body sets your "biological clock" according to the pattern of daylight where you live. This helps you naturally get sleepy at night and stay alert during the day. When people have to work at night and sleep during the day, they can have trouble getting enough sleep. When people travel to a different time zone, they can also have trouble sleeping.

### Why Can't I Fall Asleep?

Many things can make it harder for you to sleep, including:
- Stress
- Pain
- Certain health conditions
- Some medicines
- Caffeine (usually from coffee, tea, and soda)
- Alcohol and other drugs
- Untreated sleep disorders, like sleep apnea or insomnia

If you are having trouble sleeping, make changes to your routine to get the sleep you need. For example, try to:
- Follow a regular sleep schedule
- Stay away from caffeine in the afternoon
- Take a hot bath before bed to relax

### How Can I Tell If I Have a Sleep Disorder?

Signs of a sleep disorder can include:
- Difficulty falling asleep
- Trouble staying asleep

- Sleepiness during the day that makes it difficult to do tasks like driving a car

- Frequent loud snoring

- Pauses in breathing or gasping while sleeping

- Pain or itchy feelings in your legs or arms at night that feel better when you move or massage the area

If you have any of these signs, talk to a doctor or nurse. You may need to be tested or treated for a sleep disorder.

## Take Action!

Making small changes to your daily routine can help you get the sleep you need.

### Change What You Do during the Day

- Exercise earlier in the day, not right before you go to bed.

- Stay away from caffeine (including coffee, tea, and soda) late in the day.

- If you have trouble sleeping at night, limit daytime naps to 20 minutes or less.

- If you drink alcohol, drink only in moderation. This means no more than 1 drink a day for women and no more than 2 drinks a day for men. Alcohol can keep you from sleeping soundly.

- Don't eat a big meal close to bedtime.

- Quit smoking. The nicotine in cigarettes can make it harder for you to sleep.

### Create a Good Sleep Environment

- Make sure your bedroom is dark. If there are street lights near your window, try putting up light-blocking curtains.

- Keep your bedroom quiet.

- Consider keeping electronic devices – like TVs, computers, and smart phones – out of the bedroom.

### Set a Bedtime Routine.

- Go to bed at the same time every night.

- Get the same amount of sleep each night.

- Avoid eating, talking on the phone, reading, or watching TV in bed.

- Try not to lie in bed worrying about things.

If you are still awake after staying in bed for more than 20 minutes, get up. Do something relaxing, like reading or meditating, until you feel sleepy.

### If You Are Concerned about Your Sleep, See a Doctor.

Talk with a doctor or nurse if you have any of the following signs of a sleep disorder:

- Frequent, loud snoring

- Pauses in breathing during sleep

- Trouble waking up in the morning

- Pain or itchy feelings in your legs or arms at night that feel better when you move or massage the area

- Trouble staying awake during the day

Even if you aren't aware of problems like these, talk with a doctor if you feel like you often have trouble sleeping.

Keep a sleep diary for a week and share it with your doctor. A doctor can suggest different sleep routines or medicines to treat sleep disorders. Talk with a doctor before trying over-the-counter sleep medicine.

# Section 3.2

# *Physical Activity and Mental Health*

This section includes excerpts from "Exercise Can Enhance Mental Health," Defense Health Agency (DHA), September 10, 2014; and text from "Physical Activity and Health," Centers for Disease Control and Prevention (CDC), June 4, 2015.

## *Exercise Can Enhance Mental Health*

You're probably aware of the physical benefits of exercise, but exercise also plays a key role in mental health. It helps people manage stress and prevent or treat depression and anxiety, and it confers overall mental strength and resilience. What's more, exercise is something almost everyone can do, and it's inexpensive.

Physical activity helps with stress management. Experts describe exercise as a "stress buffer" because it can cushion people from the full effects of stress. It protects individuals from repeated emotional stressors and can increase positive feelings after exercise. Those who engage in regular exercise also have fewer health problems, even when stressed.

It isn't clear what type or amount of exercise is optimal to receive all of these stress-busting benefits, but moderate-intensity physical exercise of at least 30 minutes a day most days of the week (or the equivalent weekly amount) has been shown to be effective in treating mild to moderate depression. That's similar to the amount recommended to improve physical health: at least 150 minutes a week of moderate-intensity aerobic physical activity.

Researchers have found that depression has been eased by exercise programs with durations from four to twelve weeks, with an average of around nine weeks.

Exercise has also been found to be helpful in the reduction of anxiety, although a recommended amount hasn't been established.

Mental health benefits can be had from just about any kind of exercise. It can be as simple as walking indoors or outdoors or using a stationary cycle or cross-training machine. Some studies have found resistance training to be beneficial, too. The activity can be solo or with a group (or a combination of both). It's important that the activity be suitable to the current fitness level of the individual.

Exercise provides benefits to the brain that can enhance resilience. It protects the brain from degeneration and increases its ability to adapt after new experiences.

New research also suggests that exercise doesn't just stop degeneration: it can even help grow healthy brain matter. This impact isn't just for adults; being physically fit has been linked to healthy brain development and better cognitive and academic performance in children too.

## The Benefits of Physical Activity

Regular physical activity is one of the most important things you can do for your health. It can help:

- Control your weight

- Reduce your risk of cardiovascular disease

- Reduce your risk for type 2 diabetes and metabolic syndrome

- Reduce your risk of some cancers

- Strengthen your bones and muscles

- Improve your mental health and mood

- Improve your ability to do daily activities and prevent falls, if you're an older adult

- Increase your chances of living longer

If you're not sure about becoming active or boosting your level of physical activity because you're afraid of getting hurt, the good news is that moderate-intensity aerobic activity, like brisk walking, is generally safe for most people.

Start slowly. Cardiac events, such as a heart attack, are rare during physical activity. But the risk does go up when you suddenly become much more active than usual. For example, you can put yourself at risk if you don't usually get much physical activity and then all of a sudden do vigorous-intensity aerobic activity, like shoveling snow. That's why it's important to start slowly and gradually increase your level of activity.

If you have a chronic health condition such as arthritis, diabetes, or heart disease, talk with your doctor to find out if your condition limits, in any way, your ability to be active. Then, work with your doctor to come up with a physical activity plan that matches your abilities. If your condition stops you from meeting the minimum guidelines, try to do as much as you can. What's important is that you avoid being inactive. Even 60 minutes a week of moderate-intensity aerobic activity is good for you.

The bottom line is—the health benefits of physical activity far outweigh the risks of getting hurt.

If you want to know more about how physical activity improves your health, the section below gives more detail on what research studies have found.

## Control Your Weight

Looking to get to or stay at a healthy weight? Both diet and physical activity play a critical role in controlling your weight. You gain weight when the calories you burn, including those burned during physical activity, are less than the calories you eat or drink. For more information see our section on balancing calories. When it comes to weight management, people vary greatly in how much physical activity they need. You may need to be more active than others to achieve or maintain a healthy weight.

To maintain your weight: Work your way up to 150 minutes of moderate-intensity aerobic activity, 75 minutes of vigorous-intensity aerobic activity, or an equivalent mix of the two each week. Strong scientific evidence shows that physical activity can help you maintain your weight over time. However, the exact amount of physical activity needed to do this is not clear since it varies greatly from person to person. It's possible that you may need to do more than the equivalent of 150 minutes of moderate-intensity activity a week to maintain your weight.

To lose weight and keep it off: You will need a high amount of physical activity unless you also adjust your diet and reduce the amount of calories you're eating and drinking. Getting to and staying at a healthy weight requires both regular physical activity and a healthy eating plan.

## Reduce Your Risk of Cardiovascular Disease

Heart disease and stroke are two of the leading causes of death in the United States. But following the guidelines and getting at least 150 minutes a week (2 hours and 30 minutes) of moderate-intensity aerobic activity can put you at a lower risk for these diseases. You can reduce your risk even further with more physical activity. Regular physical activity can also lower your blood pressure and improve your cholesterol levels.

### Reduce Your Risk of Type 2 Diabetes and Metabolic Syndrome

Regular physical activity can reduce your risk of developing type 2 diabetes and metabolic syndrome. Metabolic syndrome is a condition in which you have some combination of too much fat around the waist, high blood pressure, low HDL cholesterol, high triglycerides, or high blood sugar. Research shows that lower rates of these conditions are seen with 120 to 150 minutes (2 hours to 2 hours and 30 minutes) a week of at least moderate-intensity aerobic activity. And the more physical activity you do, the lower your risk will be.

Already have type 2 diabetes? Regular physical activity can help control your blood glucose levels.

### Reduce Your Risk of Some Cancers

Being physically active lowers your risk for two types of cancer: colon and breast. Research shows that:

- Physically active people have a lower risk of colon cancer than do people who are not active.

- Physically active women have a lower risk of breast cancer than do people who are not active.

Reduce your risk of endometrial and lung cancer. Although the research is not yet final, some findings suggest that your risk of endometrial cancer and lung cancer may be lower if you get regular physical activity compared to people who are not active.

Improve your quality of life. If you are a cancer survivor, research shows that getting regular physical activity not only helps give you a better quality of life, but also improves your physical fitness.

### Strengthen Your Bones and Muscles

As you age, it's important to protect your bones, joints and muscles. Not only do they support your body and help you move, but keeping bones, joints and muscles healthy can help ensure that you're able to do your daily activities and be physically active. Research shows that doing aerobic, muscle-strengthening and bone-strengthening physical activity of at least a moderately-intense level can slow the loss of bone density that comes with age.

Hip fracture is a serious health condition that can have life-changing negative effects, especially if you're an older adult. But research shows that people who do 120 to 300 minutes of at least moderate-intensity aerobic activity each week have a lower risk of hip fracture.

Regular physical activity helps with arthritis and other conditions affecting the joints. If you have arthritis, research shows that doing 130 to 150 (2 hours and 10 minutes to 2 hours and 30 minutes) a week of moderate-intensity, low-impact aerobic activity can not only improve your ability to manage pain and do everyday tasks, but it can also make your quality of life better.

Build strong, healthy muscles. Muscle-strengthening activities can help you increase or maintain your muscle mass and strength. Slowly increasing the amount of weight and number of repetitions you do will give you even more benefits, no matter your age.

### Improve Your Mental Health and Mood

Regular physical activity can help keep your thinking, learning, and judgment skills sharp as you age. It can also reduce your risk of depression and may help you sleep better. Research has shown that doing aerobic or a mix of aerobic and muscle-strengthening activities 3 to 5 times a week for 30 to 60 minutes can give you these mental health benefits. Some scientific evidence has also shown that even lower levels of physical activity can be beneficial.

### Improve Your Ability to Do Daily Activities and Prevent Falls

A functional limitation is a loss of the ability to do everyday activities such as climbing stairs, grocery shopping, or playing with your grandchildren.

- How does this relate to physical activity?
- If you're a physically active middle-aged or older adult, you have a lower risk of functional limitations than people who are inactive
- Already have trouble doing some of your everyday activities?

Aerobic and muscle-strengthening activities can help improve your ability to do these types of tasks.

• Are you an older adult who is at risk for falls?

Research shows that doing balance and muscle-strengthening activities each week along with moderate-intensity aerobic activity, like brisk walking, can help reduce your risk of falling.

## *Increase Your Chances of Living Longer*

Science shows that physical activity can reduce your risk of dying early from the leading causes of death, like heart disease and some cancers. This is remarkable in two ways:

1.  Only a few lifestyle choices have as large an impact on your health as physical activity. People who are physically active for about 7 hours a week have a 40 percent lower risk of dying early than those who are active for less than 30 minutes a week.

2.  You don't have to do high amounts of activity or vigorous-intensity activity to reduce your risk of premature death. You can put yourself at lower risk of dying early by doing at least 150 minutes a week of moderate-intensity aerobic activity.

Everyone can gain the health benefits of physical activity-age, ethnicity, shape or size do not matter.

## Section 3.3

# *Keeping Mentally Fit as You Age*

This section includes excerpts from "Brain Health: You Can
Make a Difference!" Administration on Aging (AOA), November 20,
2014; and text from "Depression and Anxiety," Office on
Women's Health (OWH), September 20, 2013.

## Memory and Learning

As you grow older, you may notice differences in the way your mind
works. You may have difficulty finding the correct words, multitasking
or paying attention. The good news is that even if you have already
noticed some of these changes, you are still able to learn new things,
create new memories and improve vocabulary and language skills.

## Potential Threats to Brain Health

### *Health Conditions*

Some health conditions can negatively affect your brain. Heart
disease, high blood pressure and diabetes can alter or damage blood
vessels throughout your body, including the brain. Alzheimer disease
and other types of dementia also harm the brain. While no one knows
how to prevent dementia, many approaches that are good for your
health in other ways, including engaging in exercise and eating a
healthy diet, are being tested.

### *Medicines*

Some medications and certain combinations of drugs can affect
your thinking and the way your brain works. Older adults taking
medications should be particularly careful when consuming alcohol,
as drugs may interact negatively with it.

### *Alcohol*

Drinking alcohol can slow or impair communication among your
brain cells. This can cause slurred speech, a fuzzy memory, drowsiness

and dizziness; it can also lead to long-term difficulties with your balance, memory, coordination and body temperature.

### Smoking

The risks associated with smoking are heart attacks, stroke and lung disease.

### Brain Injury

Older adults are at higher risk of falling and other accidents that can cause brain injury.

## Action You Can Take to Help Protect Your Brain

### Take Charge

Get recommended health screenings regularly.

- Manage health conditions, such as diabetes, high blood pressure, and high cholesterol.
- Be sure to talk with your doctor or pharmacist about the medications you take and any possible side effects on memory, sleep and how your brain works.
- To learn more about how to move or exercise in a healthy way, ask your health care provider about your personal situation.

### Eat Right

Try to maintain a balanced diet of fruits and vegetables, whole grains, lean meats (including fish and poultry) and low-fat or non-fat dairy products. Monitor your intake of solid fat, sugar and salt, and eat proper portion sizes.

### Get Moving

Being physically active may help reduce the risk of conditions that can harm brain health, such as diabetes, heart disease, depression and stroke; it may also help improve connections among your brain cells. Older adults should get at least 150 minutes of exercise each week.

### Drink Moderately, If At All

Staying away from alcohol can reverse some negative changes related to brain health.

## *Don't Smoke*

Quitting smoking at any age will be beneficial to the health of your mind and body. Non-smokers have a lower risk of heart attacks, stroke and lung diseases, as well as increased blood circulation.

## *Be Safe*

To reduce the risk of falling, exercise to improve balance and coordination, take a falls prevention class, and make your home safer.

## *Think and Connect*

Keep your mind active by doing mentally stimulating activities like reading, playing games, learning new things, teaching or taking a class and being social. Older adults who remain active and engaged with others by doing activities like volunteering report being happier and healthier overall.

## Taking the First Step

You can start to support your brain health with some small, first steps and build from there.

- Begin an exercise routine, such as a daily walk, with the goal of increasing the amount of time and speed.
- Add an extra serving of fruit and vegetables each day.
- Make an appointment for a health screening or a physical exam.
- Seek out volunteer opportunities that interest you.
- Sign up for a class or program at your community college or community center.

## Depression and Anxiety

Money worries, health problems, and the loss of loved ones become more common as we age. So it might seem "normal" for an older adult to feel depressed or anxious a lot of the time. It's not. Just like at any other age, constant worrying could be due to an anxiety disorder. And, ongoing feelings of sadness or numbness could be signs of depression.

In recent years, you have probably heard more and more about depression, anxiety, and other mental health problems. You may know how common they are and that they are real illnesses and not signs of personal weakness. Yet, many women still don't seek treatment for mental health problems because they play down or dismiss their symptoms or are embarrassed or unwilling to talk about them.

It may be hard to accept that you need help. But it's important to get it. Untreated mental health problems can reduce your quality of life. The damage can be both emotional and physical. In fact, depression may be a symptom of a physical problem. People with diabetes, heart disease, and some other health problems have a higher risk of depression. Depression and other mental health problems can make it more difficult, and more costly, to treat these and other conditions. That makes it even more important to see your doctor.

Also, untreated depression is a primary risk factor for suicide. In fact, older adults commit suicide at a higher rate than any other age group. That's why you need to get help right away if you or a loved one is having mental health problems.

## *Before You Say, "I'm Fine"...*

Ask yourself if you feel:

- Nervous or "empty"
- Guilty or worthless
- Very tired and slowed down
- You don't enjoy things the way you used to
- Restless and irritable
- Like no one loves you
- Like life is not worth living

Or if you are:

- Sleeping more or less than usual
- Eating more or less than usual
- Having persistent headaches, stomach aches, or chronic pain

If these symptoms keep occurring and are interfering with your daily life, see your doctor. They may be signs of depression or an anxiety disorder, treatable medical illnesses. But your doctor can only treat

41

you if you say how you are really feeling. Depression is not a normal part of aging. Talk to your doctor.

Reach out. It's important that you talk to someone—anyone. It could be a friend, family member, a religious leader, or your doctor. Talking to them may help you feel better, and they can help make sure you get treatment.

# Chapter 4

# *Developing and Reinforcing Mental Wellness*

## *Chapter Contents*

# Section 4.1

# *Becoming More Resilient*

Text in this section is excerpted from "Resilience Annotated
Bibliography," Substance Abuse and Mental Health Services
Administration (SAMHSA), March 15, 2013.

## *Introduction*

Resilience, as a concept and construct, is the context-specific ability
to respond to stress, anxiety, trauma, crisis, or disaster. Resilience
develops over time and is the culmination of multiple internal and
external factors. For those who develop mental and/or substance use
disorders, the influence of both internal development and external
environments converge to either promote or restrict the development
of personal resilience.

The work of enhancing resilience for persons with mental and/
or substance use problems has its greatest impact during the forma-
tive stages to prevent more severe conditions and to promote health.
Additionally, although more research is needed to fully examine the
possible effects, resilience is also critical in the recovery stage where
life skills and other supports can be accessed to manage future stress.
It is the interaction of risk and protective factors that plays the central
role in the development, enhancement, and activation of resilience.

- Individual factors such as development of a desirable personal
  identity; a feeling of power and control over one's life; a feeling
  of self-worth; a sense of social justice; a sense of cohesion with
  others; good self-regulation skills; close relationships with competent adults; ; connections to prosocial organizations; tolerance
  for delayed gratification; a sense of humor; development of good
  coping and problem-solving skills; an ability to see and set long-
  term goals; and a positive outlook for the future

- Family factors such as consistent, appropriate parental involvement, discipline, and supervision; good parenting skills; trusting
  relationships; a safe environment; well-defined and appropriate
  family roles and responsibilities; opportunities to learn to deal

appropriately with criticism, rejection, and silence; prosocial values and ethics; and good goal-setting and decision-making skills exhibited by parents

- Community factors such as participation in school, work, and the community that create an environment in which an individual has opportunities to develop and practice social and cognitive skills, develop a sense of belonging, contribute to the work of the community, This develop a social network of peers, and learn to handle challenges and practice prosocial behavioral skills and self-efficacy

Risk factors come in many different forms, but at their core they are attitudes, beliefs, or environmental circumstances that put an individual in jeopardy of developing a mental and/or substance use disorder. Depending on the source, risk factors may include:

- Individual temperament characteristics related to locus of control (external versus internal), poor self-control, negative emotionality, a need for immediate gratification, and even physical activity level.

- Family-related risk factors, which may include parental and sibling drug use, poor child-rearing and socialization practices, ineffective parental supervision of the child, ineffective parental discipline skills, negative parent-child relationships, family conflict, marital discord, domestic violence, abuse and neglect, family disorganization, and family social isolation.

- Community/environmental risk factors or the social determinants of health, e.g., limited resources, low socioeconomic status, and communities that lack the knowledge, skills, and programming necessary to reach out to those in need of assistance

# Section 4.2

# *Handling Stress*

Text in this section is excerpted from "Coping with Stress," Centers for Disease Control and Prevention (CDC), October 2, 2015; and text from "Stress and the Mental Health of Children," U.S. Department of Health and Human Services (HHS), June 10, 2014.

## *Coping with Stress*

Everyone—adults, teens, and even children—experiences stress at times. Stress can be beneficial by helping people develop the skills they need to cope with and adapt to new and potentially threatening situations throughout life. However, the beneficial aspects of stress diminish when it is severe enough to overwhelm a person's ability to take care of themselves and family. Using healthy ways to cope and getting the right care and support can put problems in perspective and help stressful feelings and symptoms subside.

Stress is a condition that is often characterized by symptoms of physical or emotional tension. It is a reaction to a situation where a person feels threatened or anxious. Stress can be positive (e.g., preparing for a wedding) or negative (e.g., dealing with a natural disaster).

Sometimes after experiencing a traumatic event that is especially frightening—including personal or environmental disasters, or being threatened with an assault—people have a strong and lingering stress reaction to the event. Strong emotions, jitters, sadness, or depression may all be part of this normal and temporary reaction to the stress of an overwhelming event.

## *Common Reactions to a Stressful Event Can Include:*

- Disbelief, shock, and numbness

- Feeling sad, frustrated, and helpless

- Fear and anxiety about the future

- Feeling guilty

- Anger, tension, and irritability

- Difficulty concentrating and making decisions
- Crying
- Reduced interest in usual activities
- Wanting to be alone
- Loss of appetite
- Sleeping too much or too little
- Nightmares or bad memories
- Reoccurring thoughts of the event
- Headaches, back pains, and stomach problems
- Increased heart rate, difficulty breathing
- Smoking or use of alcohol or drugs

### *Healthy Ways to Cope with Stress*

Feeling emotional and nervous or having trouble sleeping and eating can all be normal reactions to stress. Engaging in healthy activities and getting the right care and support can put problems in perspective and help stressful feelings subside in a few days or weeks. Some tips for beginning to feel better are:

- Take care of yourself.
- Eat healthy, well-balanced meals
- Exercise on a regular basis
- Get plenty of sleep
- Give yourself a break if you feel stressed out
- Talk to others. Share your problems and how you are feeling and coping with a parent, friend, counselor or doctor.
- Avoid drugs and alcohol. Drugs and alcohol may seem to help with the stress. In the long run, they create additional problems and increase the stress you are already feeling.
- Take a break. If your stress is caused by a national or local event, take breaks from listening to the news stories, which can increase your stress.

Recognize when you need more help. If problems continue or you are thinking about suicide, talk to a psychologist, social worker, or professional counselor.

## Helping Youth Cope with Stress

Because of their level of development, children and adolescents often struggle with how to cope well with stress. Youth can be particularly overwhelmed when their stress is connected to a traumatic event—like a natural disaster (earthquakes, tornados, wildfires), family loss, school shootings, or community violence. Parents and educators can take steps to provide stability and support that help young people feel better.

# Tips

## Tips for Parents

It is natural for children to worry, especially when scary or stressful events happen in their lives. Talking with children about these stressful events and monitoring what children watch or hear about the events can help put frightening information into a more balanced context. Some suggestions to help children cope are:

- Maintain a normal routine. Helping children wake up, go to sleep, and eat meals at regular times provide them a sense of stability. Going to school and participating in typical after-school activities also provide stability and extra support.

- Talk, listen, and encourage expression. Create opportunities to have your children talk, but do not force them. Listen to your child's thoughts and feelings and share some of yours. After a traumatic event, it is important for children to feel like they can share their feelings and to know that their fears and worries are understandable. Keep these conversations going by asking them how they feel in a week, then in a month, and so on.

- Watch and listen. Be alert for any change in behavior. Are children sleeping more or less? Are they withdrawing from friends or family? Are they behaving in any way out of the ordinary? Any changes in behavior, even small changes, may be signs that the child is having trouble coming to terms with the event and may support.

- Reassure. Stressful events can challenge a child's sense of physical and emotional safety and security. Take opportunities to reassure your child about his or her safety and well-being and discuss ways that you, the school, and the community are taking steps to keep them safe.

- Connect with others. Make an on-going effort to talk to other parents and your child's teachers about concerns and ways to help your child cope. You do not have to deal with problems alone-it is often helpful for parents, schools, and health professionals to work together to support and ensuring the wellbeing of all children in stressful times.

## Tips for Kids and Teens

After a traumatic or violent event, it is normal to feel anxious about your safety and security. Even if you were not directly involved, you may worry about whether this type of event may someday affect you. How can you deal with these fears? Start by looking at the tips below for some ideas.

- Talk to and stay connected to others. This connection might be your parent, another relative, a friend, neighbor, teacher, coach, school nurse, counselor, family doctor, or member of your church or temple. Talking with someone can help you make sense out of your experience and figure out ways to feel better. If you are not sure where to turn, call your local crisis intervention center or a national hotline.

- Get active. Go for a walk, play sports, write a play or poem, play a musical instrument, or join an after-school program. Volunteer with a community group that promotes nonviolence or another school or community activity that you care about. Trying any of these can be a positive way to handle your feelings and to see that things are going to get better.

- Take care of yourself. As much as possible, try to get enough sleep, eat right, exercise, and keep a normal routine. It may be hard to do, but by keeping yourself healthy you will be better able to handle a tough time.

- Take information breaks. Pictures and stories about a disaster can increase worry and other stressful feelings. Taking breaks from the news, Internet, and conversations about the disaster can help calm you down.

## Tips for School Personnel

Kids and teens who experience a stressful event, or see it on television, may react with shock, sadness, anger, fear, and confusion. They may be reluctant to be alone or fearful of leaving secure areas such as the house or classroom. School personnel can help their students restore their sense of safety by talking with the children about their fears. Other tips for school personnel include:

- Reach out and talk. Create opportunities to have students talk, but do not force them. Try asking questions like, what do you think about these events, or how do you think these things happen? You can be a model by sharing some of your own thoughts as well as correct misinformation. Children talking about their feelings can help them cope and to know that different feelings are normal.

- Watch and listen. Be alert for any change in behavior. Are students talking more or less? Withdrawing from friends? Acting out? Are they behaving in any way out of the ordinary? These changes may be early warning signs that a student is struggling and needs extra support from the school and family.

- Maintain normal routines. A regular classroom and school schedule can provide reassurance and promote a sense of stability and safety. Encourage students to keep up with their schoolwork and extracurricular activities but do not push them if they seem overwhelmed.

- Take care of yourself. You are better able to support your students if you are healthy, coping well, and taking care of yourself first.

- Eat healthy, well-balanced meals

- Exercise on a regular basis

- Get plenty of sleep

- Give yourself a break if you feel stressed out

# Section 4.3

# *Managing Anger*

This section includes excerpts from "Anger Management," Department of Veterans Affairs (VA), July 2013; and text from "Anger Management for Substance Abuse and Mental Health Clients," Substance Abuse and Mental Health Services Administration (SAMHSA), 2013.

## *What Is Anger?*

Anger is a complex and confusing emotion that you may experience in response to specific stressors. It is a feeling, an emotion, and is quite different than aggression, which is an action and intended to cause harm to others. Anger is created by how you think about external events that are occurring, therefore you can have control over your anger. Consider the diagram below and the following example:

Example: As you are driving home from work one late afternoon, you get cut-off by a person in another car (External Event). You begin to think, "What a jerk!" (Internal Event/Thought). You become frustrated and angry (Emotion). Finally, you begin to yell out your window at the person, plan revenge, and speed up to try to catch them (Behavior).

## *What Are the Functions of Anger?*

Anger may have both positive and negative effects on you. When you learn how to appropriately express your anger, it can lead to beneficial consequences.

Some examples of positive functions include:

1. Anger can serve as a signal to you that you are becoming frustrated or annoyed.

2. It can be an energizer and may help you to deal with conflict and solve problems.

3. Anger can prompt us to communicate with others to resolve a conflict.

51

4.  It may create a sense of control and allow us to be more assertive.

Some examples of negative functions include:

1.  Being in a state of anger may cause increased heart rate, blood pressure, and tension headaches (among other negative physical effects).

2.  Excess anger may disrupt thoughts and make it difficult to think clearly.

3.  It may help us to avoid other feelings like sadness, anxiety, or embarrassment.

4.  Anger can lead to aggression

5.  It may cause problems in relationships, if it builds up.

## What Causes Anger?

Anger is an internal response to things in your environment that happen (external factors), based on how you experience and think about those things. It is important to remember that while you may have no control over the external factors, you do have control over how you think about and interpret them. The following are examples of external and internal factors, which may cause you to become angry.

1.  Frustrations: When you try to do something and you are prevented, blocked or disappointed.

2.  Tension: When you are feeling "strung out" and your stress level is high, you may be quicker to anger.

3.  Ill Humor: When you take things too seriously and are unable to "roll with the punches"; when you become moody or crabby and are more inclined to become angry easily.

4.  Withdrawal Avoidance: When you actively avoid conflict and walk away without resolving an issue, you tend to internalize the feelings and become angry.

## How Can You Control Your Anger?

Controlling your anger means learning how to manage the frequency and duration of your anger. Anger that happens often and lasts a long time can be a heavy burden. The continuous increased emotional state can drain your energy and affect you physically. Learning anger management will help you to become aware of your triggers to anger and will teach you more productive ways to respond to the feeling. It also provides you with skills to learn how to control those internal factors which you have control over. There are several strategies you can use to help you gain control over your anger. They include:

- Relaxation Techniques
- Quick Stress Relievers
- Time-Out
- Humor
- Thought Stopping
- Conflict Negotiation
- Problem Solving
- Challenging Negative Thinking
- Choosing Assertiveness vs Aggression

## When Does Anger Become a Problem?

Anger becomes a problem when it is felt too intensely, is felt too frequently, or is expressed inappropriately. Feeling anger too intensely or frequently places extreme physical strain on the body. During prolonged and frequent episodes of anger, certain divisions of the nervous system become highly activated. Consequently, blood pressure and heart rate increase and stay elevated for long periods. This stress on the body may produce many different health problems, such as hypertension, heart disease, and diminished immune system efficiency. Thus, from a health standpoint, avoiding physical illness is a motivation for controlling anger.

Another compelling reason to control anger concerns the negative consequences that result from expressing anger inappropriately. In the extreme, anger may lead to violence or physical aggression, which can result in numerous negative consequences, such as being arrested or jailed, being physically injured, being retaliated against, losing loved ones, being terminated from a substance abuse treatment or social service program, or feeling guilt, shame, or regret. Even when anger does not lead to violence, the inappropriate expression of anger, such as verbal abuse or intimidating or threatening behavior, often results in negative consequences. For example, it is likely that others will

53

develop fear, resentment, and lack of trust toward those who subject them to angry outbursts, which may cause alienation from individuals, such as family members, friends, and coworkers.

## Anger as a Habitual Response

Not only is the expression of anger learned, but it can become a routine, familiar, and predictable response to a variety of situations. When anger is displayed frequently and aggressively, it can become a maladaptive habit because it results in negative consequences. Habits, by definition, are performed over and over again, without thinking. People with anger management problems often resort to aggressive displays of anger to solve their problems, without thinking about the negative consequences they may suffer or the debilitating effects it may have on the people around them.

## Breaking the Anger Habit

Becoming Aware of Anger. To break the anger habit, you must develop an awareness of the events, circumstances, and behaviors of others that "trigger" your anger. This awareness also involves understanding the negative consequences that result from anger. For example, you may be in line at the supermarket and become impatient because the lines are too long. You could become angry, then boisterously demand that the checkout clerk call for more help. As your anger escalates, you may become involved in a heated exchange with the clerk or another customer. The store manager may respond by having a security officer remove you from the store. The negative consequences that result from this event are not getting the groceries that you wanted and the embarrassment and humiliation you suffer from being removed from the store.

## Strategies for Controlling Anger.

In addition to becoming aware of anger, you need to develop strategies to effectively manage it. These strategies can be used to stop the escalation of anger before you lose control and experience negative consequences. An effective set of strategies for controlling anger should include both immediate and preventive strategies. Immediate strategies include taking a timeout, deep-breathing exercises, and thought stop ping. Preventive strategies include developing an exercise program and changing your irrational beliefs.

# Section 4.4

# *Coping with Grief*

This section includes excerpts from "End of Life," National Institute on Aging (NIA), March 26, 2014; text from "Mourning the Death of a Spouse," National Institute on Aging (NIA), March 2013; and text from "Tips for Survivors," Substance Abuse and Mental Health Services Administration (SAMHSA), November 25, 2014.

## *End of Life*

### *Symptoms of Grief*

Losing a family member or someone close to you can make you feel sad, lost, and alone. You may have been so busy with caregiving that it now seems you have nothing to do. This is all part of grieving, the natural reaction to losing someone in your life. Grieving can start before the dying person is gone.

Bereavement is the formal term for the period of grief and mourning after a death. You may experience grief as a mental, physical, social, and/or emotional reaction.

- Mental reactions can include having trouble concentrating and making decisions.

- Physical reactions can include sleeping problems, changes in appetite, physical problems, or illness.

- Social reactions can include avoiding the people, places, and activities you enjoyed with the person you lost.

- Emotional reactions can include cycling repeatedly through feelings of numbness, disbelief, anger, and despair.

- You may cry more easily. It's common to have rollercoaster emotions for a while. It's a good idea to wait for a while before making big decisions like moving or changing jobs when you are grieving.

## The Grieving Period

How long bereavement lasts can depend on how close you were to the person who died, if the person's death was expected, and other factors. Friends, family, and faith may be sources of support. Grief counseling or grief therapy is also helpful to some people.

Some people may feel better sooner than they expect. Others may take longer. As time passes, you may still miss your loved one, but for most people, the intense pain will lessen. There will be good and bad days. You will know that you are feeling better when the good days begin to outnumber the bad.

There are many paths to healing after the loss of an important person in your life. Try not to ignore your grief. Support may be available until you can manage the grief on your own. It is especially important to get help with your loss if you feel overwhelmed, consumed, or very depressed by it.

## Support from Family and Friends

Let your family and friends know when you want to talk about the person you've lost. They are grieving, too, and may welcome the chance to share memories. It may help to be with people who let you say what you're feeling. Accept offers of help or companionship from family and friends. It's good for you and for them.

## Hospice Support

An essential part of hospice is providing grief counseling to the family of someone who was under their care. Even if hospice was not used before the death, you can ask hospice workers for bereavement support at this time.

If the death happened at a nursing home or hospital, there is often a social worker you can ask for resources that can help. Funeral homes may also be able to suggest where to find counseling.

## Support Groups

Sometimes it helps to talk to other people who are grieving. Check with hospitals, religious groups, local agencies, or your healthcare provider to find out about grief or bereavement support groups.

Choose a support group where you feel comfortable sharing your feelings and concerns. Members of support groups often have helpful ideas or know of useful resources based on their own experiences.

Online support groups make it possible for people to receive support without having to leave home.

### Therapy, Individual or Group

Sometimes short-term talk therapy with a counselor can help. You can choose between seeing a therapist one-on-one or joining a group, known as "group therapy," which is similar to a support group. Groups may be specialized—for people who have lost a child or a spouse--or they can be for anyone who is learning to manage grief.

### Spiritual Support

People who are grieving may also find comfort in their faith. Visits with a representative of your religious community (such as a minister, priest, rabbi, or Muslim cleric) may help you move through the grieving process and come to terms with your loss. Praying, talking with others of your faith, reading religious or spiritual texts, or listening to uplifting music may also bring comfort.

## Mourning the Death of a Spouse

When your spouse dies, your world changes. You are in mourning—feeling grief and sorrow at the loss. You may feel numb, shocked, and fearful. You may feel guilty for being the one who is still alive. If your spouse died in a nursing home, you may wish that you had been able to care for him or her at home. At some point, you may even feel angry at your spouse for leaving you. All these feelings are normal. There are no rules about how you should feel. There is no right or wrong way to mourn.

When you grieve, you can feel both physical and emotional pain. People who are grieving often cry easily and can have:

- Trouble sleeping
- Little interest in food
- Problems with concentration
- A hard time making decisions

If you are grieving, in addition to dealing with feelings of loss, you may also need to put your own life back together. This can be hard work. Some people may feel better sooner than they expect. Others may take longer. As time passes, you may still miss your spouse, but for most people, the intense pain will lessen. There will be good and bad days. You will know that you are feeling better when the good days begin to outnumber the bad.

For some people, mourning can go on so long that it becomes unhealthy. This can be a sign of serious depression and anxiety. If sadness keeps you from carrying on with your day-to-day life, talk to your doctor.

## What Can You Do?

In the beginning, you may find that taking care of details and keeping busy helps. For a while, family and friends may be around to assist you. But, there comes a time when you will have to face the change in your life.

Here are some ideas to keep in mind:

- Take care of yourself. Grief can be hard on your health. Try to eat right, make exercise a part of your daily routine, take your medicine, and get enough sleep. Bad habits, such as drinking too much alcohol or smoking, can put your health at risk. Keep up with your usual visits to your healthcare provider.

- Talk to caring friends. Let family and friends know when you want to talk about your husband or wife. It may help to be with people who let you say what you're feeling.

- Join a grief support group. Sometimes it helps to talk to people who are also grieving. Check with hospitals, religious communities, and local agencies to find out about support groups.

- Try not to make any major changes right away. It's a good idea to wait for a while before making big decisions like moving or changing jobs.

- See your doctor. If you're having trouble taking care of your everyday activities, like getting dressed or fixing meals, talk to your healthcare provider.

- Don't be afraid to seek professional help. Sometimes short-term talk therapy with a counselor can help.

- Remember your children are grieving, too. You may find that your relationship with your children has changed. It will take time for the whole family to adjust to life without your spouse.

- Mourning takes time. It's common to have rollercoaster emotions for a while.

### Do Men and Women Feel the Same Way?

Men and women share many of the same feelings when their spouse dies. Both may deal with the pain of loss, and both may worry about the future. But, there can also be differences. Often, married couples divide up their household tasks. One person may pay bills and handle car repairs. The other person may cook meals and mow the lawn. Splitting up jobs often works well until there is only one person who has to do it all. Learning to manage new tasks, from chores to household repairs to finances, takes time, but it can be done.

Being alone can increase concerns about safety. It's a good idea to make sure there are working locks on the doors and windows. If you need help, ask your family or friends.

Facing the future without a husband or wife can be scary. Many people have never lived alone. Those who are both widowed and retired may feel very lonely and become depressed. Talk to your doctor about how you are feeling.

### Taking Charge of Your Life

After years of being part of a couple, it can be upsetting to be alone. Many people find it helps to have things to do every day. Write down your weekly plans. You might:

- Take a walk with a friend.
- Go to the library to check out books.
- Volunteer at a local school as a tutor or playground aide.
- Join a community exercise class or a senior swim group.
- Join a singing group.
- Sign up for bingo or bridge at a nearby recreation center.
- Think about a part-time job.
- Join a bowling league.
- Offer to watch your grandchildren.
- Consider adopting a pet.
- Take a class from the recreation center or local college.
- Learn a new skill.

Some widowed people lose interest in cooking and eating. It may help to have lunch with friends at a senior center or cafeteria.

Sometimes eating at home alone feels too quiet. Turning on a radio or TV during meals can help. For information on nutrition and cooking for one, look for helpful books at your local library or bookstore.

## Is There More to Do?

When you feel stronger, you should think about:

- Writing a new will

- Looking into a durable power of attorney for legal matters and a power of attorney for health care in case you are unable to make your own medical decisions

- Putting joint property (such as a house or car) in your name

- Checking on your health insurance as well as your current life, car, and homeowner's insurance

- Signing up for Medicare by your 65th birthday

- Making a list of bills you will need to pay in the next few months; for instance, State and Federal taxes, rent, or mortgage

When you are ready, go through your husband's or wife's clothes and other personal items. It may be hard to give away these belongings. Instead of parting with everything at once, you might make three piles: one to keep, one to give away, and one "not sure." Ask your children or others to help. Think about setting aside items like a special piece of clothing, watch, favorite book, or picture to give to your children or grandchildren as personal reminders of your spouse.

## What about Going Out?

Having a social life can be tough. It may be hard to think about going to parties alone. It can be hard to think about coming home alone. You may be anxious about dating. Many people miss the feeling of closeness that marriage brings. After time, some are ready to have a social life again.

Here are some things to remember:

- Go slowly. There's no rush.

- It's okay to make the first move when it comes to planning things to do.

- Try group activities. Invite friends for a potluck dinner or go to a senior center.

- With married friends, think about informal outings like walks or picnics rather than couples events that remind you of the past.

- Find an activity you like. You may have fun and meet people who like to do the same thing.

- Many people find that pets provide important companionship.

- You can develop meaningful relationships with friends and family members of all ages.

### Don't Forget

Take care of yourself. Get help from your family or professionals if you need it. Be open to new experiences. Don't feel guilty if you laugh at a joke or enjoy a visit with a friend. You are adjusting to life without your spouse.

## Coping with Grief after Community Violence

It is not uncommon for individuals and communities as a whole to experience grief reactions and anger after an incident of community violence. Grief is the normal response of sorrow, emotion, and confusion that comes from losing someone or something important to you. Most people will experience a natural occurrence of grief after the death of a loved one, but grief and anger can be the result of other types of losses. In situations of community violence, people may experience the loss of their sense of safety, their trust in those who live in their neighborhood, or their trust in local government. The trauma and grief of community violence can be experienced by all involved.

### Grief Reactions to Violence

Often after a death or loss of some kind, many people express feeling empty and numb, or unable to feel. Some people complain that they become angry at others or at situations, or they just feel angry in general, even without a reason. Some of the physical reactions to grief and anger may include the following:

- Trembling or shakiness
- Muscle weakness
- Nausea, trouble eating
- Trouble sleeping, trouble breathing
- Dry mouth

People experiencing grief may have nightmares, withdraw socially, and may have no desire to participate in their usual activities, work, or school.

### How Long Do Grief Reactions Last?

Grief lasts as long as it takes you to accept and learn to live with the changes that have occurred in your community due to the violence and its aftermath. For some people, grief lasts a few months; for others, it may take more than a year. It's different for each person depending on his or her health, coping styles, culture, family supports, and other life experiences. How long people grieve may also depend on the resilience of the community and the ability of its members to take on roles and responsibilities that will help restore the basic needs of the community, such as getting children back to school and businesses back to working again.

### Reactions to Community Violence in Children

Witnessing community violence and death can be traumatic experiences that cause negative mental health outcomes, particularly for children. Close relationships are important to children's development, and the loss of family or a community member can represent the loss of social capital—the emotional support that enhances their well-being. Children may experience depression, posttraumatic stress, anxiety, aggression, poor academic achievement, hopelessness, and risky behavior. These losses can even affect their capacity for relationships and diminish future expectations.

### Tips for Helping Children Cope with Grief

- Allow children to talk about their feelings and to express their grief (e.g., crying, being sad).

- Try to follow the same routines as usual.

- Encourage them to play and laugh.

- Limit exposure to violence on TV news.

- Encourage them to get adequate rest and to eat healthy meals.

### What Can Communities Do to Cope with Their Grief?

Often the community needs to come together to honor those who died and find meaning in their deaths in a way that will help everyone in the community recover. People may create a memorial and decide together that this will remind them never to allow such violence in their community again. It may help them be determined to work out their differences in other ways in the future—for example, by forming a community advisory group or identifying a local leader to be their liaison with law enforcement and other government entities.

## What Can Individuals Do to Cope with Their Grief?

Talking to others who understand and respect how you feel— family members, faith leaders, people you trust—is a helpful way to ease your grief. Recognize that although you might still have these feelings over a long period, they will likely be less and less intense over time. Make sure to exercise and eat healthy meals. Do the things that you used to enjoy doing, even if you don't always feel like it. This will help you get back into your routines. Allow yourself to feel joy at times and to cry when you need to.

Even though they may be experiencing grief, some individuals also exhibit positive changes from their experience of loss, such as the following:

- Becoming more understanding and tolerant

- Having increased appreciation for relationships and loved ones

- Being grateful for what they have and for those in their community who are loving and caring

- Experiencing enhanced spiritual connection

- Becoming more socially active

If you have experienced the death of a friend or loved one—or if you have been exposed to community violence—feelings of grief and anger are a normal reaction.

# Section 4.5

# *Pets Are Good for Mental Health*

This section includes excerpts from "The Health Benefits of
Companion Animals," National Park Service (NPS), 2008. Reviewed
March 2016; and text from "Pets Promote Public Health!" U.S. Public
Health Service (USPHS), May 5, 2015.

## *Human-Animal Bond*

Many people intuitively believe that they and others derive
health benefits from relationships with their animal companions,
and numerous scientific studies performed over the past 25 years
support this belief. Among other benefits, animals have been demonstrated to improve human cardio-vascular health, reduce stress,
decrease loneliness and depression, and facilitate social interactions
among people who choose to have pets. Additionally, many terminally ill, pregnant, or immunocompromised people are urged to
relinquish their animal companions due to concerns about zoonoses
(diseases that may be transmitted between humans and non-human
animals). However, giving up their beloved friends may have a detrimental, rather than beneficial, effect on their overall health. In
many instances, human health professionals can contribute to the
welfare of their patients by encouraging them to maintain bonds
with their pets, even in the face of serious illnesses and other
challenges.

## *Physiological Benefits*

Numerous studies highlight physiologic benefits. Pet interaction, whether active or passive, tends to lower anxiety levels in
subjects, and thus decrease the onset, severity, or progression
of stress-related conditions. Furthermore, it is thought that the
reduction in blood pressure achieved through dog ownership can
be equal to the reduction achieved by changing to a low salt diet or
cutting down on alcohol. Pet ownership and other animal contact,
such as petting animals and watching fish in an aquarium, have

specifically been demonstrated to provide cardiovascular benefits. Examples include:

- Increased survival time after myocardial infarction for dog owners.
- Decreased risk factors for cardiovascular disease, particularly lower systolic blood pressure, plasma cholesterol and plasma triglycerides.
- Decreased heart rate from petting a dog or watching fish in an aquarium

These beneficial effects of pets may be mediated by increased exercise associated with pet ownership as well as decreased stress levels.

In addition to providing cardiovascular benefits, decreased physiological stress is associated with animal interaction, contributing to better overall health:

- Greater reduction of cardiovascular stress response in the presence of a dog in comparison to friends or spouses.
- Decreased pulse rate, increased skin temperature, and decreased muscle tension in elderly people watching an aquarium.
- Enhanced hormone levels of dopamine and endorphins associated with happiness and well-being and decreased levels of cortisol, a stress hormone, following a quiet 30-minute session of interacting with a dog.
- Reduced levels of the stress hormone cortisol in health- care professionals after as little as 5 minutes interacting with a therapy dog.

Other studies document that children exposed to pets in early life experience enhanced immune function:

- Fewer allergies and less wheezing and asthma in children exposed to pets during infancy.
- Protection against adult asthma and allergies in adults at age 28 when exposed to pets before 18.

Several studies document overall general health benefits of pet ownership and animal interaction:

- Less frequent illness and less susceptibility to upper respiratory infection related to a significant increase in 18 IgA (Immunoglobulin A) levels occurred after petting a dog.

- Increased lung function and overall quality of life in lung transplant patients who are allowed to have a pet.

- Perceived pain significantly reduced in children undergoing major operations after participation in pet therapy programs.

- A significant reduction in minor health problems for at least 10 months after acquiring a dog.

- Fewer doctor visits per year for elderly dog owners than non-owners.

Companion animals have been shown to provide valuable physiological, psychological, and social benefits. These benefits are often especially significant in vulnerable individuals. Because many individuals who visit health care professionals are especially sensitive due to illness and the effects illness can have on one's quality of life, it is important for health care professionals to support the vital role of animal companionship in their patients' lives.

## Psychological Benefits

Many studies have addressed the contribution of pets to human psychological well-being. One general study found that Australian cat owners scored better on psychological health ratings than did non-owners. Other studies have been more specific, focusing on groups facing stressful life events such as bereavement, illness, and homelessness. Findings from these studies often indicate that pets play a significant supportive role, reducing depression and loneliness and providing companionship and a need for responsibility.

One group of studies, performed with recently bereaved elderly subjects, demonstrated that:

- Recently widowed women who owned pets experienced significantly fewer symptoms of physical and psychological disease and reported lower medication use than widows who did not own pets.

- In bereaved elderly subjects with few social confidants, pet ownership and strong attachment were associated with less depression.

Another group of studies, looking at AIDS patients, found that:

- Patients with AIDS reported that their pets provided companionship and support, reduced stress, and provided a sense of purpose.

- Patients with AIDS reported that cats were an important part of a support system to prevent loneliness.

- Patients with AIDS who owned pets, especially those with few confidants, reported less depression and other benefits compared to those who did not have pets.

A third group of studies, carried out using homeless subjects, showed that:

- Homeless pet owners that were attached to their pets, often reported that their relationships with their pets were their only relationships, and most would not live in housing that would not allow pets.

- Over 40% of homeless adolescents reported that their dogs were a main means of coping with loneliness.

Studies focused on service dogs have shown overall improved quality of life for their human companions:

- Mobility-impaired individuals indicated increased "freedom to be capable" since receiving an assistance dog. Participants additionally reported increased independence and self-esteem, decreased loneliness, and experienced frequent friendliness from strangers.

- Quality of life improved in families of epileptic children when a dog that responds to seizures is present in the home.

Psychological studies reviewing the relationship between animals and children have revealed:

- The mere presence of animals positively alters children's attitudes about themselves and increases their ability to relate to others.

- Pets help children develop in various areas including love, attachment, and comfort; sensorimotor and nonverbal learning; responsibility, nurturance, and competence; learning about the life cycle; therapeutic benefits; and nurturing humanness, ecological awareness, and ethical responsibilities.

- Children exhibited a more playful mood, were more focused, and were more aware of their social environments when in the presence of a therapy dog.

Additional studies have shown:

- Alzheimer's patients still living at home with pets had fewer mood disorders and fewer episodes of aggression and anxiety than did non-pet owners.

- Female pet-owners that have suffered physical abuse report their pets are an important source of emotional support.

- Dog owners were found to be as emotionally close to their dogs as they were their closest family members.

- Psychiatric disability patients who participated in a 10 week horseback riding program had increased self-esteem and an augmented sense of self efficacy.

## Social Benefits

Animals often serve to facilitate social interactions between people. For individuals with visible disabilities who may frequently be socially avoided by others, and in settings such as nursing homes, the role of animals as social catalysts is especially important.

- One study found that elderly people who live in mobile homes and walk their dogs in the area had more conversations focused in the present rather than in the past than those people who walked without their dogs.

- Disabled individuals in wheelchairs accompanied by service dogs during shopping trips received a median of eight friendly approaches from strangers, versus only one approach on trips without a dog.

- Observations of passersby encountering persons in wheelchairs revealed that passersby smiled and conversed more when a service dog was present.

In addition to acting as social catalysts, service dogs provide obvious practical benefits such as alerting their owners to visual hazards, auditory warnings, and impending seizures; assisting with mobility; and seeking help in emergencies. However, studies also indicate that they promote improved psychological well-being and reduce the number of assistance hours required by disabled owners.

## Mental Well-Being

- Companion animals improve mental and emotional well-being in humans.

- Pet owners are less likely to suffer from stress, anxiety, and depression than non-pet owners.
- Pet therapy improves a wide array of mental health disabilities, including anxiety, panic, posttraumatic stress, mood obsessive compulsive, and other disorders.

## Obesity Preventions

- The National Institutes of Health (NIH) found that dog owners who walk their dogs are significantly more likely to meet physical activity guidelines are less likely to be obese than non-dog owners or walkers.
- By providing motivation and social support, pets make it easier for owners to adopt long-term behavior changes that lead to weight loss and other positive health outcomes.
- Pet ownership is associated with key indicators of cardiovascular health such as lower blood pressure, cholesterol, and triglycerides.

## Tobacco Cessation

- 28.4% of smokers said knowing the adverse impact of cigarette smoke on pet health would motivate them to stop smoking. Secondhand smoke exposure is associated with certain cancers in cats and dogs, allergies in dogs, and eye, skin, and respiratory diseases in birds.

# Chapter 5

# *Mental Health in the Workplace*

Mental health is critical to individual well-being, workplace effectiveness, and the functioning of a community. Every employee plays a vital role in creating a positive work environment, understanding what it means to be mentally healthy, and supporting those who may be facing challenges. This chapter will help you gain insight into mental health statistics and issues and learn what you can do if you are concerned about someone.

## 1. Did you know . . .

- Nearly one quarter of the U.S. workforce experiences a mental health or substance use problem each year.

- Many workers have children, spouses, or other loved ones experiencing symptoms of mental illness or a substance abuse condition.

- Mental health and substance abuse conditions and disorders can lead to increased absenteeism and turnover, as well as decreased work quality and productivity.

---

This chapter includes excerpts from "Federal Workplace Supports Mental Health," U.S. Office of Personnel Management (OPM), June 21, 2014; and text from "Mental Health and Chronic Diseases," Centers for Disease Control and Prevention (CDC), October 2, 2012. Reviewed March 2016.

- An average of 100 Americans die each day as a result of suicide, a leading cause of death among working aged Americans.

## 2. What are the signs of a mental health problem?

- Individuals with deteriorating mental health may exhibit changes in their mood, interactions, or performance at work. These include difficulties in making decisions, repeatedly missing deadlines, missing and/or being late to work, reduced quality of work, distractibility, and a general lack of interest and focus.

- Individuals at risk of suicide may talk about wanting to die, feeling hopeless or having no reason to live, or about feeling trapped, in unbearable pain, or being a burden to others. Other indicators include increased use of alcohol or drugs, sleeping too little or too much, withdrawing or becoming isolated.

## 3. Where can I learn more?

- Visit http://www.mentalhealth.gov or call the Substance Abuse and Mental Health Service Administration (SAMHSA) toll-free at 877-SAMHSA-7 (877-726-4727).

- For information on local mental health or substance abuse services, see SAMHSA's Behavioral Health Treatment Locator at: http://findtreatment.samhsa.gov.

## 4. If you are concerned about symptoms in yourself, a co-worker, or a loved one, help is available.

- Mental health problems are treatable and best addressed before they escalate. Your Agency's Employee Assistance Program is a great resource. Contact them through your local Human Resources office, health unit, or your Agency's intranet site.

## 5. If you are concerned about symptoms in yourself, a co-worker, or a loved one, help is available.

- Mental health problems are treatable and best addressed before they escalate. Your Agency's Employee Assistance Program is a great resource. Contact them through your local Human Resources office, health unit, or your Agency's intranet site.

- If you believe someone is in immediate danger, call 911 or seek care at the nearest hospital or emergency room.

- Don't be afraid to reach out to those you believe need help. Asking if an individual is thinking about killing themselves communicates your concern and will not put the idea into their heads or make it more likely that they will attempt suicide. If you need assistance assessing the situation or talking to a friend or co-worker in distress, call the National Suicide Prevention Lifeline toll-free at 800-273-TALK (8255). You will be connected to a trained crisis worker immediately.

## How Does Mental Health and Chronic Disease Affect Employees and the Workplace?

The cost to treat those with chronic diseases is approximately 75% of the total national health expenditures. Expenses related to cardiovascular disease alone were estimated to be $503 billion in 2010.

Direct and indirect costs associated with mental health are also costly. The Agency for Healthcare Research and Quality found that in 2006, $57.5 billion was spent on mental health care in the Unites States. It is estimated that about one-third of those with mental illnesses are employed. One study estimates nearly a quarter of the U.S. workforce (28 million workers aged 18–54 years) experience a mental or substance abuse disorder. The most common mental illnesses in the workplace are alcohol abuse or dependence (9% of workers); major depression (8%); and social anxiety disorder (7%). Most importantly for employees and employers is that 71% of workers with mental illnesses have never sought help from a medical or mental health specialist for their symptoms.

For depression in particular, approximately 80% of persons with depression report some level of functional impairment because of their depression, and 27% reported serious difficulties in work and home life. The condition can also have a large effect on productivity. In a 3 month period, patients with depression miss an average of 4.8 workdays and suffer 11.5 days of reduced productivity. Depression alone is estimated to cause 200 million lost workdays each year at a cost to employers of $17 to $44 billion.

Employers and employees have, in turn, had to bear the burden of rising health care costs. There has been a 97% increase in premiums for employer-sponsored health coverage since 2002. Most of the financial burden of mental health disorders is not from the cost to treat the illness. It is because of income loss from unemployment, expenses for social supports, and indirect costs—such as workers' compensation, short-and long-term disability, presenteeism (the measurable extent to which health symptoms, conditions, and diseases adversely affect the work productivity of individuals who choose to remain at work) and absenteeism.

Complications because of untreated chronic diseases and mental health disorders are the primary cause of missed work and increased presenteeism. Even though there have been increased attention on mental health in recent years, social stigma and discrimination associated with mental illnesses remains a significant barrier to an individual's health and employment. These issues often affect whether or not an individual will apply for a job or promotion when qualified. Stigma and discrimination may also prevent an employee from seeking help contributing to presenteeism and absenteeism and if treatment is sought out it may complicate the transition back to work. Both managers and coworkers alike are often unaware or uncertain how to interact with someone recovering from a mental health disorder.

Many employees will not voluntarily disclose that they suffer from a chronic disease or mental health disorder for fear of being stigmatized. This burden leads to added stress that can exacerbate their condition. In addition, not divulging this information prevents the employer from understanding to what extent some of these health issues are problems and subsequently taking action, such as changing the work environment through a workplace health program.

For example, some instances of this include how organizing and structuring work can contribute to job related stress that can put the individual at an increased risk for chronic disease such as cardiovascular disease. These organizational stressors include psychosocial stressors such as high job demands, low job control for the worker, or social isolation; scheduling issues including shiftwork or long hours;, the physical demands of work whether the position is mostly sedentary or involves heavy physical exertion; exposure to hazardous chemicals such as tobacco smoke or lead; and the broader work environmental conditions(e.g., noise, heat, cold, little access to healthy food).

Through a workplace health program, employers can identify and take steps to improve the work environment to minimize the effect these organizational factors have on employee physical and mental health.

## What Are the Best Practices for Maintaining Employees' Mental Health and Chronic Disease Status?

The Substance Abuse and Mental Health Services Administration (SAMHSA) has developed a toolkit to help workplaces become more mental health-friendly. It describes program and practice strategies that address overall well-being by placing emphasis on both physical and mental health. The main elements of a Mental Health-Friendly Workplace include—

- A workforce where diversity is valued.

- Health care that treats mental illnesses with the same urgency as physical illnesses.

- Programs and practices that promote and support employee health-wellness and work-life balance.

- Training for managers and supervisors in mental health workplace issues, including identifying problems and processes for referral and evaluation.

- Protections for the confidentiality of employee health information.

- An Employee Assistance Program (EAP) or other appropriate referral resources to assist managers and employees.

- Support for employees who seek treatment or who require hospitalization such as disability leave and planning for a return to work.

- Regular communication and education to all employees regarding health and wellness, and similar topics that promote a climate of acceptance that reduces stigma and discrimination in the workplace.

Successful programs take a comprehensive approach to health. A comprehensive program includes education, early detection and screening, program integration, and changes to the work environment to encourage healthy behaviors. The example below shows how both employers and employees can take steps to prevent and reduce work-related stress.

Establishing a workplace culture that recognizes employees for their good work, values each individual, requires that management actions are consistent with company values, and provides career development opportunities for employees, enhances employee self-confidence and productivity. Offering stress-reduction classes and employee options such as physical activity programs improve employees' physical and emotional resiliency and helps them recognize and manage their own stress responses. Stress is better tolerated when employees protect their overall health through healthy behaviors such as physical activity.

EAPs can play a critical role in reducing individual employee stress related to family caregiving or other work-life balance issues. EAPs are designed to offer confidential short-term counseling and information to employees for work and personal concerns that may affect workplace performance. These programs may be in-house or contracted services for counseling, education, and referral. EAPs may include information on child and elder care services, support groups, stress reduction classes, alcohol and substance misuse treatment, mental health including depression, marital counseling, management consultation, and a variety of other important topics for managers and employees. EAPs provide support for all levels of employees from the front line to management personnel and often for employee family members as well.

Employers can use various policy approaches that can decrease the stress effects of shiftwork and long work hours such as interference with family life through organizational change. The amount of time workers spend with family and friends depends on the flexibility of their work schedule and other social and leisure time commitments. Employers can consider several strategies to design work schedules to improve work-life balance, worker satisfaction, and productivity. There is currently a limited amount of knowledge and research regarding shiftwork schedules and these strategies are only suggestions. It is important to remember that alterations to shift schedules affect all aspects of work and home life, so caution should be exercised when considering these strategies including: planning some free weekends, examining start and end times, and keeping the schedule regular and predictable.

# Chapter 6

# *Mental Health Stigma*

## *Stigma and Mental Illness*

Stigma has been defined as an attribute that is deeply discrediting. This stigmatized trait sets the bearer apart from the rest of society, bringing with it feelings of shame and isolation. Often, when a person with a stigmatized trait is unable to perform an action because of the condition, other people view the person as the problem rather than viewing the condition as the problem. More recent definitions of stigma focus on the results of stigma—the prejudice, avoidance, rejection and discrimination directed at people believed to have an illness, disorder or other trait perceived to be undesirable. Stigma causes needless suffering, potentially causing a person to deny symptoms, delay treatment and refrain from daily activities. Stigma can exclude people from access to housing, employment, insurance, and appropriate medical care. Thus, stigma can interfere with prevention efforts, and examining and combating stigma is a public health priority.

The Substance Abuse and Mental Health Services Administration (SAMHSA) and the Centers for Disease Control and Prevention (CDC) have examined public attitudes toward mental illness in two surveys.

This chapter includes excerpts from "Stigma and Mental Illness," Centers for Disease Control and Prevention (CDC), June 18, 2015; and text from "Mental Health Stigma: 10 Things You Should Know About," U.S. Department of Veterans Affairs (VA), June 3, 2015.

77

In the 2006 *HealthStyles* survey, only one-quarter of young adults between the ages of 18–24 believed that a person with mental illness can eventually recover. In 2007, adults in 37 states and territories were surveyed about their attitudes toward mental illness, using the 2007 Behavioral Risk Factor Surveillance System Mental Illness and Stigma module. This study found that

- 78% of adults with mental health symptoms and 89% of adults without such symptoms agreed that treatment can help persons with mental illness lead normal lives.

- 57% of adults without mental health symptoms believed that people are caring and sympathetic to persons with mental illness.

- Only 25% of adults with mental health symptoms believed that people are caring and sympathetic to persons with mental illness.

These findings highlight both the need to educate the public about how to support persons with mental illness and the need to reduce barriers for those seeking or receiving treatment for mental illness.

## Mental Health Stigma: 9 Things You Should Know About

1.   Stigma is defined as "a mark, blemish, or defect; a symbol of disgrace, shame or reproach and often involves fear of that which is different."

2.   Stigma has been identified as a major reason that only about half of all Americans with a serious mental illness seek treatment.

3.   In one survey, many people reported they would rather tell employers they committed a petty crime and served time in jail, than admit to having been in a psychiatric hospital.

4.   Stigma is perpetuated in the media, which often portrays individuals with mental illness as violent and unable to contribute to society. However, research consistently shows that mental illness—by itself—is not significantly linked to violence. In fact, those with serious mental illnesses are much more likely to be a victim of violence than a perpetrator.

5.   Language is closely related to stigma. Using negative labels such as calling someone "crazy" or "a schizophrenic" (not "a

person with schizophrenia") or language that emphasizes limitations, not abilities, strongly influences our and others' perceptions.

6. Science tells us that mental illness is caused by a combination of genetic and life experiences, much of which a person has little or no control over.

7. Organizations such as the National Alliance for Mental Illness (NAMI), the Depression and Bipolar Support Alliance (DBSA), and the "It's Up 2 Us" campaign, serve as advocates and educators to reduce the impact of stigma.

8. The VA has an interactive website "Make the Connection" to reduce stigma of Veterans obtaining mental health services at the VA.

9. What can you do to fight stigma? Communication is key. Seek knowledge, and don't be afraid to talk to trusted others about your mental health concerns.

# Chapter 7

# *Mental Health Statistics*

## Mental Illness Surveillance among Adults in the United States

### How Widespread Is Mental Illness?

Mental illness results in more disability in developed countries than any other group of illnesses, including cancer and heart disease. In 2004, an estimated 25% of adult Americans reported having a mental illness within the previous year.

### What Is Mental Illness Surveillance?

Public health surveillance is the ongoing and systematic collection, analysis, interpretation, and dissemination of data used to develop public health interventions that reduce morbidity and mortality and improve health. Surveillance for a particular condition—such as mental illness—might depend either on collecting new data or using data obtained from existing health information systems.

---

This chapter includes excerpts from "CDC Report: Mental Illness Surveillance among Adults in the United States," Centers for Disease Control and Prevention (CDC), December 2, 2013; text from "Any Mental Illness (AMI) among U.S. Adults," National Institute of Mental Health (NIMH), January 8, 2014; and text from "Serious Mental Illness (SMI) among U.S. Adults," National Institute of Mental Health (NIMH), January 8, 2014.

## Why Is Monitoring Mental Illness Important?

Surveillance activities that monitor mental illness are essential because mental illness is a significant public health problem. For example, according to the World Health Organization, mental illnesses account for more disability in developed countries than any other group of illnesses, including cancer and heart disease. Published studies report that about 25% of all U.S. adults have a mental illness and that nearly 50% of U.S. adults will develop at least one mental illness during their lifetime.

Mental illness is associated with:

- increased occurrence of chronic diseases such as cardiovasculardisease, diabetes, obesity, asthma, epilepsy, and cancer

- lower use of medical care, reduced adherence to treatment therapies for chronic diseases, and higher risks of adverse health outcomes

- use of tobacco products and abuse of alcohol

Rates for both intentional (e.g., homicide, suicide) and unintentional (e.g., motor vehicle) injuries are 2 to 6 times higher among people with a mental illness than in the population overall. Population-based surveys and surveillance systems provide much of the evidence needed to guide effective mental health promotion, mental illness prevention, and treatment programs. Monitoring mental illness is an important way to provide appropriate organizations the data they need to assess the need for mental and behavioral health services and to inform the provision of those services. Many mental illnesses can be managed successfully, and increasing access to and use of mental health treatment services could substantially reduce the associated morbidity.

Many chronic illnesses are associated with mental illnesses, and it's been shown that treatment of mental illnesses associated with chronic diseases can reduce the effects of both and support better outcomes. CDC surveillance systems provide several types of mental health information, such as estimates of the prevalence of diagnosed mental illness from self-report or recorded diagnosis, estimates of the prevalence of symptoms associated with mental illness, and estimates of the effect of mental illness on health and well-being.

## Any Mental Illness (AMI) among U.S. Adults

- Mental illnesses are common in the United States.

- The data presented here are from the National Survey on Drug Use and Health (NSDUH), which defines any mental illness(AMI) as:

  - A mental, behavioral, or emotional disorder (excluding developmental and substance use disorders);

  - Diagnosable currently or within the past year; and

  - Of sufficient duration to meet diagnostic criteria specified within the 4th edition of the Diagnostic and Statistical Manual of Mental Disorders (DSM-IV).

- AMI can range in impact from no or mild impairment to significantly disabling impairment, such as in individuals with serious mental illness (SMI), defined as individuals with a mental disorder with serious functional impairment which substantially interferes with or limits one or more major life activities.

- As noted, these estimates of AMI do not include substance use disorders, such as drug- or alcohol-related disorders.

- In 2014, there were an estimated 43.6 million adults aged 18 or older in the United States with AMI in the past year. This number represented 18.1% of all U.S. adults.

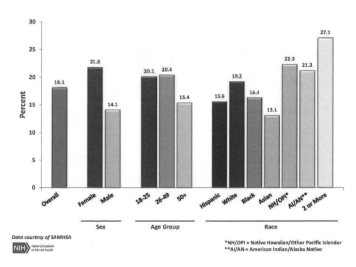

**Figure 7.1.** *Prevalence of Any Mental Illness among U.S. Adults (2014)*

## Serious Mental Illness (SMI) among U.S. Adults

- While mental disorders are common in the United States, their burden of illness is particularly concentrated among those who experience disability due to serious mental illness (SMI).

- The data presented here are from the National Survey on Drug Use and Health (NSDUH), which defines SMI as:

  - A mental, behavioral, or emotional disorder (excluding developmental and substance use disorders);

  - Diagnosable currently or within the past year;

  - Of sufficient duration to meet diagnostic criteria specified within the 4th edition of the Diagnostic and Statistical Manual of Mental Disorders (DSM-IV); and

  - Resulting in serious functional impairment, which substantially interferes with or limits one or more major life activities.

- In 2014, there were an estimated 9.8 million adults aged 18 or older in the United States with SMI. This number represented 4.2% of all U.S. Adults.

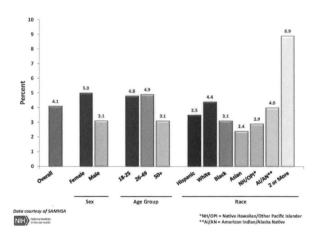

Data courtesy of SAMHSA

*NH/OPI = Native Hawaiian/Other Pacific Islander
**AI/AN = American Indian/Alaska Native

**Figure 7.2.** *Prevalence of Serious Mental Illness Among U.S. Adults (2014)*

# Part Two

# Mental Illnesses

# Chapter 8

# *Suicide and Mental Illness*

## *Chapter Contents*

# Section 8.1

# *Facts about Suicide*

Text in this section is excerpted from "Suicide," Centers for
Disease Control and Prevention (CDC), 2015.

## *Suicide*

- Suicide was the tenth leading cause of death for all ages in 2013.

- There were 41,149 suicides in 2013 in the United States—a rate
  of 12.6 per 100,000 is equal to 113 suicides each day or one every
  13 minutes.

- Based on data about suicides in 16 National Violent Death
  Reporting System states in 2010, 33.4% of suicide decedents
  tested positive for alcohol, 23.8% for antidepressants, and 20.0%
  for opiates, including heroin and prescription painkillers.

- Suicide results in an estimated $51 billion in combined medical
  and work loss costs.

## *Nonfatal Suicidal Thoughts and Behavior*

Among adults aged ≥18 years in the United States during 2013:

- An estimated 9.3 million adults (3.9% of the adult U.S. population) reported having suicidal thoughts in the past year.

- The percentage of adults having serious thoughts about suicide was highest among adults aged 18 to 25 (7.4%), followed
  by adults aged 26 to 49 (4.0%), then by adults aged 50 or older
  (2.7%).

- An estimated 2.7 million people (1.1% ) made a plan about how
  they would attempt suicide in the past year.

- The percentage of adults who made a suicide plan in the past
  year was higher among adults aged 18 to 25 (2.5%) than among
  adults aged 26 to 49 (1.35%) and those aged 50 or older (0.6%).

- An estimated 1.3 million adults aged 18 or older (0.6%) attempted suicide in the past year. Among these adults who attempted suicide, 1.1 million also reported making suicide plans (0.2 million did not make suicide plans).

Among students in grades 9–12 in the U.S. during 2013:

- 17.0% of students seriously considered attempting suicide in the previous 12 months (22.4% of females and 11.6% of males).

- 13.6% of students made a plan about how they would attempt suicide in the previous 12 months (16.9% of females and 10.3% of males).

- 8.0% of students attempted suicide one or more times in the previous 12 months (10.6% of females and 5.4% of males).

- 2.7% of students made a suicide attempt that resulted in an injury, poisoning, or an overdose that required medical attention (3.6% of females and 1.8% of males).

## Gender Disparities

- Males take their own lives at nearly four times the rate of females and represent 77.9% of all suicides.

- Females are more likely than males to have suicidal thoughts.

- Suicide is the seventh leading cause of death for males and the fourteenth leading cause for females.

- Firearms are the most commonly used method of suicide among males (56.9%).

- Poisoning is the most common method of suicide for females (34.8%).

## Racial and Ethnic Disparities

- Suicide is the eighth leading cause of death among American Indians/Alaska Natives across all ages.

- Among American Indians/Alaska Natives aged 10 to 34 years, suicide is the second leading cause of death.

- The suicide rate among American Indian/Alaska Native adolescents and young adults ages 15 to 34 (19.5 per 100,000) is 1.5

times higher than the national average for that age group (12.9 per 100,000).

- The percentages of adults aged 18 or older having suicidal thoughts in the previous 12 months were 2.9% among blacks, 3.3% among Asians, 3.6% among Hispanics, 4.1% among whites, 4.6% among Native Hawaiians /Other Pacific Islanders, 4.8% among American Indians/Alaska Natives, and 7.9% among adults reporting two or more races.

- Among Hispanic students in grades 9–12, the prevalence of having seriously considered attempting suicide (18.9%), having made a plan about how they would attempt suicide (15.7%), having attempted suicide (11.3%), and having made a suicide attempt that resulted in an injury, poisoning, or overdose that required medical attention (4.1%) was consistently higher than white and black students.

## Age Group Differences

- Suicide is the third leading cause of death among persons aged 10–14, the second among persons aged 15–34 years, the fourth among persons aged 35–44 years, the fifth among persons aged 45–54 years, the eighth among person 55–64 years, and the seventeenth among persons 65 years and older.

- In 2011, middle-aged adults accounted for the largest proportion of suicides (56%), and from 1999–2010, the suicide rate among this group increased by nearly 30%.

- Among adults aged 18–22 years, similar percentages of full-time college students and other adults in this age group had suicidal thoughts (8.0 and 8.7%, respectively) or made suicide plans (2.4 and 3.1%).

- Full-time college students aged 18–22 years were less likely to attempt suicide (0.9 vs. 1.9 percent) or receive medical attention as a result of a suicide attempt in the previous 12 months (0.3 vs. 0.7%).

## Nonfatal, Self-Inflicted Injuries

- In 2013, 494,169 people were treated in emergency departments for self-inflicted injuries.

- Nonfatal, self-inflicted injuries (including hospitalized and emergency department treated and released) resulted in an estimated $10.4 billion in combined medical and work loss costs.

# Section 8.2

## *Questions about Suicide Risk*

This section includes excerpts from "Does Depression Increase the Risk for Suicide?" U.S. Department of Health and Human Services (HHS), September 16, 2014; and text from "Suicide in America: Frequently Asked Questions (2015)," National Institute of Mental Health (NIMH), April 2015.

### *Does Depression Increase the Risk for Suicide?*

Although the majority of people who have depression do not die by suicide, having major depression does increase suicide risk compared to people without depression. The risk of death by suicide may, in part, be related to the severity of the depression.

New data on depression that has followed people over long periods of time suggests that about 2 percent of those people ever treated for depression in an outpatient setting will die by suicide. Among those ever treated for depression in an inpatient hospital setting, the rate of death by suicide is twice as high (4 percent). Those treated for depression as inpatients following suicide ideation or suicide attempts are about three times as likely to die by suicide (6 percent) as those who were only treated as outpatients. There are also dramatic gender differences in lifetime risk of suicide in depression. Whereas about 7 percent of men with a lifetime history of depression will die by suicide, only 1 percent of women with a lifetime history of depression will die by suicide.

Another way about thinking of suicide risk and depression is to examine the lives of people who have died by suicide and see what proportion of them were depressed. From that perspective, it is estimated that about 60 percent of people who commit suicide have had a mood disorder (e.g., major depression, bipolar disorder, dysthymia).

91

Younger persons who kill themselves often have a substance abuse disorder, in addition to being depressed.

## *Suicide in America: Frequently Asked Questions*

Suicide does not discriminate. People of all genders, ages, and ethnicities can be at risk for suicide. But people most at risk tend to share certain characteristics. The main risk factors for suicide are:

- Depression, other mental disorders, or substance abuse disorder
- A prior suicide attempt
- Family history of a mental disorder or substance abuse
- Family history of suicide
- Family violence, including physical or sexual abuse
- Having guns or other firearms in the home
- Incarceration, being in prison or jail
- Being exposed to others' suicidal behavior, such as that of family members, peers, or media figures.

The risk for suicidal behavior is complex. Research suggests that people who attempt suicide differ from others in many aspects of how they think, react to events, and make decisions. There are differences in aspects of memory, attention, planning, and emotion, for example. These differences often occur along with disorders like depression, substance use, anxiety, and psychosis. Sometimes suicidal behavior is triggered by events such as personal loss or violence. In order to be able to detect those at risk and prevent suicide, it is crucial that we understand the role of both long-term factors—such as experiences in childhood—and more immediate factors like mental health and recent life events. Researchers are also looking at how genes can either increase risk or make someone more resilient to loss and hardships.

Many people have some of these risk factors but do not attempt suicide. Suicide is not a normal response to stress. It is, however, a sign of extreme distress, not a harmless bid for attention.

### *What about Gender?*

Men are more likely to die by suicide than women, but women are more likely to attempt suicide. Men are more likely to use deadlier methods, such as firearms or suffocation. Women are more likely than men to attempt suicide by poisoning.

### What about Children?

Children and young people are at risk for suicide. Suicide is the second leading cause of death for young people ages 15 to 34.

### What about Older Adults?

Older adults are at risk for suicide, too. While older adults were the demographic group with the highest suicide rates for decades, suicide rates for middle-aged adults has increased to comparable levels (ages 24–62). Among those age 65+, white males comprise over 80 percent of all late-life suicides.

### What about Different Ethnic Groups?

Among ethnicities, American Indians and Alaska Natives (AI/AN) tend to have the highest rate of suicides, followed by non-Hispanic Whites. Hispanics, African Americans, and Asian/Pacific Islanders each have suicide rates that are about half their White and AI/AN counterparts.

### How Can Suicide Be Prevented?

Effective suicide prevention is based on sound research. Programs that work take into account people's risk factors and promote interventions that are appropriate to specific groups of people. For example, research has shown that mental and substance abuse disorders are risk factors for suicide. Therefore, many programs focus on treating these disorders in addition to addressing suicide risk specifically.

Psychotherapy, or "talk therapy," can effectively reduce suicide risk. One type is called cognitive behavioral therapy (CBT). CBT can help people learn new ways of dealing with stressful experiences by training them to consider alternative actions when thoughts of suicide arise.

Another type of psychotherapy called dialectical behavior therapy (DBT) has been shown to reduce the rate of suicide among people with borderline personality disorder, a serious mental illness characterized by unstable moods, relationships, self- image, and behavior. A therapist trained in DBT helps a person recognize when his or her feelings or actions are disruptive or unhealthy, and teaches the skills needed to deal better with upsetting situations.

Medications may also help; promising medications and psychosocial treatments for suicidal people are being tested.

Still other research has found that many older adults and women who die by suicide saw their primary care providers in the year before death. Training doctors to recognize signs that a person may be considering suicide may help prevent even more suicides.

## What Should I Do If Someone I Know Is Considering Suicide?

If you know someone who is considering suicide, do not leave him or her alone. Try to get your loved one to seek immediate help from his or her doctor or the nearest hospital emergency room, or call 911. Remove any access he or she may have to firearms or other potential tools for suicide, including medications.

### If You Are in Crisis

Call the toll-free National Suicide Prevention Lifeline at 1-800-273-TALK (8255), available 24 hours a day, 7 days a week. The service is available to anyone. All calls are confidential.

# Section 8.3

# *Suicide Risks and Prevention*

This section includes excerpts from "Suicide: Risk and Protective Factors," Centers for Disease Control and Prevention (CDC), August 28, 2015; and text from "Preventing Suicide," Centers for Disease Control and Prevention (CDC), September 9, 2015.

## Suicide: Risk and Protective Factors

### Risk Factors for Suicide

A combination of individual, relational, community, and societal factors contribute to the risk of suicide. Risk factors are those characteristics associated with suicide—they might not be direct causes.

*Risk Factors*

- Family history of suicide

- Family history of child maltreatment

- Previous suicide attempt(s)

- History of mental disorders, particularly clinical depression

- History of alcohol and substance abuse

- Feelings of hopelessness

- Impulsive or aggressive tendencies

- Cultural and religious beliefs (e.g., belief that suicide is noble resolution of a personal dilemma)

- Local epidemics of suicide

- Isolation, a feeling of being cut off from other people

- Barriers to accessing mental health treatment

- Loss (relational, social, work, or financial)

- Physical illness

- Easy access to lethal methods

- Unwillingness to seek help because of the stigma attached to mental health and substance abuse disorders or to suicidal thoughts

## Protective Factors for Suicide

Protective factors buffer individuals from suicidal thoughts and behavior. To date, protective factors have not been studied as extensively or rigorously as risk factors. Identifying and understanding protective factors are, however, equally as important as researching risk factors.

*Protective Factors*

- Effective clinical care for mental, physical, and substance abuse disorders

- Easy access to a variety of clinical interventions and support for help seeking

- Family and community support (connectedness)

- Support from ongoing medical and mental health care relationships

- Skills in problem solving, conflict resolution, and nonviolent ways of handling disputes

- Cultural and religious beliefs that discourage suicide and support instincts for self-preservation

## *Preventing Suicide*

Suicide can be prevented. Each year, more than 41,000 Americans take their own lives and more than 494,000 Americans receive medical care for self-inflicted injuries. September 10th is World Suicide Prevention Day, and the entire month is dedicated to suicide prevention awareness in the United States. Help prevent suicide in your community by knowing the facts, warning signs, and where to get help.

Suicide is a serious public health problem that affects people of all ages. It is the tenth leading cause of death for Americans. The top three methods used in suicides include firearms (51.5%), suffocation (24.5%), and poisoning (16.1%).

Deaths from suicide are only part of the problem. Many more people survive suicide attempts than actually die. In 2013, nearly half a million people (494,169) received medical care for self-inflicted injuries at emergency departments across the United States. More than one million adults self-reported a suicide attempt, and 9.3 million adults self-reported serious thoughts of suicide.

Suicide is often the result of multiple risk factors. Having these risk factors, however, does not mean that suicide will occur. Some of the risk factors researchers identified include the following:

- History of previous suicide attempts

- Family history of suicide

- History of depression or other mental illness

- History of alcohol or drug abuse

- Stressful life event or loss (e.g., job, financial, relationship)

- Easy access to lethal methods

- History of interpersonal violence

- Stigma associated with mental illness and help-seeking

Protective factors buffer individuals from suicidal thoughts and behavior. Some of the protective factors researchers identified are listed below.

- Skills in problem solving, conflict resolution, and nonviolent ways of handling disputes

- Effective clinical care for mental, physical, and substance abuse disorders

- Easy access to various clinical interventions and support

- Family and community support (connectedness)

- Cultural or religious beliefs that discourage suicide and support seeking help

Many people are uncomfortable with the topic of suicide. Too often, victims are blamed and their families and friends are left stigmatized. As a result, people rarely communicate openly about suicide. Thus, an important public health problem is left hidden in secrecy, which hinders effective prevention.

## *Know the Warning Signs and Get Help*

There are warning signs for suicide. Research has uncovered a wealth of information about the causes of suicide and prevention strategies. For more information, visit American Association of Suicidology. If you or someone you know is having thoughts of suicide, contact the National Suicide Prevention Lifeline at 1-800-273-TALK (1-800-273-8255).

# Chapter 9

# *Depressive Disorders*

## *Chapter Contents*

Section 9.1

# *Depression*

Text in this section is excerpted from "Depression:
What You Need to Know," National Institute of
Mental Health (NIMH), December 13, 2015.

## *Depression Is a Real Illness*

Sadness is something we all experience. It is a normal reaction to difficult times in life and usually passes with a little time.

When a person has depression, it interferes with daily life and normal functioning. It can cause pain for both the person with depression and those who care about him or her. Doctors call this condition "depressive disorder," or "clinical depression." It is a real illness. It is not a sign of a person's weakness or a character flaw. You can't "snap out of" clinical depression. Most people who experience depression need treatment to get better.

### *Signs and Symptoms*

Sadness is only a small part of depression. Some people with depression may not feel sadness at all. Depression has many other symptoms, including physical ones. If you have been experiencing any of the following signs and symptoms for at least 2 weeks, you may be suffering from depression:

- Persistent sad, anxious, or "empty" mood

- Feelings of hopelessness, pessimism

- Feelings of guilt, worthlessness, helplessness

- Loss of interest or pleasure in hobbies and activities

- Decreased energy, fatigue, being "slowed down"

- Difficulty concentrating, remembering, making decisions

- Difficulty sleeping, early-morning awakening, or oversleeping

- Appetite and/or weight changes

- Thoughts of death or suicide, suicide attempts
- Restlessness, irritability
- Persistent physical symptoms

### Factors That Play a Role in Depression

Many factors may play a role in depression, including genetics, brain biology and chemistry, and life events such as trauma, loss of a loved one, a difficult relationship, an early childhood experience, or any stressful situation.

Depression can happen at any age, but often begins in the teens or early 20s or 30s. Most chronic mood and anxiety disorders in adults begin as high levels of anxiety in children. In fact, high levels of anxiety as a child could mean a higher risk of depression as an adult.

Depression can co-occur with other serious medical illnesses such as diabetes, cancer, heart disease, and Parkinson disease. Depression can make these conditions worse and vice versa. Sometimes medications taken for these illnesses may cause side effects that contribute to depression. A doctor experienced in treating these complicated illnesses can help work out the best treatment strategy.

Research on depression is ongoing, and one day these discoveries may lead to better diagnosis and treatment.

## Types of Depression

There are several types of depressive disorders.

**Major depression:** Severe symptoms that interfere with the ability to work, sleep, study, eat, and enjoy life. An episode can occur only once in a person's lifetime, but more often, a person has several episodes.

**Persistent depressive disorder:** A depressed mood that lasts for at least 2 years. A person diagnosed with persistent depressive disorder may have episodes of major depression along with periods of less severe symptoms, but symptoms must last for 2 years.

Some forms of depression are slightly different, or they may develop under unique circumstances. They include:

**Psychotic depression,** which occurs when a person has severe depression plus some form of psychosis, such as having disturbing false beliefs or a break with reality (delusions), or hearing or seeing upsetting things that others cannot hear or see (hallucinations).

**Postpartum depression,** which is much more serious than the "baby blues" that many women experience after giving birth, when hormonal and physical changes and the new responsibility of caring for a newborn can be overwhelming. It is estimated that 10 to 15 percent of women experience postpartum depression after giving birth.

**Seasonal affective disorder** (SAD), which is characterized by the onset of depression during the winter months, when there is less natural sunlight. The depression generally lifts during spring and summer. SAD may be effectively treated with light therapy, but nearly half of those with SAD do not get better with light therapy alone. Antidepressant medication and psychotherapy can reduce SAD symptoms, either alone or in combination with light therapy.

**Bipolar disorder** is different from depression. The reason it is included in this list is because someone with bipolar disorder experiences episodes of extreme low moods (depression). But a person with bipolar disorder also experiences extreme high moods (called "mania").

## Depression Affects People in Different Ways

Not everyone who is depressed experiences every symptom. Some people experience only a few symptoms. Some people have many. The severity and frequency of symptoms, and how long they last, will vary depending on the individual and his or her particular illness. Symptoms may also vary depending on the stage of the illness.

### Women

Women with depression do not all experience the same symptoms. However, women with depression typically have symptoms of sadness, worthlessness, and guilt.

Depression is more common among women than among men. Biological, life cycle, hormonal, and psychosocial factors that are unique to women may be linked to their higher depression rate. For example, women are especially vulnerable to developing postpartum depression after giving birth, when hormonal and physical changes and the new responsibility of caring for a newborn can be overwhelming.

### Men

Men often experience depression differently than women. While women with depression are more likely to have feelings of sadness, worthlessness, and excessive guilt, men are more likely to be very tired, irritable, lose interest in once-pleasurable activities, and have difficulty sleeping.

Men may turn to alcohol or drugs when they are depressed. They also may become frustrated, discouraged, irritable, angry, and sometimes abusive. Some men may throw themselves into their work to avoid talking about their depression with family or friends, or behave recklessly. And although more women attempt suicide, many more men die by suicide in the United States.

## *Children*

Before puberty, girls and boys are equally likely to develop depression. A child with depression may pretend to be sick, refuse to go to school, cling to a parent, or worry that a parent may die. Because normal behaviors vary from one childhood stage to another, it can be difficult to tell whether a child is just going through a temporary "phase" or is suffering from depression. Sometimes the parents become worried about how the child's behavior has changed, or a teacher mentions that "your child doesn't seem to be himself." In such a case, if a visit to the child's pediatrician rules out physical symptoms, the doctor will probably suggest that the child be evaluated, preferably by a mental health professional who specializes in the treatment of children. Most chronic mood disorders, such as depression, begin as high levels of anxiety in children.

## *Teens*

The teen years can be tough. Teens are forming an identity apart from their parents, grappling with gender issues and emerging sexuality, and making independent decisions for the first time in their lives. Occasional bad moods are to be expected, but depression is different.

Older children and teens with depression may sulk, get into trouble at school, be negative and irritable, and feel misunderstood. If you're unsure if an adolescent in your life is depressed or just "being a teenager," consider how long the symptoms have been present, how severe they are, and how different the teen is acting from his or her usual self. Teens with depression may also have other disorders such as anxiety, eating disorders, or substance abuse. They may also be at higher risk for suicide.

Children and teenagers usually rely on parents, teachers, or other caregivers to recognize their suffering and get them the treatment they need. Many teens don't know where to go for mental health treatment or believe that treatment won't help. Others don't get help because they think depression symptoms may be just part of the typical stress of school or being a teen. Some teens worry what other people will think if they seek mental health care.

## Quick Tips for Talking to Your Depressed Child or Teen

- Offer emotional support, understanding, patience, and encouragement.

- Talk to your child, not necessarily about depression, and listen carefully.

- Never discount the feelings your child expresses, but point out realities and offer hope.

- Never ignore comments about suicide.

- Remind your child that with time and treatment, the depression will lift.

Depression often persists, recurs, and continues into adulthood, especially if left untreated. If you suspect a child or teenager in your life is suffering from depression, speak up right away.

### Older People

Having depression for a long period of time is not a normal part of growing older. Most older adults feel satisfied with their lives, despite having more illnesses or physical problems. But depression in older adults may be difficult to recognize because they may show different, less obvious symptoms.

Sometimes older people who are depressed appear to feel tired, have trouble sleeping, or seem grumpy and irritable. Confusion or attention problems caused by depression can sometimes look like Alzheimer disease or other brain disorders. Older adults also may have more medical conditions such as heart disease, stroke, or cancer, which may cause depressive symptoms. Or they may be taking medications with side effects that contribute to depression.

Some older adults may experience what doctors call vascular depression, also called arteriosclerotic depression or subcortical ischemic depression. Vascular depression may result when blood vessels become less flexible and harden over time, becoming constricted. The hardening of vessels prevents normal blood flow to the body's organs, including the brain. Those with vascular depression may have or be at risk for heart disease or stroke.

Sometimes it can be difficult to distinguish grief from major depression. Grief after loss of a loved one is a normal reaction and generally does not require professional mental health treatment. However, grief that is complicated and lasts for a very long time following a loss may require treatment.

Older adults who had depression when they were younger are more at risk for developing depression in late life than those who did not have the illness earlier in life.

## Depression Is Treatable

Depression, even the most severe cases, can be treated. The earlier treatment begins, the more effective it is. Most adults see an improvement in their symptoms when treated with antidepressant drugs, talk therapy (psychotherapy), or a combination of both.

If you think you may have depression, start by making an appointment to see your doctor or healthcare provider. This could be your primary doctor or a health provider who specializes in diagnosing and treating mental health conditions (psychologist or psychiatrist). Certain medications, and some medical conditions, such as viruses or a thyroid disorder, can cause the same symptoms as depression. A doctor can rule out these possibilities by doing a physical exam, interview, and lab tests. If the doctor can find no medical condition that may be causing the depression, the next step is a psychological evaluation.

### Talking to Your Doctor

How well you and your doctor talk to each other is one of the most important parts of getting good healthcare. But talking to your doctor isn't always easy. It takes time and effort on your part as well as your doctor's.

To prepare for your appointment, make a list of:

- Any symptoms you've had, including any that may seem unrelated to the reason for your appointment
- When did your symptoms start?
- How severe are your symptoms?
- Have the symptoms occurred before?

- If the symptoms have occurred before, how were they treated?

- Key personal information, including any major stresses or recent life changes

- All medications, vitamins, or other supplements that you're taking, including how much and how often

- Questions to ask your health provider

If you don't have a primary doctor or are not at ease with the one you currently see, now may be the time to find a new doctor. Whether you just moved to a new city, changed insurance providers, or had a bad experience with your doctor or medical staff, it is worthwhile to spend time finding a doctor you can trust.

## Section 9.2

# *Major Depression*

Text in this section is excerpted from "What Is Major Depression?" U.S. Department of Veterans Affairs (VA), March 15, 2012. Reviewed March 2016.

## *Basic Facts*

Major depression is a medical condition distinguished by one or more major depressive episodes. A major depressive episode is characterized by at least two weeks of depressed mood or loss of interest (pleasure) and accompanied by at least four more symptoms of depression. Such symptoms can include changes in appetite, weight, difficulty in thinking and concentrating, and recurrent thoughts of death or suicide. Depression differs from feeling "blue" in that it causes severe enough problems to interfere with a person's day-to-day functioning.

People's experience with major depression varies. Some people describe it as a total loss of energy or enthusiasm to do anything. Others may describe it as constantly living with a feeling of impending doom. There are treatments that help improve functioning and relieve many symptoms of depression. Recovery is possible!

## Prevalence

Major depression is a common psychiatric disorder. It is more common in adolescent and adult women than in adolescent and adult men. Between 15 to 20 out of every 100 people (15–20%) experience an episode of major depression during their lifetime. Prevalence has not been found to be related to ethnicity, income, education, or marital status.

## Diagnosis

Major depression cannot be diagnosed with a blood test, CAT-scan, or any other laboratory test. The only way to diagnose major depression is with a clinical interview. The interviewer checks to See if the person has experienced severe symptoms for at least two weeks. If the symptoms are less severe, but last over long periods of time, the person may be diagnosed with persistent depressive disorder. The clinician must also check to be sure there are no physical problems that could cause symptoms like those of major depression, such as a brain tumor or a thyroid problem.

## Course of Illness

The average age of onset is in the mid-20s, however, major depression can begin at any age in life. The frequency of episodes varies from person to person. Some people have isolated episodes over many years, while others suffer from frequent episodes clustered together. The number of episodes generally increases as the person grows older. The severity of the initial episode of major depression seems to indicate persistence. Episodes also seem to follow major stressors, such as the death of a loved one or a divorce. Chronic medical conditions and substance abuse may further exacerbate depressive episodes.

## Causes

There is no simple answer to what causes depression because several factors play a part in the onset of the disorder. These include a genetic or family history of depression, environmental stressors, life events, biological factors, and psychological vulnerability to depression.

Research shows that the risk for depression results from the influence of multiple genes acting together with environmental factors. This is called the stress-vulnerability model. A family history of depression does not necessarily mean children or other relatives will develop major depression. However, those with a family history of depression

107

have a slightly higher chance of becoming depressed at some stage in their lives. Although genetic research suggests that depression can run in families, genetics alone are unlikely to cause depression. Environmental factors, such as a traumatic childhood or adult life events, may act as triggers. Studies show that early childhood trauma and losses, such as the death or separation of parents, or adult life events, such as the death of a loved one, divorce, loss of a job, retirement, serious financial problems, and family conflict, can lead to the onset of depression. Subsequent episodes are usually caused by more mild stressors or even none at all.

Many scientists believe the cause is biological, such as an imbalance in brain chemicals, specifically serotonin and norepinephrine. There are also theories that physical changes to the body may play a role in depression. Such physical changes can include viral and other infections, heart attack, cancer, or hormonal disorders.

Personality style may also contribute to the onset of depression. people are at a greater risk of becoming depressed if they have low self-esteem, tend to worry a lot, are overly dependent on others, are perfectionists, or expect too much from themselves and others.

## Symptoms of Depression

To meet criteria for major depressive disorder, a person must meet at least five symptoms of depression for at least a two week period. Social, occupational, and other areas of functioning must be significantly impaired, or at least require increased effort. Depressed mood caused by substances (such as drugs, alcohol, or medications) or related to another medical condition is not considered to be major depressive disorder. Major depressive disorder also cannot be diagnosed if a person has a history of manic, hypomanic, or mixed episodes (e.g., bipolar disorder) or if the depressed mood is better accounted for by schizoaffective disorder.

Not all symptoms must be present for a person to be diagnosed with depression. Five (or more) of the following symptoms have to be present during the same 2-week period and represent a change from previous functioning. At least one of the symptoms must be either (1) depressed mood or (2) loss of interest or pleasure.

1.  Depressed mood most of the day, nearly everyday, as indicated by either subjective report (e.g., feels sad or empty) or observation made by others (e.g., appears tearful). In children and adolescents, this may be characterized as irritable mood rather than sad mood.

2.  Markedly diminished interest or pleasure in all, or almost all, activities most of the day, nearly every day. This includes activities that were previously found enjoyable.

3.  Significant weight loss when not dieting or weight gain (e.g., a change of more than 5% of body weight in a month), or a decrease or increase in appetite nearly every day.

4.  Insomnia or hypersomnia nearly every day. The person may have difficulty falling asleep, staying asleep, or waking early in the morning and not being able to get back to sleep. Alternatively, the person may sleep excessively (such as over 12 hours per night) and spend much of the day in bed.

5.  Psychomotor agitation (e.g., inability to sit still or pacing) or psychomotor retardation (e.g., slowed speech, thinking, and body movements) nearly every day. Changes in activity level are common in depression. The person may feel agitated, "on edge," and restless. Alternatively, they may experience decreased activity level reflected by slowness and lethargy, both in terms of the person's behavior and thought processes.

6.  Fatigue or loss of energy nearly every day.

7.  Feelings of worthlessness or excessive or inappropriate guilt nearly every day. Depressed people may feel they are worthless or that there is no hope for improving their lives. Feelings of guilt may be present about events with which the person had no involvement, such as a catastrophe, a crime, or an illness.

8.  Diminished ability to think or concentrate, or indecisiveness, nearly every day. A significant decrease in the ability to concentrate makes it difficult to pay attention to others or contemplate simple tasks. The person may be quite indecisive about even minor things.

9.  Recurrent thoughts of death (not just fear of dying), recurrent suicidal ideation without a specific plan, a specific plan for committing suicide, or a suicide attempt.

There are other psychiatric symptoms that depressed people often experience. They might complain of bodily aches and pains rather than feelings of sadness. They might report or exhibit persistent anger, angry outbursts, and an exaggerated sense of frustration over seemingly minor events. Symptoms of anxiety are also very common among people with depression. Other symptoms include hallucinations (false perceptions, such as hearing voices) and delusions (false beliefs, such as paranoid delusions). These symptoms usually disappear when the symptoms of depression have been controlled.

## Similar Psychiatric Disorders

Major depression shares symptoms with some of the other psychiatric disorders. If the person experiences very high or euphoric moods called mania, they would be given a diagnosis of bipolar disorder. If the person exhibits psychotic symptoms while not depressed, they might be diagnosed with schizoaffective disorder. Major depression must also be distinguished from a depressive disorder due to another medical condition. In this case, the mood disturbances are caused by physiological changes due to a medical condition.

## Treatment

There are a variety of antidepressant medications and therapies available to those suffering from depression. Antidepressant medications help to stabilize mood. People can also learn to manage their symptoms with psychotherapy. People with a milder form of depression may benefit from psychotherapy alone, while those with more severe symptoms and episodes may benefit from antidepressants. A combination of both types of treatment is often most helpful to people. The treatments listed here are ones which research have shown to be effective for people with depression. They are considered to be evidence-based practices.

### Cognitive Behavioral Therapy (CBT)

Cognitive behavioral therapy (CBT) is a well established treatment for people with depression. CBT is a blend of two therapies: cognitive therapy and behavioral therapy. Cognitive therapy focuses on a person's thoughts and beliefs, and how they influence a person's mood and actions, and aims to change a person's thinking to be more adaptive and healthy. Behavioral therapy focuses on a person's actions and aims to change unhealthy behavior patterns.

CBT helps a person focus on his or her current problems and how to solve them. Both patient and therapist need to be actively involved in this process. The therapist helps the patient learn how to identify and correct distorted thoughts or negative self-talk often associated with depressed feelings, recognize and change inaccurate beliefs, engage in more enjoyable activities, relate to self and others in more positive ways, learn problem-solving skills, and change behaviors. another focus of CBT is behavioral activation (i.e., increasing activity levels and helping the patient take part in rewarding activities which can improve mood). CBT is a structured, weekly intervention. Weekly homework assignments help the individual apply the learned techniques.

## *Family Psychoeducation*

Mental illness affects the whole family. Family treatment can play an important role to help both the person with depression and his or her relatives. Family psychoeducation is one way families can work together towards recovery. The family and clinician will meet together to discuss the problems they are experiencing. Families will then attend educational sessions where they will learn basic facts about mental illness, coping skills, communication skills, problem-solving skills, and ways to work together toward recovery.

## *Assertive Community Treatment (ACT)*

Assertive community treatment (ACT) is an approach that is most effective with individuals with the greatest service needs, such as those with a history of multiple hospitalizations. In ACT, the person receives treatment from an interdisciplinary team of usually 10 to 12 professionals, including case managers, a psychiatrist, several nurses and social workers, vocational specialists, substance abuse treatment specialists, and peer specialists. The team provides coverage 24 hours a day, 7 days a week, and utilizes small caseloads, usually one staff for every 10 clients. services provided include case management, comprehensive treatment planning, crisis intervention, medication management, individual supportive therapy, substance abuse treatment, rehabilitation services (i.e, supported employment), and peer support.

## *Electroconvulsive Therapy (ECT)*

Electroconvulsive therapy (ECT) is a procedure used to treat severe or life-threatening depression. It is used when other treatments such as psychotherapy and antidepressant medications have not worked. Electrical currents are briefly sent to the brain through electrodes placed on the head. The electrical current can last up to 8 seconds, producing a short seizure.

It is believed this brain stimulation helps relieve symptoms of depression by altering brain chemicals, including neurotransmitters like serotonin and natural pain relievers called endorphins. ECT treatments are usually done two to three times a week for two to three weeks. Maintenance treatments may be done one time each week, tapering down to one time each month. They may continue for several months to a year, to reduce the risk of relapse. ECT is usually given in combination with medication, psychotherapy, family therapy, and behavioral therapy.

The family environment is important to the recovery of people who are depressed. even though depression can be a frustrating illness, family members can help the process of recovering from depression in many ways.

## Encourage Treatment and Rehabilitation

Depression is a treatable illness. Medications, psychotherapies, and self-help measures can help a depressed person feel better, engage in meaningful activities, and improve their quality of life. The first step is to visit a doctor for a thorough evaluation. If possible, it is often helpful for family members to be present at the evaluation to offer support, help answer the doctor's questions, and learn about the illness. If medication is prescribed, family members can provide support in regularly taking those medications. Taking medication can be difficult—there will be times when the individual with depression may not want to take it or may just forget to take it. Encouragement and reminders are helpful. Family members can help the person fit taking medication into their daily routine. An individual with depression may also be referred to psychosocial treatment and rehabilitation. Family members can be very helpful in supporting therapy attendance. Some ways to encourage therapy attendance are giving reminders, offering support, and providing transportation to the clinic.

## Provide Support

Family stress is a powerful predictor of relapse. Conversely, family support decreases the rate of relapse. Support can be provided in different ways. For example, family members can be a sympathetic ear. Talking about their feelings often helps depressed people feel better. engagement in enjoyable activities can be very beneficial in the process of recovery. Family members can help an individual with depression by encouraging enjoyable activities (e.g., inviting the person out for walks or dinner). It is best if family members try to be understanding rather than critical, negative, or blaming. It may be difficult at times, but families often do best when they are patient and appreciate any progress that is being made, however slow it may be.

If family members are having difficulty being supportive, it might be because of what they believe is causing the depression. Studies show that family members try to make sense of depression by determining its cause. There is a tendency to think of the causes of depression as "moral" or "organic." Family members who believe the cause of depression is "moral" believe it is caused by the individual's personality (i.e., the individual is weak, lazy, or lacking self-discipline). Family members who believe the cause of depression is "organic" believe in the medical model of disease (i.e., it is a medical illness).

The belief that depression is caused by moral weakness, laziness, or lack of self-discipline leads family members to believe that individuals with depression are able to control their symptoms. The belief that people have control over, and, as a result, are responsible for their symptoms, can lead to feelings of anger and may prevent family members from being supportive of their ill relative. In contrast, belief in the medical model of depression may lead family members to believe that the symptoms are not controllable, and, therefore individuals are not responsible for their symptoms. This leads to greater feelings of warmth and sympathy and a greater willingness to help. Research has shown that family members who hold a medical view of depression are less critical of their relative than those who hold a moral view of depression. Family member's views on what causes depression are important because critical and hostile attitudes have been shown to be predictive of relapse.

## Take Care of Themselves

Family member often feel guilty about spending time away from their ill relative; however, it is important that they take good care of themselves. There are many ways to do this. Family members should not allow their ill relative to monopolize their time. spending time alone or with other family members and friends is important for their own well-being. Family members may also consider joining a support or therapy group. Counseling can often help family and friends better cope with a loved one's illness. Finally, family members should not feel responsible for solving the problem themselves. They can't. They should get the help of a mental health professional if needed.

## Section 9.3

# *Dysthymia*

This section includes excerpts from "Persistent Depressive Disorder," Office of Personnel Management, June 21, 2014; text from "Dysthymic Disorder Among Children," Centers for Disease Control and Prevention (CDC), December 12, 2010. Reviewed March 2016; and text from "Dysthymic Disorder among Adults," Centers for Disease Control and Prevention (CDC), December 12, 2010. Reviewed March 2016.

### *Persistent Depressive Disorder*

Persistent depressive disorder, also called dysthymia, is a continuous long-term (chronic) form of depression. You may lose interest in normal daily activities, feel hopeless, lack productivity, and have low self-esteem and an overall feeling of inadequacy. These feelings last for years and may significantly interfere with your relationships, school, work and daily activities.

If you have persistent depressive disorder, you may find it hard to be upbeat even on happy occasions—you may be described as having a gloomy personality, constantly complaining or incapable of having fun. Though persistent depressive disorder is not as severe as major depression, your current depressed mood may be mild, moderate or severe.

### *Dysthymic Disorder among Children*

Dysthymic disorder is characterized by chronic low-level depression. While the depression is not as severe as that characterizing major depressive disorder, a diagnosis of dysthymia requires having experienced a combination of depressive symptoms for two years or more.

The National Comorbidity Survey–Adolescent Supplement (NCS–A) examines both dysthymic disorder and major depressive disorder together. These depressive disorders have affected approximately 11.2 percent of 13 to 18 year olds in the United States at some point during their lives. Girls are more likely than boys to experience depressive disorders. Additionally, 3.3 percent of 13 to 18 year olds have experienced a seriously debilitating depressive disorder.

## Dysthymic Disorder among Adults

Dysthymic disorder is characterized by chronic low-level depression. While the depression is not as severe as that characterizing major depressive disorder, a diagnosis of dysthymia requires having experienced a combination of depressive symptoms for two years or more. Dysthymic disorder affects approximately 1.5 percent of the adult population in the United States.

# Section 9.4

# *Seasonal Affective Disorder*

This section includes excerpts from "Beat the Winter Blues," *NIH News in Health,* National Institutes of Health (NIH), January 2013; and text from "Cognitive Behavioral Therapy as Effective as Light Therapy for Seasonal Affective Disorder," U.S. Department of Veterans Affairs (VA), May 13, 2015.

## Shedding Light on Seasonal Sadness

As the days get shorter, many people find themselves feeling sad. You might feel blue around the winter holidays, or get into a slump after the fun and festivities have ended. Some people have more serious mood changes year after year, lasting throughout the fall and winter when there's less natural sunlight. What is it about the darkening days that can leave us down in the dumps? And what can we do about it?

NIH-funded researchers have been studying the "winter blues" and a more severe type of depression called seasonal affective disorder (SAD), for more than 3 decades. They've learned about possible causes and found treatments that seem to help most people. Still, much remains unknown about these winter-related shifts in mood.

"Winter blues is a general term, not a medical diagnosis. It's fairly common, and it's more mild than serious. It usually clears up on its own in a fairly short amount of time," says Dr. Matthew Rudorfer, a mental health expert at NIH. The so-called winter blues are often linked to something specific, such as stressful holidays or reminders of absent loved ones.

"Seasonal affective disorder, though, is different. It's a well-defined clinical diagnosis that's related to the shortening of daylight hours," says Rudorfer. "It interferes with daily functioning over a significant period of time." A key feature of SAD is that it follows a regular pattern. It appears each year as the seasons change, and it goes away several months later, usually during spring and summer.

SAD is more common in northern than in southern parts of the United States, where winter days last longer. "In Florida only about 1% of the population is likely to suffer from SAD. But in the northern-most parts of the United States, about 10% of people in Alaska may be affected," says Rudorfer.

As with other forms of depression, SAD can lead to a gloomy outlook and make people feel hopeless, worthless and irritable. They may lose interest in activities they used to enjoy, such as hobbies and spending time with friends.

"Some people say that SAD can look like a kind of hibernation," says Rudorfer. "People with SAD tend to be withdrawn, have low energy, oversleep and put on weight. They might crave carbohydrates," such as cakes, candies and cookies. Without treatment, these symptoms generally last until the days start getting longer.

Shorter days seem to be a main trigger for SAD. Reduced sunlight in fall and winter can disrupt your body's internal clock, or circadian rhythm. This 24-hour "master clock" responds to cues in your surroundings, especially light and darkness. During the day, your brain sends signals to other parts of the body to help keep you awake and ready for action. At night, a tiny gland in the brain produces a chemical called melatonin, which helps you sleep. Shortened daylight hours in winter can alter this natural rhythm and lead to SAD in certain people.

NIH researchers first recognized the link between light and seasonal depression back in the early 1980s. These scientists pioneered the use of light therapy, which has since become a standard treatment for SAD. "Light therapy is meant to replace the missing daylight hours with an artificial substitute," says Rudorfer.

In light therapy, patients generally sit in front of a light box every morning for 30 minutes or more, depending on the doctor's recommendation. The box shines light much brighter than ordinary indoor lighting.

Studies have shown that light therapy relieves SAD symptoms for as much as 70% of patients after a few weeks of treatment. Some improvement can be detected even sooner. "Our research has found that patients report an improvement in depression scores after even the first administration of light," says Dr. Teodor Postolache, who treats anxiety and mood disorders at the University of Maryland School of Medicine. "Still, a sizable proportion of patients improve but do not fully respond to light treatment alone."

Once started, light therapy should continue every day well into spring. "Sitting 30 minutes or more in front of a light box every day can put a strain on some schedules," says Postolache. So some people tend to stop using the light boxes after a while. Other options have been tested, such as light-emitting visors that allow patients to move around during therapy. "But results with visors for treating SAD haven't been as promising as hoped," Postolache says.

Light therapy is usually considered a first line treatment for SAD, but it doesn't work for everyone. Studies show that certain antidepressant drugs can be effective in many cases of SAD. The antidepressant bupropion (Wellbutrin) has been approved by the U.S. Food and Drug Administration for treating SAD and for preventing winter depression. Doctors sometimes prescribe other antidepressants as well.

Growing evidence suggests that cognitive behavioral therapy (CBT)—a type of talk therapy—can also help patients who have SAD. "For the 'cognitive' part of CBT, we work with patients to identify negative self-defeating thoughts they have," says Dr. Kelly Rohan, a SAD specialist at the University of Vermont. "We try to look objectively at the thought and then reframe it into something that's more accurate, less negative, and maybe even a little more positive. The 'behavioral' part of CBT tries to teach people new behaviors to engage in when they're feeling depressed, to help them feel better."

Behavioral changes might include having lunch with friends, going out for a walk or volunteering in the community. "We try to identify activities that are engaging and pleasurable, and we work with patients to try to schedule them into their daily routine," says Rohan.

A preliminary study by Rohan and colleagues compared CBT to light therapy. Both were found effective at relieving SAD symptoms over 6 weeks in the winter. "We also found that people treated with CBT have less depression and less return of SAD the following winter compared to people who were treated with light therapy," Rohan says. A larger NIH-funded study is now under way to compare CBT to light therapy over 2 years of follow up.

If you're feeling blue this winter, and if the feelings last for several weeks, talk to a health care provider. "It's true that SAD goes away on its own, but that could take 5 months or more. Five months of every year is a long time to be impaired and suffering," says Rudorfer. "SAD is generally quite treatable, and the treatment options keep increasing and improving."

## Cognitive Behavioral Therapy as Effective as Light Therapy for Seasonal Affective Disorder

People with winter seasonal affective disorder, or SAD, could benefit as much from cognitive behavioral therapy as they do from light therapy, the current gold-standard for treatment, according to new research. The findings could offer patients additional treatment options, and perhaps a better long-term solution, says Dr. Kelly Rohan, a professor of psychological science at the University of Vermont.

In a new study, published online in the American Journal of Psychiatry on April 10, 2015, Rohan found cognitive behavioral therapy, or CBT, was every bit as effective as the current gold-standard for treatment, light therapy.

"People would like for us to split these treatments out and say one is more effective than the other or that one works better for certain patients, but in terms of the data it is neck and neck. The treatments were not distinguishable in terms of their performance," says Rohan, who completed her residency and post-doctoral fellowship at the G.V. Montgomery VA Medical Center in Jackson, Miss.

For the study Rohan, along with researchers from the University of Maryland and VA, randomized 177 adults who were experiencing a current bout of SAD. Eighty-eight were given light therapy. The rest underwent cognitive behavioral therapy.

In the end, both groups experienced remission rates of 47 percent.

### SAD Is 'Serious Mental Health Problem'

"It is important to understand that seasonal affective disorder is clinical depression. It occurs in fall and winter and increases by latitude. The farther north you get, the higher the prevalence," says Rohan. "There is a misconception that SAD is just the winter blues. This is seasonally recurrent clinical depression. It is a serious mental health problem that can negatively impact quality of life and health."

Previous studies support the effectiveness of light therapy in treating seasonal affective disorder, although the reasons are not entirely clear. Many researchers suspect the light may replace lost sun exposure due to shorter days and reset the body's internal clock, or circadian rhythms. For this reason, most clinicians who use light therapy advocate morning treatment.

The light therapy used in Rohan's study involved exposure to a 10,000-lux cool-white fluorescent light for 30 minutes every morning upon waking initially. The duration was then individually adjusted each week, up to two hours maximum, and monitored, for six weeks. The participants were then encouraged to continue daily light therapy until the spring, when SAD typically goes into remission.

### 'CBT Boot Camp' for Half the Participants

The CBT used with the other 89 participants was an adaptation of traditional cognitive therapy. "We had to condense the treatment into a shorter time frame in order to fit the winter season," says Rohan. "It's kind of a CBT boot camp." The participants underwent twelve 1.5-hour sessions, delivered twice per week over six weeks, in groups with a community therapist. Participants focused on behaviors that would help them cope with winter, such as changing negative thoughts related to the weather or season, and were encouraged to engage in pleasurable activities during the winter to counteract avoidance.

Though the remission rates were nearly identical between the two study arms, Rohan feels for many patients, CBT may be a better long-term option.

### Light Therapy Demands Daily Commitment

Light therapy is effective, says Rohan, but it requires a person to commit to daily therapy every winter. Not all patients may be willing or able to adhere. CBT, on the other hand, is based on the assumption that people learn skills in treatment to fortify themselves against recurrence after treatment ends.

"In CBT, we try to get people to approach rather than avoid winter, and to take control of their moods rather than letting the environment dictate how to feel. I'm not pushing people to be outside if they're averse to the cold," says Rohan. "These are people who need to identify pleasurable activities that can be added to their winter routine. People with SAD often gravitate toward things that aren't possible in the winter, like gardening or going to the beach. If so, these can be substituted with fun winter activities, including indoor activities.

Join a gym. Join a club. Stay socially connected. See movies. Take advantage of free activities in your community. The premise here is that rather than continuing to treat a patient every winter, wouldn't it be nice if we could teach people skills so they could proactively cope with winter on their own?"

Chapter 10

# *Bipolar Disorder*

## What Is Bipolar Disorder?

Bipolar disorder, also known as manic-depressive illness, is a brain disorder that causes unusual shifts in mood, energy, activity levels, and the ability to carry out day-to-day tasks. Symptoms of bipolar disorder are severe. They are different from the normal ups and downs that everyone goes through from time to time. Bipolar disorder symptoms can result in damaged relationships, poor job or school performance, and even suicide. But bipolar disorder can be treated, and people with this illness can lead full and productive lives.

## Causes

Scientists are studying the possible causes of bipolar disorder. Most scientists agree that there is no single cause. Rather, many factors likely act together to produce the illness or increase risk.

### Genetics

Bipolar disorder tends to run in families. Some research has suggested that people with certain genes are more likely to develop bipolar disorder than others. Children with a parent or sibling who has bipolar disorder are much more likely to develop the illness, compared with children who do not have a family history of bipolar disorder. However, most children with a family history of bipolar disorder will not develop the illness.

Text in this chapter is excerpted from "Bipolar Disorder," National Institute of Mental Health (NIMH), February 11, 2013.

Technological advances are improving genetic research on bipolar disorder. One example is the launch of the Bipolar Disorder Phenome Database, funded in part by NIMH. Using the database, scientists will be able to link visible signs of the disorder with the genes that may influence them.

Scientists are also studying illnesses with similar symptoms such as depression and schizophrenia to identify genetic differences that may increase a person's risk for developing bipolar disorder. Finding these genetic "hotspots" may also help explain how environmental factors can increase a person's risk.

But genes are not the only risk factor for bipolar disorder. Studies of identical twins have shown that the twin of a person with bipolar illness does not always develop the disorder, despite the fact that identical twins share all of the same genes. Research suggests that factors besides genes are also at work. It is likely that many different genes and environmental factors are involved. However, scientists do not yet fully understand how these factors interact to cause bipolar disorder.

## Brain Structure and Functioning

Brain-imaging tools, such as functional magnetic resonance imaging (fMRI) and positron emission tomography (PET), allow researchers to take pictures of the living brain at work. These tools help scientists study the brain's structure and activity.

Some imaging studies show how the brains of people with bipolar disorder may differ from the brains of healthy people or people with other mental disorders. For example, one study using MRI found that the pattern of brain development in children with bipolar disorder was similar to that in children with "multidimensional impairment," a disorder that causes symptoms that overlap somewhat with bipolar disorder and schizophrenia. This suggests that the common pattern of brain development may be linked to general risk for unstable moods.

Another MRI study found that the brain's prefrontal cortex in adults with bipolar disorder tends to be smaller and function less well compared to adults who don't have bipolar disorder. The prefrontal cortex is a brain structure involved in "executive" functions such as solving problems and making decisions. This structure and its connections to other parts of the brain mature during adolescence, suggesting that abnormal development of this brain circuit may account for why the disorder tends to emerge during a person's teen years. Pinpointing brain changes in youth may help us detect illness early or offer targets for early intervention.

The connections between brain regions are important for shaping and coordinating functions such as forming memories, learning, and emotions, but scientists know little about how different parts of the human brain connect. Learning more about these connections, along with information gained from genetic studies, helps scientists better understand bipolar disorder. Scientists are working towards being able to predict which types of treatment will work most effectively.

## Signs and Symptoms

People with bipolar disorder experience unusually intense emotional states that occur in distinct periods called "mood episodes." Each mood episode represents a drastic change from a person's usual mood and behavior. An overly joyful or overexcited state is called a manic episode, and an extremely sad or hopeless state is called a depressive episode. Sometimes, a mood episode includes symptoms of both mania and depression. This is called a mixed state. People with bipolar disorder also may be explosive and irritable during a mood episode.

Extreme changes in energy, activity, sleep, and behavior go along with these changes in mood. Symptoms of bipolar disorder are described below.

**Table 10.1.** Symptoms of Bipolar Disorder

| Symptoms of mania or a manic episode include: | Symptoms of depression or a depressive episode include: |
|---|---|
| **Mood Changes**<br>• A long period of feeling "high," or an overly happy or outgoing mood<br>• Extreme irritability<br><br>**Behavioral Changes**<br>• Talking very fast, jumping from one idea to another, having racing thoughts<br>• Being easily distracted<br>• Increasing activities, such as taking on new projects<br>• Being overly restless<br>• Sleeping little or not being tired<br>• Having an unrealistic belief in one's abilities<br>• Behaving impulsively and engaging in pleasurable, high-risk behaviors | **Mood Changes**<br>• An overly long period of feeling sad or hopeless<br>• Loss of interest in activities once enjoyed, including sex.<br><br>**Behavioral Changes**<br>• Feeling tired or "slowed down"<br>• Having problems concentrating, remembering, and making decisions<br>• Being restless or irritable<br>• Changing eating, sleeping, or other habits<br>• Thinking of death or suicide, or attempting suicide. |

Bipolar disorder can be present even when mood swings are less extreme. For example, some people with bipolar disorder experience hypomania, a less severe form of mania. During a hypomanic episode, you may feel very good, be highly productive, and function well. You may not feel that anything is wrong, but family and friends may recognize the mood swings as possible bipolar disorder. Without proper treatment, people with hypomania may develop severe mania or depression.

Bipolar disorder may also be present in a mixed state, in which you might experience both mania and depression at the same time. During a mixed state, you might feel very agitated, have trouble sleeping, experience major changes in appetite, and have suicidal thoughts. People in a mixed state may feel very sad or hopeless while at the same time feel extremely energized.

Sometimes, a person with severe episodes of mania or depression has psychotic symptoms too, such as hallucinations or delusions. The psychotic symptoms tend to reflect the person's extreme mood. For example, if you are having psychotic symptoms during a manic episode, you may believe you are a famous person, have a lot of money, or have special powers. If you are having psychotic symptoms during a depressive episode, you may believe you are ruined and penniless, or you have committed a crime. As a result, people with bipolar disorder who have psychotic symptoms are sometimes misdiagnosed with schizophrenia.

People with bipolar disorder may also abuse alcohol or substances, have relationship problems, or perform poorly in school or at work. It may be difficult to recognize these problems as signs of a major mental illness.

Bipolar disorder usually lasts a lifetime. Episodes of mania and depression typically come back over time. Between episodes, many people with bipolar disorder are free of symptoms, but some people may have lingering symptoms.

## Who Is At Risk?

Bipolar disorder often develops in a person's late teens or early adult years. At least half of all cases start before age 25. Some people have their first symptoms during childhood, while others may develop symptoms late in life.

## Diagnosis

Doctors diagnose bipolar disorder using guidelines from the *Diagnostic and Statistical Manual of Mental Disorders* (DSM). To be diagnosed with bipolar disorder, the symptoms must be a major change from your normal mood or behavior. There are four basic types of bipolar disorder:

1. **Bipolar I Disorder**—defined by manic or mixed episodes that last at least seven days, or by manic symptoms that are so severe that the person needs immediate hospital care. Usually, depressive episodes occur as well, typically lasting at least 2 weeks.

2. **Bipolar II Disorder**—defined by a pattern of depressive episodes and hypomanic episodes, but no full-blown manic or mixed episodes.

3. **Bipolar Disorder Not Otherwise Specified (BP-NOS)**— diagnosed when symptoms of the illness exist but do not meet diagnostic criteria for either bipolar I or II. However, the symptoms are clearly out of the person's normal range of behavior.

4. **Cyclothymic Disorder, or Cyclothymia**—a mild form of bipolar disorder. People with cyclothymia have episodes of hypomania as well as mild depression for at least 2 years. However, the symptoms do not meet the diagnostic requirements for any other type of bipolar disorder.

A severe form of the disorder is called **rapid-cycling bipolar disorder.**. Rapid cycling occurs when a person has four or more episodes of major depression, mania, hypomania, or mixed states, all within a year. Rapid cycling seems to be more common in people who have their first bipolar episode at a younger age. One study found that people with rapid cycling had their first episode about 4 years earlier—during the mid to late teen years—than people without rapid cycling bipolar disorder. Rapid cycling affects more women than men. Rapid cycling can come and go.

When getting a diagnosis, a doctor or healthcare provider should conduct a physical examination, an interview, and lab tests. Currently, bipolar disorder cannot be identified through a blood test or a brain scan, but these tests can help rule out other factors that may contribute to mood problems, such as a stroke, brain tumor, or thyroid condition. If the problems are not caused by other illnesses, your healthcare provider may conduct a mental health evaluation or provide a referral to a trained mental health professional, such as a psychiatrist, who is experienced in diagnosing and treating bipolar disorder.

The doctor or mental health professional should discuss with you any family history of bipolar disorder or other mental illnesses and get a complete history of symptoms. The doctor or mental health professional should also talk to your close relatives or spouse about your symptoms and family medical history.

People with bipolar disorder are more likely to seek help when they are depressed than when experiencing mania or hypomania. Therefore, a careful medical history is needed to assure that bipolar disorder is not mistakenly diagnosed as major depression. Unlike people with bipolar disorder, people who have depression only (also called unipolar depression) do not experience mania.

Bipolar disorder can worsen if left undiagnosed and untreated. Episodes may become more frequent or more severe over time without treatment. Also, delays in getting the correct diagnosis and treatment can contribute to personal, social, and work-related problems. Proper diagnosis and treatment help people with bipolar disorder lead healthy and productive lives. In most cases, treatment can help reduce the frequency and severity of episodes.

Substance abuse is very common among people with bipolar disorder, but the reasons for this link are unclear. Some people with bipolar disorder may try to treat their symptoms with alcohol or drugs. However, substance abuse may trigger or prolong bipolar symptoms, and the behavioral control problems associated with mania can result in a person drinking too much.

Anxiety disorders, such as posttraumatic stress disorder (PTSD) and social phobia, also co-occur often among people with bipolar disorder. Bipolar disorder also co-occurs with attention deficit hyperactivity disorder (ADHD), which has some symptoms that overlap with bipolar disorder, such as restlessness and being easily distracted.

People with bipolar disorder are also at higher risk for thyroid disease, migraine headaches, heart disease, diabetes, obesity, and other physical illnesses. These illnesses may cause symptoms of mania or depression. They may also result from treatment for bipolar disorder.

## Treatments

Bipolar disorder cannot be cured, but it can be treated effectively over the long term. Proper treatment helps many people with bipolar disorder—even those with the most severe forms of the illness—gain better control of their mood swings and related symptoms. But because it is a lifelong illness, long-term, continuous treatment is needed to control symptoms. However, even with proper treatment, mood changes can occur. In the NIMH-funded Systematic Treatment Enhancement Program for Bipolar Disorder (STEP-BD) study—the largest treatment study ever conducted for bipolar disorder—almost half of those who recovered still had lingering symptoms. Having another mental disorder in addition to bipolar disorder increased one's chances for a relapse.

Treatment is more effective if you work closely with a doctor and talk openly about your concerns and choices. An effective maintenance treatment plan usually includes a combination of medication and psychotherapy.

## *Medications*

Different types of medications can help control symptoms of bipolar disorder. Not everyone responds to medications in the same way. You may need to try several different medications before finding ones that work best for you.

Keeping a daily life chart that makes note of your daily mood symptoms, treatments, sleep patterns, and life events can help you and your doctor track and treat your illness most effectively. If your symptoms change or if side effects become intolerable, your doctor may switch or add medications.

The types of medications generally used to treat bipolar disorder include mood stabilizers, atypical antipsychotics, and antidepressants. For the most up-to-date information on medication use and their side effects, contact the U.S. Food and Drug Administration (FDA).

**Mood stabilizers** are usually the first choice to treat bipolar disorder. In general, people with bipolar disorder continue treatment with mood stabilizers for years. Lithium (also known as Eskalith or Lithobid) is an effective mood stabilizer. It was the first mood stabilizer approved by the FDA in the 1970s for treating both manic and depressive episodes.

Anticonvulsants are also used as mood stabilizers. They were originally developed to treat seizures, but they also help control moods. Anticonvulsants used as mood stabilizers include:

- Valproic acid or divalproex sodium (Depakote), approved by the FDA in 1995 for treating mania. It is a popular alternative to lithium. However, young women taking valproic acid face special precautions.

- Lamotrigine (Lamictal), FDA-approved for maintenance treatment of bipolar disorder. It is often effective in treating depressive symptoms.

127

- Other anticonvulsant medications, including gabapentin (Neurontin), topiramate (Topamax), and oxcarbazepine (Trileptal).

Valproic acid, lamotrigine, and other anticonvulsant medications have an FDA warning. The warning states that their use may increase the risk of suicidal thoughts and behaviors. People taking anticonvulsant medications for bipolar or other illnesses should be monitored closely for new or worsening symptoms of depression, suicidal thoughts or behavior, or any unusual changes in mood or behavior. If you take any of these medications, do not make any changes to your dosage without talking to your doctor.

## What Are the Side Effects of Mood Stabilizers?

Lithium can cause side effects such as:

- Restlessness
- Dry mouth
- Bloating or indigestion
- Acne
- Unusual discomfort to cold temperatures
- Joint or muscle pain
- Brittle nails or hair

When taking lithium, your doctor should check the levels of lithium in your blood regularly, and will monitor your kidney and thyroid function as well. Lithium treatment may cause low thyroid levels in some people. Low thyroid function, called hypothyroidism, has been associated with rapid cycling in some people with bipolar disorder, especially women.

Because too much or too little thyroid hormone can lead to mood and energy changes, it is important that your doctor check your thyroid levels carefully. You may need to take thyroid medication, in addition to medications for bipolar disorder, to keep thyroid levels balanced.

Common side effects of other mood stabilizing medications include:

- Drowsiness
- Dizziness
- Headache

- Diarrhea
- Constipation
- Heartburn
- Mood swings
- Stuffed or runny nose, or other cold-like symptoms.

These medications may also be linked with rare but serious side effects. Talk with your doctor or a pharmacist to make sure you understand signs of serious side effects for the medications you're taking. If extremely bothersome or unusual side effects occur, tell your doctor as soon as possible.

### Should Young Women Take Valproic Acid?

Valproic acid may increase levels of testosterone (a male hormone) in teenage girls. It could lead to a condition called polycystic ovary syndrome (PCOS) in women who begin taking the medication before age 20. PCOS can cause obesity, excess body hair, an irregular menstrual cycle, and other serious symptoms. Most of these symptoms will improve after stopping treatment with valproic acid. Young girls and women taking valproic acid should be monitored carefully by a doctor.

**Atypical antipsychotics** are sometimes used to treat symptoms of bipolar disorder. Often, these medications are taken with other medications, such as antidepressants. Atypical antipsychotics include:

- Olanzapine (Zyprexa), which when given with an antidepressant medication, may help relieve symptoms of severe mania or psychosis. Olanzapine can be taken as a pill or a shot. The shot is often used for urgent treatment of agitation associated with a manic or mixed episode. Olanzapine can be used as maintenance treatment as well, even when psychotic symptoms are not currently present.

- Aripiprazole (Abilify), which is used to treat manic or mixed episodes. Aripiprazole is also used for maintenance treatment. Like olanzapine, aripiprazole can be taken as a pill or a shot. The shot is often used for urgent treatment of severe symptoms.

- Quetiapine (Seroquel), risperidone (Risperdal) and ziprasidone (Geodon) also are prescribed to relieve the symptoms of manic episodes.

## What Are the Side Effects of Atypical Antipsychotics?

If you are taking antipsychotics, you should not drive until you have adjusted to your medication. Side effects of many antipsychotics include:

- Drowsiness

- Dizziness when changing positions

- Blurred vision

- Rapid heartbeat

- Sensitivity to the sun

- Skin rashes

- Menstrual problems for women

Atypical antipsychotic medications can cause major weight gain and changes in your metabolism. This may increase your risk of getting diabetes and high cholesterol. Your doctor should monitor your weight, glucose levels, and lipid levels regularly while you are taking these medications.

In rare cases, long-term use of atypical antipsychotic drugs may lead to a condition called tardive dyskinesia (TD). The condition causes uncontrollable muscle movements, frequently around the mouth. TD can range from mild to severe. Some people with TD recover partially or fully after they stop taking the drug, but others do not.

**Antidepressants** are sometimes used to treat symptoms of depression in bipolar disorder. Fluoxetine (Prozac), paroxetine (Paxil), sertraline (Zoloft), and bupropion (Wellbutrin) are examples of antidepressants that may be prescribed to treat symptoms of bipolar depression.

However, taking only an antidepressant can increase your risk of switching to mania or hypomania, or of developing rapid-cycling symptoms. To prevent this switch, doctors usually require you to take a mood-stabilizing medication at the same time as an antidepressant.

## What Are the Side Effects of Antidepressants?

Antidepressants can cause:

- Headache

- Nausea (feeling sick to your stomach)

- Agitation (feeling jittery)

- Sexual problems, which can affect both men and women. These include reduced sex drive and problems having and enjoying sex.

Report any concerns about side effects to your doctor right away. You may need a change in the dose or a different medication. You should not stop taking a medication without talking to your doctor first. Suddenly stopping a medication may lead to "rebound" or worsening of bipolar disorder symptoms. Other uncomfortable or potentially dangerous withdrawal effects are also possible.

Some antidepressants are more likely to cause certain side effects than other types. Your doctor or pharmacist can answer questions about these medications. Any unusual reactions or side effects should be reported to a doctor immediately.

### Should Women Who Are Pregnant or May Become Pregnant Take Medication for Bipolar Disorder?

Women with bipolar disorder who are pregnant or may become pregnant face special challenges. Mood stabilizing medications can harm a developing fetus or nursing infant. But stopping medications, either suddenly or gradually, greatly increases the risk that bipolar symptoms will recur during pregnancy.

Lithium is generally the preferred mood-stabilizing medication for pregnant women with bipolar disorder. However, lithium can lead to heart problems in the fetus. In addition, women need to know that most bipolar medications are passed on through breast milk. The FDA has also issued warnings about the potential risks associated with the use of antipsychotic medications during pregnancy. If you are pregnant or nursing, talk to your doctor about the benefits and risks of all available treatments.

### FDA Warning on Antidepressants

Antidepressants are safe and popular, but some studies have suggested that they may have unintentional effects on some people, especially in adolescents and young adults. The FDA warning says that patients of all ages taking antidepressants should be watched closely, especially during the first few weeks of treatment. Possible side effects to look for are depression that gets worse, suicidal thinking or behavior, or any unusual changes in behavior such as trouble sleeping, agitation, or withdrawal from normal social situations.

*Psychotherapy*

When done in combination with medication, psychotherapy can be an effective treatment for bipolar disorder. It can provide support, education, and guidance to people with bipolar disorder and their families. Some psychotherapy treatments used to treat bipolar disorder include:

- **Cognitive behavioral therapy (CBT)**, which helps people with bipolar disorder learn to change harmful or negative thought patterns and behaviors.

- **Family-focused therapy**, which involves family members. It helps enhance family coping strategies, such as recognizing new episodes early and helping their loved one. This therapy also improves communication among family members, as well as problem-solving.

- **Interpersonal and social rhythm therapy**, which helps people with bipolar disorder improve their relationships with others and manage their daily routines. Regular daily routines and sleep schedules may help protect against manic episodes.

- **Psychoeducation**, which teaches people with bipolar disorder about the illness and its treatment. Psychoeducation can help you recognize signs of an impending mood swing so you can seek treatment early, before a full-blown episode occurs. Usually done in a group, psychoeducation may also be helpful for family members and caregivers.

In a STEP-BD study on psychotherapies, researchers compared people in two groups. The first group was treated with collaborative care (three sessions of psychoeducation over 6 weeks). The second group was treated with medication and intensive psychotherapy (30 sessions over 9 months of CBT, interpersonal and social rhythm therapy, or family-focused therapy). Researchers found that the second group had fewer relapses, lower hospitalization rates, and were better able to stick with their treatment plans. They were also more likely to get well faster and stay well longer. Overall, more than half of the study participants recovered over the course of 1 year.

A licensed psychologist, social worker, or counselor typically provides psychotherapy. He or she should work with your psychiatrist to track your progress. The number, frequency, and type of sessions should be based on your individual treatment needs. As with medication, following the doctor's instructions for any psychotherapy will provide the greatest benefit.

## *Other Treatments*

**Electroconvulsive Therapy (ECT)**—For cases in which medication and psychotherapy do not work, electroconvulsive therapy (ECT) may be useful. ECT, formerly known as "shock therapy," once had a bad reputation. But in recent years, it has greatly improved and can provide relief for people with severe bipolar disorder who have not been able to recover with other treatments.

Before ECT is administered, a patient takes a muscle relaxant and is put under brief anesthesia. He or she does not consciously feel the electrical impulse administered in ECT. On average, ECT treatments last from 30–90 seconds. People who have ECT usually recover after 5–15 minutes and are able to go home the same day.

Sometimes ECT is used for bipolar symptoms when other medical conditions, including pregnancy, make the use of medications too risky. ECT is a highly effective treatment for severely depressive, manic, or mixed episodes. But it is generally not used as a first-line treatment.

ECT may cause some short-term side effects, including confusion, disorientation, and memory loss. People with bipolar disorder should discuss possible benefits and risks of ECT with an experienced doctor.

**Sleep Medications**—People with bipolar disorder who have trouble sleeping usually sleep better after getting treatment for bipolar disorder. However, if sleeplessness does not improve, your doctor may suggest a change in medications. If the problems still continue, your doctor may prescribe sedatives or other sleep medications.

**Herbal Supplements**—In general, not much research has been conducted on herbal or natural supplements and how they may affect bipolar disorder. An herb called St. John's wort (Hypericum perforatum), often marketed as a natural antidepressant, may cause a switch to mania in some people with bipolar disorder. St. John's wort can also make other medications less effective, including some antidepressant and anticonvulsant medications. Scientists are also researching omega-3 fatty acids (most commonly found in fish oil) to measure their usefulness for long-term treatment of bipolar disorder. Study results have been mixed.

Be sure to tell your doctor about all prescription drugs, over-the-counter medications, or supplements you are taking. Certain medications and supplements taken together may cause unwanted or dangerous effects.

## What Research Is NIMH Doing to Improve Treatments for Bipolar Disorder?

Scientists are working to identify new targets for improving current medications or developing new treatments for bipolar disorder. In addition, NIMH researchers have made promising advances toward finding fast-acting medication treatment. In a small study of people with bipolar disorder whose symptoms had not responded to prior treatments, a single dose of ketamine—an anesthetic medication—significantly reduced symptoms of depression in as little as 40 minutes. These effects lasted about a week on average.

Ketamine itself is unlikely to become widely available as a treatment because it can cause serious side effects at high doses, such as hallucinations. However, scientists are working to understand how the drug works on the brain in an effort to develop treatments with fewer side effects and that act similarly to ketamine. Such medications could also be used for longer term management of symptoms.

In addition, NIMH is working to better understand bipolar disorder and other mental disorders by spearheading the Research Domain Criteria (RDoC) Project, which is an ongoing effort to map our current understanding of the brain circuitry that is involved in behavioral and cognitive functioning. By essentially breaking down mental disorders into their component pieces—RDoC aims to add to the knowledge we have gained from more traditional research approaches that focus solely on understanding mental disorders based on symptoms. The hope is that by changing the way we approach mental disorders, RDoC will help us open the door to new targets of preventive and treatment interventions.

## Living With

If you know someone who has bipolar disorder, it affects you too. The first and most important thing you can do is help him or her get the right diagnosis and treatment. You may need to make the appointment and go with him or her to see the doctor. Encourage your loved one to stay in treatment.

### To Help a Friend or Relative, You Can:

- Offer emotional support, understanding, patience, and encouragement

- Learn about bipolar disorder so you can understand what your friend or relative is experiencing

- Talk to your friend or relative and listen carefully
- Listen to feelings your friend or relative expresses and be understanding about situations that may trigger bipolar symptoms
- Invite your friend or relative out for positive distractions, such as walks, outings, and other activities
- Remind your friend or relative that, with time and treatment, he or she can get better

Never ignore comments from your friend or relative about harming himself or herself. Always report such comments to his or her therapist or doctor.

### How Can Caregivers Find Support?

Like other serious illnesses, bipolar disorder can be difficult for spouses, family members, friends, and other caregivers. Relatives and friends often have to cope with the person's serious behavioral problems, such as wild spending sprees during mania, extreme withdrawal during depression, or poor work or school performance. These behaviors can have lasting consequences.

Caregivers usually take care of the medical needs of their loved ones. But caregivers have to deal with how this affects their own health as well. Caregiver's stress may lead to missed work or lost free time, strained relationships with people who may not understand the situation, and physical and mental exhaustion.

It can be very hard to cope with a loved one's bipolar symptoms. One study shows that if a caregiver is under a lot of stress, his or her loved one has more trouble following the treatment plan, which increases the chance for a major bipolar episode. If you are a caregiver of someone with bipolar disorder, it is important that you also make time to take care of yourself.

### How Can I Help Myself If I Have Bipolar Disorder?

It may be very hard to take that first step to help yourself. It may take time, but you can get better with treatment. To help yourself:

- Talk to your doctor about treatment options and progress.
- Keep a regular routine, such as going to sleep at the same time every night and eating meals at the same time every day.
- Try hard to get enough sleep.

- Stay on your medication.

- Learn about warning signs signaling a shift into depression or mania.

- Expect your symptoms to improve gradually, not immediately.

## *Where Can I Go for Help?*

If you are unsure where to go for help, ask your family doctor. Others who can help are listed below.

- Mental health specialists, such as psychiatrists, psychologists, social workers, or mental health counselors

- Health maintenance organizations

- Community mental health centers

- Hospital psychiatry departments and outpatient clinics

- Mental health programs at universities or medical schools

- State hospital outpatient clinics

- Family services, social agencies, or clergy

- Peer support groups

- Private clinics and facilities

- Employee assistance programs

- Local medical and/or psychiatric societies

You can also check the phone book under "mental health," "health," "social services," "hotlines," or "physicians" for phone numbers and addresses. An emergency room doctor can also provide temporary help and can tell you where and how to get further help.

## *What If I or Someone I Know Is in Crisis?*

If you are thinking about harming yourself, or know someone who is, tell someone who can help immediately.

- Call your doctor.

- Call 911 or go to a hospital emergency room to get immediate help or ask a friend or family member to help you do these things.

- Call the toll-free, 24-hour National Suicide Prevention Lifeline at 1-800-273-TALK (1-800-273-8255); TTY: 1-800-799-4TTY (4889) to talk to a trained counselor.

Make sure you or the suicidal person is not left alone.

# Chapter 11

# *Anxiety, Fears, and Phobias*

Everyone, from the youngest child to the oldest adult, experiences anxieties and fears at one time or another. Feeling anxious in a particularly uncomfortable situation never feels very good. However, with kids, such feelings are not only normal, they're also necessary. Dealing with anxieties can prepare young people to handle the unsettling experiences and challenging situations of life.

## *Many Anxieties and Fears Are Normal*

Anxiety is defined as "apprehension without apparent cause." It usually occurs when there's no immediate threat to a person's safety or well-being, but the threat feels real.

Anxiety makes someone want to escape the situation — fast. The heart beats quickly, the body might begin to perspire, and "butterflies" in the stomach soon follow. However, a little bit of anxiety can actually help people stay alert and focused.

Having fears or anxieties about certain things can also be helpful because it makes kids behave in a safe way. For example, a kid with a fear of fire would avoid playing with matches.

The nature of anxieties and fears change as kids grow and develop:

- Babies experience stranger anxiety, clinging to parents when confronted by people they don't recognize.

- Toddlers around 10 to 18 months old experience separation anxiety, becoming emotionally distressed when one or both parents leave.

- Kids ages 4 through 6 have anxiety about things that aren't based in reality, such as fears of monsters and ghosts.

- Kids ages 7 through 12 often have fears that reflect real circumstances that may happen to them, such as bodily injury and natural disaster.

As kids grow, one fear may disappear or replace another. For example, a child who couldn't sleep with the light off at age 5 may enjoy a ghost story at a slumber party years later. And some fears may extend only to one particular kind of stimulus. In other words, a child may want to pet a lion at the zoo but wouldn't dream of going near the neighbor's dog.

## Signs of Anxiety

Typical childhood fears change with age. They include fear of strangers, heights, darkness, animals, blood, insects, and being left alone. Kids often learn to fear a specific object or situation after having an unpleasant experience, such as a dog bite or an accident.

Separation anxiety is common when young children are starting school, whereas adolescents may experience anxiety related to social acceptance and academic achievement.

If anxious feelings persist, they can take a toll on a child's sense of well-being. The anxiety associated with social avoidance can have long-term effects. For example, a child with fear of being rejected can fail to learn important social skills, causing social isolation.

Many adults are tormented by fears that stem from childhood experiences. An adult's fear of public speaking may be the result of embarrassment in front of peers many years before. It's important for parents to recognize and identify the signs and symptoms of kids' anxieties so that fears don't get in the way of everyday life.

Some signs that a child may be anxious about something may include:

- becoming clingy, impulsive, or distracted

- nervous movements, such as temporary twitches

- problems getting to sleep and/or staying asleep longer than usual

- sweaty hands

- accelerated heart rate and breathing

- nausea

- headaches

- stomachaches

Apart from these signs, parents can usually tell when their child is feeling excessively uneasy about something. Lending a sympathetic ear is always helpful, and sometimes just talking about the fear can help a child move beyond it.

## What's a Phobia?

When anxieties and fears persist, problems can arise. As much as a parent hopes the child will grow out of it, sometimes the opposite occurs, and the cause of the anxiety looms larger and becomes more prevalent. The anxiety becomes a phobia, or a fear that's extreme, severe, and persistent.

A phobia can be very difficult to tolerate, both for kids and those around them, especially if the anxiety-producing stimulus (whatever is causing the anxiety) is hard to avoid (e.g., thunderstorms).

"Real" phobias are one of the top reasons kids are referred to mental health professionals. But the good news is that unless the phobia hinders the everyday ability to function, the child sometimes won't need treatment by a professional because, in time, the phobia will be resolved.

## Focusing on Anxieties, Fears, or Phobias

*Try to answer the following questions honestly:*

*Is your child's fear and behavior related to it typical for your child's age?*

If the answer to this question is yes, it's a good bet that your child's fears will resolve before they become a serious cause for concern. This isn't to say that the anxiety should be discounted or ignored; rather, it should be considered as a factor in your child's normal development.

Many kids experience age-appropriate fears, such as being afraid of the dark. Most, with some reassurance and perhaps a nightlight, will overcome or outgrow it. However, if they continue to have trouble or there's anxiety about other things, the intervention may have to be more intensive.

*What are the symptoms of the fear and how do they affect your child's personal, social, and academic functioning?*

If symptoms can be identified and considered in light of your child's everyday activities, adjustments can be made to alleviate some of the stress factors.

*Does the fear seem unreasonable in relation to the reality of the situation; could it be a sign of a more serious problem?*

If your child's fear seems out of proportion to the cause of the stress, this may signal the need to seek outside help, such as a counselor, psychiatrist, or psychologist.

Parents should look for patterns. If an isolated incident is resolved, don't make it more significant than it is. But if a pattern emerges that's persistent or pervasive, you should take action. If you don't, the phobia is likely to continue to affect your child.

Contact your doctor and/or a mental health professional who has expertise in working with kids and adolescents.

## Helping Your Child

Parents can help kids develop the skills and confidence to overcome fears so that they don't evolve into phobic reactions.

To help your child deal with fears and anxieties:

- Recognize that the fear is real. As trivial as a fear may seem, it feels real to your child and it's causing him or her to feel anxious and afraid. Being able to talk about fears helps — words often take some of the power out of the negative feeling. If you talk about it, it can become less powerful.

- Never belittle the fear as a way of forcing your child to overcome it. Saying, "Don't be ridiculous! There are no monsters in your closet!" may get your child to go to bed, but it won't make the fear go away.

- Don't cater to fears, though. If your child doesn't like dogs, don't cross the street deliberately to avoid one. This will just reinforce that dogs should be feared and avoided. Provide support and gentle care as you approach the feared object or situation with your child.

- Teach kids how to rate fear. A child who can visualize the intensity of the fear on a scale of 1 to 10, with 10 being the strongest, may be able to "see" the fear as less intense than first imagined. Younger kids can think about how "full of fear" they are, with being full "up to my knees" as not so scared, "up to my stomach" as more frightened, and "up to my head" as truly petrified.

- Teach coping strategies. Try these easy-to-implement techniques. Using you as "home base," your child can venture out toward the feared object, and then return to you for safety before venturing out again. Kids also can learn some positive self-statements (such as "I can do this" and "I will be OK") to say to themselves when feeling anxious. Relaxation techniques are helpful, including visualization (of floating on a cloud or lying on a beach, for example) and deep breathing (imagining that the lungs are balloons and letting them slowly deflate).

The key to resolving fears and anxieties is to overcome them. Using these suggestions, you can help your child better cope with life's situations.

# Chapter 12

# *Anxiety Disorders*

## *Chapter Contents*

# Section 12.1

# *Anxiety Disorders—An Overview*

Text in this section is excerpted from "Anxiety Disorders,"
National Institutes of Health (NIH), May 2015.

## *What are Anxiety Disorders?*

Occasional anxiety is a normal part of life. You might feel anxious when faced with a problem at work, before taking a test, or making an important decision. Anxiety disorders involve more than temporary worry or fear. For a person with an anxiety disorder, the anxiety does not go away and can get worse over time. These feelings can interfere with daily activities such as job performance, school work, and relationships.

There are a variety of anxiety disorders. Collectively they are among the most common mental disorders.

## *Types of Anxiety Disorders*

There are three types of anxiety disorders:

- Generalized Anxiety Disorder (GAD)

- Panic Disorder

- Social Anxiety Disorder (Social Phobia)

## *Signs and Symptoms*

Unlike the relatively mild, brief anxiety caused by a specific event (such as speaking in public or a first date), severe anxiety that lasts at least six months is generally considered to be problem that might benefit from evaluation and treatment. Each anxiety disorder has different symptoms, but all the symptoms cluster around excessive, irrational fear and dread.

Anxiety disorders commonly occur along with other mental or physical illnesses, including alcohol or substance abuse, which may mask anxiety symptoms or make them worse. In some cases, these other problems need to be treated before a person can respond well to treatment for anxiety.

While some symptoms, such as fear and worry, occur in all anxiety disorders, each disorder also has distinctive symptoms. For more information, visit:

- Generalized Anxiety Disorder (GAD)

- Panic Disorder

- Social Anxiety Disorder (Social Phobia)

## Diagnosis and Treatment

Anxiety disorders are treatable. If you think you have an anxiety disorder, talk to your doctor.

Sometimes a physical evaluation is advisable to determine whether a person's anxiety is associated with a physical illness. If anxiety is diagnosed, the pattern of co-occurring symptoms should be identified, as well as any coexisting conditions, such as depression or substance abuse. Sometimes alcoholism, depression, or other coexisting conditions have such a strong effect on the individual that treating the anxiety should wait until the coexisting conditions are brought under control.

With proper treatment, many people with anxiety disorders can lead normal, fulfilling lives. If your doctor thinks you may have an anxiety disorder, the next step is usually seeing a mental health professional. It is advisable to seek help from professionals who have particular expertise in diagnosing and treating anxiety. Certain kinds of cognitive and behavioral therapy and certain medications have been found to be especially helpful for anxiety.

You should feel comfortable talking with the mental health professional you choose. If you do not, you should seek help elsewhere. Once you find a clinician with whom you are comfortable, the two of you should work as a team and make a plan to treat your anxiety disorder together.

In general, anxiety disorders are treated with medication, specific types of psychotherapy, or both. Treatment choices depend on the type of disorder, the person's preference, and the expertise of the clinician.

People with anxiety disorders who have already received treatment should tell their clinician about that treatment in detail. If they received medication, they should tell their doctor what medication was used, what the dosage was at the beginning of treatment, whether the dosage was increased or decreased while they were under treatment,

147

what side effects occurred, and whether the treatment helped them become less anxious. If they received psychotherapy, they should describe the type of therapy, how often they attended sessions, and whether the therapy was useful.

Often people believe that they have "failed" at treatment or that the treatment didn't work for them when, in fact, it was not given for an adequate length of time or was administered incorrectly. Sometimes people must try different treatments or combinations of treatment before they find the one that works for them.

Most insurance plans, including health maintenance organizations (HMOs), will cover treatment for anxiety disorders. Check with your insurance company and find out. If you don't have insurance, the Health and Human Services division of your county government may offer mental health care at a public mental health center that charges people according to how much they are able to pay. If you are on public assistance, you may be able to get care through your state Medicaid plan.

## Medication

Medication does not necessarily cure anxiety disorders, but it often reduces the symptoms. Medication typically must be prescribed by a doctor. A psychiatrist is a doctor who specializes in mental disorders. Many psychiatrists offer psychotherapy themselves or work as a team with psychologists, social workers, or counselors who provide psychotherapy. The principal medications used for anxiety disorders are antidepressants, anti- anxiety drugs, and beta-blockers. Be aware that some medications are effective only if they are taken regularly and that symptoms may recur if the medication is stopped.

Choosing the right medication, medication dose, and treatment plan should be based on a person's individual needs and medical situation, and done under an expert's care. Only an expert clinician can help you decide whether the medicine's ability to help is worth the risk of a side effect. Your doctor may try several medicines before finding the right one.

You and your doctor should discuss:

- How well medicines are working or might work to improve your symptoms.
- Benefits and side effects of each medicine.
- Risk for a serious side effects based on your medical history.

- How likely the medicines will require lifestyle changes.

- Costs of each medicine.

- Other alternative therapies, medicines, vitamins, and supplements you are taking and how these may affect your treatment.

- How the medication should be stopped. Some drugs can't be stopped abruptly but must be tapered off slowly under a doctor's supervision.

# Section 12.2

# *Panic Disorder*

Text in this section is excerpted from "Panic Disorder: When Fear Overwhelms," National Institutes of Health (NIH), 2013.

## *Introduction*

- Do you sometimes have sudden attacks of fear that last for several minutes?

- Do you feel like you are having a heart attack or can't breathe?

- Do these attacks occur at unpredictable times causing you to worry about the possibility of having another one at any time?

If so, you may have a type of anxiety disorder called panic disorder.

## *What Is Panic Disorder?*

People with panic disorder have sudden and repeated attacks of fear that last for several minutes or longer. These are called panic attacks. Panic attacks are characterized by a fear of disaster or of losing control even when there is no real danger. A person may also have a strong physical reaction during a panic attack. It may feel like having a heart attack. Panic attacks can occur at any time, and many people with panic disorder worry about and dread the possibility of having another attack.

149

A person with panic disorder may become discouraged and feel ashamed because he or she cannot carry out normal routines like going to the grocery store or driving. Having panic disorder can also interfere with school or work.

Panic disorder often begins in the late teens or early adulthood. More women than men have panic disorder. But not everyone who experiences panic attacks will develop panic disorder.

## What Are the Signs and Symptoms of Panic Disorder?

People with panic disorder may have:

- Sudden and repeated attacks of fear

- A feeling of being out of control during a panic attack

- An intense worry about when the next attack will happen

- A fear or avoidance of places where panic attacks have occurred in the past

- Physical symptoms during an attack, such as a pounding or racing heart, sweating, breathing problems, weakness or dizziness, feeling hot or a cold chill, tingly or numb hands, chest pain, or stomach pain

## How Is Panic Disorder Treated?

First, talk to your doctor about your symptoms. Your doctor should do an exam to make sure that another physical problem isn't causing the symptoms. The doctor may refer you to a mental health specialist.

Panic disorder is generally treated with psychotherapy, medication, or both.

**Psychotherapy.** A type of psychotherapy called cognitive behavioral therapy (CBT) is especially useful for treating panic disorder. Your doctor should do an exam to make sure that an unrelated physical problem isn't causing the symptoms.

**Medication.** Doctors also may prescribe medication to help treat panic disorder. The most commonly prescribed medications for panic disorder are anti-anxiety medications and antidepressants. Anti- anxiety medications are powerful and there are different types. Many types begin working right away, but they generally should not be taken for long periods.

Antidepressants are used to treat depression, but they also are helpful for panic disorder. They may take several weeks to start working. Some of these medications may cause side effects such as headache, nausea, or difficulty sleeping. These side effects are usually not a problem for most people, especially if the dose starts off low and is increased slowly over time. Talk to your doctor about any side effects you may have.

It's important to know that although antidepressants can be safe and effective for many people, they may be risky for some, especially children, teens, and young adults. A "black box"—the most serious type of warning that a prescription drug can have—has been added to the labels of antidepressant medications. These labels warn people that antidepressants may cause some people to have suicidal thoughts or make suicide attempts. Anyone taking antidepressants should be monitored closely, especially when they first start treatment with medications.

Another type of medication called beta-blockers can help control some of the physical symptoms of panic disorder such as excessive sweating, a pounding heart, or dizziness. Although beta blockers are not commonly prescribed, they may be helpful in certain situations that bring on a panic attack.

Some people do better with CBT, while others do better with medication. Still others do best with a combination of the two. Talk with your doctor about the best treatment for you.

## *What Is It Like to Have Panic Disorder?*

"One day, without any warning or reason, I felt terrified. I was so afraid, I thought I was going to die. My heart was pounding and my head was spinning. I would get these feelings every couple of weeks. I thought I was losing my mind."

"The more attacks I had, the more afraid I got. I was always living in fear. I didn't know when I might have another attack. I became so afraid that I didn't want to leave my house."

"My friend saw how afraid I was and told me to call my doctor for help. My doctor told me I was physically healthy but that I have panic disorder. My doctor gave me medicine that helps me feel less afraid. I've also been working with a counselor learning ways to cope with my fear. I had to work hard, but after a few months of medicine and therapy, I'm starting to feel like myself again."

Section 12.3

# *Obsessive-Compulsive Disorder (OCD)*

Text in this section is excerpted from "Obsessive-Compulsive
Disorder: When Unwanted Thoughts Take Over,"
National Institutes of Health (NIH), 2013.

## *Introduction: Obsessive-Compulsive Disorder*

- Do you feel the need to check and re-check things over and over?

- Do you have the same thoughts constantly?

- Do you feel a very strong need to perform certain rituals repeatedly and feel like you have no control over what you are doing?

If so, you may have a type of anxiety disorder called obsessive-compulsive disorder (OCD).

## *What Is OCD?*

Everyone double checks things sometimes. For example, you might double check to make sure the stove or iron is turned off before leaving the house. But people with OCD feel the need to check things repeatedly, or have certain thoughts or perform routines and rituals over and over. The thoughts and rituals associated with OCD cause distress and get in the way of daily life.

The frequent upsetting thoughts are called obsessions. To try to control them, a person will feel an overwhelming urge to repeat certain rituals or behaviors called compulsions. People with OCD can't control these obsessions and compulsions.

For many people, OCD starts during childhood or the teen years. Most people are diagnosed by about age 19. Symptoms of OCD may come and go and be better or worse at different times.

## *What Causes OCD?*

OCD sometimes runs in families, but no one knows for sure why some people have it, while others don't. Researchers have found that several parts of the brain are involved in obsessive thoughts and compulsive behavior, as well as fears and anxiety associated with them. By learning more about fear and anxiety in the brain, scientists may be able to create better treatments. Researchers are also looking for ways in which stress and environmental factors may play a role.

## What Are the Signs and Symptoms of OCD?

People with OCD generally:

- Have repeated thoughts or images about many different things, such as fear of germs, dirt, or intruders; acts of violence; hurting loved ones; sexual acts; conflicts with religious beliefs; or being overly tidy

- Do the same rituals over and over such as washing hands, locking and unlocking doors, counting, keeping unneeded items, or repeating the same steps again and again

- Can't control the unwanted thoughts and behaviors

- Don't get pleasure when performing the behaviors or rituals, but get brief relief from the anxiety the thoughts cause

- Spend at least 1 hour a day on the thoughts and rituals, which cause distress and get in the way of daily life.

## How Is OCD Treated?

First, talk to your doctor about your symptoms. Your doctor should do an exam to make sure that another physical problem isn't causing the symptoms. The doctor may refer you to a mental health specialist.

OCD is generally treated with psychotherapy, medication, or both.

**Psychotherapy.** A type of psychotherapy called cognitive behavioral therapy (CBT) is especially useful for treating OCD. It teaches a person different ways of thinking, behaving, and reacting to situations that help him or her better manage obsessive thoughts, reduce compulsive behavior, and feel less anxious. One specific form of CBT, exposure and response prevention, has been shown to be helpful in reducing the intrusive thoughts and behaviors associated with OCD.

**Medication.** Doctors may also prescribe medication to help treat OCD. The most commonly prescribed medications for OCD are antidepressants. Although antidepressants are used to treat depression, they are also particularly helpful for OCD. They may take several weeks—10 to 12 weeks for some—to start working. Some of these medications may cause side effects such as headache, nausea, or difficulty sleeping. These side effects are usually not severe for most people, especially if the dose starts off low and is increased slowly over time. Talk to your doctor about any side effects you may have.

It's important to know that although antidepressants can be safe and effective for many people, they may be risky for some, especially children, teens, and young adults. A "black box"—the most serious type of warning that a prescription drug can have—has been added to the labels of antidepressant medications. These labels warn people that antidepressants may cause some people to have suicidal thoughts or make suicide attempts. Anyone taking antidepressants should be monitored closely, especially when they first start treatment with medications.

In addition to prescribing antidepressants, doctors may prescribe other medications such as benzodiazepines to address the anxiety and distress that accompany OCD. Not all medications are effective for everyone. Talk to your doctor about the best treatment choice for you.

Combination. Some people with OCD do better with CBT, especially exposure and response prevention. Others do better with medication. Still others do best with a combination of the two. Many studies have shown that combining CBT with medication is the best approach for treating OCD, particularly in children and adolescents. Talk with your doctor about the best treatment for you.

## What Is It Like Having OCD?

"I couldn't do anything without rituals. They invaded every aspect of my life. Counting really bogged me down. I would wash my hair three times as opposed to once because three was a good luck number and one wasn't. It took me longer to read because I'd count the lines in a paragraph. When I set my alarm at night, I had to set it to a number that wouldn't add up to a 'bad' number."

"Getting dressed in the morning was tough, because I had a routine, and if I didn't follow the routine, I'd get anxious and would have to get dressed again. I always worried that if I didn't do something, my parents were going to die. I'd have these terrible thoughts of harming my parents. I knew that was completely irrational, but the thoughts triggered more anxiety and more senseless behavior. Because of the time I spent on rituals, I was unable to do a lot of things that were important to me."

"I knew the rituals didn't make sense, and I was deeply ashamed of them, but I couldn't seem to overcome them until I got treatment."

# Section 12.4

# *Compulsive Hoarding*

Text in this section is excerpted from "Distinct Brain Activity in
Hoarders," National Institutes of Health (NIH),
August 20, 2012. Reviewed March 2016.

## *Distinct Brain Activity in Hoarders*

Certain brain regions underactivate in people with hoarding disorder when dealing with others' possessions but over-activate when deciding whether to keep or discard their own things. The new findings give insight into the biology of hoarding and may guide future treatment strategies.

People with hoarding disorder have trouble making decisions about when to throw things away. Possessions can pile up and result in debilitating clutter. Until recently, hoarding disorder has been considered a type of obsessive-compulsive disorder (OCD). Many experts, however, now consider it a unique diagnosis.

Previous studies of brain function in hoarders implicated regions associated with decision-making, attachment, reward processing, impulse control and emotional regulation. But the patient populations and research methods varied between the studies, making it difficult to draw clear conclusions.

In the new study, a research team led by Dr. David Tolin of Hartford Hospital and Yale University used functional magnetic resonance imaging (fMRI) to investigate the neural basis for hoarding disorder. They compared the brains of patients with hoarding disorder to patients with OCD and healthy controls as they decided whether to keep or discard possessions. The study was funded by NIH's National Institute of Mental Health (NIMH).

The researchers analyzed brain images of 43 hoarders, 31 people with OCD and 33 healthy controls. Participants were given 6 seconds to make a decision about whether to keep or discard junk mail that either belonged to them or to someone else. Participants later watched as the items they chose to discard were placed in a paper shredder. They were then asked to rate their emotions and describe how they felt

155

during the decision-making tasks. The results appeared in the August 2012 issue of the Archives of General Psychiatry.

The hoarders chose to keep more mail that belonged to them than those in the OCD or healthy control groups. Hoarders also took longer to make decisions and reported greater anxiety, indecisiveness and sadness than the other groups.

The imaging analysis revealed that hoarders differ from both healthy controls and patients with OCD in 2 specific brain regions: the anterior cingulate cortex and insula. Scientists believe that these areas are part of a brain network involved in processing emotion. Both regions were more active in hoarders when they were making decisions about mail that belonged to them, but less active when making decisions about mail that didn't belong to them.

These results suggest that hoarders' decisions about possessions are hampered by abnormal activity in brain regions used to identify the emotional significance of things. "They lose the ability to make relative judgments, so the decision becomes absolutely overwhelming and aversive to them," Tolin says.

The scientists believe that these brain abnormalities are specific to hoarding and separate the disorder from OCD. In addition to further exploring the unique traits of hoarders, the researchers are now using this information to help assess potential treatments.

# Section 12.5

# *Social Anxiety Disorder*

Text in this section is excerpted from "Social Phobia
(Social Anxiety Disorder): Always Embarrassed,"
National Institutes of Health (NIH), 2013.

## *Introduction*

- Are you afraid of being judged by others or of being embarrassed all the time?

- Do you feel extremely fearful and unsure around other people most of the time?

- Do these worries make it hard for you to do everyday tasks like run errands, or talk to people at work or school?

If so, you may have a type of anxiety disorder called social phobia, also called social anxiety disorder.

## What Is Social Phobia?

Social phobia is a strong fear of being judged by others and of being embarrassed. This fear can be so strong that it gets in the way of going to work or school or doing other everyday things.

Everyone has felt anxious or embarrassed at one time or another. For example, meeting new people or giving a public speech can make anyone nervous. But people with social phobia worry about these and other things for weeks before they happen.

People with social phobia are afraid of doing common things in front of other people. For example, they might be afraid to sign a check in front of a cashier at the grocery store, or they might be afraid to eat or drink in front of other people, or use a public restroom. Most people who have social phobia know that they shouldn't be as afraid as they are, but they can't control their fear. Sometimes, they end up staying away from places or events where they think they might have to do something that will embarrass them. For some people, social phobia is a problem only in certain situations, while others have symptoms in almost any social situation.

Social phobia usually starts during youth. A doctor can tell that a person has social phobia if the person has had symptoms for at least 6 months. Without treatment, social phobia can last for many years or a lifetime.

## What Are the Signs and Symptoms of Social Phobia?

People with social phobia tend to:

- Be very anxious about being with other people and have a hard time talking to them, even though they wish they could

- Be very self-conscious in front of other people and feel embarrassed

- Be very afraid that other people will judge them

- Worry for days or weeks before an event where other people will be

- Stay away from places where there are other people

157

- Have a hard time making friends and keeping friends

- Blush, sweat, or tremble around other people

- Feel nauseous or sick to their stomach when with other people.

## What Causes Social Phobia?

Social phobia sometimes runs in families, but no one knows for sure why some people have it, while others don't. Researchers have found that several parts of the brain are involved in fear and anxiety. Some researchers think that misreading of others' behavior may play a role in causing social phobia. For example, you may think that people are staring or frowning at you when they truly are not. Weak social skills are another possible cause of social phobia. For example, if you have weak social skills, you may feel discouraged after talking with people and may worry about doing it in the future. By learning more about fear and anxiety in the brain, scientists may be able to create better treatments. Researchers are also looking for ways in which stress and environmental factors may play a role.

## How Is Social Phobia Treated?

First, talk to your doctor about your symptoms. Your doctor should do an exam to make sure that an unrelated physical problem isn't causing the symptoms. The doctor may refer you to a mental health specialist.

Social phobia is generally treated with psychotherapy, medication, or both.

**Psychotherapy.** A type of psychotherapy called cognitive behavioral therapy (CBT) is especially useful for treating social phobia. It teaches a person different ways of thinking, behaving, and reacting to situations that help him or her feel less anxious and fearful. It can also help people learn and practice social skills.

**Medication.** Doctors also may prescribe medication to help treat social phobia. The most commonly prescribed medications for social phobia are anti- anxiety medications and antidepressants. Anti- anxiety medications are powerful and there are different types. Many types begin working right away, but they generally should not be taken for long periods.

Antidepressants are used to treat depression, but they are also helpful for social phobia. They are probably more commonly prescribed for social phobia than anti-anxiety medications. Antidepressants may take several weeks to start working. Some may cause side effects such as headache, nausea, or difficulty sleeping. These side effects are usually not a problem for most people, especially if the dose starts off low and is increased slowly over time. Talk to your doctor about any side effects you may have.

A type of antidepressant called monoamine oxidase inhibitors (MAOIs) are especially effective in treating social phobia. However, they are rarely used as a first line of treatment because when MAOIs are combined with certain foods or other medicines, dangerous side effects can occur.

It's important to know that although antidepressants can be safe and effective for many people, they may be risky for some, especially children, teens, and young adults. A "black box"—the most serious type of warning that a prescription drug can have—has been added to the labels of antidepressant medications. These labels warn people that antidepressants may cause some people to have suicidal thoughts or make suicide attempts.

Anyone taking antidepressants should be monitored closely, especially when they first start treatment.

Another type of medication called beta-blockers can help control some of the physical symptoms of social phobia such as excessive sweating, shaking, or a racing heart. They are most commonly prescribed when the symptoms of social phobia occur in specific situations, such as "stage fright."

Some people do better with CBT, while others do better with medication. Still others do best with a combination of the two. Talk with your doctor about the best treatment for you.

## What Is It Like Having Social Phobia?

"In school I was always afraid of being called on, even when I knew the answers. When I got a job, I hated to meet with my boss. I couldn't eat lunch with my co-workers. I worried about being stared at or judged, and worried that I would make a fool of myself. My heart would pound and I would start to sweat when I thought about meetings. The feelings got worse as the time of the event got closer. Sometimes I couldn't sleep or eat for days before a staff meeting."

"I'm taking medicine and working with a counselor to cope better with my fears. I had to work hard, but I feel better. I'm glad I made that first call to my doctor."

159

## Section 12.6

# *Generalized Anxiety Disorder*

Text in this section is excerpted from "Generalized Anxiety
Disorder (GAD): When Worry Gets Out of Control,"
National Institutes of Health (NIH), 2013.

## *Introduction*

- Are you extremely worried about everything in your life, even if there is little or no reason to worry?

- Are you very anxious about just getting through the day?

- Are you afraid that everything will always go badly?

If so, you may have an anxiety disorder called generalized anxiety disorder (GAD).

## *What Is GAD?*

All of us worry about things like health, money, or family problems. But people with GAD are extremely worried about these or other things, even when there is little or no reason to worry about them. They are very anxious about just getting through the day. They think things will always go badly. At times, worrying keeps people with GAD from doing everyday tasks.

GAD develops slowly. It often starts during the teen years or young adulthood. Symptoms may get better or worse at different times, and often are worse during times of stress.

People with GAD may visit a doctor many times before they find out they have this disorder. They ask their doctors to help them with headaches or trouble falling asleep, which can accompany GAD but they don't always get the help they need right away. It may take doctors some time to be sure that a person has GAD instead of something else.

## *What Causes GAD?*

GAD sometimes runs in families, but no one knows for sure why some people have it, while others don't. Researchers have found that several parts of the brain are involved in fear and anxiety. Research suggests that the extreme worries of GAD may be a way for a person to avoid or ignore some deeper concern. If the person deals with this concern, then the worries of GAD would also disappear. By learning more about fear and anxiety in the brain, scientists may be able to create better treatments. Researchers are also looking for ways in which stress and environmental factors may play a role.

## What Are the Signs and Symptoms of GAD?

A person with GAD may:

- Worry very much about everyday things

- Have trouble controlling their constant worries

- Know that they worry much more than they should

- Have trouble relaxing

- Have a hard time concentrating

- Be easily startled

- Have trouble falling asleep or staying asleep

- Feel tired all the time

- Have headaches, muscle aches, stomach aches, or unexplained pains

- Have a hard time swallowing

- Tremble or twitch

- Be irritable, sweat a lot, and fccl light-headed or out of breath

- Have to go to the bathroom a lot.

## How Is GAD Treated?

First, talk to your doctor about your symptoms. Your doctor should do an exam to make sure that an unrelated physical problem isn't causing the symptoms. The doctor may refer you to a mental health specialist.

GAD is generally treated with psychotherapy, medication, or both.

**Psychotherapy.** A type of psychotherapy called cognitive behavioral therapy (CBT) is especially useful for treating GAD. It teaches a person different ways of thinking, behaving, and reacting to situations that help him or her feel less anxious and worried.

**Medication.** Doctors also may prescribe medication to help treat GAD. Two types of medications are commonly used to treat GAD—anti-anxiety medications and antidepressants. Anti-anxiety medications are powerful and there are different types. These side effects are usually not severe for most people, especially if the dose starts off low and is increased slowly over time.

Antidepressants are used to treat depression, but they also are helpful for GAD. They may take several weeks to start working. These medications may cause side effects such as headache, nausea, or difficulty sleeping. These side effects are usually not a problem for most people, especially if the dose starts off low and is increased slowly over time. Talk to your doctor about any side effects you may have.

It's important to know that although antidepressants can be safe and effective for many people, they may be risky for some, especially children, teens, and young adults. A "black box"—the most serious type of warning that a prescription drug can have—has been added to the labels of antidepressant medications. These labels warn people that antidepressants may cause some people to have suicidal thoughts or make suicide attempts. Anyone taking antidepressants should be monitored closely, especially when they first start treatment.

Some people do better with CBT, while others do better with medication. Still others do best with a combination of the two. Talk with your doctor about the best treatment for you.

## What Is It Like to Have GAD?

"I was worried all the time about everything. It didn't matter that there were no signs of problems, I just got upset. I was having trouble falling asleep at night, and I couldn't keep my mind focused at work. I felt angry at my family all the time.

"I saw my doctor and explained my constant worries. My doctor sent me to someone who knows about GAD. Now I am taking medicine and working with a counselor to cope better with my worries. I had to work hard, but I feel better. I'm glad I made that first call to my doctor."

# Chapter 13

# *Posttraumatic Stress Disorder*

## Definition

Posttraumatic stress disorder (PTSD) is a disorder that develops in some people who have seen or lived through a shocking, scary, or dangerous event.

It is natural to feel afraid during and after a traumatic situation. Fear triggers many split-second changes in the body to help defend against danger or to avoid it. This "fight-or-flight" response is a healthy reaction meant to protect a person from harm. Nearly everyone will experience a range of reactions after trauma, yet most people recover from initial symptoms naturally. Those who continue to experience problems may be diagnosed with PTSD. People who have PTSD may feel stressed or frightened even when they are not in danger.

## Signs and Symptoms

Not every traumatized person develops ongoing (chronic) or even short-term (acute) PTSD. Symptoms usually begin early, within 3 months of the traumatic incident, but sometimes they begin years

This chapter includes excerpts from "Post-Traumatic Stress Disorder," National Institute of Mental Health (NIMH), February 2016; text from "How is PTSD Measured?" U.S. Department of Veterans Affairs (VA), August 10, 2015; and text from "FAQs about PTSD Assessment," U.S. Department of Veterans Affairs (VA), August 13, 2015.

afterward. Symptoms must last more than a month to be considered PTSD. The course of the illness varies. Some people recover within 6 months, while others have symptoms that last much longer. In some people, the condition becomes chronic.

A doctor who has experience helping people with mental illnesses, such as a psychiatrist or psychologist, can diagnose PTSD.

To be diagnosed with PTSD, an adult must have all of the following for at least 1 month:

- At least one re-experiencing symptom

- At least one avoidance symptom

- At least two arousal and reactivity symptoms

- At least two cognition and mood symptoms

## Re-Experiencing Symptoms Include:

- Flashbacks—reliving the trauma over and over, including physical symptoms like a racing heart or sweating

- Bad dreams

- Frightening thoughts

Re-experiencing symptoms may cause problems in a person's everyday routine. The symptoms can start from the person's own thoughts and feelings. Words, objects, or situations that are reminders of the event can also trigger re-experiencing symptoms.

## Avoidance Symptoms Include:

- Staying away from places, events, or objects that are reminders of the traumatic experience

- Feeling emotionally numb

- Feeling strong guilt, depression, or worry

- Losing interest in activities that were enjoyable in the past

- Having trouble remembering the dangerous event

Things that remind a person of the traumatic event can trigger avoidance symptoms. These symptoms may cause a person to change his or her personal routine. For example, after a bad car accident, a person who usually drives may avoid driving or riding in a car.

*Arousal and Reactivity Symptoms Include:*

- Being easily startled
- Feeling tense or "on edge"
- Having difficulty sleeping
- Having angry outbursts

Arousal symptoms are usually constant, instead of being triggered by things that remind one of the traumatic events. These symptoms can make the person feel stressed and angry. They may make it hard to do daily tasks, such as sleeping, eating, or concentrating.

*Cognition and Mood Symptoms Include:*

- Trouble remembering key features of the traumatic event
- Negative thoughts about oneself or the world
- Distorted feelings like guilt or blame
- Loss of interest in enjoyable activities

Cognition and mood symptoms can begin or worsen after the traumatic event, but are not due to injury or substance use. These symptoms can make the person feel alienated or detached from friends or family members.

It is natural to have some of these symptoms after a dangerous event. Sometimes people have very serious symptoms that go away after a few weeks. This is called acute stress disorder, or ASD. When the symptoms last more than a few weeks and become an ongoing problem, the person may have developed PTSD. Some people with PTSD don't show any symptoms for weeks or months. PTSD is often accompanied by depression, substance abuse, or one or more of the other anxiety disorders.

## Do Children React Differently than Adults?

Children and teens can have extreme reactions to trauma, but their symptoms may not be the same as adults. In very young children (less than 6 years of age), these symptoms can include:

- Wetting the bed after having learned to use the toilet
- Forgetting how to or being unable to talk

- Acting out the scary event during playtime

- Being unusually clingy with a parent or other adult

Older children and teens are more likely to show symptoms similar to those seen in adults. They may also develop disruptive, disrespectful, or destructive behaviors. Older children and teens
may feel guilty for not preventing injury or deaths. They may also have thoughts of revenge.

## Risk Factors

Anyone can develop PTSD at any age. This includes war veterans, children, and people who have been through a physical or sexual assault, abuse, accident, disaster, or many other serious events. According to the National Center for PTSD, about 7 or 8 out of every 100 people will experience PTSD at some point in their lives. Women are more likely to develop PTSD than men, and genes may make some people more likely to develop PTSD than others.

Not everyone with PTSD has been through a dangerous event. Some people develop PTSD after a friend or family member experiences danger or harm. The sudden, unexpected death of a loved one can also lead to PTSD.

## Why Do Some People Develop PTSD and Other People Do Not?

It is important to remember that not everyone who lives through a dangerous event gets PTSD. In fact, most people will not get the disorder.

Many factors play a part in whether a person will develop PTSD. Some examples are listed below. Risk factors make a person more likely to get PTSD. Other factors, called resilience factors, can help reduce the risk of the disorder.

## Risk Factors and Resilience Factors for PTSD

Some factors that increase risk for PTSD include:

- Living through dangerous events and traumas

- Getting hurt

- Seeing another person hurt, or seeing a dead body

- Childhood trauma

- Feeling horror, helplessness, or extreme fear

- Having little or no social support after the event
- Dealing with extra stress after the event, such as loss of a loved one, pain and injury, or loss of a job or home
- Having a history of mental illness

Some resilience factors that may reduce the risk of PTSD include:

- Seeking out support from other people, such as friends and family
- Finding a support group after a traumatic event
- Learning to feel good about one's own actions in the face of danger
- Having a positive coping strategy, or a way of getting through the bad event and learning from it
- Being able to act and respond effectively despite feeling fear

Researchers are studying the importance of these and other risk and resilience factors, including genetics and neurobiology. With more research, someday it may be possible to predict who is likely to get PTSD and to prevent it.

## Treatments and Therapies

The main treatments for people with PTSD are medications, psychotherapy ("talk" therapy), or both. Everyone is different, and PTSD affects people differently so a treatment that works for one person may not work for another. It is important for anyone with PTSD to be treated by a mental health provider who is experienced with PTSD. Some people with PTSD need to try different treatments to find what works for their symptoms.

If someone with PTSD is going through an ongoing trauma, such as being in an abusive relationship, both of the problems need to be addressed. Other ongoing problems can include panic disorder, depression, substance abuse, and feeling suicidal.

## Medications

The most studied medications for treating PTSD include antidepressants, which may help control PTSD symptoms such as sadness, worry, anger, and feeling numb inside. Antidepressants and other medications may be prescribed along with psychotherapy.

Doctors and patients can work together to find the best medication or medication combination, as well as the right dose. Check the U.S. Food and Drug Administration website (http://www.fda.gov/ ) for the latest information on patient medication guides, warnings, or newly approved medications.

Psychotherapy (sometimes called "talk therapy") involves talking with a mental health professional to treat a mental illness. Psychotherapy can occur one-on-one or in a group. Talk therapy treatment for PTSD usually lasts 6 to 12 weeks, but it can last longer. Research shows that support from family and friends can be an important part of therapy.

Many types of psychotherapy can help people with PTSD. Some types target the symptoms of PTSD directly. Other therapies focus on social, family, or job-related problems. The doctor or therapist may combine different therapies depending on each person's needs.

Effective psychotherapies tend to emphasize a few key components, including education about symptoms, teaching skills to help identify the triggers of symptoms, and skills to manage the symptoms. One helpful form of therapy is called cognitive behavioral therapy, or CBT. CBT can include:

- **Exposure therapy.** This helps people face and control their fear. It gradually exposes them to the trauma they experienced in a safe way. It uses imagining, writing, or visiting the place where the event happened. The therapist uses these tools to help people with PTSD cope with their feelings.

- **Cognitive restructuring.** This helps people make sense of the bad memories. Sometimes people remember the event differently than how it happened. They may feel guilt or shame about something that is not their fault. The therapist helps people with PTSD look at what happened in a realistic way.

There are other types of treatment that can help as well. People with PTSD should talk about all treatment options with a therapist. Treatment should equip individuals with the skills to manage their symptoms and help them participate in activities that they enjoyed before developing PTSD.

## How Talk Therapies Help People Overcome PTSD?

Talk therapies teach people helpful ways to react to the frightening events that trigger their PTSD symptoms. Based on this general goal, different types of therapy may:

- Teach about trauma and its effects

- Use relaxation and anger-control skills

- Provide tips for better sleep, diet, and exercise habits

- Help people identify and deal with guilt, shame, and other feelings about the event

- Focus on changing how people react to their PTSD symptoms. For example, therapy helps people face reminders of the trauma.

## Beyond Treatment: How Can I Help Myself?

It may be very hard to take that first step to help yourself. It is important to realize that although it may take some time, with treatment, you can get better. If you are unsure where to go for help, ask your family doctor. You can also check the Internet under "mental health providers," "social services," "hotlines," or "physicians" for phone numbers and addresses. An emergency room doctor can also provide temporary help and can tell you where and how to get further help.

To help yourself while in treatment:

- Talk to your doctor about treatment options

- Engage in mild physical activity or exercise to help reduce stress

- Set realistic goals for yourself

- Break up large tasks into small ones, set some priorities, and do what you can as you can

- Try to spend time with other people, and confide in a trusted friend or relative. Tell others about things that may trigger symptoms.

- Expect your symptoms to improve gradually, not immediately

- Identify and seek out comforting situations, places, and people

Caring for yourself and others is especially important when large numbers of people are exposed to traumatic events (such as natural disasters, accidents, and violent acts).

## Next Steps for PTSD Research

In the last decade, progress in research on the mental and biological foundations of PTSD has lead scientists to focus on better understanding the underlying causes of why people experience a range of reactions to trauma.

- NIMH-funded researchers are exploring patients in acute care settings to better understand the changes that occur in individuals who do not recover compared with those who are resilient.

- Other research is looking at how fear memories are affected by learning, changes in the body, or even sleep.

- Research on preventing the development of PTSD soon after trauma exposure is also under way.

- Still other research is attempting to identify what factors determine whether someone with PTSD will respond well to one type of intervention or another, aiming to develop more personalized, effective, and efficient treatments.

- As gene research and brain imaging technologies continue to improve, scientists are more likely to be able to pinpoint when and where in the brain PTSD begins. This understanding may then lead to better targeted treatments to suit each person's own needs or even prevent the disorder before it causes harm.

## Join a Study

### What are Clinical Trials?

Clinical trials are research studies that look at new ways to prevent, detect, or treat diseases and conditions, including PTSD. During clinical trials, treatments might be new drugs or new combinations of drugs, new surgical procedures or devices, or new ways to use existing treatments. The goal of clinical trials is to determine if a new test or treatment works and is safe. Although individual participants may benefit from being part of a clinical trial, participants should be aware that the primary purpose of a clinical trial is to gain new scientific knowledge so that others may be better helped in the future.

## How Is PTSD Measured?

To develop PTSD, a person must have gone through a trauma. Almost all people who go through trauma have some symptoms for a short time after the trauma. Yet most people do not get PTSD. A certain pattern of symptoms is involved in PTSD. There are four major types of symptoms: re-experiencing, avoidance, arousal, and negative changes in beliefs and feelings.

Deciding if someone has PTSD can involve several steps. The diagnosis of PTSD is most often made by a mental health provider. To diagnose PTSD, a mental health provider "measures," "assesses," or "evaluates" PTSD symptoms you may have had since the trauma.

### *What Is a PTSD Screen?*

A person who went through trauma might be given a screen to see if he or she could have PTSD. A screen is a very short list of questions just to see if a person needs to be assessed further. The results of the screen do not show whether a person has PTSD. A screen can only show whether this person should be assessed further.

### *What Can I Expect from an Assessment for PTSD?*

The length of a PTSD assessment can vary widely depending on the purpose as well as the training of the evaluator. While some evaluations may take as little as 15 minutes, a more thorough evaluation takes about one hour. Some PTSD assessments can take eight or more one-hour sessions. This is more likely when the information is needed for legal reasons or disability claims.

You can expect to be asked questions about events that may have been traumatic for you. You will be asked about symptoms you may have had since these events. Assessments that are more complete are likely to involve structured sets of questions. You may be asked to complete surveys that ask about your thoughts and feelings. Your spouse or partner may be asked to provide extra information. Although it is uncommon, you may also be asked to go through a test that looks at how your body reacts to mild reminders of your trauma.

No matter what your case involves, you should always be able to ask questions in advance. The evaluator should be able to tell you what the assessment will include, how long it will take, and how the results of the assessment will be used.

### *What Are Some of the Common Measures Used?*

There are two main types of measures used in PTSD evaluations:

*Structured Interviews*

A structured interview is a standard set of questions that an interviewer asks. Some examples of structured interviews are:

- Clinician-Administered PTSD Scale (CAPS). Created by the National Center for PTSD staff, the CAPS is one of the most widely used PTSD interviews. The questions ask how often you have PTSD symptoms and how intense they are. The CAPS also asks about other symptoms that commonly occur with PTSD.

- Structured Clinical Interview for DSM (SCID). The SCID is another widely used interview. The SCID can be used to assess a range of mental health disorders including PTSD.

Other interviews include:

- Anxiety Disorders Interview Schedule-Revised (ADIS)

- PTSD-Interview

- Structured Interview for PTSD (SI-PTSD)

- PTSD Symptom Scale Interview (PSS-I)

Each has special features that might make it a good choice for a particular evaluation.

*Self-Report Questionnaires*

A self-report questionnaire is a set of questions, usually printed out, that you are given to answer. This kind of measure often takes less time and may be less costly than an interview. An example of a self-report measure is:

An example of a self-report measure is:

- PTSD Checklist (PCL). The PCL is another widely used measure developed by National Center for PTSD staff.

Other self-report measures are:

- Impact of Events Scale-Revised (IES-R)

- Keane PTSD Scale of the MMPI-2

- Mississippi Scale for Combat Related PTSD and the Mississippi Scale for Civilians

- Posttraumatic Diagnostic Scale (PDS)

- Penn Inventory for Posttraumatic Stress

- Los Angeles Symptom Checklist (LASC)

## FAQs about PTSD Assessment

The following frequently asked questions provide answers on topics that are commonly asked about PTSD assessment by Veterans and the general public.

### How Can I Tell If I Have PTSD?

Many people ask us how they can decide for themselves whether they have PTSD. It is natural to want to know why you are feeling or acting a certain way. However, trying to figure out on your own whether or not you have PTSD is difficult. Since many common reactions after trauma look like the symptoms of PTSD, a mental health provider must decide if you have PTSD.

Providers who have been trained to understand the thoughts and behaviors that go along with PTSD are best able to make that decision. A provider must use his or her training and judgment to select the best test or set of questions to use. Then he or she must interpret the results of the test.

The American Psychological Association suggests that only trained professionals give tests to assess for PTSD. If you think you may have PTSD, talk to your doctor or a mental health provider.

### How Can I Find out If a Mental Health Provider Is Able to Evaluate Me for PTSD?

You can ask questions about the provider's training and experience. Here are some questions you might ask:

#### "What Is Your Specialty Area?"

Many providers specialize in assessing and treating people who have experienced trauma. Providers who specialize in trauma will likely have expertise in evaluating PTSD. Some providers may specialize in working with certain kinds of trauma survivors. For example, a provider may work with adult survivors of childhood traumas. You may find a provider who specializes in a different trauma area than what you need, or who does not specialize at all. A provider who has experience assessing trauma survivors like you is most likely to have the expertise to do a good job on your assessment.

173

*"How Many PTSD Assessments Have You Done?"*

If possible, find a professional who has experience conducting PTSD assessments.

*"What Formal Training Have You Had That Will Allow You to Evaluate Me for PTSD?"*

If possible, find a professional who has completed training focused on PTSD assessment. Such providers are preferred over those trained only in general assessment.

*"What Formal Training Have You Had That Will Allow You to Evaluate Me for PTSD?"*

If possible, find a professional who has completed training focused on PTSD assessment. Such providers are preferred over those trained only in general assessment.

*"Can You Tell Me a Little about How You Assess PTSD?"*

You should feel comfortable with the assessment methods that a provider will use. A good assessment of PTSD can be done without the use of any special equipment. Most often, providers will have you fill out surveys or they will use a standard interview in which the provider will read a series of questions from a printed document.

## Who Can Request a PTSD or Trauma Measure from the National Center for PTSD?

The American Psychological Association requires that anyone who gives and interprets psychological tests must have advanced training. That is why we only give out measures to people with at least a master's degree in psychology or a related clinical area.

## What Is the Difference between an Evaluation That Measures Trauma Exposure and an Evaluation That Measures PTSD?

An evaluation that measures trauma exposure looks at whether you've gone through a traumatic event. Examples of traumatic events include combat, a car accident, or child sexual abuse. Sometimes the evaluation asks when the event happened. For example, you might be asked your age at the time of the experience. A measure of trauma exposure may also assess how you felt at the time of the event. You might be asked if you felt your life or the life of someone else was in danger.

By contrast, an evaluation that measures PTSD looks at how you felt or acted after you went through the traumatic event. You might be asked about the effect the trauma has had on your life, or any symptoms you may have had since the trauma. Some PTSD evaluations also ask about other problems such as depression or relationship problems. These other problems do not lead to a PTSD diagnosis, however.

### *If an Organization Is Asking for Proof of a PTSD Diagnosis, What Should I Provide?*

Only the results of a complete evaluation given by a professional can determine whether you have PTSD. Any organization with which you might be dealing will likely need the results of your evaluation. Therefore, you should see a healthcare provider who has experience in this area. As a patient, you can typically request a copy of your evaluation results from the professional who completes your assessment.

If you are a Veteran, the Veterans Benefits Administration has fact sheets on how to submit a compensation claim for PTSD. You can also call your local VA Medical Center to ask about benefits. Veterans Service Organizations (VSOs) also offer free guidance on completing claims.

# Chapter 14

# *Psychotic Disorders*

## *Chapter Contents*

# Section 14.1

# *Psychosis*

Text in this section is excerpted from "RAISE
Questions and Answers," National Institute of
Mental Health (NIMH), October 7, 2015.

## *Questions and Answers about Psychosis*

**Q: What is psychosis?**

A: The word psychosis is used to describe conditions that affect the mind, where there has been some loss of contact with reality. When someone becomes ill in this way it is called a psychotic episode. During a period of psychosis, a person's thoughts and perceptions are disturbed and the individual may have difficulty understanding what is real and what is not. Symptoms of psychosis include delusions (false beliefs) and hallucinations (seeing or hearing things that others do not see or hear). Other symptoms include incoherent or nonsense speech, and behavior that is inappropriate for the situation. A person in a psychotic episode may also experience depression, anxiety, sleep problems, social withdrawal, lack of motivation and difficulty functioning overall.

**Q: What causes psychosis?**

A: There is not one specific cause of psychosis. Psychosis may be a symptom of a mental illness, such as schizophrenia or bipolar disorder, but there are other causes, as well. Sleep deprivation, some general medical conditions, certain prescription medications, and the abuse of alcohol or other drugs, such as marijuana, can cause psychotic symptoms. Because there are many different causes of psychosis, it is important to see a qualified healthcare professional (e.g., psychologist, psychiatrist, or trained social worker) in order to receive a thorough assessment and accurate diagnosis. A mental illness, such as schizophrenia, is typically diagnosed by excluding all of these other causes of psychosis.

**Q: How common is psychosis?**

A: Approximately 3 percent of the people in the U.S. (3 out of 100 people) will experience psychosis at some time in their lives. About

100,000 adolescents and young adults in the U.S. experience a first episode of psychosis each year.

**Q: What is the connection between psychosis and schizophrenia?**

A: Schizophrenia is a mental illness characterized by periods of psychosis. An individual must experience psychotic symptoms for at least six months in order to be diagnosed with schizophrenia. However, a person may experience psychosis and never be diagnosed with schizophrenia, or any other mental health condition. This is because there are many different causes of psychosis, such as sleep deprivation, general medical conditions, the use of certain prescription medications, and the abuse of alcohol or other drugs.

**Q: What are the early warning signs of psychosis?**

A: Typically, a person will show changes in their behavior before psychosis develops. The list below includes behavioral warning signs for psychosis.

- Worrisome drop in grades or job performance

- New trouble thinking clearly or concentrating

- Suspiciousness, paranoid ideas or uneasiness with others

- Withdrawing socially, spending a lot more time alone than usual

- Unusual, overly intense new ideas, strange feelings or having no feelings at all

- Decline in self-care or personal hygiene

- Difficulty telling reality from fantasy

- Confused speech or trouble communicating

Any one of these items by itself may not be significant, but someone with several of the items on the list should consult a mental health professional. A qualified psychologist, psychiatrist or trained social worker will be able to make a diagnosis and help develop a treatment plan. Early treatment of psychosis increases the chance of a successful recovery. If you notice these changes in behavior and they begin to intensify or do not go away, it is important to seek help.

**Q: What does "duration of untreated psychosis" mean?**

A: The length of time between the start of psychotic symptoms and the beginning of treatment is called the duration of untreated psychosis or DUP. In general, research has shown that treatments for psychosis work better when they are delivered closer to the time when symptoms

179

first appear. This was the case in the RAISE-ETP study. Individuals who had a shorter DUP when they started treatment showed even greater improvements than those with longer DUP. The RAISE-ETP project also found average DUP in the United States to be longer than what is considered acceptable by international standards. Future RAISE-related efforts are working to find ways of decreasing DUP so that individuals receive care as early as possible after symptoms appear.

**Q: Do people recover from psychosis?**
A: With early diagnosis and appropriate treatment, it is possible to recover from psychosis. Many people who receive early treatment never have another psychotic episode. For other people, recovery means the ability to live a fulfilling and productive life, even if psychotic symptoms return sometimes.

**Q: What should I do if I think someone is having a psychotic episode?**
A: If you think someone you know is experiencing psychosis, encouraging them to seek treatment as early as possible is important. Psychosis can be treated effectively, and early intervention increases the chance of a successful outcome. To find a qualified treatment program, contact your health care professional. If someone having a psychotic episode is in distress or you are concerned about their safety, consider taking them to the nearest emergency room, or calling 911.

## Questions and Answers about Treatment

**Q: Why is early treatment important?**
Left untreated, psychotic symptoms can lead to disruptions in school and work, strained family relations, and separation from friends. The longer the symptoms go untreated, the greater the risk of additional problems. These problems can include substance abuse, going to the emergency department, being admitted to the hospital, having legal trouble, or becoming homeless.

Studies have shown that many people experiencing a first episode of psychosis in the United States typically have symptoms for more than a year before receiving treatment. It is important to reduce this duration of untreated psychosis because people tend to do better when they receive effective treatment as early as possible.

**Q: What is coordinated specialty care (CSC)?**
A: Coordinated specialty care (CSC) is a recovery-oriented treatment program for people with first episode psychosis (FEP). CSC

uses a team of specialists who work with the client to create a personal treatment plan. The specialists offer psychotherapy, medication management geared to individuals with FEP, case management, family education, and support, and work or education support, depending on the individual's needs and preferences. The client and the team work together to make treatment decisions, involving family members as much as possible. The goal is to link the individual with a CSC team as soon as possible after psychotic symptoms begin.

Coordinated specialty care is a general term used to describe a certain type of treatment for FEP. There are many different programs that are considered CSC. In the United States, examples of CSC programs include (but are not limited to) NAVIGATE, the Connection Program, OnTrackNY, the Specialized Treatment Early in Psychosis (STEP) program, and the Early Assessment and Support Alliance (EASA). RAISE is not a CSC program. RAISE is the name of a research initiative developed and funded by the National Institute of Mental Health to test CSC programs. Navigate and the Connection Program were the two CSC programs tested as part of the RAISE Project. For more information, read, "Evidence-Based Treatments for First Episode Psychosis: Components of Coordinated Specialty Care."

### Q. What is shared decision making and how does it work in early treatment?

A: Shared decision making means individuals and their health care providers work together to find the best treatment options based on the individual's unique needs and preferences. More information about how to participate in decisions with health care providers can be found on the SAMHSA website.

### Q: What is the role of medication in treatment?

A: Antipsychotic medications help reduce psychotic symptoms. Like medications for any illness, antipsychotic drugs have benefits and risks. Individuals should talk with their healthcare providers about the benefits of taking antipsychotic medication as well as potential side effects, dosage, and preferences like taking a daily pill or a monthly injection. For more information about how to work with your healthcare provider, visit the SAMHSA website.

### Q: What is Supported Employment/Education (SEE) and why is it important?

A: For young adults, psychosis can hurt school attendance and academic performance or make it difficult to find or keep a job. Supported

Employment/Education (SEE) is one way to help individuals return to work or school. A SEE specialist helps clients develop the skills they need to achieve school and work goals. In addition, the specialist can be a bridge between clients and educators or employers. SEE services are an important part of coordinated specialty care and are valued by many clients. Findings from RAISE-IES showed that SEE services often brought people into care and engaged them in treatment because it directly addressed their personal goals.

## Section 14.2

## *Schizophrenia*

Text in this section is excerpted from "schizophrenia," National Institute of Mental Health (NIMH), December 4, 2015.

### *What Is schizophrenia?*

Schizophrenia is a chronic and severe disorder that affects how a person thinks, feels, and acts. Although schizophrenia is not as common as other mental disorders, it can be very disabling. Approximately 7 or 8 individuals out of 1,000 will have schizophrenia in their lifetime.

People with the disorder may hear voices or see things that aren't there. They may believe other people are reading their minds, controlling their thoughts, or plotting to harm them. This can be scary and upsetting to people with the illness and make them withdrawn or extremely agitated. It can also be scary and upsetting to the people around them.

People with schizophrenia may sometimes talk about strange or unusual ideas, which can make it difficult to carry on a conversation. They may sit for hours without moving or talking. Sometimes people with schizophrenia seem perfectly fine until they talk about what they are really thinking.

Families and society are impacted by schizophrenia too. Many people with schizophrenia have difficulty holding a job or caring for themselves, so they may rely on others for help. Stigmatizing attitudes and beliefs about schizophrenia are common and sometimes interfere with people's willingness to talk about and get treatment for the disorder.

People with schizophrenia may cope with symptoms throughout their lives, but treatment helps many to recover and pursue their life goals. Researchers are developing more effective treatments and using new research tools to understand the causes of schizophrenia. In the years to come, this work may help prevent and better treat the illness.

## What Are the Symptoms of schizophrenia?

The symptoms of schizophrenia fall into three broad categories: positive, negative, and cognitive symptoms.

### Positive Symptoms

Positive symptoms are psychotic behaviors not generally seen in healthy people. People with positive symptoms may "lose touch" with some aspects of reality. For some people, these symptoms come and go. For others, they stay stable over time. Sometimes they are severe, and at other times hardly noticeable. The severity of positive symptoms may depend on whether the individual is receiving treatment. Positive symptoms include the following:

Hallucinations are sensory experiences that occur in the absence of a stimulus. These can occur in any of the five senses (vision, hearing, smell, taste, or touch). "Voices" (auditory hallucinations) are the most common type of hallucination in schizophrenia. Many people with the disorder hear voices. The voices can either be internal, seeming to come from within one's own mind, or they can be external, in which case they can seem to be as real as another person speaking. The voices may talk to the person about his or her behavior, command the person to do things, or warn the person of danger. Sometimes the voices talk to each other, and sometimes people with schizophrenia talk to the voices that they hear. People with schizophrenia may hear voices for a long time before family and friends notice the problem.

Other types of hallucinations include seeing people or objects that are not there, smelling odors that no one else detects, and feeling things like invisible fingers touching their bodies when no one is near.

Delusions are strongly held false beliefs that are not consistent with the person's culture. Delusions persist even when there is evidence that the beliefs are not true or logical. People with schizophrenia can have delusions that seem bizarre, such as believing that neighbors can control their behavior with magnetic waves. They may also believe that people on television are directing special messages to them, or that radio stations are broadcasting their thoughts aloud to others. These are called "delusions of reference."

Sometimes they believe they are someone else, such as a famous historical figure. They may have paranoid delusions and believe that others are trying to harm them, such as by cheating, harassing, poisoning, spying on, or plotting against them or the people they care about. These beliefs are called "persecutory delusions."

Thought disorders are unusual or dysfunctional ways of thinking. One form is called "disorganized thinking." This is when a person has trouble organizing his or her thoughts or connecting them logically. He or she may talk in a garbled way that is hard to understand. This is often called "word salad." Another form is called "thought blocking." This is when a person stops speaking abruptly in the middle of a thought. When asked why he or she stopped talking, the person may say that it felt as if the thought had been taken out of his or her head. Finally, a person with a thought disorder might make up meaningless words, or "neologisms."

Movement disorders may appear as agitated body movements. A person with a movement disorder may repeat certain motions over and over. In the other extreme, a person may become catatonic. Catatonia is a state in which a person does not move and does not respond to others. Catatonia is rare today, but it was more common when treatment for schizophrenia was not available.

## Negative Symptoms

Negative symptoms are associated with disruptions to normal emotions and behaviors. These symptoms are harder to recognize as part of the disorder and can be mistaken for depression or other conditions. These symptoms include the following:

- "Flat affect" (reduced expression of emotions via facial expression or voice tone)

- Reduced feelings of pleasure in everyday life

- Difficulty beginning and sustaining activities

- Reduced speaking

- People with negative symptoms may need help with everyday tasks. They may neglect basic personal hygiene.

This may make them seem lazy or unwilling to help themselves, but the problems are symptoms caused by schizophrenia.

*Cognitive Symptoms*

For some people, the cognitive symptoms of schizophrenia are subtle, but for others, they are more severe and patients may notice changes in their memory or other aspects of thinking. Similar to negative symptoms, cognitive symptoms may be difficult to recognize as part of the disorder. Often, they are detected only when specific tests are performed. Cognitive symptoms include the following:

- Poor "executive functioning" (the ability to understand information and use it to make decisions)

- Trouble focusing or paying attention

- Problems with "working memory" (the ability to use information immediately after learning it) Poor cognition is related to worse employment and social outcomes and can be distressing to individuals with schizophrenia.

## When Does Schizophrenia Start, and Who Gets It?

Schizophrenia affects slightly more males than females. It occurs in all ethnic groups around the world. Symptoms such as hallucinations and delusions usually start between ages 16 and 30. Males tend to experience symptoms a little earlier than females. Most commonly, schizophrenia occurs in late adolescence and early adulthood. It is uncommon to be diagnosed with schizophrenia after age 45. Schizophrenia rarely occurs in children, but awareness of childhood-onset schizophrenia is increasing.

It can be difficult to diagnose schizophrenia in teens. This is because the first signs can include a change of friends, a drop in grades, sleep problems, and irritability—behaviors that are common among teens. A combination of factors can predict schizophrenia in up to 80 percent of youth who are at high risk of developing the illness. These factors include isolating oneself and withdrawing from others, an increase in unusual thoughts and suspicions, and a family history of psychosis. This pre-psychotic stage of the disorder is called the "prodromal" period.

## Are People with Schizophrenia Violent?

Most people with schizophrenia are not violent. In fact, most violent crimes are not committed by people with schizophrenia. People with schizophrenia are much more likely to harm themselves than others. Substance abuse may increase the chance a person will become violent. The risk of violence is greatest when psychosis is untreated and decreases substantially when treatment is in place.

## Schizophrenia and Suicide

Suicidal thoughts and behaviors are very common among people with schizophrenia. People with schizophrenia die earlier than people without a mental illness, partly because of the increased suicide risk. It is hard to predict which people with schizophrenia are more likely to die by suicide, but actively treating any co-existing depressive symptoms and substance abuse may reduce suicide risk. People who take their antipsychotic medications as prescribed are less likely to attempt suicide than those who do not. If someone you know is talking about or has attempted suicide, help him or her find professional help right away or call 911.

## Schizophrenia and Substance Use Disorders

Substance use disorders occur when frequent use of alcohol and/ or drugs interferes with a person's health, family, work, school, and social life. Substance use is the most common co-occurring disorder in people with schizophrenia, and the complex relationships between substance use disorders and schizophrenia have been extensively studied. Substance use disorders can make treatment for schizophrenia less effective, and individuals are also less likely to engage in treatment for their mental illness if they are abusing substances. It is commonly believed that people with schizophrenia who also abuse substances are trying to "self-medicate" their symptoms, but there is little evidence that people begin to abuse substances in response to symptoms or that abusing substances reduces symptoms.

Nicotine is the most common drug abused by people with schizophrenia. People with schizophrenia are much more likely to smoke than people without a mental illness, and researchers are exploring whether there is a biological basis for this. There is some evidence that nicotine may temporarily alleviate a subset of the cognitive deficits commonly observed in schizophrenia, but these benefits are outweighed by the detrimental effects of smoking on other aspects of cognition and general health. Bupropion has been found to be effective for smoking cessation in people with schizophrenia.

Most studies find that reducing or stopping smoking does not make schizophrenia symptoms worse. Cannabis (marijuana) is also frequently abused by people with schizophrenia, which can worsen health outcomes. Heavy cannabis use is associated with more severe and earlier onset of schizophrenia symptoms, but research has not yet definitively determined whether cannabis directly causes schizophrenia.

Drug abuse can increase rates of other medical illnesses (such as hepatitis, heart disease, and infectious disease) as well as suicide, trauma, and homelessness in people with schizophrenia. It is generally understood that schizophrenia and substance use disorders have strong genetic risk factors.

While substance use disorder and a family history of psychosis have individually been identified as risk factors for schizophrenia, it is less well understood if and how these factors are related. When people have both schizophrenia and a substance abuse disorder, their best chance for recovery is a treatment program that integrates the schizophrenia and substance abuse treatment.

## What Causes Schizophrenia?

Research has identified several factors that contribute to the risk of developing schizophrenia.

### Genes and Environment

Scientists have long known that schizophrenia sometimes runs in families. The illness occurs in less than 1 percent of the general population, but it occurs in 10 percent of people who have a first-degree relative with the disorder, such as a parent, brother, or sister. People who have second- degree relatives (aunts, uncles, grandparents, or cousins) with the disease also develop schizophrenia more often than the general population. The risk is highest for an identical twin of a person with schizophrenia. He or she has a 40 to 65 percent chance of developing the disorder. Although these genetic relationships are strong, there are many people who have schizophrenia who don't have a family member with the disorder and, conversely, many people with one or more family members with the disorder who do not develop it themselves.

Scientists believe that many different genes contribute to an increased risk of schizophrenia, but that no single gene causes the disorder by itself. In fact, recent research has found that people with schizophrenia tend to have higher rates of rare genetic mutations. These genetic differences involve hundreds of different genes and probably disrupt brain development in diverse and subtle ways.

Research into various genes that are related to schizophrenia is ongoing, so it is not yet possible to use genetic information to predict who will develop the disease. Despite this, tests that scan a person's genes can be bought without a prescription or a health professional's advice. Ads for the tests suggest that with a saliva sample, a company can determine if a client is at risk for developing specific diseases, including schizophrenia. However, scientists don't yet know all of the gene variations that contribute to schizophrenia and those that are known raise the risk only by very small amounts. Therefore, these "genome scans" are unlikely to provide a complete picture of a person's risk for developing a mental disorder like schizophrenia.

In addition, it certainly takes more than genes to cause the disorder. Scientists think that interactions between genes and aspects of the individual's environment are necessary for schizophrenia to develop. Many environmental factors may be involved, such as exposure to viruses or malnutrition before birth, problems during birth, and other, not yet known, psychosocial factors.

## Different Brain Chemistry and Structure

Scientists think that an imbalance in the complex, interrelated chemical reactions of the brain involving the neurotransmitters dopamine and glutamate, and possibly others, plays a role in schizophrenia. Neurotransmitters are substances that brain cells use to communicate with each other. Scientists are learning more about how brain chemistry is related to schizophrenia.

Also, the brain structures of some people with schizophrenia are slightly different than those of healthy people. For example, fluid-filled cavities at the center of the brain, called ventricles, are larger in some people with schizophrenia. The brains of people with the illness also tend to have less gray matter, and some areas of the brain may have less or more activity. These differences are observed when brain scans from a group of people with schizophrenia are compared with those from a group of people without schizophrenia. However, the differences are not large enough to identify individuals with the disorder and are not currently used to diagnose schizophrenia.

Studies of brain tissue after death also have revealed differences in the brains of people with schizophrenia. Scientists have found small changes in the location or structure of brain cells that are formed before birth. Some experts think problems during brain development before birth may lead to faulty connections. The problem may not show up in a person until puberty. The brain undergoes major changes during puberty, and these changes could trigger psychotic symptoms in people who are vulnerable due to genetics or brain differences.

Scientists have learned a lot about schizophrenia, but more research is needed to help explain how it develops.

## How Is Schizophrenia Treated?

Because the causes of schizophrenia are still unknown, treatments focus on eliminating the symptoms of the disease. Treatments include antipsychotic medications and various psychosocial treatments. Research on "coordinated specialty care," where a case manager, the patient, and a medication and psychosocial treatment team work together, has shown promising results for recovery.

### Antipsychotic Medications

Antipsychotic medications have been available since the mid-1950s. The older types are called conventional or typical antipsychotics. In the 1990s, new antipsychotic medications were developed. These new medications are called second-generation or atypical antipsychotics.

### What Are the Side Effects?

Some people have side effects when they start taking medications. Most side effects go away after a few days. Others are persistent but can often be managed successfully. People who are taking antipsychotic medications should not drive until they adjust to their new medication. Side effects of many antipsychotics include:

- Drowsiness
- Dizziness when changing positions
- Blurred vision
- Rapid heartbeat
- Sensitivity to the sun
- Skin rashes
- Menstrual problems for women

Atypical antipsychotic medications can cause major weight gain and changes in a person's metabolism. This may increase a person's risk of getting diabetes and high cholesterol. A doctor should monitor a person's weight, glucose levels, and lipid levels regularly while the individual is taking an atypical antipsychotic medication.

Typical antipsychotic medications can cause side effects related to physical movement, such as:

- Rigidity

- Persistent muscle spasms

- Tremors

- Restlessness

Doctors and individuals should work together to choose the right medication, medication dose, and treatment plan, which should be based on a person's individual needs and medical situation. Information about medications is frequently updated. Check the U.S. Food and Drug Administration (FDA) website ( http://www.fda.gov ) for the latest information on warnings, patient medication guides, or newly approved medications.

Long-term use of typical antipsychotic medications may lead to a condition called tardive dyskinesia (TD). TD causes muscle movements a person can't control. The movements commonly happen around the mouth. TD can range from mild to severe, and in some people the problem cannot be cured. Sometimes people with TD recover partially or fully after they stop taking the medication.

TD happens to fewer people who take the atypical antipsychotics, but some people may still get TD. People who think that they might have TD should check with their doctor before stopping their medication.

## How Are Antipsychotic Medications Taken, and How Do People Respond to Them?

Antipsychotic medications are usually taken daily in pill or liquid form. Some antipsychotics are injections that are given once or twice a month.

Symptoms of schizophrenia, such as feeling agitated and having hallucinations, usually improve within days after starting antipsychotic treatment. Symptoms like delusions usually improve within a few weeks. After about 6 weeks, many people will experience improvement in their symptoms. Some people will continue to have some symptoms, but usually medication helps to keep the symptoms from getting very intense.

However, people respond in different ways to antipsychotic medications, and no one can tell beforehand how a person will respond. Sometimes a person needs to try several medications before finding the right one. Doctors and patients can work together to find the best medication or medication combination, as well as the right dose.

Most people will have one or more periods of relapse—their symptoms come back or get worse. Usually, relapses happen when people stop taking their medication or when they take it less often than prescribed.

Some people stop taking the medication because they feel better or they may feel they don't need it anymore. But no one should stop taking an antipsychotic medication without first talking to his or her doctor. Medication should be gradually tapered off, never stopped suddenly.

## *How Do Antipsychotic Medications Interact with Other Medications?*

Antipsychotic medications can produce unpleasant or dangerous side effects when taken with certain other medications. For this reason, all doctors treating a patient need to be aware of all the medications that person is taking. Doctors need to know about prescription and over-the- counter medicine, vitamins, minerals, and herbal supplements. People also need to discuss any alcohol or street drug use with their doctor.

## *Psychosocial Treatments*

Psychosocial treatments can help people with schizophrenia who are already stabilized. Psychosocial treatments help individuals deal with the everyday challenges of their illness, such as difficulty with communication, work, and forming and keeping relationships. Learning and using coping skills to address these problems helps people with schizophrenia to pursue their life goals, such as attending school or work. Individuals who participate in regular psychosocial treatment are less likely to have relapses or be hospitalized.

## *Illness Management Skills*

People with schizophrenia can take an active role in managing their own illness. Once they learn basic facts about schizophrenia and its treatment, they can make informed decisions about their care. If they know how to watch for the early warning signs of relapse and make a plan to respond, patients can learn to prevent relapses. Patients can also use coping skills to deal with persistent symptoms.

## Rehabilitation

Rehabilitation emphasizes social and vocational training to help people with schizophrenia participate fully in their communities. Because schizophrenia usually develops during the critical career-development years (ages 18 to 35), the career and life trajectories for individuals with schizophrenia are usually interrupted and they need to learn new skills to get their work life back on track. Rehabilitation programs can include employment services, money management counseling, and skills training to maintain positive relationships.

### Family Education and Support

Family education and support teaches relatives or interested individuals about schizophrenia and its treatment and strengthens their capacity to aid in their loved one's recovery.

### Cognitive Behavioral Therapy

Cognitive behavioral therapy (CBT) is a type of psychotherapy that focuses on changing unhelpful patterns of thinking and behavior. The CBT therapist teaches people with schizophrenia how to test the reality of their thoughts and perceptions, how to "not listen" to their voices, and how to manage their symptoms overall. CBT can help reduce the severity of symptoms and reduce the risk of relapse. CBT can be delivered individually or in groups.

### Self-Help Groups

In self-help groups for people with schizophrenia, group members support and comfort each other and share information on helpful coping strategies and services. Professional therapists usually are not involved. People in self-help groups know that others are facing the same problems, which can help everyone feel less isolated and more connected.

## How Can You Help a Person with Schizophrenia?

Family and friends can help their loved one with schizophrenia by supporting their engagement in treatment and pursuit of their recovery goals. Positive communication approaches will be most helpful. It can be difficult to know how to respond to someone with schizophrenia who makes strange or clearly false statements. Remember that these beliefs or hallucinations seem very real to the person. It is not helpful to say they are wrong or imaginary. But going along with the delusions is not helpful, either. Instead, calmly say that you see things differently. Tell them that you acknowledge that everyone has the right to see things his or her own way. In addition, it is important to understand that schizophrenia is a biological illness. Being respectful, supportive, and kind without tolerating dangerous or inappropriate behavior is the best way to approach people with this disorder

## What Is the Outlook for the Future?

The outlook for people with schizophrenia continues to improve. Treatments that work well are available, and new ones are being developed. Many people with schizophrenia experience recovery and lead independent, satisfying lives. Continued research and understanding in genetics, neuroscience, and behavioral science will help scientists and health professionals understand the causes of the disorder and how it may be predicted and prevented. This work will help experts develop better treatments to help people with schizophrenia achieve their full potential. In 2009, NIMH launched the Recovery After an Initial Schizophrenia Episode (RAISE) research project (http://www.nimh.nih.gov/raise). RAISE seeks to fundamentally change the trajectory and prognosis of schizophrenia through coordinated treatment in the earliest stages of the disorder. RAISE is designed to reduce the likelihood of long-term disability that people with schizophrenia often experience and help people with this disorder lead productive, independent lives.

Families and individuals who are living with schizophrenia are encouraged to participate in clinical research.

# Section 14.3

# *Schizoaffective Disorder*

Text in this section is excerpted from "Facts about
Schizoaffective Disorder," U.S. Department of
Veterans Affairs (VA), February 1, 2001. Reviewed March 2016

## What Is Schizoaffective Disorder?

Schizoaffective disorder is a major psychiatric disorder that is quite similar to schizophrenia. The disorder can affect all aspects of daily living, including work, social relationships, and self- care skills (such as grooming and hygiene). People with schizoaffective disorder can have a wide variety of different symptoms, including having unusual perceptual experiences (hallucinations) or beliefs others do not share (delusions), mood (such as marked depression), low motivation, inability to experience pleasure, and poor attention. The serious nature of the symptoms of schizoaffective disorder sometimes requires consumers to go to the hospital to get care. The experience of schizoaffective disorder can be described as similar to "dreaming when you are wide awake"; that is, it can be hard for the person with the disorder to distinguish between reality and fantasy.

## How Common Is Schizoaffective Disorder?

About one in every two hundred people (1/2 percent) develops schizoaffective disorder at some time during his or her life. Schizoaffective disorder, along with schizophrenia, is one of the most common serious psychiatric disorders. More hospital beds are occupied by persons with these disorders than any other psychiatric disorder. However, as with other types of mental illness, individuals with schizoaffective disorder can engage in treatment and other mental health recovery efforts that have the potential to dramatically improve the wellbeing of the individual.

## How Is the Disorder Diagnosed?

Schizoaffective disorder can only be diagnosed by a clinical interview. The purpose of the interview is to determine whether the person has experienced specific "symptoms" of the disorder, and whether these symptoms have been present long enough to merit the diagnosis. In addition to conducting the interview, the diagnostician must also check to make sure the person is not experiencing any physical problems that could cause symptoms similar to schizoaffective disorder, such as a brain tumor or alcohol or drug abuse.

Schizoaffective disorder cannot be diagnosed with a blood test, X-ray, CAT-scan, or any other laboratory test. An interview is necessary to establish the diagnosis.

## The Characteristic Symptoms of Schizoaffective Disorder

The diagnosis of schizoaffective disorder requires that t he person experience some decline in social functioning for at least a six-month period, such as problems with school or work, social relationships, or self-care. In addition, some other symptoms must be commonly present. The symptoms of schizoaffective disorder can be divided into five broad classes: positive symptoms, negative symptoms, symptoms of mania, symptoms of depression, and other symptoms. A person with schizoaffective disorder will usually have some (but not all) of the symptoms described below.

## Positive Symptoms

Positive symptoms refer to thoughts, perceptions, and behaviors that are ordinarily absent in persons who are not diagnosed with schizophrenia or schizoaffective disorder, but are present in persons with schizoaffective disorder. These symptoms often vary over time in their severity, and may be absent for long periods in some persons.

**Hallucinations.** Hallucinations are "false perceptions"; that is, hearing, seeing, feeling, or smelling things that are not actually there. The most common type of hallucinations is auditory hallucinations. Individuals sometimes report hearing voices talking to them or about them, often saying insulting things, such as calling them names. These voices are usually heard through the ears and sound like other human voices.

**Delusions.** Delusions are "false beliefs"; that is, a belief which the person holds, but which others do not share. Some individuals have paranoid delusions, believing that they are not safe or others want to hurt them. Delusions of reference are common, in which the individual believes that something in the environment is referring to him or her when it is not (such as the television talking to the person). Delusions of control are beliefs that others can control one's actions. Individuals may hold these beliefs strongly and cannot usually be "talked out" of them.

**Thinking Disturbances.** This problem is reflected in a difficulty in communication. The individual talks in a manner that is difficult to follow. For example, the individual may jump from one topic to the next, stop in the middle of the sentence, make up new words, or simply be difficult to understand.

## Negative Symptoms

Negative symptoms are the opposite of positive symptoms. They are the absence of thoughts, perceptions, or behaviors that are ordinarily present in people who are not diagnosed with schizophrenia or schizoaffective disorder. These symptoms can often persist for a long period of time, though with effort on the individual's part they can often be improved. Many professionals think these symptoms reflect a sense of hopelessness about the future.

**Blunted Affect.** The expressiveness of the individual's face, voice tone, and gestures is less. However, this does not mean that the person is not reacting to his or her environment or having feelings.

**Apathy.** The individual does not feel motivated to pursue goals and activities. The individual may feel lethargic or sleep y, and have trouble following through on even simple plans. Individuals with apathy often have little sense of purpose in their lives and have few interests.

**Anhedonia.** The individual experiences little or no pleasure from activities that he or she used to enjoy or that others enjoy. For example, the person may not enjoy watching a sunset, going to the movies, or a close relationship with another person.

**Poverty of Speech or Content of Speech.** The individual says very little, or when he or she talks, there does not seem to be much information being conveyed. Sometimes conversing with the person with schizoaffective disorder can be very difficult.

**Inattention.** The individual has difficulty paying attention and is easily distracted. This can interfere with activities such as work, interacting with others, and personal care skills

## *Symptoms of Mania*

In general, the symptoms of mania involve an excess in behavioral activity, mood states (in particular, irritability or positive feelings), and self-esteem and confidence.

**Euphoric or Expansive Mood.** The individual's mood is abnormally elevated, such as extremely happy or excited (euphoria). The person may tend to talk more and with greater enthusiasm or emphasis on certain topics (expansiveness).

**Irritability.** The individual is easily angered or persistently irritable, especially when others seem to interfere with his or her plans or goals, however unrealistic they may be.

**Inflated Self-Esteem or Grandiosity.** The individual is extremely self- confident and may be unrealistic about his or her abilities (grandiosity). For example, the individual may believe he or she is a brilliant artist or inventor, a wealthy person, a shrewd businessperson, or a healer when he or she has no special competence in these areas.

**Decreased Need for Sleep.** Only a few hours of sleep are needed each night (such as less than four hours) for the individual to feel rested.

**Talkativeness.** The individual talks excessively and may be difficult to interrupt. The individual may jump quickly from one topic to another (called flight of ideas), making it hard for others to understand.

**Racing Thoughts.** Thoughts come so rapidly that the individual finds it hard to keep up with them or express them.

**Distractibility.** The individual's attention is easily drawn to irrelevant stimuli, such as the sound of a car honking outside on the street.

**Increased Goal-Directed Activity.** A great deal of time is spent pursuing specific goals, at work, school, or sexually. Often these behaviors put the person at risk.

**Excessive Involvement in Pleasurable Activities with High Potential for Negative Consequences.** Common problem areas include spending sprees, sexual indiscretions, increased substance abuse, or making foolish business investments.

## Symptoms of Depression

Depressive symptoms reflect the opposite end of the continuum of mood from manic symptoms, with a low mood and behavioral inactivity as the major features.

**Depressed Mood.** Mood is low most of the time, according to the person or significant others.

**Diminished Interest or Pleasure.** The individual has few interests and gets little pleasure from anything, including activities previously found enjoyable.

**Change in Appetite and/or Weight.** Loss of appetite (and weight) when not dieting, or increased appetite (and weight gain) are evident.

**Change in Sleep Pattern.** The individual may have difficulty falling asleep, staying asleep, or wake early in the morning and not be able to get back to sleep. Alternatively, the person may sleep excessively (such as over twelve hours per night), spending much of the day in bed.

**Change in Activity Level.** Decreased activity level is reflected by slowness and lethargy, both in terms of the individual' s behavior and thought processes. Alternatively, the individual may feel agitated, "on edge," and restless.

**Fatigue or Loss of Energy.** The individual experiences fatigue throughout the day or there is a chronic feeling of loss of energy.

**Feelings of Worthlessness, Hopelessness, Helplessness.** Individuals may feel they are worthless as people, that there is no hope for improving their lives, or that there is no point in trying to improve their unhappy situation.

**Inappropriate Guilt.** Feelings of guilt may be present about events that the individual did not even do, such as a catastrophe, a crime, or an illness.

**Recurrent Thoughts about Death.** The individual thinks about death a great deal and may contemplate (or even attempt) suicide.

**Decreased Concentration or Ability to Make Decisions.** Significant decreases in the ability to concentrate make it difficult for the individual to pay attention to others or complete simple tasks. The individual may be quite indecisive about even minor things.

## Other Symptoms

Individuals with schizoaffective disorder are prone to alcohol or drug abuse. Some individuals may use alcohol and drugs excessively either because of their disturbing symptoms, to experience pleasure, or when socializing with others.

## How Is Schizoaffective Disorder Distinguished from Schizophrenia and Affective (Mood) Disorders?

Many persons with a diagnosis of schizoaffective disorder have had, at a prior time, diagnoses of schizophrenia or bipolar disorder. Frequently, this previous diagnosis is revised to schizo affective disorder when it becomes clear, over time, that the person experiences symptoms of mania or depression much of the time, but on other occasions has experienced psychotic symptoms such as hallucinations or delusions even when his or her mood i s stable.

## What Is the Course of Schizoaffective Disorder?

The disorder usually begins in late adolescence or early adulthood, often between the ages of sixteen and thirty. The severity of symptoms usually varies over time, at times requiring hospitalization for treatment. The disorder is often life-long, although the symptoms tend to improve gradually over the person's life and many individuals who were diagnosed with the disorder when they were younger appear to have few or no symptoms from middle age on. With schizoaffective disorder, as with other major psychiatric illnesses, individuals can work to achieve their goals and live very full lives.

## What Causes Schizoaffective Disorder?

The cause of schizoaffective disorder is not known, although many scientists believe it is a variant of the disorder of schizophrenia. Schizoaffective disorder (and schizophrenia) may actually be several disorders. Current theories suggest that an imbalance in brain chemicals (specifically, dopamine) may be at the root o f these two disorders. Vulnerability to developing schizoaffective disorder appears to be partly determined by genetic factors and partly by early environmental factors (such as subtle insults to the brain of the baby in the womb before and during birth).

## *How Is Schizoaffective Disorder Treated?*

Many of the same methods used to treat schizophrenia are also effective for schizoaffective disorder. Antipsychotic medications are an effective treatment for schizoaffective disorder for most, but not all, persons with the disorder. These drugs are not a "cure" for the disorder, but they can reduce symptoms and prevent relapses among the majority of people with the disorder. Antidepressant medications and mood stabilizing medications (such as lithium) are occasionally used to treat affective symptoms (depressive or manic symptoms) in schizoaffective disorder.

Other important treatments include social skills training, vocational rehabilitation and supported employment, peer support, and intensive case management. Family therapy helps reduce stress in the family and teaches family members how to monitor the disorder. In addition, individual supportive counseling can help the person with the disorder learn to manage the disorder more successfully and obtain emotional support in coping with the distress resulting from the disorder.

Individuals with schizoaffective disorder who work actively toward mental health recovery can positively affect the course of their illness and improve the quality of their lives. Family support for the individual's recovery efforts can lend meaningful benefits.

Chapter 15

# *Personality Disorders*

## *Chapter Contents*

# Section 15.1

# *Borderline Personality Disorder*

Text in this section is excerpted from "An Introduction to Co-Occurring Borderline Personality Disorder and Substance Use Disorders," Substance Abuse and Mental Health Services Administration (SAMHSA), December 10, 2014.

## *What Is Borderline Personality Disorder?*

BPD is one among several personality disorders (e.g., narcissistic personality disorder, paranoid personality disorder, antisocial personality disorder). According to the *Diagnostic and Statistical Manual of Mental Disorders, Fifth Edition* (DSM-5), personality disorders are generally characterized by:

- Entrenched patterns of behavior that deviate significantly from the usual expectations of behavior of the individual's culture.

- Behavior patterns that are pervasive, inflexible, and resistant to change.

- Emergence of the disorder's features no later than early adulthood (unlike depression, for example, which can begin at any age).

- Lack of awareness that behavior patterns and personality characteristics are problematic or that they differ from those of other individuals.

- Distress and impairment in one or more areas of a person's life (often only after other people get upset about his or her behavior).

- Behavior patterns that are not better accounted for by the effects of substance abuse, medication, or some other mental disorder or medical condition (e.g., head injury).

BPD is a complex and serious mental illness. Individuals with BPD are often misunderstood and misdiagnosed. A history of childhood trauma (e.g., physical or sexual abuse, neglect, early parental loss) is more common for individuals with BPD. In fact, many individuals with BPD may have developed BPD symptoms as a way to cope with childhood trauma. However, it is important to note that not all individuals with BPD have a history of childhood trauma. It is also important to note that some of the symptoms of BPD overlap with those of several other DSM-5 diagnoses, such as bipolar disorder and posttraumatic stress disorder (PTSD). Therefore, a diagnosis of BPD should be made only by a licensed and experienced mental health professional (whose scope of practice includes diagnosing mental disorders) and then only after a thorough assessment over time. Individuals with BPD often require considerable attention from their therapists and are generally considered to be challenging clients to treat. However, BPD may not be the chronic disorder it was once thought to be. Individuals with BPD often respond to appropriate treatment and may have a good long-term prognosis, experiencing a remission of symptoms with a relatively low occurrence of relapse.

The DSM-5 indicates that BPD is diagnosed more often in women than in men (75 percent and 25 percent, respectively). Other research, however, has suggested that there may be no gender difference in prevalence in the general population, but that BPD is associated with a significantly higher level of mental and physical disability for women than it is for men. In addition, the types of co-occurring conditions tend to be different for women than for men. In women, the most common co-occurring disorders are major depression, anxiety disorders, eating disorders, and PTSD. Men with BPD are more likely to have co-occurring SUDs and antisocial personality disorder, and they are more likely to experience episodes of intense or explosive anger.

## *What Are the Symptoms of BPD?*

The DSM-5 classifies mental disorders and includes specific diagnostic criteria for all currently recognized mental disorders. It is a tool for diagnosis and treatment, but it is also a tool for communication, providing a common language for clinicians and researchers to discuss symptoms and disorders. According to the DSM-5, the symptoms of BPD include:

- Intense fear of abandonment and efforts to avoid abandonment (real or imagined).

- Turbulent, erratic, and intense relationships that often involve vacillating perceptions of others (from extremely positive to extremely negative).

203

- Lack of a sense of self or an unstable sense of self.

- Impulsive acts that can be hurtful to oneself (e.g., excessive spending, reckless driving, risky sex).

- Repeated suicidal behavior or gestures or self-mutilating behavior.

- Chronic feelings of emptiness.

- Episodes of intense (and sometimes inappropriate) anger or difficulty controlling anger (e.g., repeated physical fights, inappropriate displays of anger).

- Temporary feelings of paranoia (often stress-related) or severe dissociative symptoms (e.g., feeling detached from oneself, trancelike).

Anyone with some of these symptoms may need to be referred to a licensed mental health professional for a complete assessment. Exhibit 1 presents some examples of how a person with BPD might behave.

### *Suicide and Nonsuicidal Self-Injury*

BPD is unique in that it is the only mental disorder diagnosis that includes suicide attempts or self-harming behaviors among its diagnostic criteria. The risk of suicide is high among individuals with BPD, with as many as 79 percent reporting a history of suicide attempts and 8 percent to 10 percent dying by suicide—a rate that may be 50 times greater than the rate among the general population.

More than 75 percent of individuals with BPD engage in deliberate self-harming behaviors known as nonsuicidal self-injury (NSSI) (e.g., cutting or burning themselves). Unlike suicide attempts, NSSI does not usually involve a desire or intent to die. Sometimes the person with BPD does not consider these behaviors harmful. One study involving 290 patients with BPD found that 90 percent of patients reported a history of NSSI, and over 70 percent reported the use of multiple methods of NSSI. Reasons for NSSI vary from person to person and, for some individuals, there may be more than one reason. The behaviors may be:

- A way to express anger or pain.

- A way to relieve pain (i.e., shifting from psychic pain to physical pain).

- A way to "feel" something.

- A way to "feel real."

- An attempt to regulate emotions.

- A form of self-punishment.

- An effort to get attention or care from others.

NSSI may include:

- Cutting.

- Burning.

- Skin picking or excoriation

- Head banging.

- Hitting.

- Hair pulling

## What Are the Symptoms of Substance Use Disorders (SUD)?

SUDs involve patterns of recurrent substance use that result in significant problems, which fall into the following categories:

- **Impaired control**—taking more of the substance than intended, trying unsuccessfully to cut down on use, spending an increasing amount of time obtaining and using the substance, craving or having a strong desire for substance use

- **Social impairment**—failing to fulfill obligations at work, school, or home; continuing substance use in spite of the problems it causes; giving up or reducing other activities because of substance use

- **Risky use**—using the substance(s) in situations in which it may be physically dangerous to do so (e.g., driving) or in spite of physical or psychological problems that may have been caused or may be made worse by substance use (e.g., liver problems, depression)

- **Pharmacological criteria**—displaying symptoms of *tolerance* (need for increased amounts of the substance to achieve the desired effect) or *withdrawal* (a constellation of physical symptoms that occurs when the use of the substance has ceased)

# Section 15.2

# *Antisocial and Avoidant Personality Disorders*

This section includes excerpts from "Antisocial Personality Disorder," U.S. Department of Health and Human Services (HHS), January 4, 2013 ; and text from "Major Depression among Adults," National Institute of Mental Health (NIMH), July 18, 2014.

## *What Is Antisocial Personality Disorder?*

Antisocial personality disorder is a mental health condition in which a person has a long-term pattern of manipulating, exploiting, or violating the rights of others. This behavior is often criminal.

## *Causes*

Cause of antisocial personality disorder is unknown. Genetic factors and environmental factors, such as child abuse, are believed to contribute to the development of this condition. People with an antisocial or alcoholic parent are at increased risk. Far more men than women are affected. The condition is common among people who are in prison.

Fire-setting and cruelty to animals during childhood are linked to the development of antisocial personality.

Some doctors believe that psychopathic personality (psychopathy) is the same disorder. Others believe that psychopathic personality is a similar but more severe disorder.

## *Symptoms*

A person with antisocial personality disorder may:

• Be able to act witty and charming

• Be good at flattery and manipulating other people's emotions

• Break the law repeatedly

• Disregard the safety of self and others

- Have problems with substance abuse
- Lie, steal, and fight often
- Not show guilt or remorse
- Often be angry or arrogant

## Avoidant Personality Disorder

Avoidant personality disorder is characterized by extreme social inhibition (shyness), feelings of inadequacy, and acute sensitivity to actual or perceived rejection. While most people have certainly feelings of insecurity, for people with avoidant personality disorder these feelings are extremely intense and lead to an avoidance of social interaction that negatively impacts their day-to-day life.

# Chapter 16

# *Eating and Body Image Disorders*

## *Chapter Contents*

Section 16.1

# *Anorexia Nervosa and Bulimia Nervosa*

Text in this section is excerpted from "Eating Disorders: About More than Food," National Institute of Mental Health (NIMH), 2014.

## *What Are Eating Disorders?*

The eating disorders anorexia nervosa, bulimia nervosa, and binge-eating disorder, and their variants, all feature serious disturbances in eating behavior and weight regulation. They are associated with a wide range of adverse psychological, physical, and social consequences. A person with an eating disorder may start out just eating smaller or larger amounts of food, but at some point, their urge to eat less or more spirals out of control. Severe distress or concern about body weight or shape, or extreme efforts to manage weight or food intake, also may characterize an eating disorder.

Eating disorders are real, treatable medical illnesses. They frequently coexist with other illnesses such as depression, substance abuse, or anxiety disorders. Other symptoms can become life-threatening if a person does not receive treatment, which is reflected by anorexia being associated with the highest mortality rate of any psychiatric disorder.

Eating disorders affect both genders, although rates among women and girls are 2½ times greater than among men and boys. Eating disorders frequently appear during the teen years or young adulthood but also may develop during childhood or later in life.

## *What Are the Different Types of Eating Disorders?*

### *Anorexia Nervosa*

Many people with anorexia nervosa see themselves as overweight, even when they are clearly underweight. Eating, food, and weight control become obsessions. People with anorexia nervosa typically weigh themselves repeatedly, portion food carefully, and eat very small quantities of only certain foods. Some people with anorexia nervosa also may engage in binge eating followed by extreme dieting, excessive exercise, self-induced vomiting, or misuse of laxatives, diuretics, or enemas.

Symptoms of anorexia nervosa include:

- Extremely low body weight
- Severe food restriction
- Relentless pursuit of thinness and unwillingness to maintain a normal or healthy weight
- Intense fear of gaining weight
- Distorted body image and self-esteem that is heavily influenced by perceptions of body weight and shape, or a denial of the seriousness of low body weight
- Lack of menstruation among girls and women.

Some who have anorexia nervosa recover with treatment after only one episode. Others get well but have relapses. Still others have a more chronic, or long-lasting, form of anorexia nervosa, in which their health declines as they battle the illness.

Other symptoms and medical complications may develop over time, including:

- Thinning of the bones (osteopenia or osteoporosis)
- Brittle hair and nails
- Dry and yellowish skin
- Growth of fine hair all over the body (lanugo)
- Mild anemia, muscle wasting, and weakness
- Severe constipation
- Low blood pressure, or slowed breathing and pulse
- Damage to the structure and function of the heart
- Brain damage
- Multi-organ failure
- Drop in internal body temperature, causing a person to feel cold all the time
- Lethargy, sluggishness, or feeling tired all the time
- Infertility

## Bulimia Nervosa

People with bulimia nervosa have recurrent and frequent episodes of eating unusually large amounts of food and feel a lack of control over these episodes. This binge eating is followed by behavior that compensates for the overeating such as forced vomiting, excessive use of laxatives or diuretics, fasting, excessive exercise, or a combination of these behaviors.

Unlike anorexia nervosa, people with bulimia nervosa usually maintain what is considered a healthy or normal weight, while some are slightly overweight. But like people with anorexia nervosa, they often fear gaining weight, want desperately to lose weight, and are intensely unhappy with their body size and shape. Usually, bulimic behavior is done secretly because it is often accompanied by feelings of disgust or shame. The binge eating and purging cycle can happen anywhere from several times a week to many times a day.

Other symptoms include:

- Chronically inflamed and sore throat
- Swollen salivary glands in the neck and jaw area
- Worn tooth enamel, and increasingly sensitive and decaying teeth as a result of exposure to stomach acid
- Acid reflux disorder and other gastrointestinal problems
- Intestinal distress and irritation from laxative abuse
- Severe dehydration from purging of fluids
- Electrolyte imbalance—too low or too high levels of sodium, calcium, potassium, and other minerals that can lead to a heart attack or stroke

## Binge-Eating Disorder

People with binge-eating disorder lose control over their eating. Unlike bulimia nervosa, periods of binge eating are not followed by compensatory behaviors like purging, excessive exercise, or fasting. As a result, people with binge-eating disorder often are overweight or obese. People with binge-eating disorder who are obese are at higher risk for developing cardiovascular disease and high blood pressure. They also experience guilt, shame, and distress about their binge eating, which can lead to more binge eating.

## How Are Eating Disorders Treated?

Typical treatment goals include restoring adequate nutrition, bringing weight to a healthy level, reducing excessive exercise, and stopping binging and purging behaviors. Specific forms of psychotherapy, or talk therapy—including a family-based therapy called the Maudsley approach and cognitive behavioral approaches—have been shown to be useful for treating specific eating disorders. Evidence also suggests that antidepressant medications approved by the U.S. Food and Drug Administration (FDA) may help for bulimia nervosa and also may be effective for treating co-occurring anxiety or depression for other eating disorders.

Treatment plans often are tailored to individual needs and may include one or more of the following:

- Individual, group, or family psychotherapy

- Medical care and monitoring

- Nutritional counseling

- Medications (for example, antidepressants).

Some patients also may need to be hospitalized to treat problems caused by malnutrition or to ensure they eat enough if they are very underweight. Complete recovery is possible.

## What Is Being Done to Better Understand and Treat Eating Disorders?

Researchers are finding that eating disorders are caused by a complex interaction of genetic, biological, psychological, and social factors. But many questions still need answers. Researchers are studying questions about behavior, genetics, and brain function to better understand risk factors, identify biological markers, and develop specific psychotherapies and medications that can target areas in the brain that control eating behavior. Brain imaging and genetic studies may provide clues for how each person may respond to specific treatments for these medical illnesses. Ongoing efforts also are aimed at developing and refining strategies for preventing and treating eating disorders among adolescents and adults.

# Section 16.2

# *Binge Eating Disorder*

Text in this section is excerpted from "Binge Eating Disorder,"
National Institute of Diabetes and Digestive and
Kidney Diseases (NIDDK), December 2012.

## *Understanding Binge Eating*

Binge eating means eating a large amount of food in a short period of time. Most of us may overeat during a special occasion, like a holiday. But people who have this disorder binge eat on a regular basis and feel a lack of control over their eating.

People with binge eating disorder are usually very upset by their binge eating and may experience stress, trouble sleeping, and depression. Binge eating disorder may lead to weight gain and to related health problems, such as heart disease and diabetes.

Most people who binge eat feel ashamed and try to hide their problem. Often they become so good at hiding it that even close friends and family members may not know that their loved one binge eats.

Binge eating disorder can be successfully treated. If you are concerned that you or someone close to you may have binge eating disorder, talking to a health care provider may be an important first step.

### *How common is binge eating disorder?*

Binge eating disorder is the most common eating disorder in the United States. Among adults, about 3.5 percent of women and 2 percent of men are estimated to have binge eating disorder. About 1.6 percent of adolescents may also be affected.

Among women, binge eating disorder is most common in early adulthood, while among men it is most common in midlife. Binge eating disorder affects blacks as often as whites, but it is not known how often it affects people in other racial and ethnic groups.

People with obesity are at a higher risk for developing the disorder than people of normal weight. Although most people with obesity do not have binge eating disorder, about 2 in 3 people who have the disorder are obese. People of normal weight can also have binge eating disorder.

## How do I know if I have binge eating disorder?

People who have binge eating disorder

- eat a large amount of food in a short period of time (for example, within 2 hours).
- feel a lack of control over their eating. For example, they may feel that they cannot stop eating or control what or how much they are eating.

People who have binge eating disorder may also

- eat much more quickly than usual
- eat until uncomfortably full
- eat large amounts of food even when not really hungry
- eat alone
- feel disgusted, depressed, or guilty after overeating

If you think that you or someone close to you may have binge eating disorder, share your concerns with a health care provider. He or she can connect you to helpful sources of care.

## What causes binge eating disorder?

No one knows for sure what causes binge eating disorder. Like other eating disorders, binge eating disorder may result from a mix of genetic, psychological, emotional, social, and other factors. Binge eating disorder has been linked to depression and anxiety. Painful childhood experiences—such as family problems and critical comments about shape, weight, or eating—may also make some people more likely to develop the disorder.

Although binge eating is related to dieting, it is not clear if dieting causes binge eating disorder. Among some people, trying to diet in unhealthy ways—such as by skipping meals, not eating enough food each day, or avoiding certain kinds of food—may lead to binge eating. Studies suggest that changes to eating habits that are made as part of obesity treatment are not harmful to people with binge eating disorder and may promote weight loss.

## What are the health risks of binge eating disorder?

People with binge eating disorder are usually very upset by their binge eating and may become depressed. They may also miss school, social activities, or work to binge eat.

Research suggests that people with binge eating disorder report more health problems, stress, trouble sleeping, and suicidal thoughts than do people without an eating disorder. Other problems that may result from binge eating disorder could include digestive problems, headaches, joint pains, menstrual problems, and muscle pains. In addition, binge eating disorder may lead to weight gain and to health problems related to obesity.

## Should people with binge eating disorder try to lose weight?

Many people with binge eating disorder have excess weight and related health problems. Losing weight may help prevent or reduce some of these problems. However, binge eating may make it difficult to lose weight and keep it off. People with binge eating disorder who are obese may benefit from a weight-loss program that also offers treatment for eating disorders. However, some people with binge eating disorder may do just as well in a standard weight-loss program as people who do not binge eat.

## How is binge eating disorder treated?

People with binge eating disorder should get help from a specialist in eating disorders, such as a psychiatrist or a psychologist. Treatment may include the use of behavior change therapy, counseling on eating patterns, and/or drugs. The goal is to change the thoughts and beliefs that lead to binge eating and promote healthy eating and physical activity habits.

In addition to treatment from specialists, self-help books and DVDs have been found to help some people control their binge eating. Support groups may also be a good source of encouragement, hope, and advice on coping with the disorder.

If you have any symptoms of binge eating disorder, talk to your health care provider about the type of help that may be best for you. Ask for a referral to a specialist or a support group in your area.

The good news is that most people do well in treatment and can overcome binge eating.

# Section 16.3

# *Body Dysmorphic Disorder*

## *Focusing on Appearance*

Most of us spend time in front of the mirror checking our appearance. Some people spend more time than others, but taking care of our bodies and being interested in our appearance is natural.

How we feel about our appearance is part of our body image and self-image. Many people have some kind of dissatisfaction with their bodies. This can be especially true during the teen years when our bodies and appearance go through lots of changes.

Although many people feel dissatisfied with some aspect of their appearance, these concerns usually don't constantly occupy their thoughts or cause them to feel tormented. But for some people, concerns about appearance become quite extreme and upsetting.

Some people become so focused on imagined or minor imperfections in their looks that they can't seem to stop checking or obsessing about their appearance. Being constantly preoccupied and upset about body imperfections or appearance flaws is called body dysmorphic disorder.

## *What Is Body Dysmorphic Disorder?*

Body dysmorphic disorder (BDD) is a condition that involves obsessions, which are distressing thoughts that repeatedly intrude into a person's awareness. With BDD, the distressing thoughts are about perceived appearance flaws.

People with BDD might focus on what they think is a facial flaw, but they can also worry about other body parts, such as short legs, breast size, or body shape. Just as people with eating disorders obsess about their weight, those with BDD become obsessed over an aspect of their appearance. They may worry their hair is thin, their face is scarred, their eyes aren't exactly the same size, their nose is too big, or their lips are too thin.

BDD has been called "imagined ugliness" because the appearance issues the person is obsessing about usually are so small that others don't even notice them. Or, if others do notice them, they consider them minor. But for someone with BDD, the concerns feel very real, because the obsessive thoughts distort and magnify any tiny imperfection.

Because of the distorted body image caused by BDD, a person might believe that he or she is too horribly ugly or disfigured to be seen.

## Behaviors That Are Part of BDD

Besides obsessions, BDD also involves compulsions and avoidance behaviors.

A **compulsion** is something a person does to try to relieve the tension caused by the obsessive thoughts. For example, someone with obsessive thoughts that her nose is horribly ugly might check her appearance in the mirror, apply makeup, or ask someone many times a day whether her nose looks ugly. These types of checking, fixing, and asking are compulsions.

Somebody with obsessions usually feels a strong or irresistible urge to do compulsions because they can provide temporary relief from the terrible distress. The compulsions seem like the only way to escape bad feelings caused by bad thoughts. Compulsive actions often are repeated many times a day, taking up lots of time and energy.

**Avoidance behaviors** are also a part of BDD. A person might stay home or cover up to avoid being seen by others. Avoidance behaviors also include things like not participating in class or socializing, or avoiding mirrors.

With BDD, a pattern of obsessive thoughts, compulsive actions, and avoidance sets in. Even though the checking, fixing, asking, and avoiding seem to relieve terrible feelings, the relief is just temporary. In reality, the more someone performs compulsions or avoids things, the stronger the pattern of obsessions, compulsions, and avoidance becomes.

After a while, it takes more and more compulsions to relieve the distress caused by the bad thoughts. A person with BDD doesn't want to be preoccupied with these thoughts and behaviors, but with BDD it can seem impossible to break the pattern.

## What Causes BDD?

Although the exact cause of BDD is still unclear, experts believe it is related to problems with serotonin, one of the brain's chemical neurotransmitters. Poor regulation of serotonin also plays a role in obsessive compulsive disorder (OCD) and other anxiety disorders, as well as depression.

Some people may be more prone to problems with serotonin balance, including those with family members who have problems with anxiety or depression. This may help explain why some people develop BDD but others don't.

Cultural messages can also play a role in BDD by reinforcing somebody's concerns about appearance. Critical messages or unkind teasing about appearance as someone is growing up may also contribute to a person's sensitivity to BDD. But while cultural messages, criticism, and teasing might harm someone's body image, these things alone usually do not result in BDD.

It's hard to know exactly how common BDD is because most people with BDD are unwilling to talk about their concerns or seek help. But compared with those who feel somewhat dissatisfied with their appearance, very few people have true BDD. BDD usually begins in the teen years, and if it's not treated, can continue into adulthood.

## How Can BDD Affect a Person's Life?

Sometimes people with BDD feel ashamed and keep their concerns secret. They may think that others will consider them vain or superficial.

Other people might become annoyed or irritated with somebody's obsessions and compulsions about appearance. They don't understand BDD or what the person is going through. As a result, those with BDD may feel misunderstood, unfairly judged, or alone. Because they avoid contact with others, they may have few friends or activities to enjoy.

It's extremely upsetting to be tormented by thoughts about appearance imperfections. These thoughts intrude into a person's awareness throughout the day and are hard to ignore. People with mild to moderate symptoms of BDD usually spend a great deal of time grooming themselves in the morning. Throughout the day, they may frequently check their appearance in mirrors or windows. In addition, they may repeatedly seek reassurance from people around them that they look OK.

Although people with mild BDD usually continue to go to school, the obsessions can interfere with their daily lives. For example, someone might measure or examine the "flawed" body part repeatedly or spend large sums of money and time on makeup to cover the problem.

Some people with BDD hide from others, and avoid going places because of fear of being seen. Spending so much time and energy on appearance concerns robs a person of pleasure and happiness, and of opportunities for fun and socializing.

People with severe symptoms may drop out of school, quit their jobs, or refuse to leave their homes. Many people with BDD also develop depression. Those with the most severe BDD might even consider or attempt suicide.

Many people with BDD seek the help of a dermatologist or cosmetic surgeon to try to correct appearance flaws. But dermatology treatments or plastic surgery don't change the BDD. Those who find cosmetic surgeons willing to perform surgery are often not satisfied with the results. They may find that even though their appearance has changes, the obsessive thinking is still present, and they begin to focus on some other imperfection.

## Getting Help for BDD

If you or someone you know has BDD, the first step is recognizing what might be causing the distress. Many times, people with BDD are so focused on their appearance that they believe the answer lies in correcting how they look, not with their thoughts.

The real problem with BDD lies in the obsessions and compulsions, which distort body image, making someone feel ugly. Because people with BDD believe what they're perceiving is true and accurate, sometimes the most challenging part of overcoming the disorder is being open to new ideas about what might help.

BDD can be treated by an experienced mental health professional. Usually, the treatment involves a type of talk therapy called cognitive-behavioral therapy. This approach helps to correct the pattern that's causing the body image distortion and the extreme distress.

In cognitive behavioral therapy, a therapist helps a person to examine and change faulty beliefs, resist compulsive behaviors, and face stressful situations that trigger appearance concerns. Sometimes doctors prescribe medication along with the talk therapy.

Treatment for BDD takes time, hard work, and patience. It helps if a person has the support of a friend or loved one. If someone with BDD is also dealing with depression, anxiety, feeling isolated or alone, or other life situations, the therapy can address those issues, too.

Body dysmorphic disorder, like other obsessions, can interfere with a person's life, robbing it of pleasure and draining energy. An experienced psychologist or psychiatrist who is knowledgeable about BDD can help break the grip of the disorder so that a person can fully enjoy life.

Section 16.4

# *Emotional Eating*

## *What Is Emotional Eating?*

Emotional eating is when people use food as a way to deal with feelings instead of to satisfy hunger. We've all been there, finishing a whole bag of chips out of boredom or downing cookie after cookie while cramming for a big test. But when done a lot—especially without realizing it—emotional eating can affect weight, health, and overall well-being.

Not many of us make the connection between eating and our feelings. But understanding what drives emotional eating can help people take steps to change it.

One of the biggest myths about emotional eating is that it's prompted by negative feelings. Yes, people often turn to food when they're stressed out, lonely, sad, anxious, or bored. But emotional eating can be linked to positive feelings too, like the romance of sharing dessert on Valentine's Day or the celebration of a holiday feast.

Sometimes emotional eating is tied to major life events, like a death or a divorce. More often, though, it's the countless little daily stresses that cause someone to seek comfort or distraction in food.

Emotional eating patterns can be learned: A child who is given candy after a big achievement may grow up using candy as a reward for a job well done. A kid who is given cookies as a way to stop crying may learn to link cookies with comfort.

It's not easy to "unlearn" patterns of emotional eating. But it is possible. And it starts with an awareness of what's going on.

## *"Comfort" Foods*

We all have our own comfort foods. Interestingly, they may vary according to moods and gender. One study found that happy people seem to want to eat things like pizza, while sad people prefer ice cream and cookies. Bored people crave salty, crunchy things, like chips.

221

Researchers also found that guys seem to prefer hot, homemade comfort meals, like steaks and casseroles. Girls go for chocolate and ice cream.

This brings up a curious question: Does no one take comfort in carrots and celery sticks? Researchers are looking into that, too. What they're finding is that high-fat foods, like ice cream, may activate certain chemicals in the body that create a sense of contentment and fulfillment. This almost addictive quality may actually make you reach for these foods again when feeling upset.

## Physical Hunger vs. Emotional Hunger

We're all emotional eaters to some extent (who hasn't suddenly found room for dessert after a filling dinner?). But for some people, emotional eating can be a real problem, causing serious weight gain or cycles of binging and purging.

The trouble with emotional eating (aside from the health issues) is that once the pleasure of eating is gone, the feelings that cause it remain. And you often may feel worse about eating the amount or type of food you did. That's why it helps to know the differences between physical hunger and emotional hunger.

Next time you reach for a snack, check in and see which type of hunger is driving it.

## Questions to Ask Yourself

You can also ask yourself these questions about your eating:

- Have I been eating larger portions than usual?
- Do I eat at unusual times?
- Do I feel a loss of control around food?
- Am I anxious over something, like school, a social situation, or an event where my abilities might be tested?
- Has there been a big event in my life that I'm having trouble dealing with?
- Am I overweight, or has there recently been a big jump in my weight?
- Do other people in my family use food to soothe their feelings too?

If you answered yes to many of these questions, then it's possible that eating has become a coping mechanism instead of a way to fuel your body.

## Breaking the Cycle

Managing emotional eating means finding other ways to deal with the situations and feelings that make someone turn to food.

For example, do you come home from school each day and automatically head to the kitchen? Stop and ask yourself, "Am I really hungry?" Is your stomach growling? Are you having difficulty concentrating or feeling irritable? If these signs point to hunger, choose something light and healthy to take the edge off until dinner.

Not really hungry? If the post-school food foraging has just become part of your routine, think about why.

## Tips to Try

These three techniques can help:

1. Explore why you're eating and find a replacement activity. For example:

   - If you're bored or lonely, call or text a friend or family member.

   - If you're stressed out, try a yoga routine. Or listen to some feel-good tunes and let off some steam by jogging in place, doing jumping jacks, or dancing around your room until the urge to eat passes.

   - If you're tired, rethink your bedtime routine. Tiredness can feel a lot like hunger, and food won't help if sleepless nights are causing daytime fatigue.

   - If you're eating to procrastinate, open those books and get that homework over with. You'll feel better afterwards (honestly!).

2. Write down the emotions that trigger your eating. One of the best ways to keep track is with a mood and food journal. Write down what you ate, how much, and how you felt as you ate (e.g., bored, happy, worried, sad, mad) and whether you were really hungry or just eating for comfort.

   Through journaling, you'll start to see patterns emerging between what you feel and what you eat. You'll be able to use this information to make better choices (like choosing to clear your head with a walk around the block instead of a bag of Doritos).

3.  Pause and "take 5" before you reach for food. Too often, we rush through the day without really checking in with ourselves. We're so stressed, overscheduled, and plugged-in that we lose out on time to reflect.

    Instead of eating when you get in the door, take a few minutes to transition from one part of your day to another. Go over the things that happened that day. Acknowledge how they made you feel: Happy? Grateful? Excited? Angry? Worried? Jealous? Left out?

## *Getting Help*

Even when we understand what's going on, many of us still need help breaking the cycle of emotional eating. It's not easy—especially when emotional eating has already led to weight and self-esteem issues. So don't go it alone when you don't have to.

Take advantage of expert help. Counselors and therapists can help you deal with your feelings. Nutritionists can help you identify your eating patterns and get you on track with a better diet. Fitness experts can get your body's feel-good chemicals firing through exercise instead of food.

If you're worried about your eating, talk to your doctor. He or she can make sure you reach your weight-loss goals safely and put you in touch with professionals who can put you on a path to a new, healthier relationship with food.

# Chapter 17

# *Addictions*

## *Chapter Contents*

225

## Section 17.1

# *Alcoholism, Substance Abuse, and Addictive Behavior*

Text in this section is excerpted from "Alcoholism, Substance Abuse, and Addictive Behavior," Office on Women's Health (OWH), August 13, 2015.

## *Alcoholism*

Alcohol abuse is a pattern of drinking that is harmful to the drinker or others. The following situations, occurring repeatedly in a 12-month period, would be indicators of alcohol abuse:

- Missing work or skipping child care responsibilities because of drinking

- Drinking in situations that are dangerous, such as before or while driving

- Being arrested for driving under the influence of alcohol or for hurting someone while drunk

- Continuing to drink even though there are ongoing alcohol-related tensions with friends and family

Alcoholism is a disease. It is chronic, or lifelong, and it can get worse over time and be life-threatening. Alcoholism is based in the brain. These are some of the typical characteristics of alcoholism:

- Craving: a strong need to drink

- Loss of control: the inability to stop drinking

- Physical dependence: withdrawal symptoms, such as nausea, sweating, shakiness, and anxiety, when alcohol use is stopped after a period of heavy drinking

- Tolerance: the need for increasing amounts of alcohol to get "high"

## Know the Risks

Research suggests that a woman is more likely to drink too much if she has any of the following:

- Parents and siblings (or other blood relatives) with alcohol problems
- A partner who drinks too much
- The ability to "hold her liquor" more than others
- A history of depression
- A history of childhood physical or sexual abuse

The presence of any of these factors is a good reason to be especially careful with drinking.

## How Do You Know If You Have a Problem?

Answering the following four questions can help you find out if you or someone close to you has a drinking problem.

- Have you ever felt you should cut down on your drinking?
- Have people annoyed you by criticizing your drinking?
- Have you ever felt bad or guilty about your drinking?
- Have you ever had a drink first thing in the morning to steady your nerves or to get rid of a hangover?

One "yes" answer suggests a possible alcohol problem. If you responded "yes" to more than one question, it is very likely that you have a problem with alcohol. In either case, it is important that you see your health care provider right away to discuss your responses to these questions.

Even if you answered "no" to all of the above questions, if you are having drinking-related problems with your job, relationships, health, or with the law, you should still seek help.

## Treatment for Alcohol Problems

Treatment for an alcohol problem depends on its severity. Routine doctor visits are an ideal time to discuss alcohol use and its potential problems. Health care professionals can help a woman take a good hard look at what effect alcohol is having on her life and can give advice on ways to stop drinking or to cut down.

Alcoholism treatment works for many people. But like other chronic illnesses, such as diabetes, high blood pressure, and asthma, there are varying levels of success when it comes to treatment. Some people stop drinking and remain sober. Others have long periods of sobriety with bouts of relapse. And still others cannot stop drinking for any length of time. With treatment, one thing is clear, however: the longer a person stops drinking alcohol, the more likely he or she will be able to stay sober.

## Substance Abuse

Many people do not understand why people become addicted to drugs. The truth is: drugs change the brain and cause repeated drug abuse. Drug addiction is a brain disease. Drug use leads to changes in the structure and function of the brain. Although it is true that for most people the initial decision to take drugs is voluntary, over time, the changes in the brain caused by repeated drug abuse can affect a person's self control and ability to make sound decisions. At the same time, drugs cause the brain to send intense impulses to take more drugs.

### Treatment

Drug abuse is a treatable disease. There are many effective treatments for drug abuse. Some important points about substance abuse treatment include:

- Medical and behavioral therapy, alone or used together, are used to treat drug abuse.

- Sometimes treatment can be done on an outpatient basis.

- Severe drug abuse usually requires residential treatment, where the patient sleeps at the treatment center.

- Treatment can take place within the criminal justice systems, which can stop a convicted person from returning to criminal behavior.

- Studies show that treatment does not need to be voluntary to work.

## Addictive Behavior

### Why Do Some People Become Addicted, While Others Do Not?

Nothing can predict whether or not a person will become addicted to drugs. But there are some risk factors for drug addiction, including:

- **Biology.** Genes, gender, ethnicity, and the presence of other mental disorders may increase risk for drug abuse and addiction.

- **Environment.** Peer pressure, physical and sexual abuse, stress, and family relationships can influence the course of drug abuse and addiction in a person's life.

- **Development.** Although taking drugs at any age can lead to addiction, the earlier that drug use begins, the more likely it is to progress to more serious abuse.

## Section 17.2

# *Comorbidity: Addiction and Other Mental Disorders*

This section includes excerpts from "Mental and Substance Use Disorders," Substance Abuse and Mental Health Services Administration (SAMHSA), December 4, 2015; and text from "Substance Use Disorders," Substance Abuse and Mental Health Services Administration (SAMHSA), October 27, 2015.

## *Overview*

Mental and substance use disorders affect people from all walks of life and all age groups. These illnesses are common, recurrent, and often serious, but they are treatable and many people do recover. Learning about some of the most common mental and substance use disorders can help people recognize their signs and to seek help.

According to SAMHSA's 2014 National Survey on Drug Use and Health (NSDUH) an estimated 43.6 million (18.1%) Americans ages 18 and up experienced some form of mental illness. In the past year, 20.2 million adults (8.4%) had a substance use disorder. Of these, 7.9 million people had both a mental disorder and substance use disorder, also known as co-occurring mental and substance use disorders.

Various mental and substance use disorders have prevalence rates that differ by gender, age, race, and ethnicity.

# Mental Disorders

Mental disorders involve changes in thinking, mood, and/or behavior. These disorders can affect how we relate to others and make choices. Mental disorders take many different forms, with some rooted in deep levels of anxiety, extreme changes in mood, or reduced ability to focus or behave appropriately. Others involve unwanted, intrusive thoughts and some may result in auditory and visual hallucinations or false beliefs about basic aspects of reality. Reaching a level that can be formally diagnosed often depends on a reduction in a person's ability to function as a result of the disorder.

Anxiety disorders are the most common type of mental disorders, followed by depressive disorders. Different mental disorders are more likely to begin and occur at different stages in life and are thus more prevalent in certain age groups. Lifetime anxiety disorders generally have the earliest age of first onset, most commonly around age 6. Other disorders emerge in childhood, approximately 11% of children 4 to 17 years of age (6.4 million) have been diagnosed with attention deficit hyperactivity disorder (ADHD) as of 2011. Schizophrenia spectrum and psychotic disorders emerge later in life, usually in early adulthood.

Not all mental health issues first experienced during childhood or adolescence continue into adulthood, and not all mental health issues are first experienced before adulthood. Mental disorders can occur once, reoccur intermittently, or be more chronic in nature. Mental disorders frequently co-occur with each other and with substance use disorders. Because of this and because of variation in symptoms even within one type of disorder, individual situations and symptoms are extremely varied.

## Serious Mental Illness

Serious mental illness among people ages 18 and older is defined at the federal level as having, at any time during the past year, a diagnosable mental, behavior, or emotional disorder that causes serious functional impairment, that substantially interferes with or limits one or more major life activities. Serious mental illnesses include major depression, schizophrenia, and bipolar disorder, and other mental disorders that cause serious impairment. In 2014, there were an estimated 9.8 million adults (4.1%) ages 18 and up with a serious mental illness in the past year. People with serious mental illness are more likely to be unemployed, arrested, and/or face inadequate housing compared to those without mental illness.

*Serious Emotional Disturbance*

The term serious emotional disturbance (SED) is used to refer to children and youth who have had a diagnosable mental, behavioral, or emotional disorder in the past year, which resulted in functional impairment that substantially interferes with or limits the child's role or functioning in family, school, or community activities. A Centers for Disease Control and Prevention (CDC) review of population-level information found that estimates of the number of children with a mental disorder range from 13 to 20%, but current national surveys do not have an indicator of SED.

## Substance Use Disorders

Substance use disorders occur when the recurrent use of alcohol and/or drugs causes clinically significant impairment, including health problems, disability, and failure to meet major responsibilities at work, school, or home.

In 2014, about 21.5 million Americans ages 12 and older (8.1%) were classified with a substance use disorder in the past year. Of those, 2.6 million had problems with both alcohol and drugs, 4.5 million had problems with drugs but not alcohol, and 14.4 million had problems with alcohol only.

## Co-Occurring Mental and Substance Use Disorders

The coexistence of both a mental illness and a substance use condition is referred to as co-occurring mental and substance use disorders. There are no specific combinations of substance use disorders and mental disorders that are defined uniquely as co-occurring disorders. Co-occurring disorders may include any combination of two or more substance use disorders and mental disorders identified in the *Diagnostic and Statistical Manual of Mental Disorders, Fifth Edition* (DSM-5). They are also referred to as having a dual diagnosis.

People with a mental health issue are more likely to experience an alcohol or substance use disorder than those not affected by a mental illness. Approximately 7.9 million adults had co-occurring disorders in 2014.

Co-occurring disorders can be difficult to diagnose due to the complexity of symptoms. Both disorders may be severe or mild, or one may be more severe than the other. In many cases, one disorder is addressed while the other disorder remains untreated. Both substance use disorders and mental disorders have biological, psychological, and social components.

There are many consequences of undiagnosed, untreated, or under-treated co-occurring disorders including higher likelihood of experiencing homelessness, incarceration, medical illnesses, suicide, and early death.

## Substance Use Disorders

The *Diagnostic and Statistical Manual of Mental Disorders, Fifth Edition* (DSM-5), no longer uses the terms substance abuse and substance dependence, rather it refers to substance use disorders, which are defined as mild, moderate, or severe to indicate the level of severity, which is determined by the number of diagnostic criteria met by an individual. Substance use disorders occur when the recurrent use of alcohol and/or drugs causes clinically and functionally significant impairment, such as health problems, disability, and failure to meet major responsibilities at work, school, or home. According to the DSM-5, a diagnosis of substance use disorder is based on evidence of impaired control, social impairment, risky use, and pharmacological criteria.

The following is a list with descriptions of the most common substance use disorders in the United States.

### Alcohol Use Disorder (AUD)

Excessive alcohol use can increase a person's risk of developing serious health problems in addition to those issues associated with intoxication behaviors and alcohol withdrawal symptoms. According to the Centers for Disease Control and Prevention (CDC), excessive alcohol use causes 88,000 deaths a year.

Data from the National Survey on Drug Use and Health (NSDUH) — 2014 show that in 2014, slightly more than half (52.7%) of Americans ages 12 and up reported being current drinkers of alcohol. Most people drink alcohol in moderation. However, of those 176.6 million alcohol users, an estimated 17 million have an AUD.

Many Americans begin drinking at an early age. In 2012, about 24% of eighth graders and 64% of twelfth graders used alcohol in the past year.

The definitions for the different levels of drinking include the following:

- Moderate Drinking—According to the *Dietary Guidelines for Americans,* moderate drinking is up to 1 drink per day for women and up to 2 drinks per day for men.

- Binge Drinking—SAMHSA defines binge drinking as drinking 5 or more alcoholic drinks on the same occasion on at least 1 day in the past 30 days. The National Institute on Alcohol Abuse and Alcoholism (NIAAA) defines binge drinking as a pattern of drinking that produces blood alcohol concentrations (BAC) of greater than 0.08 g/dL. This usually occurs after 4 drinks for women and 5 drinks for men over a 2 hour period.

- Heavy Drinking—SAMHSA defines heavy drinking as drinking 5 or more drinks on the same occasion on each of 5 or more days in the past 30 days.

Excessive drinking can put you at risk of developing an alcohol use disorder in addition to other health and safety problems. Genetics have also been shown to be a risk factor for the development of an AUD.

To be diagnosed with an AUD, individuals must meet certain diagnostic criteria. Some of these criteria include problems controlling intake of alcohol, continued use of alcohol despite problems resulting from drinking, development of a tolerance, drinking that leads to risky situations, or the development of withdrawal symptoms. The severity of an AUD— mild, moderate, or severe—is based on the number of criteria met.

## Tobacco Use Disorder

According to the CDC, more than 480,000 deaths each year are caused by cigarette smoking. Tobacco use and smoking do damage to nearly every organ in the human body, often leading to lung cancer, respiratory disorders, heart disease, stroke, and other illnesses.

In 2014, an estimated 66.9 million Americans aged 12 or older were current users of a tobacco product (25.2%). Young adults aged 18 to 25 had the highest rate of current use of a tobacco product (35%), followed by adults aged 26 or older (25.8%), and by youths aged 12 to 17 (7%).

In 2014, the prevalence of current use of a tobacco product was 37.8% for American Indians or Alaska Natives, 27.6% for whites, 26.6% for blacks, 30.6% for Native Hawaiians or other Pacific Islanders, 18.8% for Hispanics, and 10.2% for Asians.

## Cannabis Use Disorder

Marijuana is the most-used drug after alcohol and tobacco in the United States. According to SAMHSA data:

- In 2014, about 22.2 million people ages 12 and up reported using marijuana during the past month.

- Also in 2014, there were 2.6 million people in that age range who had used marijuana for the first time within the past 12 months. People between the ages of 12 and 49 report first using the drug at an average age of 18.5.

In the past year, 4.2 million people ages 12 and up met criteria for a substance use disorder based on marijuana use.

Marijuana's immediate effects include distorted perception, difficulty with thinking and problem solving, and loss of motor coordination. Long-term use of the drug can contribute to respiratory infection, impaired memory, and exposure to cancer-causing compounds. Heavy marijuana use in youth has also been linked to increased risk for developing mental illness and poorer cognitive functioning.

Some symptoms of cannabis use disorder include disruptions in functioning due to cannabis use, the development of tolerance, cravings for cannabis, and the development of withdrawal symptoms, such as the inability to sleep, restlessness, nervousness, anger, or depression within a week of ceasing heavy use.

## Stimulant Use Disorder

Stimulants increase alertness, attention, and energy, as well as elevate blood pressure, heart rate, and respiration. They include a wide range of drugs that have historically been used to treat conditions, such as obesity, attention deficit hyperactivity disorder and, occasionally, depression. Like other prescription medications, stimulants can be diverted for illegal use. The most commonly abused stimulants are amphetamines, methamphetamine, and cocaine. Stimulants can be synthetic (such as amphetamines) or can be plant-derived (such as cocaine). They are usually taken orally, snorted, or intravenously.

In 2014, an estimated 913,000 people ages 12 and older had a stimulant use disorder because of cocaine use, and an estimated 476,000 people had a stimulant use disorder as a result of using other stimulants besides methamphetamines. In 2014, almost 569,000 people in the United States ages 12 and up reported using methamphetamines in the past month.

Symptoms of stimulant use disorders include craving for stimulants, failure to control use when attempted, continued use despite interference with major obligations or social functioning, use of larger amounts over time, development of tolerance, spending a great deal of time to obtain and use stimulants, and withdrawal symptoms that occur after stopping or reducing use, including fatigue, vivid and unpleasant dreams, sleep problems, increased appetite, or irregular problems in controlling movement.

## Hallucinogen Use Disorder

Hallucinogens can be chemically synthesized (as with lysergic acid diethylamide or LSD) or may occur naturally (as with psilocybin mushrooms, peyote). These drugs can produce visual and auditory hallucinations, feelings of detachment from one's environment and oneself, and distortions in time and perception.

In 2014, approximately 246,000 Americans had a hallucinogen use disorder. Symptoms of hallucinogen use disorder include craving for hallucinogens, failure to control use when attempted, continued use despite interference with major obligations or social functioning, use of larger amounts over time, use in risky situations like driving, development of tolerance, and spending a great deal of time to obtain and use hallucinogens.

## Opioid Use Disorder

Opioids reduce the perception of pain but can also produce drowsiness, mental confusion, euphoria, nausea, constipation, and, depending upon the amount of drug taken, can depress respiration. Illegal opioid drugs, such as heroin and legally available pain relievers such as oxycodone and hydrocodone can cause serious health effects in those who misuse them. Some people experience a euphoric response to opioid medications, and it is common that people misusing opioids try to intensify their experience by snorting or injecting them. These methods increase their risk for serious medical complications, including overdose. Other users have switched from prescription opiates to heroin as a result of availability and lower price. Because of variable purity and other chemicals and drugs mixed with heroin on the black market, this also increases risk of overdose. Overdoses with opioid pharmaceuticals led to almost 17,000 deaths in 2011. Since 1999, opiate overdose deaths have increased 265% among men and 400% among women.

In 2014, an estimated 1.9 million people had an opioid use disorder related to prescription pain relievers and an estimated 586,000 had an opioid use disorder related to heroin use.

Symptoms of opioid use disorders include strong desire for opioids, inability to control or reduce use, continued use despite interference with major obligations or social functioning, use of larger amounts over time, development of tolerance, spending a great deal of time to obtain and use opioids, and withdrawal symptoms that occur after stopping or reducing use, such as negative mood, nausea or vomiting, muscle aches, diarrhea, fever, and insomnia.

## Section 17.3

# *Link between Marijuana Use and Mental Illness*

Text in this section is excerpted from "Marijuana,"
National Institute on Drug Abuse (NIDA), September 2015.

### *Is There a Link between Marijuana Use and Mental Illness?*

Several studies have linked marijuana use to increased risk for mental illnesses, including psychosis (schizophrenia), depression, and anxiety, but whether and to what extent it actually causes these conditions is not always easy to determine. The amount of drug used, the age at first use, and genetic vulnerability have all been shown to influence this relationship. The strongest evidence to date concerns the link between marijuana use and psychotic disorders in those with a preexisting genetic or other vulnerability. Recent research has found that marijuana users who carry a specific variant of the AKT1 gene, which codes for an enzyme that affects dopamine signaling in the striatum, are at increased risk of developing psychosis. The striatum is an area of the brain that becomes activated and flooded with dopamine when certain stimuli are present. One study found that the risk for those with this variant was seven times higher for daily marijuana users compared with infrequent- or non-users.

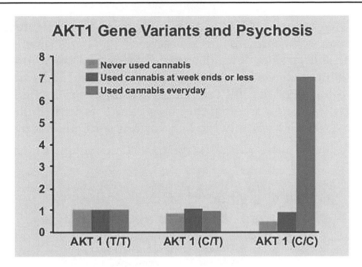

*Figure 17.1. AKT1 Gene Variants and Psychosis*

Whether adolescent marijuana use can contribute to developing psychosis later in adulthood appears to depend on whether a person already has a genetically based vulnerability to the disorder. The AKT1 gene governs an enzyme that affects brain signaling involving the neurotransmitter dopamine. Altered dopamine signaling is known to be involved in schizophrenia. AKT1 can take one of three forms in a specific region of the gene implicated in susceptibility to schizophrenia: T/T, C/T, and C/C. Daily users of marijuana (green bars) with the C/C variant have a seven times higher risk of developing psychosis than infrequent marijuana users or nonusers. The risk for psychosis among those with the T/T variant was unaffected by whether they used marijuana.

Another study found an increased risk of psychosis among adults who had used marijuana in adolescence and also carried a specific variant of the gene for catechol-O-methyltransferase (COMT), an enzyme that degrades neurotransmitters such as dopamine and norepinephrine.44 (see Genetic variation in COMT influences the harmful effects of abused drugs). Marijuana use has also been shown to worsen the course of illness in patients who already have schizophrenia. As mentioned previously, marijuana can also produce a brief psychotic reaction in non-schizophrenic users, especially at high doses, although this fades as the drug wears off.

The influence of adolescent marijuana use on adult psychosis is affected by genetic variables. This figure shows that variations in a gene can affect the likelihood of developing psychosis in adulthood, following exposure to cannabis in adolescence. The COMT gene governs an enzyme that breaks down dopamine, a brain chemical involved in schizophrenia. It comes in two forms: "Met" and "Val." Individuals with one or two copies of the Val variant have a higher risk of developing schizophrenic-type disorders if they used cannabis during adolescence (dark bars). Those with only the Met variant were unaffected by cannabis use.

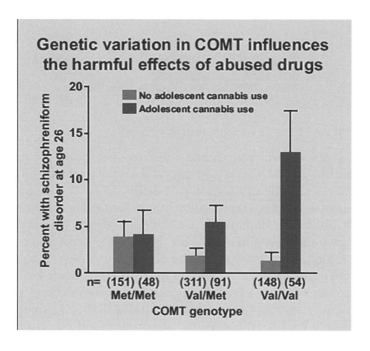

*Figure 17.2.* Genetic variation in COMT influences the harmful effects of abused drugs

## Adverse Consequences of Marijuana Use

### Acute (Present during Intoxication)

- Impaired short-term memory
- Impaired attention, judgment, and other cognitive functions
- Impaired coordination and balance
- Increased heart rate

- Anxiety, paranoia
- Psychosis (uncommon)

***Persistent (Lasting Longer than Intoxication, but May Not Be Permanent)***

- Impaired learning and coordination
- Sleep problems

***Long-Term (Cumulative Effects of Repeated Use)***

- Potential for addiction
- Potential loss of IQ
- Increased risk of chronic cough, bronchitis
- Increased risk of schizophrenia in vulnerable people
- Potentially increased risk of anxiety, depression, and amotivational syndrome

# Chapter 18

# *Impulse Control Disorders*

## *Chapter Contents*

# Section 18.1

# *What Are Impulse Control Disorders?*

Text in this section is excerpted from "Mental
Disorders," Substance Abuse and Mental Health Services
Administration (SAMHSA), October 27, 2015.

## *Impulse Control Disorder*

This class of disorders is characterized by problems with self-control of emotions or behaviors that violate the rights of others and/or bring a person into conflict with societal norms or authority figures. Oppositional defiant disorder and conduct disorder are the most prominent of this class of disorders in children.

### *Oppositional Defiant Disorder*

Children with oppositional defiant disorder (ODD) display a frequent and persistent pattern of angry or irritable mood, argumentative/defiant behavior, or vindictiveness. Symptoms are typically first seen in the preschool years, and often precede the development of conduct disorder.

The average prevalence of ODD is estimated at 3.3%, and occurs more often in boys than girls.

Children who experienced harsh, inconsistent, or neglectful child-rearing practices are at increased risk for developing ODD.

Symptoms of ODD include angry/irritable mood, argumentative/defiant behavior, or vindictiveness. A child with an angry/irritable mood may often lose their temper, be frequently resentful, or easily annoyed. Argumentative or defiant children are frequently combative with authority figures or adults and often refuse to comply with rules. They may also deliberately annoy others or blame others for their mistakes or misbehavior. These symptoms must be evident for at least six months and observed when interacting with at least one individual who is not a sibling.

### *Conduct Disorder*

Occurring in children and teens, conduct disorder is a persistent pattern of disruptive and violent behaviors that violate the basic rights of others or age-appropriate social norms or rules, and causes significant impairment in the child or family's daily life.

An estimated 8.5% of children and youth meet criteria for conduct disorder at some point in their life. Prevalence increases from childhood to adolescence and is more common among males than females.

Conduct disorder may be preceded by temperamental risk factors, such as behavioral difficulties in infancy and below-average intelligence. Similar to ODD, environmental risk factors may include harsh or inconsistent child-rearing practices and/or child maltreatment. Parental criminality, frequent changes of caregivers, large family size, familial psychopathology, and early institutional living may also contribute to risk for developing the disorder. Community-level risk factors may include neighborhood exposure to violence, peer rejection, and association with a delinquent peer group. Children with a parent or sibling with conduct disorder or other behavioral health disorders (for example, ADHD, schizophrenia, severe alcohol use disorder) are more likely to develop the condition. Children with conduct disorder often present with other disorders as well, including ADHD, learning disorders, and depression.

The primary symptoms of conduct disorder include aggression to people and animals (for example, bullying or causing physical harm), destruction of property (for example, fire-setting), deceitfulness or theft (for example, breaking and entering), and serious violations of rules (for example, truancy, elopement). Symptoms must be present for 12 months and fall into one of three subtypes depending on the age at onset (childhood, adolescent, or unspecified).

## Trichotillomania

Trichotillomania is an impulse control disorder characterized by an overwhelming urge to repeatedly pull out one's own hair (usually on the scalp), resulting in hair loss (alopecia). The eyelashes, eyebrows, and beard can also be affected. Many affected individuals feel extreme tension when they feel an impulse, followed by relief, gratification or pleasure afterwards. The condition may be mild and manageable, or severe and debilitating. Some individuals chew or swallow the hair they pull out (trichophagy), which can result in gastrointestinal problems. The exact cause of the condition is unknown. Treatment typically involves psychotherapy (including cognitive behavior therapy) and/or drug therapy, but these are not always effective.

# Section 18.2

# *Disruptive Behavior Disorders*

This section includes excerpts from "Psychosocial and
Pharmacologic Interventions for Disruptive Behavior in
Children and Adolescents," Agency for Healthcare
Research and Quality (AHRQ), October 19, 2015;
text from "Attention Deficit Hyperactivity Disorder,"
National Institute of Mental Health (NIMH),
December 23, 2008. Reviewed March 2016; and
text from "Attention-Deficit/Hyperactivity
Disorder (ADHD)," Centers for Disease Control and
Prevention (CDC), January 6, 2016.

## *Background*

Disruptive behavior disorders (DBDs) are a group of related psychiatric disorders of childhood and adolescence marked by temper
tantrums, interpersonal aggression, and defiance. These disorders
and related symptoms may manifest in young children as significant behavioral problems at home and difficulties at school. Children
with disruptive behaviors in early childhood often experience persistent impairment and are at increased risk for negative developmental outcomes, including substance abuse problems; school problems; and delinquent, violent, and antisocial or criminal behaviors in
adolescence.

DBDs are among the most common child and adolescent psychiatric disorders, with recent estimates indicating that 3.5 percent of
children ages 3–17 years had behavioral or conduct problems in the
period 2005– Examples of DBDs include oppositional defiant disorder
(ODD), conduct disorder (CD), attention deficit hyperactivity disorder
(ADHD), and DBD not otherwise specified. Estimates suggest that
disruptive behaviors that are problematic but do not meet formal
diagnostic criteria may be more common than those meeting formal
clinical diagnostic criteria. The etiology of DBDs is unknown, but
temperamental, biological, and environmental factors are associated
with increased risk.

## Behavior or Conduct Problems

Children occasionally act angry or defiant around adults or respond aggressively when they are upset. When these behaviors persist over time, or are severe, they can become a behavior disorder. Children with ADHD are more likely to be diagnosed with a behavior disorder such as Oppositional Defiant Disorder or Conduct Disorder. About 1 in 4 children with ADHD have a diagnosed behavior disorder.

## Oppositional Defiant Disorder

When children act out persistently so that it causes serious problems at home, in school, or with peers, they may be diagnosed with *Oppositional Defiant Disorder* (ODD). ODD is one of the most common disorders occurring with ADHD. ODD usually starts before 8 years of age, but can also occur in adolescents. Children with ODD may be most likely to act oppositional or defiant around people they know well, such as family members or a regular care provider. Children with ODD show these behaviors more often than other children their age.

Examples of ODD behaviors include:

- Often losing their temper

- Arguing with adults or refusing to comply with adults' rules or requests

- Often getting angry, being resentful, or wanting to hurt someone who they feel has hurt them or caused problems for them

- Deliberately annoying others; easily becoming annoyed with others

- Often blaming other people for their own mistakes or misbehavior

## Conduct Disorder

Conduct disorder (CD) is diagnosed when children show a behavioral pattern of aggression toward others, and serious violations of rules and social norms at home, in school, and with peers. These behaviors often lead to breaking the law and being jailed. Having ADHD makes a child more likely to be diagnosed with CD. Children with CD are more likely to get injured, and have difficulties getting along with peers.

Examples of CD behaviors include

- Breaking serious rules, such as running away, staying out at night when told not to, or skipping school

- Being aggressive in a way that causes harm, such as bullying, fighting, or being cruel to animals

- Lying and stealing, or damaging other people's property on purpose

## Treatment for Disruptive Behavior Disorders

Starting treatment early is important. Treatment is most effective if it fits the needs of the child and family. The first step to treatment is to have a comprehensive evaluation by a mental health professional. Some of the signs of behavior problems, such as not following rules, are also signs of ADHD, so it is important to get a careful evaluation to see if a child has both conditions. For younger children, the treatment with the strongest evidence is behavioral parent training, where a therapist helps the parent learn effective ways to strengthen the parent-child relationship and respond to the child's behavior. For school-age children and teens, an often-used effective treatment is combination training and therapy that includes the child, the family, and the school. Sometimes medication is part of the treatment.

## Learning Disorder

Many children with ADHD also have a learning disorder (LD). This is in addition to other symptoms of ADHD, such as difficulties paying attention, staying on task, or being organized, which also keep a child from doing well in school.

Having a learning disorder means that a child has a clear difficulty in one or more areas of learning, even when their intelligence is not affected. Learning disorders include:

- Dyslexia – difficulty with reading

- Dyscalculia – difficulty with math

- Dysgraphia – difficulty with writing

Data from the 2004–2006 National Health Interview Survey suggests that almost half of children 6–17 years of age diagnosed with

ADHD may also have LD. The combination of problems caused by ADHD and LD can make it particularly hard for a child to succeed in school. Properly diagnosing each disorder is crucial, so that the child can get the right kind of help for each.

## Treatment for Learning Disorders

Children with learning disorders often need extra help and instruction that is specialized for them. Having a learning disorder can qualify a child for special education services in school. Because children with ADHD often have difficulty in school, the first step is a careful evaluation to see if the problems are also caused by a learning disorder. Schools usually do their own testing to see if a child needs intervention. Parents, healthcare providers, and the school can work together to find the right referrals and treatment.

### Depression

Occasionally being sad or feeling hopeless is a part of every child's life. When children feel persistent sadness and hopelessness, it can cause problems. Children with ADHD are more likely than children without ADHD to develop childhood depression. Children may be more likely to feel hopeless and sad when they can't control their ADHD symptoms and the symptoms interfere with doing well at school or getting along with family and friends. About 1 in 7 children with ADHD have a diagnosis of depression.

Examples of behaviors often seen when children are depressed include

- Feeling sad or hopeless a lot of the time
- Not wanting to do things that are fun
- Having a hard time focusing
- Feeling worthless or useless

Children with ADHD already have a hard time focusing on things that are not very interesting to them. Depression can make it hard to focus on things that are normally fun. Changes in eating and sleeping habits can also be a sign of depression. For children with ADHD who take medication, changes in eating and sleeping can also be side effects from the medication rather than signs of depression. Talk with your doctor if you have concerns.

*Treatment for Anxiety and Depression*

The first step to treatment is to talk with a healthcare provider to get an evaluation. Some signs of depression, like having a hard time focusing, are also signs of ADHD, so it is important to get a careful evaluation to see if a child has both conditions. A mental health professional can develop a therapy plan that works best for the child and family. Early treatment is important, and can include child therapy, family therapy, or a combination of both. The school can also be included in therapy programs. For very young children, involving parents in treatment is very important. Cognitive behavioral therapy is one form of therapy that is used to treat anxiety or depression, particularly in older children. It helps the child change negative thoughts into more positive, effective ways of thinking. Consultation with a health provider can help determine if medication should also be part of the treatment.

# Section 18.3

# *Self-Harm*

Text in this section is excerpted from "Self-Harm," U.S. Department of Health and Human Services (HHS), January 8, 2013; and text from "Cutting," © 1995–2016. The Nemours Foundation/ KidsHealth®. Reprinted with permission.

Self-harm refers to a person's harming their own body on purpose. About 1 in 100 people hurts himself or herself in this way. More females hurt themselves than males. A person who self-harms usually does not mean to kill himself or herself. But they are at higher risk of attempting suicide if they do not get help.

Self-harm tends to begin in teen or early adult years. Some people may engage in self-harm a few times and then stop. Others engage in it more often and have trouble stopping.

- Examples of self-harm include

- Cutting yourself (such as using a razor blade, knife, or other sharp object to cut the skin)

- Punching yourself or punching things (like a wall)
- Burning yourself with cigarettes, matches, or candles
- Pulling out your hair
- Poking objects through body openings
- Breaking your bones or bruising yourself

Many people cut themselves because it gives them a sense of relief. Some people use cutting as a means to cope with a problem. Some teens say that when they hurt themselves, they are trying to stop feeling lonely, angry, or hopeless.

It is possible to overcome the urge to hurt yourself. There are other ways to find relief and cope with your emotions. Counseling may help.

## *What Is Cutting?*

Injuring yourself on purpose by making scratches or cuts on your body with a sharp object — enough to break the skin and make it bleed — is called cutting. Cutting is a type of self-injury, or SI. People who cut often start cutting in their young teens. Some continue to cut into adulthood.

People may cut themselves on their wrists, arms, legs, or bellies. Some people self-injure by burning their skin with the end of a cigarette or lighted match.

When cuts or burns heal, they often leave scars or marks. People who injure themselves usually hide the cuts and marks and sometimes no one else knows.

## *Why Do People Cut Themselves?*

It can be hard to understand why people cut themselves on purpose. Cutting is a way some people try to cope with the pain of strong emotions, intense pressure, or upsetting relationship problems. They may be dealing with feelings that seem too difficult to bear or bad situations they think can't change.

Some people cut because they feel desperate for relief from bad feelings. People who cut may not know better ways to get relief from emotional pain or pressure. Some people cut to express strong feelings of rage, sorrow, rejection, desperation, longing, or emptiness.

There are other ways to cope with difficulties, even big problems and terrible emotional pain. The help of a mental health professional might be needed for major life troubles or overwhelming emotions. For other tough situations or strong emotions, it can help put things in perspective to talk problems over with parents, other adults, or friends. Getting plenty of exercise also can help put problems in perspective and help balance emotions.

But people who cut may not have developed ways to cope. Or their coping skills may be overpowered by emotions that are too intense. When emotions don't get expressed in a healthy way, tension can build up — sometimes to a point where it seems almost unbearable. Cutting may be an attempt to relieve that extreme tension. For some, it seems like a way of feeling in control.

The urge to cut might be triggered by strong feelings the person can't express — such as anger, hurt, shame, frustration, or alienation. People who cut sometimes say they feel they don't fit in or that no one understands them. A person might cut because of losing someone close or to escape a sense of emptiness. Cutting might seem like the only way to find relief or express personal pain over relationships or rejection.

People who cut or self-injure sometimes have other mental health problems that contribute to their emotional tension. Cutting is sometimes (but not always) associated with depression, bipolar disorder, eating disorders, obsessive thinking, or compulsive behaviors. It can also be a sign of mental health problems that cause people to have trouble controlling their impulses or to take unnecessary risks. Some people who cut themselves have problems with drug or alcohol abuse.

Some people who cut have had a traumatic experience, such as living through abuse, violence, or a disaster. Self-injury may feel like a way of "waking up" from a sense of numbness after a traumatic experience. Or it may be a way of reliving the pain they went through, expressing anger over it, or trying to get control of it.

## What Can Happen to People Who Cut?

Although cutting may provide some temporary relief from a terrible feeling, even people who cut agree that it isn't a good way to get that relief. For one thing, the relief doesn't last. The troubles that triggered the cutting remain — they're just masked over.

People don't usually intend to hurt themselves permanently when they cut. And they don't usually mean to keep cutting once they start. But both can happen. It's possible to misjudge the depth of a cut, making it so deep that it requires stitches (or, in extreme cases, hospitalization). Cuts can become infected if a person uses nonsterile or dirty cutting instruments — razors, scissors, pins, or even the sharp edge of the tab on a can of soda.

Most people who cut aren't attempting suicide. Cutting is usually a person's attempt at feeling better, not ending it all. Although some people who cut do attempt suicide, it's usually because of the emotional problems and pain that lie behind their desire to self-harm, not the cutting itself.

Cutting can be habit forming. It can become a compulsive behavior — meaning that the more a person does it, the more he or she feels the need to do it. The brain starts to connect the false sense of relief from bad feelings to the act of cutting, and it craves this relief the next time tension builds. When cutting becomes a compulsive behavior, it can seem impossible to stop. So cutting can seem almost like an addiction, where the urge to cut can seem too hard to resist. A behavior that starts as an attempt to feel more in control can end up controlling you.

## How Does Cutting Start?

Cutting often begins on an impulse. It's not something the person thinks about ahead of time. Shauna says, "It starts when something's really upsetting and you don't know how to talk about it or what to do. But you can't get your mind off feeling upset, and your body has this knot of emotional pain. Before you know it, you're cutting yourself. And then somehow, you're in another place. Then, the next time you feel awful about something, you try it again — and slowly it becomes a habit."

Natalie, a high-school junior who started cutting in middle school, explains that it was a way to distract herself from feelings of rejection and helplessness she felt she couldn't bear. "I never looked at it as anything that bad at first — just my way of getting my mind off something I felt really awful about. I guess part of me must have known it was a bad thing to do, though, because I always hid it. Once a friend asked me if I was cutting myself and I even lied and said 'no.' I was embarrassed."

You can't force someone who self-injures to stop. It doesn't help to get mad at a friend who cuts, reject that person, lecture her, or beg him to stop. Instead, let your friend know that you care, that he or she deserves to be healthy and happy, and that no one needs to bear their troubles alone.

## Pressured to Cut?

Girls and guys who self-injure are often dealing with some heavy troubles. Many work hard to overcome difficult problems. So they find it hard to believe that some kids cut just because they think it's a way to seem tough and rebellious.

Tia tried cutting because a couple of the girls at her school were doing it. "It seemed like if I didn't do it, they would think I was afraid or something. So I did it once. But then I thought about how lame it was to do something like that to myself for no good reason. Next time they asked I just said, 'no, thanks — it's not for me.' "

If you have a friend who suggests you try cutting, say what you think. Why get pulled into something you know isn't good for you? There are plenty of other ways to express who you are.

## Getting Help

There are better ways to deal with troubles than cutting — healthier, long-lasting ways that don't leave a person with emotional and physical scars. The first step is to get help with the troubles that led to the cutting in the first place. Here are some ideas for doing that:

**Tell someone.** People who have stopped cutting often say the first step is the hardest — admitting to or talking about cutting. But they also say that after they open up about it, they often feel a great sense of relief. Choose someone you trust to talk to at first (a parent, school counselor, teacher, coach, doctor, or nurse). If it's too difficult to bring up the topic in person, write a note.

**Identify the trouble that's triggering the cutting.** Cutting is a way of reacting to emotional tension or pain. Try to figure out what feelings or situations are causing you to cut. Is it anger? Pressure to be perfect? Relationship trouble? A painful loss or trauma? Mean criticism or mistreatment? Identify the trouble you're having, then tell someone about it. Many people have trouble figuring this part out on their own. This is where a mental health professional can be helpful.

**Ask for help.** Tell someone that you want help dealing with your troubles and the cutting. If the person you ask doesn't help you get the assistance you need, ask someone else. Sometimes adults try to downplay the problems teens have or think they're just a phase. If you get the feeling this is happening to you, find another adult (such as a school counselor or nurse) who can make your case for you.

**Work on it.** Most people with deep emotional pain or distress need to work with a counselor or mental health professional to sort through strong feelings, heal past hurts, and to learn better ways to cope with life's stresses. One way to find a therapist or counselor is to ask at your doctor's office, at school, or at a mental health clinic in your community.

Although cutting can be a difficult pattern to break, it is possible. Getting professional help to overcome the problem doesn't mean that a person is weak or crazy. Therapists and counselors are trained to help people discover inner strengths that help them heal. These inner strengths can then be used to cope with life's other problems in a healthy way.

# Section 18.4

# *Problem Gambling*

Text in this section is excerpted from "Gambling Addiction," © 1995–2016. The Nemours Foundation/ KidsHealth®. Reprinted with permission.

## *What Is Gambling?*

Gambling means taking part in any activity or game where you risk money or a valuable object (like an iPod or video game) in order to win money or other stuff.

Gambling is mostly about chance, although some games can involve skill too. Some gambling (like lotteries, slot machines, or bingo) depends on luck, and no amount of knowledge or practice can help a person win. Other games—like pool or darts, for example—require skill. So knowing how to play (and practicing) can influence the results.

Card games (poker, for example) are mostly chance, but they do have some skill elements. The skill in card games comes from knowing what to do with the hand you have been dealt. The more a person knows about playing, the more it can increase the chances of winning. But a win is never guaranteed, because part of the game involves chance: A player has no control over the cards that he or she is dealt. Even the best player can carry a losing hand.

It might seem like gambling is a harmless pastime—after all, 48 U.S. states have some form of legalized gambling. But gambling— even Internet gambling—can easily become a problem that affects not just the person, but that person's family and friends as well. For some people, gambling can become as serious an addiction as drugs, tobacco, or alcohol.

## Why Do People Do It?

It might seem like the obvious reason for gambling is to make money. But that's only part of the story. For many gamblers, it's as much about the fun and excitement—the rush and high from winning (or thinking of gambling)—as it is about winning money.

Sometimes people start gambling because their friends are into it or they have a family member who gambles. In fact, the main thing that puts teens at risk for gambling problems is influence from family members and friends.

Some people gamble simply because they're bored or lonely. Some teens who develop a gambling problem say they gamble as a way to escape or to avoid problems at home. The trouble is, gambling may start out as a casual distraction. But because it works on the risk and reward part of our brains, people can end up addicted.

That's why it helps to ask yourself some questions about gambling, for example:

- "Is it really good for me?"

- "Even if it's fun, is it worth my time?"

- "What are the risks?"

## Gambling Addiction

Some people have a higher chance of becoming addicted to gambling. Those who have trouble controlling impulses, like people with ADHD, can be at greater risk for developing an addiction. So can people whose personalities mean they enjoy taking risks.

This doesn't mean people who have these issues will automatically get addicted to gambling, of course. Most don't. But they are more likely to get sucked in. So they need to be extra cautious and aware of the risks if they decide to try gambling.

## Problems Associated with Gambling Addiction

First and foremost, excessive gambling can cost you a lot of money. Gamblers may experience "hot streaks" from time to time where they win. But the odds will always be against them, and they usually end up down (that's how casinos make a profit since they couldn't stay in business if people kept winning!).

People with severe gambling addiction can gamble away everything they have and even resort to stealing money to fuel their gambling habits.

Gambling can cause someone to lose interest in other activities. When people skip school or miss work in order to gamble it affects their chances of having a good job or career. Gambling can also affect personality, causing mood swings and problems in someone's social life and personal relationships.

As gambling becomes a larger presence in someone's life, it can alienate friends and loved ones and cause friction and bad feelings at home.

Gambling can even affect a person's health, causing sleep problems, anxiety, stress, depression, unexplained anger, thoughts of suicide, and suicide attempts.

Also, since gambling is almost always against the law for minors, and because gamblers can be driven to crime to fund their addictions, teen gamblers can develop serious legal problems.

## What Signs Indicate a Gambling Problem?

Gambling problems can be tough to detect. Unlike other addictions, there generally aren't a lot of physical warnings. There may be some telltale signs, such as tiredness or irritability, money problems, turning to crime, or bad grades. But much of the time, problem gamblers won't show obvious symptoms.

As with many addictions, family members and friends often notice the problem first. The person gambling may not believe he or she has a problem.

If you suspect that you, a friend, or a family member might have a problem, ask a few questions about the gambling. Answering "yes" to any of these questions may indicate a risk for gambling addiction:

- Do you think about gambling more and more (or all the time) and find yourself planning the next time you'll play?

- Do you have a new circle of friends that only includes the people you know through gambling?

- Does it seem like you spend more time gambling than you do doing anything else?

- Has your gambling led to problems at school, such as poor grades, absenteeism, or lateness?

- Have you ever spent your lunch money or bus fare on gambling?

- Have you ever taken money from someone without their knowledge to finance your gambling?

- Have you ever lied to a friend or family member about your gambling or do you feel the need to be secretive about your gambling activities?

- Have you ever stolen money or shoplifted to finance your gambling?

- Have you ever committed (or thought about committing) another crime to get money for gambling?

- Do you gamble for longer than you planned or do you find yourself gambling for longer and longer periods of time?

- Do you spend more money on gambling than you meant to or have you ever gambled away all the money you had before you stopped?

- Do you ever gamble out of boredom or as a way to escape your problems?

- Have you ever had to ask for help with your gambling problems or have you tried to quit gambling and been unable to do so?

- Does a big win make you want to gamble again right away?

- Does a big loss make you want to gamble immediately so you can win your money back?

- Has gambling ever made you think of committing suicide or caused you to attempt suicide?

- Has gambling led to problems at home or had an effect on your relationships with your friends and family?

If you've asked yourself these questions about your gambling (or someone else's) and answered yes to more than a few of them, the next thing to do is get help.

## How to Get Help?

If you think you have a problem, tell a family member, school counselor, or someone you trust about your gambling. If you believe a friend or family member is developing a gambling habit, talk to a school counselor, parent, or other trusted adult.

Distraction can work well in breaking a gambling habit, if the habit hasn't become too much of a problem. Try finding a new hobby or something better to do. Just having something to take your mind off gambling can go a long way toward helping you stop. Be realistic, though. If this approach doesn't work, the next step should be to talk to a counselor or call a hotline.

Most states have gambling help hotlines that you can call toll free, and there are numerous support groups online. These groups also can offer advice to people who are looking for help for friends and family members who have gambling problems.

Recovery programs that include group therapy and counseling sessions have helped many gamblers overcome their addiction. Talking with people who have been through the experience can provide both support and ideas for overcoming the problem.

Different styles of treatment work better for different people, so it can sometimes take a few tries to figure out what works for you. Just be sure to keep trying if your first option doesn't work.

Gambling can be a difficult habit to break. It may seem like quitting should be easy, but — as with any strong habit — it can be hard to do alone. Counselors and therapists are trained to help people discover inner strengths that allow them to overcome problems.

# Chapter 19

# *Tourette Syndrome*

## *Facts about Tourette Syndrome*

Tourette syndrome (TS) is a condition of the nervous system. TS causes people to have "tics".

Tics are sudden twitches, movements, or sounds that people do repeatedly. People who have tics cannot stop their body from doing these things. For example, a person might keep blinking over and over again. Or, a person might make a grunting sound unwillingly.

Having tics is a little bit like having hiccups. Even though you might not want to hiccup, your body does it anyway. Sometimes people can stop themselves from doing a certain tic for awhile, but it's hard. Eventually the person has to do the tic.

## *Diagnosis*

There is no single test, like a blood test, to diagnose TS. Health professionals look at the person's symptoms to diagnose TS and other tic disorders. The tic disorders differ from each other in terms of the type of tic present (motor or vocal, or combination of the both), and how long the symptoms have lasted. TS can be diagnosed if a person has both motor and vocal tics, and has had tic symptoms for at least a year.

---

Text in this chapter is excerpted from "Facts about Tourette Syndrome," Centers for Disease Control and Prevention (CDC), November 30, 2015.

## Treatments

Although there is no cure for TS, there are treatments available to help manage the tics. Many people with TS have tics that do not get in the way of their daily life and, therefore, do not need any treatment. However, medication and behavioral treatments are available if tics cause pain or injury; interfere with school, work, or social life; or cause stress.

## Risk Factors and Causes

Doctors and scientists do not know the exact cause of TS. Research suggests that it is an inherited genetic condition. That means it is passed on from parent to child through genes.

## Other Concerns and Conditions

TS often occurs with other conditions (called co-occurring conditions). Among children diagnosed with TS, 86% also have been diagnosed with at least one additional mental, behavioral, or developmental condition. The two most common conditions are attention-deficit/hyperactivity disorder (ADHD) and obsessive-compulsive disorder (OCD). It is important to find out if a person with TS has any other conditions, and treat those conditions properly.

# Part Three

# Mental Health Treatments

# Chapter 20

# *Responding to Mental Health Crisis*

## *Introduction*

### *Crisis Have a Profound Impact on People with Serious Mental Health or Emotional Problems.*

Adults, children and older adults with a serious mental illness or emotional disorder often lead lives characterized by recurrent, significant crises. These crises are not the inevitable consequences of mental disability, but rather represent the combined impact of a host of additional factors, including lack of access to essential services and supports, poverty, unstable housing, coexisting substance use, other health problems, discrimination and victimization.

Homelessness, police contact, institutionalization and other adverse events are in themselves crises, and may also contribute to further crises. The statistics below paint a sobering picture of how crises affect the lives of people who have mental or emotional disabilities:

This chapter includes excerpts from "Core Elements in Responding to Mental Health Crises," Substance Abuse and Mental Health Services Administration (SAMHSA), 2009. Reviewed March 2016; text from "For Friends and Family Members," U.S. Department of Health and Human Services (HHS), May 31, 2013; and text from "What Is Mental Health?" U.S. Department of Health and Human Services (HHS), May 31, 2013.

- From one third to one half of homeless people have a severe psychiatric disorder.

- Approximately 7 percent of all police contacts in urban settings involve a person believed to have a mental illness.

- The likelihood of mental illness among people confined in state prisons and local jails is three to four times higher than in the general population and, compared with other inmates, it is *at least twice as likely* that these individuals will be injured during their incarceration.

- About 6 percent of all hospital emergency department visits reflect mental health emergencies.

- Due to a lack of available alternatives, 79 percent of hospital emergency departments report having to "board" psychiatric patients who are in crisis and in need of inpatient care, sometimes for *eight hours or longer*.

- Almost one in 10 individuals discharged from a state psychiatric hospital will be readmitted within 30 days; more than one in five will be readmitted within 180 days.

- About 90 percent of adult inpatients in state psychiatric hospitals report histories of trauma.

- About three quarters of youth in the juvenile justice system report mental health problems and one in five has a serious mental disorder.

- Mothers with serious mental illnesses are *more than four times as likely as* other mothers to lose custody of their children.

- People with serious mental illnesses die, on average, *25 years earlier* than the general population.

These statistics are incomplete; they reflect just a sampling of scenarios that, while commonplace, constitute significant life crises for individuals with serious mental illnesses.

Many such individuals experience a cascade of crisis events that place them in more than one of these statistical groups. For instance, readmission to a psychiatric institution—a high probability for adults who have been discharged from a state psychiatric hospital, based on these data—may feature a series of crisis events for the individual: the psychiatric emergency itself; forcible removal from one's home; being taken into police custody, handcuffed and transported in the back of a police car; evaluation in the emergency department of a general hospital; transfer to a psychiatric hospital; a civil commitment hearing; and so on. And at multiple points in this series of interventions, there is a likelihood that physical restraints, seclusion, involuntary medication or other coercion may be used. Intense feelings of disempowerment are definitional of mental health crises, yet as the individual becomes the subject of a "disposition" at each juncture, that person may experience a diminishing sense of control.

In the wake of rare but highly publicized tragedies attributed to people with mental illnesses, there is often a temporary surge in political concern about mental healthcare and expanding crisis interventions. Sadly, the more commonplace crises endured every day by many thousands of adults, older adults and children with serious mental or emotional problems tend to generate neither media attention nor political concern.

While no one with a mental or emotional disorder is immune from crises, people with what are termed serious mental illnesses—defined as schizophrenia, bipolar disorder and major depression—may be most reliant on public systems. They also may be at great risk of recurrent crises and interventions that exacerbate their clinical and social problems. These guidelines focus most specifically on individuals with serious mental or emotional problems who tend to encounter an assortment of governmental or publicly funded interveners when they are in crisis. Nevertheless, the values, principles and strategies embedded in the guidelines that follow are applicable to all individuals with mental healthcare needs, across populations and service settings.

Individuals whose diagnoses do not fit "serious mental illnesses" may be vulnerable to serious mental health crises that can have devastating outcomes. Interventions on their behalf are more likely to occur within the private healthcare sector, which mirrors public mental health systems' problems in providing early and meaningful access to help. Within these parallel systems, crisis services are provided in a broad array of settings that ultimately will require translation of the guidelines presented here into specific protocols that break cycles of crises and advance the prospects of recovery for people with mental illnesses.

## What It Means to Be in a Mental Health Crisis

Too often, public systems respond as if a *mental health crisis* and *danger to self or others* were one and the same. In fact, *danger to self or others* derives from common legal language defining when involuntary psychiatric hospitalization may occur—at best, this is a blunt measure of an extreme emergency. A narrow focus on dangerousness is not a valid approach to addressing a mental health crisis. To identify crises accurately requires a much more nuanced understanding and a perspective that looks beyond whether an individual is dangerous or immediate psychiatric hospitalization is indicated.

While behaviors that represent an imminent danger certainly indicate the need for some sort of an emergency response, these behaviors may well be the culmination of a crisis episode, rather than the episode in its entirety. Situations involving mental health crises may follow trajectories that include intense feelings of personal distress (e.g., anxiety, depression, anger, panic, hopelessness), obvious changes in functioning (e.g., neglect of personal hygiene, unusual behavior) or catastrophic life events (e.g., disruptions in personal relationships, support systems or living arrangements; loss of autonomy or parental rights; victimization or natural disasters).

Because only a portion of real-life crises may actually result in serious harm to self or others, a response that is activated only when physical safety becomes an issue is often too little, too late or no help at all in addressing the root of the crisis. And a response that does not meaningfully address the actual issues underlying a crisis may do more harm than good.

## Responding to Mental Health Crisis

### Ten Essential Values

Ten essential values are inherent in an appropriate crisis response, regardless of the nature of the crisis, the situations where assistance is offered or the individuals providing assistance:

1.  **Avoiding harm**. Sometimes mental health crises place the safety of the person, the crisis responders or others in jeopardy. An appropriate response establishes physical safety, but it also establishes the individual's psychological safety. For instance, restraints are sometimes used in situations where there is an immediate risk of physical harm, yet this intervention has inherent physical and psychological risks that can cause injury and even death. Precipitous responses to individuals in mental health crises—often initiated with the intention of establishing physical safety—sometimes result in harm to the individual. *An appropriate response to mental health crises considers the risks and benefits attendant to interventions and*

*whenever possible employs alternative approaches, such as controlling danger sufficiently to allow a period of "watchful waiting." In circumstances where there is an urgent need to establish physical safety and few viable alternatives to address an immediate risk of significant harm to the individual or others, an appropriate crisis response incorporates measures to minimize the duration and negative impact of interventions used.*

2.  **Intervening in person-centered ways.** Mental health crises may be routine in some settings and, perhaps, have even come to be routine for some people with serious mental health or emotional problems. Nevertheless, appropriate crisis assistance avoids rote interventions based on diagnostic labels, presenting complaint or practices customary to a particular setting. *Appropriate interventions seek to understand the individual, his or her unique circumstances and how that individual's personal preferences and goals can be maximally incorporated in the crisis response.*

3.  **Shared responsibility.** An acute sense of losing control over events or feelings is a hallmark of mental health crises. In fact, research has shown "feeling out of control" to be the most common reason consumers cite for being brought in for psychiatric emergency care. An intervention that is done to the individual— rather than with the individual—can reinforce these feelings of helplessness. One of the principal rationales for person-centered plans is that shared responsibility promotes engagement and better outcomes. While crisis situations may present challenges to implementing shared, person-centered plans, ultimately an intervention that considers and, to the extent possible, honors an individual's role in crisis resolution may hold long-term benefits. *An appropriate crisis response seeks to assist the individual in regaining control by considering the individual an active partner in—rather than a passive recipient of—services.*

4.  **Addressing trauma**. Crises, themselves, are intrinsically traumatic and certain crisis interventions may have the effect of imposing further trauma—both physical and emotional. In addition, people with serious mental illness have a high probability of having been victims of abuse or neglect. *It is essential that once physical safety has been established, harm resulting from the crisis or crisis response is evaluated and addressed*

*without delay by individuals qualified to diagnose and initiate needed treatment. There is also a dual responsibility relating to the individual's relevant trauma history and vulnerabilities associated with particular interventions; crisis responders should appropriately seek out and incorporate this information in their approaches, and individuals should take personal responsibility for making this crucial information available (for instance, by executing advance directives).*

5. **Establishing feelings of Personal safety**. An individual may experience a mental health crisis as a catastrophic event and, accordingly, may have an urgent need to feel safe. What is regarded as agitated behavior may reflect an individual's attempts at self-protection, though perhaps to an unwarranted threat. *Assisting the individual in attaining the subjective goal of personal safety requires an understanding of what is needed for that person to experience a sense of security (perhaps contained in a crisis plan or personal safety plan previously formulated by the individual) and what interventions increase feelings of vulnerability (for instance, confinement in a room alone). Providing such assistance also requires that staff be afforded time to gain an understanding of the individual's needs and latitude to address these needs creatively.*

6. **Based on strengths.** Sharing responsibility for crisis resolution means understanding that an individual, even while in crisis, can marshall personal strengths and assist in the resolution of the emergency. Individuals often understand the factors that precipitated a crisis as well as factors that can help ameliorate their impact. *An appropriate crisis response seeks to identify and reinforce the resources on which an individual can draw, not only to recover from the crisis event, but to also help protect against further occurrences.*

7. **The whole person.** For individuals who have a mental illness, the psychiatric label itself may shape—even dominate—decisions about which crisis interventions are offered and how they are made available. *An individual with a serious mental illness who is in crisis is a whole person, whose established psychiatric disability may be relevant but may—or may not—be immediately paramount.* That the individual may have multiple needs and an adequate understanding of the crisis means not being limited by services that are compartmentalized

according to healthcare specialty. An individual's emergency may reflect the interplay of psychiatric issues with other health factors. And while the individual is experiencing a crisis that tends to be addressed as a clinical phenomenon, there may also be a host of seemingly mundane, real-world concerns that significantly affect an individual's response: the whereabouts of the person's children, the welfare of pets, whether the house is locked, absence from work, and so on.

8. **The person as credible source**. Assertions or complaints made by individuals who have been diagnosed with a serious mental illness tend to be viewed skeptically by others. Particularly within the charged context of mental health crises, there may be a presumption that statements made by these individuals are manifestations of delusional thinking. Consequently, there is a risk that legitimate complaints relating to such matters as medical illness, pain, abuse or victimization will go unheeded. Even when an individual's assertions are not well grounded in reality and represent obviously delusional thoughts, the "telling of one's story" may represent an important step toward crisis resolution. *For these reasons, an appro priate response to an individual in mental health crisis is not dismissive of the person as a credible source of information— factual or emotional—that is important to understanding the person's strengths and needs.*

9. **Recovery, resilience, and natural supports**. Certain settings, such as hospital emergency departments, may see individuals only transiently, at a point when they are in acute crisis and in a decidedly high-stress environment. Even when not occurring within hospitals, mental health emergency interventions are often provided in settings that are alien to the individual and the natural supports that may be important parts of his or her daily life. It is important not to lose sight of the fact that an emergency episode may be a temporary relapse and not definitional of the person or that individual's broader life course. *An appropriate crisis response contributes to the individual's larger journey toward recovery and resilience and incorporates these values. Accordingly, interventions should preserve dignity, foster a sense of hope, and promote engagement with formal systems and informal resources.*

**10. Prevention**. Too often, individuals with serious mental illnesses have only temporary respite between crises. An appropriate crisis response works to ensure that crises will not be recurrent by evaluating and considering factors that contributed to the current episode and that will prevent future relapse. *Hence, an adequate crisis response requires measures that address the person's unmet needs, both through individualized planning and by promoting systemic improvements.*

## For Friends and Family Members

Anyone can experience mental health problems. Friends and family can make all the difference in a person's recovery process.

### Supporting a Friend or Family Member with Mental Health Problems

You can help your friend or family member by recognizing the signs of mental health problems and connecting them to professional help.

Talking to friends and family about mental health problems can be an opportunity to provide information, support, and guidance. Learning about mental health issues can lead to:

- Improved recognition of early signs of mental health problems

- Earlier treatment

- Greater understanding and compassion

If a friend or family member is showing signs of a mental health problem or reaching out to you for help, offer support by:

- Finding out if the person is getting the care that he or she needs and wants—if not, connect him or her to help

- Expressing your concern and support

- Reminding your friend or family member that help is available and that mental health problems can be treated

- Asking questions, listening to ideas, and being responsive when the topic of mental health problems come up

- Reassuring your friend or family member that you care about him or her

- Offering to help your friend or family member with everyday tasks

- Including your friend or family member in your plans—continue to invite him or her without being overbearing, even if your friend or family member resists your invitations

- Educating other people so they understand the facts about mental health problems and do not discriminate

- Treating people with mental health problems with respect, compassion, and empathy

## *How to Talk about Mental Health?*

Do you need help starting a conversation about mental health? Try leading with these questions and make sure to actively listen to your friend or family member's response.

- I've been worried about you. Can we talk about what you are experiencing? If not, who are you comfortable talking to?

- What can I do to help you to talk about issues with your parents or someone else who is responsible and cares about you?

- What else can I help you with?

- I am someone who cares and wants to listen. What do you want me to know about how you are feeling?

- Who or what has helped you deal with similar issues in the past?

- Sometimes talking to someone who has dealt with a similar experience helps. Do you know of others who have experienced these types of problems who you can talk with?

- It seems like you are going through a difficult time. How can I help you to find help?

- How can I help you find more information about mental health problems?

- I'm concerned about your safety. Have you thought about harming yourself or others?

When talking about mental health problems:
- Know how to connect people to help

- Communicate in a straightforward manner

- Speak at a level appropriate to a person's age and development level (preschool children need fewer details as compared to teenagers)

- Discuss the topic when and where the person feels safe and comfortable

- Watch for reactions during the discussion and slow down or back up if the person becomes confused or looks upset

Sometimes it is helpful to make a comparison to a physical illness. For example, many people get sick with a cold or the flu, but only a few get really sick with something serious like pneumonia. People who have a cold are usually able to do their normal activities. However, if they get pneumonia, they will have to take medicine and may have to go to the hospital.

Similarly, feelings of sadness, anxiety, worry, irritability, or sleep problems are common for most people. However, when these feelings get very intense, last for a long period of time, and begin to interfere with school, work, and relationships, it may be a sign of a mental health problem. And just like people need to take medicine and get professional help for physical conditions, someone with a mental health problem may need to take medicine and/or participate in therapy in order to get better.

### Get Help for Your Friend or Family Member

Seek immediate assistance if you think your friend or family member is in danger of harming themselves. You can call a crisis line or the National Suicide Prevention Line at 1.800.273.TALK (8255).

## Early Warning Signs

Not sure if you or someone you know is living with mental health problems? Experiencing one or more of the following feelings or behaviors can be an early warning sign of a problem:

- Eating or sleeping too much or too little

- Pulling away from people and usual activities

- Having low or no energy

- Feeling numb or like nothing matters

- Having unexplained aches and pains

- Feeling helpless or hopeless

- Smoking, drinking, or using drugs more than usual

- Feeling unusually confused, forgetful, on edge, angry, upset, worried, or scared

- Yelling or fighting with family and friends

- Experiencing severe mood swings that cause problems in relationships

- Having persistent thoughts and memories you can't get out of your head

- Hearing voices or believing things that are not true

- Thinking of harming yourself or others

- Inability to perform daily tasks like taking care of your kids or getting to work or school

## Mental Health and Wellness

Positive mental health allows people to:

- Realize their full potential
- Cope with the stresses of life
- Work productively
- Make meaningful contributions to their communities

Ways to maintain positive mental health include:

- Getting professional help if you need it
- Connecting with others
- Staying positive
- Getting physically active
- Helping others
- Getting enough sleep
- Developing coping skills

# Chapter 21

# *Treatments for Mental Disorders*

Mental disorders are generally characterized by changes in mood, thought, and/or behavior. They can make daily activities difficult and impair a person's ability to work, interact with family, and fulfill other major life functions. The National Survey on Drug Use and Health data — 2014 shows that 43.6 million adults ages 18 and older experienced some form of mental illness in the past year, or about 18.1% of the adult population.

SAMHSA's Community Mental Health Services Block Grant (MHBG) provides funds and technical assistance for community-based mental health services to adults with serious mental illnesses and to children with serious emotional disturbances. SAMHSA also funds a number of other grant programs to help individuals with or at risk of developing mental disorders. For more information about these programs, read about SAMHSA's grant opportunities and the grant application, review, and management process.

## *Treatment for Anxiety Disorders*

Anxiety disorders range from specific phobias, such as the fear of flying, to more generalized feelings of worry and tension. This group of

Text in this chapter is excerpted from "Treatments for Mental Disorders," Substance Abuse and Mental Health Services Administration (SAMHSA), October 10, 2015.

disorders includes panic disorder, separation anxiety disorder, social phobia, and generalized anxiety disorder.

The use of medication to treat anxiety disorders may be recommended, and while medication alone does not address the underlying reasons that a person develops an anxiety disorder, the use of medication can help keep symptoms under control while other forms of treatment are implemented. Examples of medication that may be used as part of a treatment approach to anxiety disorders includes anti-anxiety drugs (benzodiazepines) such as clonazepam, lorazepam, and alprazolam. Anti-depressants such as fluoxetine, sertraline, and venlafaxine may be used. In some circumstances beta-blockers can also be prescribed to reduce physical symptoms such as sweating. Importantly, medications work differently in different people and need to be prescribed and monitored by appropriate medical personnel.

Effective treatments for anxiety disorders also include various forms of counseling, including:

• Cognitive-behavioral therapies that help people address their fears by modifying the way they think and respond to stressful events

• Mindfulness therapy that helps patients stay focused in the present and to stop struggling to control distressing thoughts and feelings resulting in greater self-acceptance

• Exposure therapies that use a method of gradual exposure to fearful situations that leads to decreased anxiety

Exercise and relaxation techniques such as meditation can be useful for people with this disorder because they help to lower stress and to manage severe worry. Positive support from family, friends, and other peers also helps to reinforce anxiety disorder treatment.

## Treatment for Attention Deficit Hyperactivity Disorder (ADHD)

Attention deficit hyperactivity disorder (ADHD) is a mental disorder characterized by excessive hyperactivity, impulsivity, or inattention. While ADHD is typically diagnosed in childhood, symptoms may persist into adulthood. ADHD is most effectively treated with a combination of medication and counseling. Prescription stimulants are the most widely used medications to treat ADHD. Seventy to 80% of children with ADHD show improved attention span, reduced impulsivity, and improved on-task behavior while taking stimulant medications.

Different types of counseling and behavioral therapies are used to treat ADHD. Providing practical assistance, such as helping a child organize tasks or complete schoolwork teaches a child how to monitor his or her own behavior. Helping a child control anger or think before acting is another goal of counseling for ADHD. Laying out clear rules, chore lists, and other structured routines helps a child control his or her behavior. Counseling can also be used to help adults by educating them about ADHD, helping develop skills such as organization and planning, and applying these skills in daily life. ADHD coaching is an emerging treatment option that may help adults with the disorder. ADHD coaches work with individuals on improving their skills on scheduling, goal setting, confidence building, organization, and persisting at life tasks.

## Treatment for Depressive Disorders

Depressive disorders are characterized by a pervading sense of sadness and/or loss of interest or pleasure in most activities, and include major depressive disorder and persistent depressive disorder (dysthymia). Like most mental illness, depressive disorders are best treated with a combination of medication and counseling.

Many medications exist for the treatment of depressive disorders. These medications, known as antidepressants, work by affecting neurotransmitters, especially serotonin and norepinephrine. These medications fall into a number of classes including selective serotonin reuptake inhibitors (SSRIs), serotonin and norepinephrine reuptake inhibitors (SNRIs), tricyclic antidepressants, and monoamine oxidase inhibitors (MAOIs). There are numerous forms of medication across these classes and each has different side effects. People sometimes need to try different medications to find a medication that relieves their depression and has tolerable side effects.

People with a depressive disorder often benefit from seeing a psychiatrist, psychologist, or other mental health counselor. If medication is needed, the person must see a psychiatrist or other healthcare professional with prescribing privileges. Interpersonal therapy, a form of behavioral therapy, is a short-term treatment option that aims to help people work through troubled relationships that may be affecting their condition.

It is important that those with major depression who experience suicidal thinking, a common symptom of major depression, and who are treated with antidepressants, have ongoing close psychiatric follow-up because energy levels may improve before mood symptoms and suicidal thinking resolve thereby potentially increasing the risk of suicide early in the course of treatment. Cognitive-behavioral therapies tailored to address the thoughts and behaviors that can accompany depressive disorders are another treatment option.

## Treatment for Bipolar Disorder

Bipolar disorder causes highs (mania) and lows (depression) in mood. Symptoms of bipolar disorder are severe and can result in damaged relationships, poor job or school performance, and even suicide. A combination of medication and counseling is recommended to treat bipolar disorder.

Bipolar disorder can be treated with a range of medications depending on the specific symptoms an individual with bipolar disorder experiences. These medications include mood stabilizers, antipsychotics, and antidepressants. Because some of these medications have serious side effects, especially mood stabilizers and antipsychotics, it is important for people with bipolar disorder to closely monitor side effects and have close support from their psychiatrist to properly manage their medication.

A number of psychotherapies can help with the treatment of bipolar disorder including cognitive-behavioral therapy to identify negative patterns and behaviors, interpersonal and family therapies that help people with bipolar disorder improve relationships and communications, and psychoeducation, which can educate people with bipolar disorder and their family members about the illness and help them to identify the signs of mood swings before they happen.

## Treatment for Schizophrenia

Schizophrenia is a serious mental illness that affects about 1% of the U.S. population. It usually appears between the ages of 16 and 30. Symptoms of schizophrenia include hallucinations and delusions, disorganized thinking, social withdrawal, flat affect, lack of pleasure, difficulty starting and sustaining activities, problems with decision making, problems with working memory (recalling what has been learned previously), and problems with attention.

Treatments for schizophrenia focus on eliminating the symptoms of the disease. They include a combination of antipsychotic medication and behavioral therapy. Hallucinations and other symptoms of agitation usually subside within days after starting medications. It typically takes about six weeks on these medications for people to experience a marked improvement. Individual response to treatment can vary widely among individuals, so people living with schizophrenia will need to work collaboratively with their psychiatrist and other treatment providers to determine the course of medication, behavioral therapy, and other recovery supports that will most effectively help them to achieve the highest possible level of function.

Those who are diagnosed with schizophrenia can benefit from behavioral therapies, including:

- Illness management—Once patients learn basic facts about schizophrenia and its treatment, they can make informed decisions about their care and watch for the early warning signs of relapse.

- Rehabilitation—This involves social and vocational training to help people with schizophrenia function better in their communities.

- Family education—People with schizophrenia are often discharged from the hospital into the care of their families, so it is important that family members learn about the illness. With the help of a therapist, family members can learn coping strategies and problem-solving skills.

- Cognitive-behavioral therapy—Therapy helps patients to understand and cope with symptoms that do not go away even when they take medication.

- Mutual support groups—These groups provide support and help people feel less isolated.

## Treatment for Posttraumatic Stress Disorder

Trauma is a widespread, harmful and costly public health concern. It may occur as a result of violence, abuse, neglect, loss, disaster, war, and other emotionally harmful experiences. Posttraumatic stress disorder (PTSD) is a reaction to traumatic stress, and people with PTSD may feel stressed or frightened even when they are no longer in danger following a traumatic event. PTSD can affect different people, from survivors of sexual or physical assault or natural disasters to military service men and women. Not everyone who experiences trauma develops PTSD. However, about 10% of women and 5% of men are diagnosed with PTSD in their lifetime. Learn more about trauma and violence.

Treatment strategies work best when they are customized to meet a person with PTSD's individual needs. The selection of treatment and services should also reflect an individual's stage of recovery. Some of the most common forms of treatment for PTSD include:

- **Exposure therapy** helps people face and control their fear by exposing them to the trauma they experienced in a safe way. It uses mental imagery, writing, or visits to the place where the event happened to encourage the development of coping strategies.

- **Cognitive restructuring** helps people make sense of bad memories and address negative thinking.

- **Psychological therapies** teach people helpful ways to react to frightening events that trigger their PTSD symptoms.

Medications are often prescribed with behavioral therapy to treat the common co-occurrence of depression, related anxiety disorders, aggression, or impulsivity. Emerging complementary and alternative treatments such as meditation, acupuncture, and relaxation therapy may help people with PTSD. Research on therapy dogs for PTSD has been called for because anecdotal reports are promising, but controlled studies have not yet been completed.

# Chapter 22

# *Recovery and the Role of Parents, Caregivers, Friends, and Family Members*

## *Recovery is Possible*

Most people with mental health problems can get better. Treatment and recovery are ongoing processes that happen over time. The first step is getting help.

## *What Is Recovery?*

Recovery from mental disorders and/or substance abuse disorders is a process of change through which individuals:

- Improve their health and wellness
- Live a self-directed life
- Strive to achieve their full potential

---

This chapter includes excerpts from "Recovery Is Possible," U.S. Department of Health and Human Services (HHS), May 31, 2013; and text from "For Parents and Caregivers," U.S. Department of Health and Human Services (HHS), May 31, 2013.

## Four Dimensions of Recovery

Four major dimensions support a life in recovery:
1.  Health: Make informed, healthy choices that support physical and emotional wellbeing.

2.  Home: Have a stable and safe place to live.

3.  Purpose: Engage in meaningful daily activities, such as a job or school, volunteering, caring for your family, or being creative. Work for independence, income, and resources to participate in society.

4.  Community: Build relationships and social networks that provide support.

## Develop a Recovery Plan

If you are struggling with a mental health problem, you may want to develop a written recovery plan.

Recovery plans:

*   Enable you to identify goals for achieving wellness

*   Specify what you can do to reach those goals

*   Include daily activities as well as longer term goals

*   Track any changes in your mental health problem

*   Identify triggers or other stressful events that can make you feel worse, and help you learn how to manage them

## For Parents and Caregivers

As a parent or caregiver, you want the best for your children or other dependents. You may be concerned or have questions about certain behaviors they exhibit and how to ensure they get help.

### What to Look For?

It is important to be aware of warning signs that your child may be struggling. You can play a critical role in knowing when your child may need help.

Consult with a school counselor, school nurse, mental health provider, or another health care professional if your child shows one or more of the following behaviors:

- Feeling very sad or withdrawn for more than two weeks

- Seriously trying to harm or kill himself or herself, or making plans to do so

- Experiencing sudden overwhelming fear for no reason, sometimes with a racing heart or fast breathing

- Getting in many fights or wanting to hurt others

- Showing severe out-of-control behavior that can hurt oneself or others

- Not eating, throwing up, or using laxatives to make himself or herself lose weight

- Having intense worries or fears that get in the way of daily activities

- Experiencing extreme difficulty controlling behavior, putting himself or herself in physical danger or causing problems in school

- Using drugs or alcohol repeatedly

- Having severe mood swings that cause problems in relationships

- Showing drastic changes in behavior or personality

Because children often can't understand difficult situations on their own, you should pay particular attention if they experience:

- Loss of a loved one

- Divorce or separation of their parents

- Any major transition – new home, new school, etc.

- Traumatic life experiences, like living through a natural disaster

- Teasing or bullying

- Difficulties in school or with classmates

### What to Do?

If you are concerned your child's behaviors, it is important to get appropriate care. You should:

- Talk to your child's doctor, school nurse, or another health care provider and seek further information about the behaviors or symptoms that worry you

- Ask your child's primary care physician if your child needs further evaluation by a specialist with experience in child behavioral problems

- Ask if your child's specialist is experienced in treating the problems you are observing

- Talk to your medical provider about any medication and treatment plans

### *How to Talk about Mental Health?*

Do you need help starting a conversation with your child about mental health? Try leading with these questions. Make sure you actively listen to your child's response.

- Can you tell me more about what is happening? How you are feeling?

- Have you had feelings like this in the past?

- Sometimes you need to talk to an adult about your feelings. I'm here to listen. How can I help you feel better?

- Do you feel like you want to talk to someone else about your problem?

- I'm worried about your safety. Can you tell me if you have thoughts about harming yourself or others?

When talking about mental health problems with your child you should:

- Communicate in a straightforward manner

- Speak at a level that is appropriate to a child or adolescent's age and development level (preschool children need fewer details than teenagers)

- Discuss the topic when your child feels safe and comfortable

- Watch for reactions during the discussion and slow down or back up if your child becomes confused or looks upset

- Listen openly and let your child tell you about his or her feelings and worries

### *For Friends and Family Members*

Anyone can experience mental health problems. Friends and family can make all the difference in a person's recovery process.

## *Supporting a Friend or Family Member with Mental Health Problems*

You can help your friend or family member by recognizing the signs of mental health problems and connecting them to professional help.

Talking to friends and family about mental health problems can be an opportunity to provide information, support, and guidance. Learning about mental health issues can lead to:

- Improved recognition of early signs of mental health problems

- Earlier treatment

- Greater understanding and compassion

If a friend or family member is showing signs of a mental health problem or reaching out to you for help, offer support by:

- Finding out if the person is getting the care that he or she needs and wants—if not, connect him or her to help

- Expressing your concern and support

- Reminding your friend or family member that help is available and that mental health problems can be treated

- Asking questions, listening to ideas, and being responsive when the topic of mental health problems come up

- Reassuring your friend or family member that you care about him or her

- Offering to help your friend or family member with everyday tasks

- Including your friend or family member in your plans—continue to invite him or her without being overbearing, even if your friend or family member resists your invitations

- Educating other people so they understand the facts about mental health problems and do not discriminate

- Treating people with mental health problems with respect, compassion, and empathy

## *How to Talk about Mental Health*

Do you need help starting a conversation about mental health? Try leading with these questions and make sure to actively listen to your friend or family member's response.

- I've been worried about you. Can we talk about what you are experiencing? If not, who are you comfortable talking to?

- What can I do to help you to talk about issues with your parents or someone else who is responsible and cares about you?

- What else can I help you with?

- I am someone who cares and wants to listen. What do you want me to know about how you are feeling?

- Who or what has helped you deal with similar issues in the past?

- Sometimes talking to someone who has dealt with a similar experience helps. Do you know of others who have experienced these types of problems who you can talk with?

- It seems like you are going through a difficult time. How can I help you to find help?

- How can I help you find more information about mental health problems?

- I'm concerned about your safety. Have you thought about harming yourself or others?

When talking about mental health problems:

- Know how to connect people to help

- Communicate in a straightforward manner

- Speak at a level appropriate to a person's age and development level (preschool children need fewer details as compared to teenagers)

- Discuss the topic when and where the person feels safe and comfortable

- Watch for reactions during the discussion and slow down or back up if the person becomes confused or looks upset

Sometimes it is helpful to make a comparison to a physical illness. For example, many people get sick with a cold or the flu, but only a few get really sick with something serious like pneumonia. People who have a cold are usually able to do their normal activities. However, if they get pneumonia, they will have to take medicine and may have to go to the hospital.

Similarly, feelings of sadness, anxiety, worry, irritability, or sleep problems are common for most people. However, when these feelings get very intense, last for a long period of time, and begin to interfere with school, work, and relationships, it may be a sign of a mental health problem. And just like people need to take medicine and get professional help for physical conditions, someone with a mental health problem may need to take medicine and/or participate in therapy in order to get better.

### *Get Help for Your Friend or Family Member*

Seek immediate assistance if you think your friend or family member is in danger of harming themselves. You can call a crisis line or the National Suicide Prevention Line at 1-800-273-TALK (8255).

# Chapter 23

# *Mental Health Care Services*

## *Chapter Contents*

# Section 23.1

# *Types of Mental Health Professionals*

This section includes excerpts from "Types of Therapists," U.S. Department of Veterans Affairs (VA), August 14, 2015; and text from "Finding a Mental Health Provider for Children and Families in Your Early Head Start/Head Start Program," U.S. Department of Health and Human Services (HHS), January 12, 2014.

## *Types of Therapists*

Mental health professionals can have different training, credentials, or licenses. Providers can also offer different services, based upon their expertise. If you are looking for a particular type of treatment (like medications) or expert focus, the license and specialized training of the mental health provider is important.

The information below reviews the most common types of licensed mental health providers and generally explains their education, training, and services offered. Whether or not a therapist needs a license to provide psychotherapy and the requirements to be licensed varies by state. Your health insurance provider may also allow you to see only certain types of mental health providers. Check your policy for details.

### *Psychologists*

Licensed clinical psychologists focus on mental health assessment and treatment. They have a doctoral degree (e.g., PhD, PsyD, EdD) from 4 or more years of graduate training in clinical or counseling psychology. To be licensed to practice, psychologists must have another 1 to 2 years of supervised clinical experience. Psychologists have the title of "doctor" because of their doctoral degree, but in most states they cannot prescribe medicine.

### *Clinical Social Workers*

The purpose of social work is to enhance human well-being by helping people meet basic human needs. Licensed social workers also focus on diagnosis and treatment, and specialize in areas such as mental health, aging, of family and children. Most licensed social workers have a master's degree from 2 years of graduate training (e.g., MSW) or a doctoral degree in social work (e.g., DSW or PhD).

## *Master's Level Clinicians*

Master's level clinicians have a master's degree in counseling, psychology, or marriage and family therapy (e.g., MA, MFT). To be licensed to provide individual and/or group counseling, master's level clinicians must meet requirements that vary by state.

## *Psychiatrists*

Psychiatrists have either a Doctor of Allopathic Medicine (MD) or Doctor of Osteopathic Medicine (DO) degree in addition to specialized training in the diagnosis and treatment of mental health problems. Since they are medical doctors, psychiatrists can prescribe medicine. Some may also provide psychotherapy.

## *Psychiatric Nurses or Nurse Practitioners*

Psychiatric mental health nurses (PMHN) can have different levels of training. Most are registered nurses (RN) with additional training in psychiatry or psychology. Psychiatric mental health advanced practice registered nurses (PMH-APRN) have a graduate degree. Psychiatric nurse practitioners are registered nurse practitioners with specialized training in the diagnosis and treatment of mental health problems. In most states, psychiatric nurses and psychiatric nurse practitioners can prescribe medicine.

## What Education, Skills, and Attributes Should a Mental Health Provider Have?

Mental health providers should have the licensure, education, experience, and attributes that support high quality services.

## *Education*

Typically, a mental health provider has a minimum of a master's degree in a human services field with licensure or certification from an accredited state board. Common types of mental health professionals include marriage and family therapists, social workers, psychiatrists, and psychologists. Table 23.1 describes the level of education and licensure each type of mental health provider requires.

**Table 23.1.** Common Types of Mental Health Providers and Level of Education

| Marriage and family therapist | Marriage and family therapists (MFT) have a master's degree and clinical experience in marriage and family therapy. |
|---|---|
| Social worker | Licensed clinical social workers (LCSW/ LICSW) have a master's in social work (MSW) along with additional clinical training. |
| Psychiatrist | A psychiatrist is a physician (MD or DO) who specializes in mental Health. Because they are medical doctors, psychiatrists can prescribe Medication. |
| Psychologist | Psychologists have a doctoral degree in psychology (PhD or PsyD) and are licensed in clinical psychology. |
| Counselor | Licensed professional counselors (LPC) or licensed mental health counselors (LMHC) have a master's degree in counseling |

## *Experience*

Services for children and families are likely to be more successful when a mental health provider is experienced in treating the specific challenges the family is facing. Often, a mental health provider has a special area of focus, such as depression, childhood trauma, or substance abuse. Experienced providers have seen the problems faced repeatedly by children and families, which can broaden their view and give them added insight.

Important to early child and family work is the mental health providers' experience with and ability to:

- conduct and interpret mental health screening and assessment s for very young children

- facilitate a family-centered approach to services

- use evidence-based practices

- have knowledge of and sensitivity to the first language of families

- use treatment methods that reflect the culture-specific values and treatment needs of clients (Center for Substance Abuse Prevention, 1994).

## *Attributes*

Mental health providers are typically required to have training in ethical conduct covering topics such as tolerance, integrity, boundaries, and self-awareness. Yet, a mental health professional's "way of being" can greatly affect the success of a child and family's experience with therapeutic work. Important attributes to look for in any mental health provider include:

Strong communication skills with the ability to listen and engage in shared decision-making.

- A strength-based perspective that supports a family's sense of hope.

- Flexibility to adjust one's schedule and expectations to the needs of the family.

- Dependability—showing up on time and regularly.

- Open-mindedness—accepting where families are in the process.

## *Approach / Orientation*

Another important component to consider when looking for mental health providers is their approach to mental health work (often referred to as their "orientation"). Mental health providers have very different approaches to their work based on their training and experience. Some therapists adopt a particular approach to their work that may be informed by a specific theoretical perspective and others use a more eclectic approach—drawing from multiple theories and orientations. Some therapists might provide their clients with guidance on how to change specific behaviors that are problematic while others may focus more on the quality of the relationships that a parent or child has with other family members. Knowing what a family expects or is most comfortable with before a referral can assist program staff in linking a family to the right mental health provider. For example, one family may prefer a therapist with a more behavioral approach who might suggest specific strategies. Another family may be more comfortable with a therapist who spends more time listening, reflecting, and asking questions about their relationships.

# Section 23.2

# *Types of Psychotherapies*

Text in this section is excerpted from "Psychotherapies," National
Institute of Mental Health (NIMH), 2008. Reviewed March 2016.

## What is Psychotherapy?

Psychotherapy, or "talk therapy," is a way to treat people with a
mental disorder by helping them understand their illness. It teaches
people strategies and gives them tools to deal with stress and unhealthy
thoughts and behaviors. Psychotherapy helps patients manage their
symptoms better and function at their best in everyday life.

Sometimes psychotherapy alone may be the best treatment for a
person, depending on the illness and its severity. Other times, psychotherapy is combined with medications. Therapists work with an
individual or families to devise an appropriate treatment plan.

## What Are the Different Types of Psychotherapy?

Many kinds of psychotherapy exist. There is no "one-size-fits-all"
approach. In addition, some therapies have been scientifically tested
more than others. Some people may have a treatment plan that
includes only one type of psychotherapy. Others receive treatment
that includes elements of several different types. The kind of psychotherapy a person receives depends on his or her needs.

This section explains several of the most commonly used psychotherapies. However, it does not cover every detail about psychotherapy. Patients should talk to their doctor or a psychotherapist about
planning treatment that meets their needs.

### *Cognitive Behavioral Therapy*

Cognitive behavioral therapy (CBT) is a blend of two therapies:
cognitive therapy (CT) and behavioral therapy. CT was developed by
psychotherapist Aaron Beck, M.D., in the 1960s. CT focuses on a person's thoughts and beliefs, and how they influence a person's mood and

actions, and aims to change a person's thinking to be more adaptive and healthy. Behavioral therapy focuses on a person's actions and aims to change unhealthy behavior patterns.

CBT helps a person focus on his or her current problems and how to solve them. Both patient and therapist need to be actively involved in this process. The therapist helps the patient learn how to identify distorted or unhelpful thinking patterns, recognize and change inaccurate beliefs, relate to others in more positive ways, and change behaviors accordingly.

CBT can be applied and adapted to treat many specific mental disorders.

## CBT for depression

Many studies have shown that CBT is a particularly effective treatment for depression, especially minor or moderate depression. Some people with depression may be successfully treated with CBT only. Others may need both CBT and medication. CBT helps people with depression restructure negative thought patterns. Doing so helps people interpret their environment and interactions with others in a positive and realistic way. It may also help a person recognize things that may be contributing to the depression and help him or her change behaviors that may be making the depression worse.

## CBT for anxiety disorders

CBT for anxiety disorders aims to help a person develop a more adaptive response to a fear. A CBT therapist may use "exposure" therapy to treat certain anxiety disorders, such as a specific phobia, post traumatic stress disorder, or obsessive compulsive disorder. Exposure therapy has been found to be effective in treating anxiety-related disorders. It works by helping a person confront a specific fear or memory while in a safe and supportive environment. The main goals of exposure therapy are to help the patient learn that anxiety can lessen over time and give him or her the tools to cope with fear or traumatic memories.

## CBT for bipolar disorder

People with bipolar disorder usually need to take medication, such as a mood stabilizer. But CBT is often used as an added treatment. The medication can help stabilize a person's mood so that he or she is receptive to psychotherapy and can get the most out of it. CBT can help a person cope with bipolar symptoms and learn to recognize when a mood shift is about to occur. CBT also helps a person with bipolar disorder stick with a treatment plan to reduce the chances of relapse (e.g., when symptoms return).

### *CBT for eating disorders*

Eating disorders can be very difficult to treat. However, some small studies have found that CBT can help reduce the risk of relapse in adults with anorexia who have restored their weight. CBT may also reduce some symptoms of bulimia, and it may also help some people reduce binge-eating behavior.

### *CBT for schizophrenia*

Treating schizophrenia with CBT is challenging. The disorder usually requires medication first. But research has shown that CBT, as an add-on to medication, can help a patient cope with schizophrenia. CBT helps patients learn more adaptive and realistic interpretations of events. Patients are also taught various coping techniques for dealing with "voices" or other hallucinations. They learn how to identify what triggers episodes of the illness, which can prevent or reduce the chances of relapse.

CBT for schizophrenia also stresses skill-oriented therapies. Patients learn skills to cope with life's challenges. The therapist teaches social, daily functioning, and problem-solving skills. This can help patients with schizophrenia minimize the types of stress that can lead to outbursts and hospitalizations.

## *Dialectical Behavior Therapy*

Dialectical behavior therapy (DBT), a form of CBT, was developed by Marsha Linehan, Ph.D. At first, it was developed to treat people with suicidal thoughts and actions. It is now also used to treat people with borderline personality disorder (BPD). BPD is an illness in which suicidal thinking and actions are more common.

The term "dialectical" refers to a philosophic exercise in which two opposing views are discussed until a logical blending or balance of the two extremes—the middle way—is found. In keeping with that philosophy, the therapist assures the patient that the patient's behavior and feelings are valid and understandable. At the same time, the therapist coaches the patient to understand that it is his or her personal responsibility to change unhealthy or disruptive behavior.

DBT emphasizes the value of a strong and equal relationship between patient and therapist. The therapist consistently reminds the patient when his or her behavior is unhealthy or disruptive—when boundaries are overstepped—and then teaches the skills needed to better deal with future similar situations. DBT involves both individual and group therapy. Individual sessions are used to teach new skills, while group sessions provide the opportunity to practice these skills.

Research suggests that DBT is an effective treatment for people with BPD. A recent NIMH-funded study found that DBT reduced suicide attempts by half compared to other types of treatment for patients with BPD.

## *Interpersonal Therapy*

Interpersonal therapy (IPT) is most often used on a one-on-one basis to treat depression or dysthymia (a more persistent but less severe form of depression). The current manual-based form of IPT used today was developed in the 1980's by Gerald Klerman, M.D., and Myrna Weissman, M.D.

IPT is based on the idea that improving communication patterns and the ways people relate to others will effectively treat depression. IPT helps identify how a person interacts with other people. When a behavior is causing problems, IPT guides the person to change the behavior. IPT explores major issues that may add to a person's depression, such as grief, or times of upheaval or transition. Sometimes IPT is used along with antidepressant medications.

IPT varies depending on the needs of the patient and the relationship between the therapist and patient. Basically, a therapist using IPT helps the patient identify troubling emotions and their triggers. The therapist helps the patient learn to express appropriate emotions in a healthy way. The patient may also examine relationships in his or her past that may have been affected by distorted mood and behavior. Doing so can help the patient learn to be more objective about current relationships.

Studies vary as to the effectiveness of IPT. It may depend on the patient, the disorder, the severity of the disorder, and other variables. In general, however, IPT is found to be effective in treating depression.

A variation of IPT called interpersonal and social rhythm therapy (IPSRT) was developed to treat bipolar disorder. IPSRT combines the basic principles of IPT with behavioral psychoeducation designed to help patients adopt regular daily routines and sleep/wake cycles, stick with medication treatment, and improve relationships. Research has found that when IPSRT is combined with medication, it is an effective treatment for bipolar disorder. IPSRT is as effective as other types of psychotherapy combined with medication in helping to prevent a relapse of bipolar symptoms.

## Family-Focused Therapy

Family-focused therapy (FFT) was developed by David Miklowitz, Ph.D., and Michael Goldstein, Ph.D., for treating bipolar disorder. It was designed with the assumption that a patient's relationship with his or her family is vital to the success of managing the illness. FFT includes family members in therapy sessions to improve family relationships, which may support better treatment results.

Therapists trained in FFT work to identify difficulties and conflicts among family members that may be worsening the patient's illness. Therapy is meant to help members find more effective ways to resolve those difficulties. The therapist educates family members about their loved one's disorder, its symptoms and course, and how to help their relative manage it more effectively. When families learn about the disorder, they may be able to spot early signs of a relapse and create an action plan that involves all family members. During therapy, the therapist will help family members recognize when they express unhelpful criticism or hostility toward their relative with bipolar disorder. The therapist will teach family members how to communicate negative emotions in a better way. Several studies have found FFT to be effective in helping a patient become stabilized and preventing relapses.

FFT also focuses on the stress family members feel when they care for a relative with bipolar disorder. The therapy aims to prevent family members from "burning out" or disengaging from the effort. The therapist helps the family accept how bipolar disorder can limit their relative. At the same time, the therapist holds the patient responsible for his or her own well being and actions to a level that is appropriate for the person's age.

Generally, the family and patient attend sessions together. The needs of each patient and family are different, and those needs determine the exact course of treatment. However, the main components of a structured FFT usually include:

- Family education on bipolar disorder,
- Building communication skills to better deal with stress, and
- Solving problems together as a family.

It is important to acknowledge and address the needs of family members. Research has shown that primary caregivers of people with bipolar disorder are at increased risk for illness themselves. For example, a 2007 study based on results from the NIMH-funded Systematic Treatment Enhancement Program for Bipolar Disorder (STEP-BD) trial found that primary caregivers of participants were at high risk for developing sleep problems and chronic conditions, such as high blood pressure. However, the caregivers were less likely to see a doctor for their own health issues. In addition, a 2005 study found that 33 percent of caregivers of bipolar patients had clinically significant levels of depression.

## Are Psychotherapies Different for Children and Adolescents?

Psychotherapies can be adapted to the needs of children and adolescents, depending on the mental disorder. For example, the NIMH-funded Treatment of Adolescents with Depression Study (TADS) found that CBT, when combined with antidepressant medication, was the most effective treatment over the short term for teens with major depression. CBT by itself was also an effective treatment, especially over the long term. Studies have found that individual and group-based CBT are effective treatments for child and adolescent anxiety disorders. Other studies have found that IPT is an effective treatment for child and adolescent depression.

Psychosocial treatments that involve a child's parents and family also have been shown to be effective, especially for disruptive disorders such as conduct disorder or oppositional defiant disorder. Some effective treatments are designed to reduce the child's problem behaviors and improve parent-child interactions. Focusing on behavioral parent management training, parents are taught the skills they need to encourage and reward positive behaviors in their children. Similar training helps parents manage their child's attention deficit/hyperactivity disorder (ADHD). This approach, which has been shown to be effective, can be combined with approaches directed at children to help them learn problem-solving, anger management and social interaction skills.

Family-based therapy may also be used to treat adolescents with eating disorders. One type is called the Maudsley approach, named after the Maudsley Hospital in London, where the approach was developed. This type of outpatient family therapy is used to treat anorexia nervosa in adolescents. It considers the active participation of parents to be essential in the recovery of their teen. The Maudsley approach proceeds through three phases:

- **Weight restoration**. Parents become fully responsible for ensuring that their teen eats. A therapist helps parents better understand their teen's disease. Parents learn how to avoid criticizing their teen, but they also learn to make sure that their teen eats.

- **Returning control over eating to the teen.** Once the teen accepts the control parents have over his or her eating habits, parents may begin giving up that control. Parents are encouraged to help their teen take more control over eating again.

- **Establishing healthy adolescent identity.** When the teen has reached and maintained a healthy weight, the therapist helps him or her begin developing a healthy sense of identity and autonomy.

Several studies have found the Maudsley approach to be successful in treating teens with anorexia. Currently a large-scale, NIMH-funded study on the approach is under way.

## What Other Types of Therapies Are Used?

In addition to the therapies listed above, many more approaches exist. Some types have been scientifically tested more than others. Also, some of these therapies are constantly evolving. They are often combined with more established psychotherapies. A few examples of other therapies are described here.

**Psychodynamic therapy.** Historically, psychodynamic therapy was tied to the principles of psychoanalytic theory, which asserts that a person's behavior is affected by his or her unconscious mind and past experiences. Now therapists who use psychodynamic therapy rarely include psychoanalytic methods. Rather, psychodynamic therapy helps people gain greater self-awareness and understanding about their own actions. It helps patients identify and explore how their nonconscious emotions and motivations can influence their behavior. Sometimes ideas from psychodynamic therapy are interwoven with other types of therapy, like CBT or IPT, to treat various types of mental disorders. Research on psychodynamic therapy is mixed. However, a review of clinical trials involving psychodynamic therapy found it to be as effective as other established psychotherapies.

**Light therapy.** Light therapy is used to treat seasonal affective disorder (SAD), a form of depression that usually occurs during the autumn and winter months, when the amount of natural sunlight decreases. Scientists think SAD occurs in some people when their bodies' daily rhythms are upset by short days and long nights. Research has found that the hormone melatonin is affected by this seasonal change. Melatonin normally works to regulate the body's rhythms and responses to light and dark. During light therapy, a person sits in front of a "light box" for periods of time, usually in the morning. The box emits a full spectrum light, and sitting in front of it appears to help reset the body's daily rhythms. Also, some research indicates that a low dose of melatonin, taken at specific times of the day, can also help treat SAD.

Other types of therapies sometimes used in conjunction with the more established therapies include:

- **Expressive or creative arts therapy.** Expressive or creative arts therapy is based on the idea that people can help heal themselves through art, music, dance, writing, or other expressive acts. One study has found that expressive writing can reduce depression symptoms among women who were victims of domestic violence. It also helps college students at risk for depression.

- **Animal-assisted therapy.** Working with animals, such as horses, dogs, or cats, may help some people cope with trauma, develop empathy, and encourage better communication. Companion animals are sometimes introduced in hospitals, psychiatric wards, nursing homes, and other places where they may bring comfort and have a mild therapeutic effect. Animal-assisted therapy has also been used as an added therapy for children with mental disorders. Research on the approach is limited, but a recent study found it to be moderately effective in easing behavioral problems and promoting emotional well-being.

- **Play therapy.** This therapy is used with children. It involves the use of toys and games to help a child identify and talk about his or her feelings, as well as establish communication with a therapist. A therapist can sometimes better understand a child's problems by watching how he or she plays. Research in play therapy is minimal.

## What Research Is Underway to Improve Psychotherapies?

Researchers are continually studying ways to better treat mental disorders with psychotherapy, and many NIMH-funded studies are underway.

## How Do I Find a Psychotherapist?

Your family doctor can help you find a psychotherapist.

## Section 23.3

# *Assertive Community Treatment*

Text in this section is excerpted from "Building Your Program,"
U.S. Department of Health and Human Services, 2008.
Reviewed March 2016.

### *How Assertive Community Treatment Began?*

Assertive Community Treatment (ACT) started when a group of mental health professionals at the Mendota Mental Health Institute in Wisconsin—Arnold Marx, M.D.; Leonard Stein, M.D.; and Mary Ann Test, Ph.D.—recognized that many consumers were discharged from inpatient care in stable condition, only to be readmitted relatively soon afterward. Practitioners and consumers were frustrated.

This group looked at how the mental health system worked and tried to figure out what could be done so that consumers could remain in their communities and have a life that was not driven by their illness.

They recognized that the type and intensity of services available to consumers immediately decreased after they left the hospital. The group also realized that, even when hospital staff spent considerable time teaching consumers skills that they needed to live in the community, consumers were often unable to apply these skills once they actually lived in the community.

Adjusting to a community setting was worsened by the fact that consumers who experience serious psychiatric symptoms may be particularly vulnerable to the stress associated with change. Consumers often had difficulty getting the services and support they needed to prevent relapse because the mental health system was complex and services were fragmented.

Many programs were available only for a limited time. Once consumers were discharged, assistance ended. Sometimes consumers were denied services or they were unable to apply for services because of problems caused by the symptoms of their mental illness. Sometimes the service consumers needed did not even exist, and no one was responsible for making sure consumers got the help they needed to stay out of the hospital.

## What the Originators Did?

The group learned from the actions of a social worker, Barb Lontz. They moved inpatient staff into the community to work with consumers in the settings where they lived and worked. They created multidisciplinary teams which gave consumers the support, treatment, and rehabilitation services they needed to continue living in the community.

The types of services that were provided and how long those services were provided depended on consumers' needs. Team members pooled their experience and knowledge and worked together to ensure that consumers had the help they needed and that the treatment they received was effective.

Every day, ACT team members met to discuss how each consumer was doing; they quickly adjusted services, when necessary. When consumers needed more support, team members met with them more frequently.

Team members responded to consumers in the community 24 hours a day, 7 days a week. As consumers improved, team members decreased their interactions with them, but remained available to give additional support any time it was needed. After 30 years, the principles of this model remain the same.

## Principles of ACT

- ACT is a service-delivery model, not a case management program.

- The primary goal of ACT is recovery through community treatment and habilitation.

  ACT is characterized by:

- a team approach—Practitioners with various professional training and general life skills work closely together to blend their knowledge and skills.

- in vivo services—Services are delivered in the places and contexts where they are needed.

- a small caseload—An ACT team consists of 10 to 12 staff members who serve about 100 consumers, resulting in a staff-to-consumer ratio of approximately 1 to 10.

- time-unlimited services—A service is provided as long as needed,

- a shared caseload—Practitioners do not have individual caseloads; rather, the team as a whole is responsible for ensuring that consumers receive the services they need to live in the community and reach their personal goals.

- a flexible service delivery—The ACT team meets daily to discuss how each consumer is doing. The team members can quickly adjust their services to respond to changes in consumers' needs.

- a fixed point of responsibility—Rather than sending consumers to various providers for services, the ACT team provides the services that consumers need. If using another provider cannot be avoided (e.g., medical care), the team makes certain that consumers receive the services they need.

- 24/7 crisis availability—Services are available 24 hours a day, 7 days a week. However, team members often find that they can anticipate and avoid crises.

- ACT is for consumers with the most challenging and persistent problems.

- Programs that adhere most closely to the ACT model are more likely to get the best outcomes.

## *What ACT Is?*

ACT is a way of delivering comprehensive and effective services to consumers who have needs that have not been well met by traditional approaches to delivering services. At the heart of ACT is a transdisciplinary team of 10 to 12 practitioners who provide services to about 100 people.

ACT teams directly deliver services to consumers instead of brokering services from other agencies or providers. For the most part, to ensure that services are highly integrated, team members are cross-trained in one another's areas of expertise.

ACT team members collaborate on assessments, treatment planning, and day-to-day interventions. Instead of practitioners having individual caseloads, team members are jointly responsible for making sure that each consumer receives the services needed to support recovery from mental illness.

The course of recovery from serious mental illness, and what it means to have a life that is not defined by a serious mental illness, differ among consumers. Consequently, ACT services are highly individualized. No arbitrary time limits dictate the length of time consumers receive services.

Most services are provided in vivo, that is, in the community settings where problems may occur and where support is needed rather than in staff offices or clinics. By providing services in this way, consumers receive the treatment and support they need to address the complex, real-world problems that can hinder their recovery.

Every day, ACT teams review each consumer's status so that the ACT team can quickly adjust the nature and intensity of services as needs change. At times, team members may meet with consumers several times a day but, as consumers' needs and goals change, the nature and frequency of contacts with them also change.

## *How We Know That ACT Is Effective?*

Since the original ACT program began in Madison, Wisconsin nearly 30 years ago, programs have been implemented in 35 States and in Canada, England, Sweden, Australia, and the Netherlands. As ACT spread, researchers carefully studied its effectiveness. Reviews of ACT research consistently conclude that, compared with other treatments (e.g., brokered or clinical case management programs), when faithfully implemented, ACT greatly reduces psychiatric hospitalization and leads to a higher level of housing stability.

Research also shows that, compared to other treatments, ACT has the same or a better effect on consumers' quality of life, symptoms, and social functioning. In addition, consumers and family members report greater satisfaction.

While studies consistently show that ACT is associated with many beneficial outcomes, the Patient Outcomes Research Team (PORT), consisting of researchers from the University of Maryland and Johns Hopkins University, found that people who might benefit from ACT often did not receive this intervention. Those findings ultimately led to creating this KIT.

In a growing trend, governmental and professional organizations see ACT as a fundamental element in a mental health service system. The Centers for Medicare and Medicaid Services (CMS) authorized ACT as a Medicaid-reimbursable treatment and ACT has been endorsed as an essential treatment for serious mental illness in the Surgeon General's Report on Mental Health (U.S. Department of Health and Human Services, 1999).

In the federal performance indicator system that the Substance Abuse and Mental Health Services Administration (SAMHSA) developed, accessibility to ACT services was one of three best-practice measures of the quality of a state's mental health system. Disseminating the ACT model has also been a top priority for the National Alliance on Mental Illness.

## *Core ACT services*

- crisis assessment and intervention;

- comprehensive assessment;

- illness management and recovery skills;

- individual supportive therapy;

- substance-abuse treatment;

- employment-support services;

- side-by-side assistance with activities of daily living;

- intervention with support networks (family, friends, landlords, neighbors, etc);

- support services, such as medical care, housing, benefits, transportation;

- case management; and

- medication prescription, administration, and monitoring.

# Chapter 24

# *Mental Health Medications for Adults*

## *Overview*

Medications can play a role in treating several mental disorders and conditions. Treatment may also include psychotherapy (also called "talk therapy") and brain stimulation therapies (less common). In some cases, psychotherapy alone may be the best treatment option. Choosing the right treatment plan should be based on a person's individual needs and medical situation, and under a mental health professional's care.

## *Understanding Your Medications*

If you are prescribed a medication, be sure that you:

- Tell the doctor about all medications and vitamin supplements you are already taking.

- Remind your doctor about any allergies and any problems you have had with medicines.

- Understand how to take the medicine before you start using it and take your medicine as instructed.

---

Text in this chapter is excerpted from "Mental Health Medications," National Institute of Mental Health (NIMH), January 2016.

- Don't take medicines prescribed for another person or give yours to someone else.

- Call your doctor right away if you have any problems with your medicine or if you are worried that it might be doing more harm than good. Your doctor may be able to adjust the dose or change your prescription to a different one that may work better for you.

- Report serious side effects to the FDA MedWatch Adverse Event Reporting program online at http://www.fda.gov/Safety/Med-Watch or by phone [1-800-332-1088]. You or your doctor may send a report.

## Antidepressants

### What Are Antidepressants?

Antidepressants are medications commonly used to treat depression. Antidepressants are also used for other health conditions, such as anxiety, pain and insomnia. Although antidepressants are not FDA-approved specifically to treat ADHD, antidepressants are sometimes used to treat ADHD in adults.

The most popular types of antidepressants are called selective serotonin reuptake inhibitors (SSRIs). Examples of SSRIs include:

- Fluoxetine

- Citalopram

- Sertraline

- Paroxetine

- Escitalopram

Other types of antidepressants are serotonin and norepinephrine reuptake inhibitors (SNRIs). SNRIs are similar to SSRIs and include-venlafaxine and duloxetine.

Another antidepressant that is commonly used is bupropion. Bupropionis a third type of antidepressant which works differently than either SSRIs or SNRIs. Bupropion is also used to treat seasonal affective disorder and to help people stop smoking.

SSRIs, SNRIs, and bupropion are popular because they do not cause as many side effects as older classes of antidepressants, and seem to help a broader group of depressive and anxiety disorders. Older antidepressant medications include tricyclics, tetracyclics, and monoamine oxidase inhibitors (MAOIs). For some people, tricyclics, tetracyclics, or MAOIs may be the best medications.

### *How Do People Respond to Antidepressants?*

According to a research review by the Agency for Healthcare Research and Quality, all antidepressant medications work about as well as each other to improve symptoms of depression and to keep depression symptoms from coming back. For reasons not yet well understood, some people respond better to some antidepressant medications than to others.

Therefore, it is important to know that some people may not feel better with the first medicine they try and may need to try several medicines to find the one that works for them. Others may find that a medicine helped for a while, but their symptoms came back. It is important to carefully follow your doctor's directions for taking your medicine at an adequate dose and over an extended period of time (often 4 to 6 weeks) for it to work.

Once a person begins taking antidepressants, it is important to not stop taking them without the help of a doctor. Sometimes people taking antidepressants feel better and stop taking the medication too soon, and the depression may return. When it is time to stop the medication, the doctor will help the person slowly and safely decrease the dose. It's important to give the body time to adjust to the change. People don't get addicted (or "hooked") on these medications, but stopping them abruptly may also cause withdrawal symptoms

### *What Are the Possible Side Effects of Antidepressants?*

Some antidepressants may cause more side effects than others. You may need to try several different antidepressant medications before finding the one that improves your symptoms and that causes side effects that you can manage.

The most common side effects listed by the FDA include:

- Nausea and vomiting
- Weight gain
- Diarrhea
- Sleepiness
- Sexual problems

Call your doctor right away if you have any of the following symptoms, especially if they are new, worsening, or worry you (U.S. Food and Drug Administration, 2011):

- Thoughts about suicide or dying
- Attempts to commit suicide
- New or worsening depression
- New or worsening anxiety
- Feeling very agitated or restless
- Panic attacks
- Trouble sleeping (insomnia)
- New or worsening irritability
- Acting aggressively, being angry, or violent
- Acting on dangerous impulses
- An extreme increase in activity and talking (mania)
- Other unusual changes in behavior or mood

Combining the newer SSRI or SNRI antidepressants with one of the commonly-used "triptan" medications used to treat migraine headaches could cause a life-threatening illness called "serotonin syndrome." A person with serotonin syndrome may be agitated, have hallucinations (see or hear things that are not real), have a high temperature, or have unusual blood pressure changes. Serotonin syndrome is usually associated with the older antidepressants called MAOIs, but it can happen with the newer antidepressants as well, if they are mixed with the wrong medications.

Antidepressants may cause other side effects that were not included in this list. To report any serious adverse effects associated with the use of antidepressant medicines, please contact the FDA MedWatch program using the contact information at the bottom of this page.

## Anti-Anxiety Medications

### What Are Anti-Anxiety Medications?

Anti-anxiety medications help reduce the symptoms of anxiety, such as panic attacks, or extreme fear and worry. The most common anti-anxiety medications are called benzodiazepines. Benzodiazepines can treat generalized anxiety disorder. In the case of panic disorder or social phobia (social anxiety disorder), benzodiazepines are usually second-line treatments, behind SSRIs or other antidepressants.

Benzodiazepines used to treat anxiety disorders include:

- Clonazepam
- Alprazolam
- Lorazepam

Short half-life (or short-acting) benzodiazepines (such as Lorazepam) and beta-blockers are used to treat the short-term symptoms of anxiety. Beta-blockers help manage physical symptoms of anxiety, such as trembling, rapid heartbeat, and sweating that people with phobias (an overwhelming and unreasonable fear of an object or situation, such as public speaking) experience in difficult situations. Taking these medications for a short period of time can help the person keep physical symptoms under control and can be used "as needed" to reduce acute anxiety.

Buspirone (which is unrelated to the benzodiazepines) is sometimes used for the long-term treatment of chronic anxiety. In contrast to the benzodiazepines, buspirone must be taken every day for a few weeks to reach its full effect. It is not useful on an "as-needed" basis.

## How Do People Respond to Anti-Anxiety Medications?

Anti-anxiety medications such as benzodiazepines are effective in relieving anxiety and take effect more quickly than the antidepressant medications (or buspirone) often prescribed for anxiety. However, people can build up a tolerance to benzodiazepines if they are taken over a long period of time and may need higher and higher doses to get the same effect. Some people may even become dependent on them. To avoid these problems, doctors usually prescribe benzodiazepines for short periods, a practice that is especially helpful for older adults people who have substance abuse problems and people who become dependent on medication easily. If people suddenly stop taking benzodiazepines, they may have withdrawal symptoms or their anxiety may return. Therefore, benzodiazepines should be tapered off slowly.

## What Are the Possible Side Effects of Anti-Anxiety Medications?

Like other medications, anti-anxiety medications may cause side effects. Some of these side effects and risks are serious. The most common side effects for benzodiazepines are drowsiness and dizziness. Other possible side effects include:

- Nausea
- Blurred vision
- Headache
- Confusion
- Tiredness
- Nightmares

Tell your doctor if any of these symptoms are severe or do not go away:

- Drowsiness
- Dizziness
- Unsteadiness
- Problems with coordination
- Difficulty thinking or remembering
- Increased saliva
- Muscle or joint pain
- Frequent urination
- Blurred vision
- Changes in sex drive or ability (The American Society of Health-System Pharmacists, Inc, 2010)

If you experience any of the symptoms below, call your doctor immediately:

- Rash
- Hives
- Swelling of the eyes, face, lips, tongue, or throat

- Difficulty breathing or swallowing
- Hoarseness
- Seizures
- Yellowing of the skin or eyes
- Depression
- Difficulty speaking
- Yellowing of the skin or eyes
- Thoughts of suicide or harming yourself
- Difficulty breathing

Common side effects of beta-blockers include:

- Fatigue
- Cold hands
- Dizziness or light-headedness
- Weakness

Beta-blockers generally are not recommended for people with asthma or diabetes because they may worsen symptoms related to both.

Possible side effects from buspirone include:

- Dizziness
- Headaches
- Nausea
- Nervousness
- Lightheadedness
- Excitement
- Trouble sleeping

Anti-anxiety medications may cause other side effects that are not included in the lists above. To report any serious adverse effects associated with the use of these medicines, please contact the FDA MedWatch program using the contact information at the bottom of this page.

## Stimulants

### What Are Stimulants?

As the name suggests, stimulants increase alertness, attention, and energy, as well as elevate blood pressure, heart rate, and respiration (National Institute on Drug Abuse, 2014). Stimulant medications are often prescribed to treat children, adolescents, or adults diagnosed with ADHD.

Stimulants used to treat ADHD include:

- Methylphenidate

- Amphetamine

- Dextroamphetamine

- Lisdexamfetamine Dimesylate

**Note:** In 2002, the FDA approved the non-stimulant medication atomoxetine for use as a treatment for ADHD. Two other non-stimulant antihypertensive medications, clonidine and guanfacine, are also approved for treatment of ADHD in children and adolescents. One of these non-stimulant medications is often tried first in a young person with ADHD, and if response is insufficient, then a stimulant is prescribed.

Stimulants are also prescribed to treat other health conditions, including narcolepsy, and occasionally depression (especially in older or chronically medically ill people and in those who have not responded to other treatments).

### How Do People Respond to Stimulants?

Prescription stimulants have a calming and "focusing" effect on individuals with ADHD. Stimulant medications are safe when given under a doctor's supervision. Some children taking them may feel slightly different or "funny."

Some parents worry that stimulant medications may lead to drug abuse or dependence, but there is little evidence of this when they are used properly as prescribed. Additionally, research shows that teens with ADHD who took stimulant medications were less likely to abuse drugs than those who did not take stimulant medications.

### What Are the Possible Side Effects of Stimulants?

Stimulants may cause side effects. Most side effects are minor and disappear when dosage levels are lowered. The most common side effects include:

- Difficulty falling asleep or staying asleep

- Loss of appetite

- Stomach pain

- Headache

Less common side effects include:

- Motor tics or verbal tics (sudden, repetitive movements or sounds)

- Personality changes, such as appearing "flat" or without emotion

Call your doctor right away if you have any of these symptoms, especially if they are new, become worse, or worry you.

Stimulants may cause other side effects that are not included in the list above. To report any serious adverse effects associated with the use of stimulants, please contact the FDA MedWatch program using the contact information at the bottom of this page.

## *What Are Antipsychotics?*

Antipsychotic medicines are primarily used to manage psychosis. The word "psychosis" is used to describe conditions that affect the mind, and in which there has been some loss of contact with reality, often including delusions (false, fixed beliefs) or hallucinations (hearing or seeing things that are not really there). It can be a symptom of a physical condition such as drug abuse or a mental disorder such as schizophrenia, bipolar disorder, or very severe depression (also known as "psychotic depression").

Antipsychotic medications are often used in combination with other medications to treat delirium, dementia, and mental health conditions, including:

- Attention-Deficit Hyperactivity Disorder (ADHD)

- Severe Depression

- Eating Disorders

- Posttraumatic Stress Disorder (PTSD)

- Obsessive Compulsive Disorder (OCD)

- Generalized Anxiety Disorder

Antipsychotic medicines do not cure these conditions. They are used to help relieve symptoms and improve quality of life.

Older or first-generation antipsychotic medications are also called conventional "typical" antipsychotics or "neuroleptics". Some of the common typical antipsychotics include:

- Chlorpromazine

- Haloperidol

- Perphenazine

- Fluphenazine

Newer or second generation medications are also called "atypical" antipsychotics. Some of the common atypical antipsychotics include:

- Risperidone

- Olanzapine

- Quetiapine

- Ziprasidone

- Aripiprazole

- Paliperidone

- Lurasidone

According to a 2013 research review by the Agency for Healthcare Research and Quality, typical and atypical antipsychotics both work to treat symptoms of schizophrenia and the manic phase of bipolar disorder.

Several atypical antipsychotics have a "broader spectrum" of action than the older medications, and are used for treating bipolar depression or depression that has not responded to an antidepressant medication alone.

## Antipsychotics

### *How Do People Respond to Antipsychotics?*

Certain symptoms, such as feeling agitated and having hallucinations, usually go away within days of starting an antipsychotic medication. Symptoms like delusions usually go away within a few weeks, but the full effects of the medication may not be seen for up to six weeks. Every patient responds differently, so it may take several trials of different antipsychotic medications to find the one that works best.

Some people may have a relapse—meaning their symptoms come back or get worse. Usually relapses happen when people stop taking their medication, or when they only take it sometimes. Some people stop taking the medication because they feel better or they may feel that they don't need it anymore, but no one should stop taking an antipsychotic medication without talking to his or her doctor. When a doctor says it is okay to stop taking a medication, it should be gradually tapered off—never stopped suddenly. Many people must stay on an antipsychotic continuously for months or years in order to stay well; treatment should be personalized for each individual.

## What are the possible side effects of antipsychotics?

Antipsychotics have many side effects (or adverse events) and risks. The FDA lists the following side effects of antipsychotic medicines:

- Drowsiness

- Dizziness

- Restlessness

- Weight gain (the risk is higher with some atypical antipsychotic medicines)

- Dry mouth

- Constipation

- Nausea

- Vomiting

- Blurred vision

- Low blood pressure

- Uncontrollable movements, such as tics and tremors (the risk is higher with typical antipsychotic medicines)

- Seizures

- A low number of white blood cells, which fight infections

A person taking an atypical antipsychotic medication should have his or her weight, glucose levels, and lipid levels monitored regularly by a doctor.

Typical antipsychotic medications can also cause additional side effects related to physical movement, such as:

- Rigidity

- Persistent muscle spasms

- Tremors

- Restlessness

Long-term use of typical antipsychotic medications may lead to a condition called tardive dyskinesia (TD). TD causes muscle movements, commonly around the mouth, that a person can't control. TD can range from mild to severe, and in some people, the problem cannot be cured. Sometimes people with TD recover partially or fully after they stop taking typical antipsychotic medication. People who think that they might have TD should check with their doctor before stopping their medication. TD rarely occurs while taking atypical antipsychotics.

Antipsychotics may cause other side effects that are not included in this list above. To report any serious adverse effects associated with the use of these medicines, please contact the FDA MedWatch program.

## Mood Stabilizers

### What Are Mood Stabilizers?

Mood stabilizers are used primarily to treat bipolar disorder, mood swings associated with other mental disorders, and in some cases, to augment the effect of other medications used to treat depression. Lithium, which is an effective mood stabilizer, is approved for the treatment of mania and the maintenance treatment of bipolar disorder. Mood stabilizers work by decreasing abnormal activity in the brain and are also sometimes used to treat:

- Depression (usually along with an antidepressant)

- Schizoaffective Disorder

- Disorders of impulse control

- Certain mental illnesses in children

Anticonvulsant medications are also used as mood stabilizers. They were originally developed to treat seizures, but they were found to help control unstable moods as well. One anticonvulsant commonly used as a mood stabilizer is valproic acid (also called divalproex sodium). For some people, especially those with "mixed" symptoms of mania and depression or those with rapid-cycling bipolar disorder, valproic acid may work better than lithium. Other anticonvulsants used as mood stabilizers include:

- Carbamazepine
- Lamotrigine
- Oxcarbazepine

**What are the possible side effects of mood stabilizers?**

Mood stabilizers can cause several side effects, and some of them may become serious, especially at excessively high blood levels. These side effects include:

- Itching, rash
- Excessive thirst
- Frequent urination
- Tremor (shakiness) of the hands
- Nausea and vomiting
- Slurred speech
- Fast, slow, irregular, or pounding heartbeat
- Blackouts
- Changes in vision
- Seizures
- Hallucinations (seeing things or hearing voices that do not exist)
- Loss of coordination
- Swelling of the eyes, face, lips, tongue, throat, hands, feet, ankles, or lower legs.

If a person with bipolar disorder is being treated with lithium, he or she should visit the doctor regularly to check the lithium levels his or her blood, and make sure the kidneys and the thyroid are working normally.

Lithium is eliminated from the body through the kidney, so the dose may need to be lowered in older people with reduced kidney function. Also, loss of water from the body, such as through sweating or diarrhea, can cause the lithium level to rise, requiring a temporary lowering of the daily dose. Although kidney functions are checked periodically during lithium treatment, actual damage of the kidney is uncommon in people whose blood levels of lithium have stayed within the therapeutic range.

Mood stabilizers may cause other side effects that are not included in this list. To report any serious adverse effects associated with the use of these medicines, please contact the FDA MedWatch program.

Some possible side effects linked anticonvulsants (such as valproic acid) include:

- Drowsiness
- Dizziness
- Headache
- Diarrhea
- Constipation
- Changes in appetite
- Weight changes
- Back pain
- Agitation
- Mood swings
- Abnormal thinking
- Uncontrollable shaking of a part of the body
- Loss of coordination
- Uncontrollable movements of the eyes
- Blurred or double vision
- Ringing in the ears
- Hair loss

These medications may also:

- Cause damage to the liver or pancreas, so people taking it should see their doctors regularly

- Increase testosterone (a male hormone) levels in teenage girls and lead to a condition called polycystic ovarian syndrome (a disease that can affect fertility and make the menstrual cycle become irregular)

Medications for common adult health problems, such as diabetes, high blood pressure, anxiety, and depression may interact badly with anticonvulsants. In this case, a doctor can offer other medication options.

## Special Groups: Children, Older Adults, Pregnant Women

All types of people take psychiatric medications, but some groups have special needs, including:

- Children and adolescents

- Older adults

- Women who are pregnant or who may become pregnant

### Children and Adolescents

Many medications used to treat children and adolescents with mental illness are safe and effective. However, some medications have not been studied or approved for use with children or adolescents.

Still, a doctor can give a young person an FDA-approved medication on an "off-label" basis. This means that the doctor prescribes the medication to help the patient even though the medicine is not approved for the specific mental disorder that is being treated or for use by patients under a certain age. Remember:

- It is important to watch children and adolescents who take these medications on an "off-label" basis.

- Children may have different reactions and side effects than adults.

- Some medications have current FDA warnings about potentially dangerous side effects for younger patients.

In addition to medications, other treatments for children and adolescents should be considered, either to be tried first, with medication added later if necessary, or to be provided along with medication. Psychotherapy, family therapy, educational courses, and behavior management techniques can help everyone involved cope with disorders that affect a child's mental health.

### Older Adults

People over 65 have to be careful when taking medications, especially when they're taking many different drugs. Older adults have a higher risk for experiencing bad drug interactions, missing doses, or overdosing.

Older adults also tend to be more sensitive to medications. Even healthy older people react to medications differently than younger people because older people's bodies process and eliminate medications more slowly. Therefore, lower or less frequent doses may be needed for older adults. Before starting a medication, older people and their family members should talk carefully with a physician about whether a medication can affect alertness, memory, or coordination, and how to help ensure that prescribed medications do not increase the risk of falls.

Sometimes memory problems affect older people who take medications for mental disorders. An older adult may forget his or her regular dose and take too much or not enough. A good way to keep track of medicine is to use a seven-day pill box, which can be bought at any pharmacy. At the beginning of each week, older adults and their caregivers fill the box so that it is easy to remember what medicine to take. Many pharmacies also have pill boxes with sections for medications that must be taken more than once a day.

### Women Who Are Pregnant or Who May Become Pregnant

The research on the use of psychiatric medications during pregnancy is limited. The risks are different depending on which medication is taken, and at what point during the pregnancy the medication is taken. Decisions on treatments for all conditions during pregnancy should be based on each woman's needs and circumstances, and based on a careful weighing of the likely benefits and risks of all available options, including psychotherapy (or "watchful waiting" during part or all of the pregnancy), medication, or a combination of the two. While no medication is considered perfectly safe for all women at all stages of pregnancy, this must be balanced for each woman against the fact that untreated serious mental disorders themselves can pose a risk to a pregnant woman and her developing fetus. Medications should be selected based on available scientific research, and they should be taken at the lowest possible dose. Pregnant women should have a medical professional who will watch them closely throughout their pregnancy and after delivery.

Most women should avoid certain medications during pregnancy. For example:

• Mood stabilizers are known to cause birth defects. Benzodiazepines and lithium have been shown to cause "floppy baby syndrome," in which a baby is drowsy and limp, and cannot breathe or feed well. Benzodiazepines may cause birth defects or other infant problems, especially if taken during the first trimester.

- According to research, taking antipsychotic medications during pregnancy can lead to birth defects, especially if they are taken during the first trimester and in combination with other drugs, but the risks vary widely and depend on the type of antipsychotic taken. The conventional antipsychotic haloperidol has been studied more than others, and has been found not to cause birth defects. Research on the newer atypical antipsychotics is ongoing.

Antidepressants, especially SSRIs, are considered to be safe during pregnancy. However, antidepressant medications do cross the placental barrier and may reach the fetus. Birth defects or other problems are possible, but they are very rare. The effects of antidepressants on childhood development remain under study.

Studies have also found that fetuses exposed to SSRIs during the third trimester may be born with "withdrawal" symptoms such as breathing problems, jitteriness, irritability, trouble feeding, or hypoglycemia (low blood sugar). Most studies have found that these symptoms in babies are generally mild and short-lived, and no deaths have been reported. Risks from the use of antidepressants need to be balanced with the risks of stopping medication; if a mother is too depressed to care for herself and her child, both may be at risk for problems.

In 2004, the FDA issued a warning against the use of certain antidepressants in the late third trimester. The warning said that doctors may want to gradually taper pregnant women off antidepressants in the third trimester so that the baby is not affected. After a woman delivers, she should consult with her doctor to decide whether to return to a full dose during the period when she is most vulnerable to postpartum depression.

After the baby is born, women and their doctors should watch for postpartum depression, especially if a mother stopped taking her medication during pregnancy. In addition, women who nurse while taking psychiatric medications should know that a small amount of the medication passes into the breast milk. However, the medication may or may not affect the baby depending s on the medication and when it is taken. Women taking psychiatric medications and who intend to breastfeed should discuss the potential risks and benefits with their doctors.

# Chapter 25

# *Mental Health Medications for Children and Adolescents*

## *Antidepressant Medications for Children and Adolescents: Information for Parents and Caregivers*

Depression is a serious disorder that can cause significant problems in mood, thinking, and behavior at home, in school, and with peers. It is estimated that major depressive disorder (MDD) affects about 5 percent of adolescents.

Research has shown that, as in adults, depression in children and adolescents is treatable. Certain antidepressant medications, called selective serotonin reuptake inhibitors (SSRIs), can be beneficial to children and adolescents with MDD. Certain types of psychological therapies also have been shown to be effective. However, our knowledge of antidepressant treatments in youth, though growing substantially, is limited compared to what we know about treating depression in adults.

Recently, there has been some concern that the use of antidepressant medications themselves may induce suicidal behavior in youths. Following a thorough and comprehensive review of all the available published and unpublished controlled clinical trials of antidepressants

Text in this chapter is excerpted from "Antidepressant Medications for Children and Adolescents: Information for Parents and Caregivers," National Institute of Mental Health (NIMH), July 9, 2010. Reviewed March 2016.

in children and adolescents, the U.S. Food and Drug Administration (FDA) issued a public warning in October 2004 about an increased risk of suicidal thoughts or behavior (suicidality) in children and adolescents treated with SSRI antidepressant medications. In 2006, an advisory committee to the FDA recommended that the agency extend the warning to include young adults up to age 25.

More recently, results of a comprehensive review of pediatric trials conducted between 1988 and 2006 suggested that the benefits of antidepressant medications likely outweigh their risks to children and adolescents with major depression and anxiety disorders. The study, partially funded by NIMH, was published in the April 18, 2007, issue of the Journal of the American Medical Association.

### What Did the FDA Review Find?

In the FDA review, no completed suicides occurred among nearly 2,200 children treated with SSRI medications. However, about 4 percent of those taking SSRI medications experienced suicidal thinking or behavior, including actual suicide attempts—twice the rate of those taking placebo, or sugar pills.

In response, the FDA adopted a "black box" label warning indicating that antidepressants may increase the risk of suicidal thinking and behavior in some children and adolescents with MDD. A black-box warning is the most serious type of warning in prescription drug labeling.

The warning also notes that children and adolescents taking SSRI medications should be closely monitored for any worsening in depression, emergence of suicidal thinking or behavior, or unusual changes in behavior, such as sleeplessness, agitation, or withdrawal from normal social situations. Close monitoring is especially important during the first four weeks of treatment. SSRI medications usually have few side effects in children and adolescents, but for unknown reasons, they may trigger agitation and abnormal behavior in certain individuals.

### What Do We Know about Antidepressant Medications?

The SSRIs include:

- fluoxetine (Prozac)
- sertraline (Zoloft)
- paroxetine (Paxil)
- citalopram (Celexa)

- escitalopram (Lexapro)

- fluvoxamine (Luvox)

Another antidepressant medication, venlafaxine (Effexor), is not an SSRI but is closely related.

SSRI medications are considered an improvement over older antidepressant medications because they have fewer side effects and are less likely to be harmful if taken in an overdose, which is an issue for patients with depression already at risk for suicide. They have been shown to be safe and effective for adults.

However, use of SSRI medications among children and adolescents ages 10 to 19 has risen dramatically in the past several years. Fluoxetine (Prozac) is the only medication approved by the FDA for use in treating depression in children ages 8 and older. The other SSRI medications and the SSRI-related antidepressant venlafaxine have not been approved for treatment of depression in children or adolescents, but doctors still sometimes prescribe them to children on an "off-label" basis. In June 2003, however, the FDA recommended that paroxetine not be used in children and adolescents for treating MDD.

Fluoxetine can be helpful in treating childhood depression, and can lead to significant improvement of depression overall. However, it may increase the risk for suicidal behaviors in a small subset of adolescents. As with all medical decisions, doctors and families should weigh the risks and benefits of treatment for each individual patient.

### What Should You Do for a Child with Depression?

A child or adolescent with MDD should be carefully and thoroughly evaluated by a doctor to determine if medication is appropriate. Psychotherapy often is tried as an initial treatment for mild depression. Psychotherapy may help to determine the severity and persistence of the depression and whether antidepressant medications may be warranted. Types of psychotherapies include "cognitive behavioral therapy," which helps people learn new ways of thinking and behaving, and "interpersonal therapy," which helps people understand and work through troubled personal relationships.

Those who are prescribed an SSRI medication should receive ongoing medical monitoring. Children already taking an SSRI medication should remain on the medication if it has been helpful, but should be carefully monitored by a doctor for side effects. Parents should promptly seek medical advice and evaluation if their child or adolescent experiences suicidal thinking or behavior, nervousness, agitation, irritability, mood instability, or sleeplessness that either emerges or worsens during treatment with SSRI medications.

Once started, treatment with these medications should not be abruptly stopped. Although they are not habit-forming or addictive, abruptly ending an antidepressant can cause withdrawal symptoms or lead to a relapse. Families should not discontinue treatment without consulting their doctor.

All treatments can be associated with side effects. Families and doctors should carefully weigh the risks and benefits, and maintain appropriate follow-up and monitoring to help control for the risks.

## What Does Research Tell Us?

An individual's response to a medication cannot be predicted with certainty. It is extremely difficult to determine whether SSRI medications increase the risk for completed suicide, especially because depression itself increases the risk for suicide and because completed suicides, especially among children and adolescents, are rare. Most controlled trials are too small to detect for rare events such as suicide (thousands of participants are needed). In addition, controlled trials typically exclude patients considered at high risk for suicide.

One major clinical trial, the NIMH-funded Treatment for Adolescents with Depression Study (TADS), has indicated that a combination of medication and psychotherapy is the most effective treatment for adolescents with depression. The clinical trial of 439 adolescents ages 12 to 17 with MDD compared four treatment groups—one that received a combination of fluoxetine and CBT, one that received fluoxetine only, one that received CBT only, and one that received a placebo only. After the first 12 weeks, 71 percent responded to the combination treatment of fluoxetine and CBT, 61 percent responded to the fluoxetine only treatment, 43 percent responded to the CBT only treatment, and 35 percent responded to the placebo treatment.

At the beginning of the study, 29 percent of the TADS participants were having clinically significant suicidal thoughts. Although the rate of suicidal thinking decreased among all the treatment groups, those in the fluoxetine/CBT combination treatment group showed the greatest reduction in suicidal thinking.

Researchers are working to better understand the relationship between antidepressant medications and suicide. So far, results are mixed. One study, using national Medicaid files, found that among adults, the use of antidepressants does not seem to be related to suicide attempts or deaths. However, the analysis found that the use of antidepressant medications may be related to suicide attempts and deaths among children and adolescents.

Another study analyzed health plan records for 65,103 patients treated for depression. It found no significant increase among adults and young people in the risk for suicide after starting treatment with newer antidepressant medications.

A third study analyzed suicide data from the National Vital Statistics and commercial prescription data. It found that among children ages five to 14, suicide rates from 1996 to 1998 were actually lower in areas of the country with higher rates of SSRI antidepressant prescriptions. The relationship between the suicide rates and the SSRI use rates, however, is unclear.

# Chapter 26

# *Brain Stimulation Therapies*

## *Noninvasive Brain Stimulation: Applications and Implications*

Though initially developed by scientists and clinicians to probe and modulate brain function, brain stimulation devices are now being sold directly to consumers with the promise they will enhance brain function or well being. These products claim they can increase cognitive performance, mathematical ability, attention span, problem solving, memory, and coordination as well as treat depression and chronic pain. It was clear from the presentations and discussions, however, that much work remains to be done to understand the short- and long-term impact of using these devices for medical and nonmedical purposes.

### *History of Brain Stimulation*

In 1831, Michael Faraday discovered electromagnetic induction, in which a varying magnetic field induces electrical current in a conductor placed within the field. The brain makes constant use of electricity to rapidly convey information via action potentials sent along axons—which are elegant biological examples of electrical conductors. Interestingly, humans have been attempting to use electricity to heal

---

Text in this chapter is excerpted from "Noninvasive Brain Stimulation: Applications and Implications," National Institute of Neurological Disorders and Stroke (NINDS), October 18, 2015.

the brain since long before this was understood. For example, stone carvings from the Fifth Dynasty of Egypt depict an electric fish being used to treat pain, and during the time of Socrates, electric fish were used to treat headaches and arthritis.

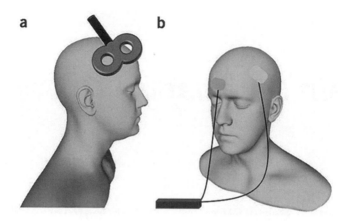

*Figure 26.1.* Typical Noninvasive Brain Stimulation (NIBS) setups

Developed in the 1940s, electroconvulsive therapy (ECT), electrical brain stimulation over one or both hemispheres to create a seizure, is highly effective in treating severe depression. In 1985 researchers seized upon Faraday's law of induction to stimulate discrete regions on the surface of the brain through the skull using a pulsed magnetic field. By connecting a wire coil to a source of electric current and placing the coil on the scalp over the motor cortex, Barker et al. gave the first example of transcranial magnetic stimulation (TMS). The mechanism by which TMS influences brain function is not completely understood, but we do know that TMS can activate axons and cause them to fire action potentials. TMS effects are not specific to inhibitory vs. excitatory neural activity, but may change the balance between excitation and inhibition.

The development of stimulators able to deliver long trains of closely spaced pulses enabled repetitive transcranial magnetic stimulation (rTMS) in the 1990s. This increased the scope of TMS from a neurophysiological probe to a tool with the potential for altering brain function. The growing scientific and clinical interest in noninvasive brain stimulation generated by TMS also led to the revitalization of transcranial direct current stimulation (tDCS), a technique originally applied to humans and animal models in the mid-20 century. Unlike TMS, which can produce a direct neuro stimulatory effect, tDCS does not usually elicit action potentials. Instead, tDCS is thought to exhibit a modulatory effect on brain function: the externally applied electric field displaces ions within neurons, altering neuronal excitability and modulating the firing rate of individual neurons. Most of the direct-to-consumer brain stimulation products are tDCS devices.

**Table 26.1.** History of Brain Stimulation

|      | Technique | How does it work? |
|------|-----------|-------------------|
| ECT  | Electroconvulsive Therapy | Electrodes are placed on the patient's scalp and a finely controlled electric current is applied while the patient is under general anesthesia. The current causes a brief seizure in the brain. |
| TMS  | Transcranial magnetic stimulation | An electromagnet placed on the scalp generates magnetic field pulses. Can activate axons and cause them to fire action potentials. |
| rTMS | Repetitive transcranial magnetic stimulation | Repeated application of TMS pulses. |
| tDCS | Transcranial direct current stimulation | Two small electrodes placed on the head deliver a constant low level of electric current, altering neuronal excitability. |

## Medical Indications for rTMS

Noninvasive brain stimulation is of great interest to clinicians and researchers, given its potential role in studying brain physiology and in treating diseases of the brain. It offers advantages as a diagnostic tool in that it can be used to observe disease-related changes in brain activation, inhibition, or connectivity. Based upon controlled studies the FDA has cleared TMS devices for therapeutic use with patients suffering from treatment-resistant major depressive disorder. Also, based on a randomized controlled clinical trial, the FDA granted premarket approval of a TMS device for the acute treatment of pain associated with migraine headache with aura. Researchers are also studying rTMS as a potential treatment for a range of other neurological diseases and disorders including stroke rehabilitation, chronic pain, epilepsy, obsessive-compulsive disorder, posttraumatic stress disorder, tinnitus, and movement disorders such as Parkinson disease. In general, researchers have found that for any given indication, patients need repeated rTMS treatment sessions, and combining rTMS with pharmacological and/or behavioral therapy may improve treatment effects. These observations are perhaps not surprising, given that neuroplasticity is likely fundamental to the therapeutic mechanism of noninvasive brain stimulation.

## Moving the Field Forward

It is reported that tDCS has the ability to improve learning of specific experimental tasks. Whether these generalize to clinically beneficial improved learning is less clear. Also reported were symptom improvements such as decreased anxiety and fatigue with tDCS. Progress in determining the medical benefit of brain stimulation devices is slowed by the lack of standardization across studies of pulse protocols, devices, and stimulation sites. With some exceptions the large randomized trials that are the norm for testing drugs have not been performed for non-invasive brain stimulation devices. This raises concern that positive results from smaller studies could occur simply by chance, due to natural variation and too small a sample size. Publication bias, which leads to the publication of positive results, but not negative results, adds to the concern. It is clear that for the science of non-invasive neuromodulation to advance, a concerted effort must occur to understand how these interventions affect neural circuit function in animals, and to conduct rigorous human studies with standardized protocols.

## Ethics of Neurostimulation to Enhance Performance

An area that was particularly fascinating concerned relevant ethical questions surrounding the distinction between enhancement and treatment. Treatment aims to restore normal functioning to people suffering from neurological, mental, or substance abuse disorders, while enhancement aims to improve the function of normal individuals.

Of course, people use various methods to achieve self-enhancement through neuromodulation, such as drinking coffee, exercising, meditating, and so on. Those methods are fairly universally embraced, but the discussion grows murky if noninvasive brain stimulation is included in the mix. rTMS is an existing technology to treat depression, but how would we think about using rTMS to help people feel 'better than normal? Or to help school children perform better on standardized testing? In general, are there special issues to consider in applying brain stimulation to the developing brains of children? There is a small but growing contingent of the public that is currently utilizing 'do it yourself' brain stimulation device despite the fact that this area of science is in its infancy and these devices are in no way regulated or approved by any group of technical experts–governmental, academic, or otherwise. Some companies are already positioning themselves to capture a bit of market share.

Going forward, research is necessary to better understand the changes that occur in the brain after both acute and chronic non-invasive brain stimulation. Not all brains are the same – some patients do not respond to non-invasive brain stimulation, and more studies are needed to determine which individuals are most likely to benefit from treatment. Broad discussions will be needed on not just the scientific, clinical, and regulatory issues, but also ethical questions surrounding noninvasive brain stimulation. Attention is needed not only on the treatment of people with neurological disease, but also the complicated ethical and social landscape of neuroenhancement.

Chapter 27

# Complementary and Alternative Medicine for Mental Health Care

## Chapter Contents

# Section 27.1

# *Herbal Remedies and Supplements for Mental Health*

This section includes excerpts from "Depression and Complementary Health Approaches," National Center for Complementary and Integrative Health (NCCIH), October 2015; text from "Ginkgo (Ginkgo Biloba)," National Institute of Diabetes and Digestive and Kidney Diseases (NIDDK), September 30, 2015; text from "Ginseng (Panax Gingseng)," National Institute of Diabetes and Digestive and Kidney Diseases (NIDDK), September 30 2015; and text from "Passionflower," National Center for Complementary and Integrative Health (NCCIH), October 2014.

## *Introduction*

Many individuals with depression turn to complementary health approaches as an adjunct to or in place of conventional treatment. Although these approaches are commonly used and readily available in the marketplace, many of these treatments have not been rigorously studied for depression. For this reason, it's important that you understand the benefits and risks of these complementary approaches to advise your patients.

A Task Force on Complementary and Alternative Medicine of the American Psychiatric Association conducted a review in 2010 of complementary approaches in psychiatry and found that, based on the quality of available evidence, there is enough evidence to support further research on some complementary approaches, including omega-3 fatty acids, St. John's wort *(Hypericum perforatum)*, folate, S-adenosyl-l-methionine (SAMe), light therapy, physical exercise, and mindfulness-based therapies for augmenting current treatments of depression in adults. However, the Task Force noted the need for more rigorous and larger studies before employing these complementary approaches.

## *Omega-3 Fatty Acids*

Some evidence suggests that omega-3 fatty acid supplementation may provide a small effect in adjunctive therapy in patients with a diagnosis of major depressive disorder (MDD) and on depressive patients without a diagnosis of MDD. Most trials have been adjunctive studies. Although the data are promising, controlled trials of omega-3 fatty acids as a monotherapy are inconclusive compared to standard antidepressant medicines, and it remains unclear that a mechanism is present to suggest that a pharmacological or biological antidepressant effect exists.

## The Evidence Base

- The evidence base on efficacy of omega-3 fatty acids for depression consists of many randomized controlled trials, as well as several systematic reviews and meta-analyses. Most randomized controlled trials of omega-3 fatty acids for MDD have been adjunctive studies, and it is important to note that evidence is limited due to variations in formulations and dosages of omega-3s, small sample size, mixed studies of augmentation and monotherapy, and durations of trials.

## Efficacy

- The 2010 American Psychiatric Association Task Force on Complementary and Alternative Medicine report found that adjunctive eicosapentaenoic acid (EPA) or the combination of EPA and docosahexaenoic acid (DHA) appear most useful, with less evidence for DHA alone. The report concluded that "the established general health benefits of omega-3 fatty acids, epidemiologic evidence, at most modest efficacy data, and low safety risks make omega-3 fatty acids a reasonable augmentation strategy in MDD."

- A 2013 review of clinical evidence of omega-3 fatty acids in psychiatry concluded that based on their safety profile and their potential efficacy, particularly in mood disorders, omega-3s deserve further study. The authors suggest that omega-3 fatty acids appear to be a well-tolerated adjunctive therapy for adults with depression, since most clinical trials have used omega-3 fatty acids as adjunctive agents.

- A 2008 Cochrane review of one study involving 75 participants investigating the efficacy of ethyl-EPA as an adjunctive treatment for participants with bipolar disorder found some positive benefits for depressive symptoms but not for mania.

- The most recent and rigorous double-blind, randomized controlled trial comparing EPA and DHA as monotherapy for MDD in 1,954 participants found that neither EPA-enriched nor DHA-enriched fatty acid supplementation was superior to placebo.

## *Safety*

- Omega-3 fatty acid supplements are generally safe and well-tolerated. When side effects do occur, they typically consist of minor gastrointestinal symptoms and fishy aftertaste.

- There is some concern that omega-3 supplements may extend bleeding time. The risk appears to be minimal, and should never be used in patients who take drugs that affect platelet function. It is important to discuss any potential herb-drug interactions with patients if they are considering using omega-3 fatty acids.

- It is uncertain whether people with fish or shellfish allergies can safely consume fish oil supplements and should not be used in such patients.

## *St. John's Wort* (Hypericum perforatum)

- There is some evidence that suggests St. John's wort *(Hypericum perforatum)* may have an effect on mild to moderate major depressive disorder (MDD) for a limited number of patients, similar to standard antidepressants, but the evidence is far from definitive. Although some studies have demonstrated a slight efficacy over placebo, others contradict these findings.

- The significant herb-drug interactions of St. John's wort *(Hypericum perforatum)* are important safety considerations and may outweigh any benefit of its use.

## *The Evidence Base*

- The evidence base on efficacy of *Hypericum perforatum* for depression consists of many randomized controlled trials and several systematic reviews and meta-analyses. Many of the studies in which findings were favorable were conducted in German-speaking countries.

## Efficacy

- The 2010 American Psychiatric Association Task Force on Complementary and Alternative Medicine report states that St. John's wort *(Hypericum perforatum)* may eventually become a reasonable treatment for mild to moderate major depressive disorder (MDD) for a limited number of individuals, although not all recent studies for the treatment of MDD demonstrated efficacy over placebo. The report also indicates any potential efficacy is only a greater consensus and support from studies in mild to moderate MDD.

- A 2015 systematic review and network meta-analysis of 66 studies involving 15,161 patients examined whether antidepressants and other agents, including St. John's wort *(Hypericum perforatum)*, may be more effective than placebo in the primary care setting. The reviewers found that St. John's wort *(Hypericum perforatum)*, as well as some other agents, showed some positive results, but because the current evidence is limited, conclusions about their place in clinical practice cannot be drawn.

- In a 2011 randomized controlled trial examining the treatment of minor depression with St. John's wort *(Hypericum perforatum)* or citalopram over the course of 12 weeks, neither St. John's wort nor citalopram showed any benefit over placebo.

- A 2012 study examined longer-term efficacy of St. John's wort *(Hypericum perforatum)* versus sertraline and placebo in patients with major depressive disorder and found that St. John's wort, sertraline, and placebo produced similar treatment effects over the course of 26 weeks.

- A 2008 Cochrane review of 29 studies involving 5,489 patients with depression concluded that the formulations of St. John's wort *(Hypericum perforatum)* extract tested in these trials were better than placebo in patients with major depression and were similarly effective as standard antidepressants.

## Safety

- Drug interactions with St. John's wort *(Hypericum perforatum)* limit use and are important safety considerations.

- Combining St. John's wort *(Hypericum perforatum)* and certain antidepressants can lead to serotonin syndrome, with dangerous symptoms ranging from tremor and diarrhea to very dangerous confusion, muscle stiffness, drop in body temperature, and even death.

• Other side effects of St. John's wort *(Hypericum perforatum)* are usually minor and uncommon and may include upset stomach and sensitivity to sunlight. Also, St. John's wort may worsen feelings of anxiety in some people.

• A rare, but possible side effect of taking St. John's wort *(Hypericum perforatum)* is psychosis. Those with certain mental health disorders, such as bipolar disorder, are at risk of experiencing this rare side effect. Therefore, it is important to discuss this potential side effect with patients who are considering using St. John's wort and encourage discontinuation of the herb if they experience a worsening of symptoms.

• Taking St. John's wort *(Hypericum perforatum)* increases the activity of cytochrome P450 3A4 (CYP3A4) enzyme and reduces plasma concentrations and can weaken many prescription medicines, such as:

• Antidepressants

• Oral contraceptives

• Cyclosporine

• Digoxin

• Some HIV drugs including indinavir

• Some chemotherapeutic agents including irinotecan

• Warfarin and other anticoagulants

## S-Adenosyl-L-Methionine (SAMe)

Current scientific evidence does not support the use of SAMe for the treatment of depression.

### The Evidence Base

• The evidence base on efficacy of SAMe for the treatment of depression consists of many randomized controlled trials; however, most of these trials were not rigorous because of their short duration, small sample size, and extensive methodological flaws. Early human studies utilized parenteral administration of SAMe, but more recent studies have used oral administration of stable SAMe preparations.

## *Efficacy*

- The 2010 American Psychiatric Association Task Force on Complementary and Alternative Medicine report suggest the need for more rigorous studies "to determine the efficacy of SAMe and its comparative efficacy to standard antidepressants."

- Preliminary results from a 2014 randomized controlled trial in a subsample of 144 participants with major depressive disorder (MDD) who received SAMe, escitalopram, or placebo for 12 weeks provided some evidence for the use of SAMe in the treatment of MDD. However, in the parent study, SAMe failed to demonstrate any advantage over placebo for MDD.

- A 2002 Agency for Healthcare Research and Quality meta-analysis of SAMe for depression found no statistically significant difference in outcomes compared to conventional antidepressants. Compared to placebo, treatment with SAMe was associated with clinically significant improvements equivalent to a partial response to treatment.

## *Safety*

- A 2009 review of evidence for SAMe for the treatment of MDD concluded that there is insufficient evidence examining whether the oral preparations of SAMe can be safe or efficacious when used as adjunctive treatment for patients with MDD who are unresponsive to antidepressants.

- Information on the long-term safety of SAMe is limited and inconclusive. However, in one study of alcohol-related liver disease in which participants took SAMe for 2 years, no serious side effects were reported.

- SAMe may decrease the effects of levodopa. It is also possible that SAMe might interact with drugs and dietary supplements that increase levels of serotonin, including some antidepressants, L-tryptophan, and St. John's wort, but the evidence for such interactions is very limited.

- SAMe promotes the growth of Pneumocystis, a fungus that can cause pneumonia in people with suppressed immune systems. It is possible that taking SAMe might increase the likelihood or severity of Pneumocystis infection in people who are HIV positive and should never be used in these patients.

- Side effects of SAMe appear to be uncommon, and when they do occur they are usually problems such as nausea or digestive upsets.

## Inositol

Current scientific evidence does not support the use of inositol for the treatment of depression.

### The Evidence Base

The current evidence for efficacy of inositol for depression consists of inadequate, small, randomized controlled trials and a single meta-analysis, as well as inclusion in a few systematic reviews along with other nutrient-based therapies for depressive disorders.

### Efficacy

- A 2014 meta-analysis of seven randomized controlled trials (two bipolar studies, one bipolar and major depressive disorder (MDD) study, two MDD studies, and two premenstrual dysphoric disorder (PMDD) studies) involving 242 participants found no significant treatment effect of inositol for depressed patients. However, inositol showed a trend of efficacy of depressive symptoms over placebo in patients with PMDD.

- A 2004 Cochrane review of four double-blind, randomized controlled trials involving a total of 141 participants found no clear evidence of a therapeutic benefit.

### Safety

- There is a paucity of data on the safety and side effects of inositol. A 2014 meta-analysis of inositol for depression and anxiety disorders found that inositol marginally caused gastrointestinal upset compared with placebo. A 2011 European review on the safety of inositol had similar findings in that inositol induced gastrointestinal side effects such as nausea, flatus, and diarrhea.

## Safe Use of Complementary Health Products and Practices

As with any treatment, it is important to consider safety before using complementary health products and practices. Safety depends

344

on the specific therapy, and each complementary product or practice should be considered on its own.

Mind and body practices such as meditation and yoga, for example, are generally considered to be safe in healthy people when practiced appropriately. Natural products such as herbal medicines or botanicals are often sold as dietary supplements and are readily available to consumers; however, there is a lot we don't know about the safety of many of these products, in part because a manufacturer does not have to prove the safety and effectiveness of a dietary supplement before it is available to the public.

Two of the main safety concerns for dietary supplements are

- The possibilities of drug interactions—for example, research has shown that St. John's wort interacts with drugs such as antidepressants in ways that can interfere with their intended effects

- The possibilities of product contamination—supplements have been found to contain hidden prescription drugs or other compounds, particularly in dietary supplements marketed for weight loss, sexual health including erectile dysfunction, and athletic performance or body-building.

## Ginko (Ginkgo Biloba)

### Introduction

Ginkgo is a popular herbal medication and extract derived from the leaves and seeds of the tree *Ginkgo biloba*. Ginkgo has not been implicated in causing liver injury.

### Background

Ginkgo is a widely used herbal derived from the leaves and seeds of the *Ginkgo biloba* tree, a "living fossil", being the only extant species of what was a large order of plants (Ginkgoales) more than 200 million years ago. Ginkgo is native to central China, but has been introduced worldwide. The word ginkgo derives from a Japanese approximation of the Chinese word for "silver apricot" referring to the tree's fruit. Extracts from ginkgo leaves and seeds were used in traditional Chinese medicine for centuries for a multitude of illnesses and conditions. Ginkgo extracts contain multiple compounds, but ginkgolides and bilobalide are unique to this herb. Ginkgo extracts have been shown to have antioxidant, anti-inflammatory and antihistaminic activity. Current uses are many and include dementia, memory loss, headache, dizziness, tinnitus, hearing problems, difficulty concentrating, mood disturbances, peripheral vascular disease, asthma, and bronchitis. Ginkgo is purported to increase mental acuity and delay the effects of aging on the brain, as well as improve peripheral circulation, prevent macular degeneration and decrease symptoms of claudication and Raynaud's syndrome. Ginkgo leaf extract is also used in foods, cosmetics, and skin lotions.

The scientific bases for the purported effects of ginkgo are not well established and clinical trials have shown no or only modest clinical effects in dementia, claudication and tinnitus. Ginkgo is available in a variety of formulations (tablets, capsules, powder, teas, and lotions) and the typical oral dosage is 120 to 240 mg per day in 2 to 3 divided doses. Side effects of ginkgo are uncommon and mild, and include gastrointestinal upset, nausea, diarrhea, headache, dizziness, increased bleeding tendency and rash. In clinical trials, both serious and common side effects have been no more frequent with ginkgo than placebo.

## *Hepatotoxicity*

Despite wide-spread use, ginkgo has not been specifically linked to liver injury, either in the form of transient serum enzyme elevations or clinically apparent acute liver injury. Indeed, ginkgo is sometimes used to treat acute or chronic liver injury. Gingko demonstrates some degree of inhibition of cytochrome P450 activity in vitro, but in doses used in humans it appears to have little effect on drug metabolism. Several instances of excessive bleeding during therapy with ginkgo have been attributed to drug interactions with antiplatelet medications or anticoagulants.

## *Ginseng (Panax Ginseng)*

### *Introduction*

Ginseng is a popular herbal medication and extract derived from the roots of a perennial plant (Panax ginseng) found mostly in China, Korea and Siberia. Ginseng is used is to promote health and improve wellness, as well as to treat stress and as a mild stimulant. Ginseng has not been implicated in causing liver injury although it may have the potential of causing significant herb-drug interactions that can lead to liver injury.

### *Background*

Ginseng is a widely used herbal derived from the roots of eleven distinct species of plants belonging to the genus Panax and family

Araliaceae. Ginseng grows in the Northern Hemisphere in eastern Asia, mostly China, Korea and Siberia. The form of ginseng most commonly used is Asian (or Chinese) ginseng made from the dried roots of Panax ginseng. American ginseng (Panax quinquefolius) has similar properties. The word ginseng derives from the Chinese character "rénshen" meaning "man root", which refers to the ginseng root's characteristic forked shape.

The botanical name Panax is derived from the Greek word meaning "all-heal" as in the term panacea. Ginseng is taken promote health and healing, as an adaptogen (to treat stress and enhance recovery from illness), aphrodisiac (to aid in sexual desire and performance) and a stimulant (wakefulness and mental acuity). Ginseng is also claimed to lower blood glucose levels and to be beneficial in diabetes. Ginseng is found in energy drinks as well as in many cosmetic preparations. The scientific bases for the purported effects of ginseng are not well established. Ginseng contains 30 different triterpene saponins, referred to as ginsenosides and panaxosides, which are considered the active compounds and which have antioxidant and stimulatory activities.

Commercial preparations of ginseng vary widely in ginsenoside content (some have none at all), which may cause variation in their biologic effects. The recommended daily dose varies widely (100 to >1,000 mg daily), depending on the preparation used (capsules, tablets, liquid, root extract, tea) and indications. Side effects of ginseng are uncommon and mild, and include inability to sleep, nausea, morning diarrhea, headaches, and nose bleeds.

## *Hepatotoxicity*

Despite wide spread use, ginseng by itself has not been linked to liver injury, either in the form of transient serum enzyme elevations or clinically apparent acute liver injury. Indeed, ginseng is sometimes used to treat acute or chronic liver injury, although its efficacy and safety in this situation have not been proven. Nevertheless, ginseng has been reported to affect cytochrome P450 activity and cause significant herb-drug interactions that can lead to adverse events including liver injury.

In vitro studies have found that different gensinosides have different effects on cytochrome P450 activity and some inhibit CYP 3A4 sufficiently to cause such interactions. Thus, different ginseng preparations may exhibit varying degrees of herb-drug interaction. Liver injury has been reported to develop 1 to 3 months after starting ginseng in patients who previously tolerated the potentially toxic agent (imatinib, raltegravir) without liver injury and who later tolerated restarting the medication without concurrent ginseng use.

## Passionflower

### Introduction

This fact sheet provides basic information about passionflower—common names, usefulness and safety, and resources for more information.

### Background

Sixteenth-century Spanish explorers learned of passionflower in Peru. Native peoples of the Americas used passionflower for boils, wounds, earaches, and liver problems.

Today, passionflower is used as a dietary supplement for anxiety, stress, and sleep, as well as for heart ailments, asthma, attention-deficit hyperactivity disorder, burns, and hemorrhoids.

Passionflower is available dried (which can be used to make tea), or as liquid extract, capsules, or tablets.

### How Much Do We Know?

Passionflower's effect on anxiety hasn't been studied extensively. A 2009 systematic review of two studies that included 198 people compared the ability of passionflower and two drugs to reduce anxiety. It concluded that the three substances had about the same degree of minimal effectiveness.

There isn't enough evidence to draw conclusions about passionflower for cardiovascular conditions, asthma, hemorrhoids, burns, or sleep.

### What Do We Know about Safety?

Passionflower is generally considered to be safe but may cause dizziness and confusion.

Taking passionflower with a sedative may increase the risk of excessive sleepiness.

Passionflower should not be used during pregnancy as it may induce contractions.

### Keep in Mind

Tell all your health care providers about any complementary health approaches you use. Give them a full picture of what you do to manage your health. This will help ensure coordinated and safe care.

Section 27.2

# *Physical Therapies for Mental Health*

This section includes excerpts from "Depression and Complementary Health Approaches," National Center for Complementary and Integrative Health (NCCIH), October 2015; text from "Massage Therapy for Health Purposes: What You Need to Know," National Center for Complementary and Integrative Health (NCCIH), May 2015; text from "Relaxation Techniques for Health," National Center for Complementary and Integrative Health (NCCIH), September 30, 2015; text from "Reiki: In Depth," National Center for Complementary and Integrative Health (NCCIH), October 2015; and text from "Meditation: In Depth," National Center for Complementary and Integrative Health (NCCIH), January 2016.

## *Acupuncture*

Current scientific evidence does not support the use of acupuncture for the treatment of depression.

### *The Evidence Base*

- The evidence base on efficacy of acupuncture for depression consists of several randomized controlled trials, systematic reviews, and meta-analyses. Findings from systematic reviews and meta-analyses have been at best inconsistent regarding efficacy, and there are only a few trials comparing manual acupuncture to control conditions. Evidence is limited due to different types of acupuncture studied, duration and frequency of sessions, and methodological flaws, including small sample sizes, and inconsistent randomization and blinding.

### *Efficacy*

- A 2010 Cochrane review of 30 studies involving 2,812 participants found insufficient evidence to support the use of acupuncture for people with depression. There was a high risk of bias in most of the trials included in the review, limiting any conclusions based on scientific rigor.

349

- The 2010 American Psychiatric Association Task Force on Complementary and Alternative Medicine report found that evidence for the efficacy of acupuncture as a primary treatment of depression is at best inconclusive, and studies to date have been unable to demonstrate efficacy of acupuncture compared to a control for the treatment of MDD.

## Safety

- Relatively few complications from using acupuncture have been reported. Still, complications have resulted from the use of non-sterile needles and improper delivery of treatments.

- When not delivered properly, acupuncture can cause serious adverse effects, including skin infections, punctured organs, pneumothoraces, and injury to the central nervous system.

## Music Therapy

There is some limited evidence that suggests music therapy may provide an improvement in mood.

### The Evidence Base

The evidence base on efficacy of music therapy for depression consists of a few randomized trials and a few systematic reviews.

### Efficacy

- Findings from a 2008 Cochrane review of five studies suggest that music therapy is accepted by people with depression and is associated with improvements in mood. However, because evidence is limited by the small number and low methodological quality of studies, its effectiveness remains unclear.

### Safety

There are no adverse effects associated with music therapy.

## Relaxation Techniques for Health

### What Are Relaxation Techniques?

Relaxation techniques include a number of practices such as progressive relaxation, guided imagery, biofeedback, self-hypnosis, and deep breathing exercises. The goal is similar in all: to produce the body's natural relaxation response, characterized by slower breathing, lower blood pressure, and a feeling of increased well-being.

Meditation and practices that include meditation with movement, such as yoga and tai chi, can also promote relaxation. Stress management programs commonly include relaxation techniques. Relaxation techniques have also been studied to see whether they might be of value in managing various health problems.

## How much do we know about relaxation techniques?

A substantial amount of research has been done on relaxation techniques. However, for many health conditions, the number or size of the studies has been small, and some studies have been of poor quality.

## What Do We Know about the Effectiveness of Relaxation Techniques?

Relaxation techniques may be helpful in managing a variety of health conditions, including anxiety associated with illnesses or medical procedures, insomnia, labor pain, chemotherapy-induced nausea, and temporomandibular joint dysfunction. Psychological therapies, which may include relaxation techniques, can help manage chronic headaches and other types of chronic pain in children and adolescents. Relaxation techniques have also been studied for other conditions, but either they haven't been shown to be useful, research results have been inconsistent, or the evidence is limited.

## What Do We Know about the Safety of Relaxation Techniques?

Relaxation techniques are generally considered safe for healthy people, although there have been a few reports of unpleasant experiences such as increased anxiety. People with serious physical or mental health problems should discuss relaxation techniques with their health care providers.

## The Importance of Practice

Relaxation techniques are skills, and like other skills, they need practice. People who use relaxation techniques frequently are more likely to benefit from them. Regular, frequent practice is particularly important if you're using relaxation techniques to help manage a chronic health problem. Continuing use of relaxation techniques is more effective than short-term use.

Relaxation techniques include the following:

## Autogenic Training

In autogenic training, you learn to concentrate on the physical sensations of warmth, heaviness, and relaxation in different parts of your body.

## Biofeedback-Assisted Relaxation

Biofeedback techniques measure body functions and give you information about them so that you can learn to control them. Biofeedback-assisted relaxation uses electronic devices to teach you to produce changes in your body that are associated with relaxation, such as reduced muscle tension.

## Deep Breathing or Breathing Exercises

This technique involves focusing on taking slow, deep, even breaths.

## Guided Imagery

For this technique, people are taught to focus on pleasant images to replace negative or stressful feelings. Guided imagery may be self-directed or led by a practitioner or a recording.

## Progressive Relaxation

This technique, also called Jacobson relaxation or progressive muscle relaxation, involves tightening and relaxing various muscle groups. Progressive relaxation is often combined with guided imagery and breathing exercises.

## Self-Hypnosis

In self-hypnosis programs, people are taught to produce the relaxation response when prompted by a phrase or nonverbal cue (called a "suggestion").

## What the Science Says about the Effectiveness of Relaxation Techniques?

Researchers have evaluated relaxation techniques to see whether they could play a role in managing a variety of health conditions, including the following:

## Anxiety

Studies have shown relaxation techniques may reduce anxiety in people with ongoing health problems such as heart disease or inflammatory bowel disease, and in those who are having medical procedures such as breast biopsies or dental treatment. Relaxation techniques have also been shown to be useful for older adults with anxiety.

On the other hand, relaxation techniques may not be the best way to help people with generalized anxiety disorder. Generalized anxiety disorder is a mental health condition, lasting for months or longer, in which a person is often worried or anxious about many things and finds it hard to control the anxiety. Studies indicate that long-term results are better in people with generalized anxiety disorder who receive a type of psychotherapy called cognitive-behavioral therapy than in those who are taught relaxation techniques.

## Depression

An evaluation of 15 studies concluded that relaxation techniques are better than no treatment in reducing symptoms of depression but are not as beneficial as psychological therapies such as cognitive-behavioral therapy.

## Posttraumatic Stress Disorder

Studies of biofeedback and other relaxation techniques for post-traumatic stress disorder have had inconsistent results.

## What the Science Says about the Safety and Side Effects of Relaxation Techniques?

Relaxation techniques are generally considered safe for healthy people. However, occasionally, people report unpleasant experiences such as increased anxiety, intrusive thoughts, or fear of losing control.

There have been rare reports that certain relaxation techniques might cause or worsen symptoms in people with epilepsy or certain psychiatric conditions, or with a history of abuse or trauma. People with heart disease should talk to their health care provider before doing progressive muscle relaxation.

## Reiki

### What Is Reiki?

Reiki is a complementary health approach in which practitioners place their hands lightly on or just above a person, with the goal of facilitating the person's own healing response.

Reiki is based on an Eastern belief in an energy that supports the body's innate or natural healing abilities. However, there isn't any scientific evidence that such an energy exists.

Reiki has been studied for a variety of conditions, including pain, anxiety, fatigue, and depression.

### How Much Do We Know about Reiki?

We don't know very much because little high-quality research has been done on Reiki.

### What Do We Know about the Effectiveness of Reiki?

Reiki hasn't been clearly shown to be useful for any health-related purpose.

### What Do We Know about the Safety of Reiki?

Reiki hasn't been shown to have any harmful effects. However, Reiki should not be used to replace conventional care or to postpone seeing a health care provider about a health problem.

### What the Science Says about the Effectiveness of Reiki?

Several groups of experts have evaluated the evidence on Reiki, and all of them have concluded that it's uncertain whether Reiki is helpful.

Only a small number of studies of Reiki have been completed, and most of them included only a few people. Different studies looked at different health conditions making it hard to compare their results. Many of the studies didn't compare Reiki with both sham (simulated) Reiki and with no treatment. Studies that include both of these comparisons are usually the most informative.

### What the Science Says about the Safety of Reiki?

Reiki appears to be generally safe. In studies of Reiki, side effects were no more common among participants who received Reiki than among those who didn't receive it.

## More to Consider

Reiki should not be used to replace conventional care or to postpone seeing a health care provider about a health problem. If you have severe or long-lasting symptoms, see your health care provider. You may have a health problem that needs prompt treatment.

Tell all your health care providers about any complementary health approaches you use. Give them a full picture of what you do to manage your health. This will help ensure coordinated and safe care.

# Meditation

## What Is Meditation?

Meditation is a mind and body practice that has a long history of use for increasing calmness and physical relaxation, improving psychological balance, coping with illness, and enhancing overall health and well-being. Mind and body practices focus on the interactions among the brain, mind, body, and behavior.

There are many types of meditation, but most have four elements in common: a quiet location with as few distractions as possible; a specific, comfortable posture (sitting, lying down, walking, or in other positions); a focus of attention (a specially chosen word or set of words, an object, or the sensations of the breath); and an open attitude (letting distractions come and go naturally without judging them).

## How Much Do We Know about Meditation?

Many studies have been conducted to look at how meditation may be helpful for a variety of conditions, such as high blood pressure, certain psychological disorders, and pain. A number of studies also have helped researchers learn how meditation might work and how it affects the brain.

## What Do We Know about the Effectiveness of Meditation?

Research suggests that practicing meditation may reduce blood pressure, symptoms of irritable bowel syndrome, anxiety and depression, insomnia, and the incidence, duration, and severity of acute respiratory illnesses (such as influenza). Evidence about its effectiveness for pain and as a smoking-cessation treatment is uncertain.

## What Do We Know about the Safety of Meditation?

Meditation is generally considered to be safe for healthy people. However, people with physical limitations may not be able to participate in certain meditative practices involving movement.

## What the Science Says about the Effectiveness of Meditation

Many studies have investigated meditation for different conditions, and there's evidence that it may reduce blood pressure as well as symptoms of irritable bowel syndrome and flare-ups in people who have had ulcerative colitis. It may ease symptoms of anxiety and depression, and may help people with insomnia. Meditation also may lower the incidence, duration, and severity of acute respiratory illnesses (such as influenza).

## Meditation and the Brain

Some research suggests that meditation may physically change the brain and body and could potentially help to improve many health problems and promote healthy behaviors.

- In a 2012 study, researchers compared brain images from 50 adult meditators and 50 adult non-meditators. Results suggested that people who practiced meditation for many years have more folds in the outer layer of the brain. This process (called gyrification) may increase the brain's ability to process information.

- A 2013 review of three studies suggests that meditation may slow, stall, or even reverse changes that take place in the brain due to normal aging.

- Results from a 2012 NCCIH-funded study suggest that meditation can affect activity in the amygdala (a part of the brain involved in processing emotions), and that different types of meditation can affect the amygdala differently even when the person is not meditating.

- Research about meditation's ability to reduce pain has produced mixed results. However, in some studies scientists suggest that meditation activates certain areas of the brain in response to pain.

## What the Science Says about Safety and Side Effects of Meditation

Meditation is generally considered to be safe for healthy people.

People with physical limitations may not be able to participate in certain meditative practices involving movement. People with physical health conditions should speak with their health care providers before starting a meditative practice, and make their meditation instructor aware of their condition.

There have been rare reports that meditation could cause or worsen symptoms in people with certain psychiatric problems like anxiety and depression. People with existing mental health conditions should speak with their health care providers before starting a meditative practice, and make their meditation instructor aware of their condition.

## Massage Therapy

### What Is Massage Therapy?

The term "massage therapy" includes many techniques, and the type of massage given usually depends on your needs and physical condition.

### For More Information

- Massage therapy dates back thousands of years. References to massage appear in ancient writings from China, Japan, India, and Egypt.

- In general, massage therapists work on muscle and other soft tissue to help you feel better.

- In Swedish massage, the therapist uses long strokes, kneading, deep circular movements, vibration, and tapping.

- Sports massage combines techniques of Swedish massage and deep tissue massage to release chronic muscle tension. It is adapted to the needs of athletes.

- Myofascial trigger point therapy focuses on trigger points— areas that are painful when pressed and are associated with pain elsewhere in the body.

- Massage therapy is sometimes done using essential oils as a form of aromatherapy.

### What the Science Says about the Effectiveness of Massage

A lot of the scientific research on massage therapy is preliminary or conflicting, but much of the evidence points toward beneficial effects on pain and other symptoms associated with a number of different conditions. Much of the evidence suggests that these effects are short term and that people need to keep getting massages for the benefits to continue.

Researchers have studied the effects of massage for many conditions.

## Effectiveness of Massage Therapy in Mental health

- A 2010 meta-analysis of 17 clinical trials concluded that massage therapy may help to reduce depression.

- Brief, twice-weekly yoga and massage sessions for 12 weeks were associated with a decrease in depression, anxiety, and back and leg pain in pregnant women with depression, a 2012 NCCIH-funded randomized controlled trial showed. Also, the women's babies weighed more than babies born to women who didn't receive the therapy.

- However, a 2013 research review concluded that there is not enough evidence to determine if massage helps pregnant mothers with depression.

- A 2010 review concluded that massage may help older people relax.

- For generalized anxiety disorder, massage therapy was no better at reducing symptoms than providing a relaxing environment and deep breathing lessons, according to a small, 2010 NCCIH-supported clinical trial.

## What the Science Says about the Safety and Side Effects of Massage Therapy

Massage therapy appears to have few risks when performed by a trained practitioner. However, massage therapists should take some precautions in people with certain health conditions.

## For More Information

- In some cases, pregnant women should avoid massage therapy. Talk with your health care provider before getting a massage if you are pregnant.

- People with some conditions such as bleeding disorders or low blood platelet counts should avoid having forceful and deep tissue massage. People who take anticoagulants (also known as blood thinners) also should avoid them. Massage should not be done in any potentially weak area of the skin, such as wounds.

- Deep or intense pressure should not be used over an area where the patient has a tumor or cancer, unless approved by the patient's health care provider.

# Section 27.3

# *Spirituality and Mental Health*

This section includes excerpts from "Spirituality and Trauma: Professionals Working Together," U.S. Department of Veterans Affairs (VA), February 23, 2016; and text from "Building Faith in Recovery: SAMHSA's Faith-Based and Community Initiatives," Substance Abuse and Mental Health Services Administration (SAMHSA), May 14, 2015.

## *Spirituality and Trauma: Professionals Working Together*

### *What Is Spirituality?*

Spirituality is a personal experience with many definitions. Spirituality might be defined as "an inner belief system providing an individual with meaning and purpose in life, a sense of the sacredness of life, and a vision for the betterment of the world." Other definitions emphasize "a connection to that which transcends the self." The connection might be to God, a higher power, a universal energy, the sacred, or to nature. Researchers in the field of spirituality have suggested three useful dimensions for thinking about one's spirituality:

- Beliefs

- Spiritual practices

- Spiritual experiences

Currently in the United States, opinion surveys consistently find that most people endorse a belief in God or higher power. In a 2007

Gallup Poll 86% of respondents indicated a belief in God, while only 6% stated they did not believe in God. Many of these individuals would describe religion or spirituality as the most important source of strength and direction for their lives. Because spirituality plays such a significant and central role in the lives of many people, it is likely to be affected by trauma, and in turn to affect the survivor's reaction to the trauma.

Historically, there have been differences between the beliefs of scientists and healthcare practitioners and those of the general population. For example, one study indicated that only 66% of psychologists report a "belief in God." These differences in viewpoint may contribute to the lack of research on spirituality. The beliefs and training experiences of practitioners may also influence whether and how spirituality is incorporated into therapy.

## *Relationship of Trauma to Spirituality*

Evidence suggests that trauma can produce both positive and negative effects on the spiritual experiences and perceptions of individuals. For example, depression and loneliness can lead to feelings of abandonment and loss of faith in God. These effects may change as time passes and a person moves further away from the acute phase of trauma recovery. On the positive side, some individuals experience increased appreciation of life, greater perceived closeness to God, increased sense of purpose in life, and enhanced spiritual well-being even following devastating events such as disasters and rape. For others, trauma can be associated with loss of faith, diminished participation in religious or spiritual activities, changes in belief, feelings of being abandoned or punished by God, and loss of meaning and purpose for living.

Aspects of spirituality are associated with positive outcomes, even when trauma survivors develop psychiatric difficulties such as PTSD or depression. Research also indicates that healthy spirituality is often associated with lower levels of symptoms and clinical problems in some trauma populations. For example, anger, rage, and a desire for revenge following trauma may be tempered by forgiveness, spiritual beliefs, or spiritual practices.

Suggestions have been made about the pathways by which spirituality might affect the recovery trajectory for survivors of traumatic events. Spirituality may improve post-trauma outcomes through: reduction of behavioral risks through healthy religious lifestyles (e.g., less drinking or smoking), expanded social support through involvement in spiritual communities, enhancement of coping skills and helpful ways of understanding trauma that result in meaning-making, and physiological mechanisms such as activation of the "relaxation response" through prayer or meditation. Feelings of isolation, loneliness, and depression related to grief and loss may be lessened by the social support of a spiritual community. Being part of a spiritual community places survivors among caring individuals who may provide encouragement and emotional support, as well as possible instrumental support in the form of physical or even financial assistance in times of trouble.

## Making Meaning of the Trauma Experience

Spiritual beliefs may influence the trauma survivor's ability to make meaning out of the trauma experience. In turn, the meaning drawn can have a significant impact on the survivor's symptoms and functioning. Several studies have indicated that negative thoughts or attributions about God, such as "God has abandoned me," and "God is punishing me," or, being angry at God are associated with a number of poor clinical outcomes. Research suggests that these types of thoughts can be associated with poorer physical and mental health, and increased use of substances. One study of Veterans being treated for PTSD found that negative religious coping and lack of forgiveness were both associated with worse PTSD and depression symptoms.

Recovery of meaning in life may be achieved through changed ways of thinking, involvement in meaningful activities, or through rituals experienced as part of religious or spiritual involvement. Some researchers have suggested that traumatic events frequently challenge one's core beliefs about safety, self worth, and the meaning of life. For individuals whose core values are spiritually grounded, traumatic events may give rise to questions about the fundamental nature of the relationship between the creator and humankind. Survivors may question their belief in a loving, all-powerful God when the innocent are subjected to traumatic victimization. In this way, traumatic experiences may become a starting point for discussion of the many ways in which survivors define what it is to have "faith."

## Guilt and Moral Injury

Additionally, in certain types of traumatic events, such as war, an individual can be both victim and perpetrator of trauma. For example, a soldier during their war-zone service could be exposed to the injury and death of others, be wounded himself or herself, and have a role in killing the enemy. It is also possible for two core elements of a person's world-view - for example, patriotism and faith - to be in conflict, creating doubt and uncertainty about the right course of action. These experiences can sometimes lead to long-lasting difficult spiritual and moral questions. The result may be loss of faith, increased guilt and self-blame, and alienation from other people and from God. Individuals may experience a disconnection between the beliefs they were raised with, their expectations about what military service would be like, and their actual war-zone experiences.

## Grief and Bereavement

Grief and loss can be significant issues that survivors must cope with in the aftermath of trauma. In U.S. society, spirituality is frequently utilized to cope with traumatic death and loss. Researchers noted after the 9/11 terrorist attacks that 90% of respondents reported turning to "prayer, religion, or spiritual feelings" as a coping mechanism. In general, research suggests there is a positive association between spirituality and grief recovery for survivors of traumatic loss. Researchers suggest that for many spirituality provides a frame through which survivors can "make sense" of the loss. Additionally survivors may benefit from supportive relationships often provided by spiritual communities.

# Part Four


# Pediatric Mental Health Concerns

Chapter 28

# Mental Health Care for Children and Teens

## Chapter Contents

# Section 28.1

# *Taking Your Child to a Therapist*

Sometimes kids, like adults, can benefit from therapy. Therapy can help kids develop problem-solving skills and also teach them the value of seeking help. Therapists can help kids and families cope with stress and a variety of emotional and behavioral issues.

Many kids need help dealing with school stress, such as homework, test anxiety, bullying, or peer pressure. Others need help to discuss their feelings about family issues, particularly if there's a major transition, such as a divorce, move, or serious illness.

## *Should My Child See a Therapist?*

Significant life events—such as the death of a family member, friend, or pet; divorce or a move; abuse; trauma; a parent leaving on military deployment; or a major illness in the family—can cause stress that might lead to problems with behavior, mood, sleep, appetite, and academic or social functioning.

In some cases, it's not as clear what's caused a child to suddenly seem withdrawn, worried, stressed, sulky, or tearful. But if you feel your child might have an emotional or behavioral problem or needs help coping with a difficult life event, trust your instincts.

Signs that a child may benefit from seeing a psychologist or licensed therapist include:

- developmental delay in speech, language, or toilet training

- learning or attention problems (such as ADHD)

- behavioral problems (such as excessive anger, acting out, bed wetting or eating disorders)

- a significant drop in grades, particularly if your child normally maintains high grades

- episodes of sadness, tearfulness, or depression
- social withdrawal or isolation
- being the victim of bullying or bullying other children
- decreased interest in previously enjoyed activities
- overly aggressive behavior (such as biting, kicking, or hitting)
- sudden changes in appetite (particularly in adolescents)
- insomnia or increased sleepiness
- excessive school absenteeism or tardiness
- mood swings (e.g., happy one minute, upset the next)
- development of or an increase in physical complaints (such as headache, stomachache, or not feeling well) despite a normal physical exam by your doctor
- management of a serious, acute, or chronic illness
- signs of alcohol, drug, or other substance use (such as solvents or prescription drug abuse)
- problems in transitions (following separation, divorce, or relocation)
- bereavement issues
- custody evaluations
- therapy following sexual, physical, or emotional abuse or other traumatic events

Kids who aren't yet school-age could benefit from seeing a developmental or clinical psychologist if there's a significant delay in achieving developmental milestones such as walking, talking, and potty training, and if there are concerns regarding autism or other developmental disorders.

## Talk to Caregivers, Teachers, and the Doctor

It's also helpful to speak to caregivers and teachers who interact regularly with your child. Is your child paying attention in class and turning in assignments on time? What's his or her behavior like at recess and with peers? Gather as much information as possible to determine the best course of action.

Discuss your concerns with your child's doctor, who can offer perspective and evaluate your child to rule out any medical conditions that could be having an effect. The doctor also may be able to refer you to a qualified therapist for the help your child needs.

## Finding the Right Therapist

**How do you find a qualified clinician who has experience working with kids and teens?** While experience and education are important, it's also important to find a counselor your child feels comfortable talking to. Look for one who not only has the right experience, but also the best approach to help your child in the current circumstances.

Your doctor can be a good source of a referral. Most doctors have working relationships with mental health specialists such as child psychologists or clinical social workers. Friends, colleagues, or family members might also be able to recommend someone.

Consider a number of factors when searching for the right therapist for your child. A good first step is to ask if the therapist is willing to meet with you for a brief consultation or to talk with you during a phone interview before you commit to regular visits. Not all therapists are able to do this, given their busy schedules. Most therapists charge a fee for this type of service; others consider it a free visit.

## Factors to Consider

Consider the following factors when evaluating a potential therapist:

- Is the therapist licensed to practice in your state? (You can check with the state board for that profession or check to see if the license is displayed in the office.)

- Is the therapist covered by your health insurance plan's mental health benefits? If so, how many sessions are covered by your plan? What will your co-pay be?

- What are his or her credentials?

- What type of experience does the therapist have?

- How long has the therapist worked with children and adolescents?

- Would your child find the therapist friendly?

- What is the cancellation policy if you're unable to keep an appointment?

- Is the therapist available by phone during an emergency?

- Who will be available to your child during the therapist's vacation or illness or during off-hours?

- What types of therapy does the therapist specialize in?

- Is the therapist willing to meet with you in addition to working with your child?

The right therapist–client match is critical, so you might need to meet with a few before you find one who clicks with both you and your child.

As with other medical professionals, therapists may have a variety of credentials and specific degrees. As a general rule, your child's therapist should hold a professional degree in the field of mental health (psychology, social work, or psychiatry) and be licensed by your state. Psychologists, social workers, and psychiatrists all diagnose and treat mental health disorders.

It's also a good idea to know what those letters that follow a therapist's name mean.

## Psychiatrists

Psychiatrists (MDs or DOs) are medical doctors who have advanced training and experience in psychotherapy and pharmacology. They can also prescribe medications.

## Clinical Psychologists

Clinical psychologists (PhDs, PsyDs, or EdDs) are therapists who have a doctorate degree that includes advanced training in the practice of psychology, and many specialize in treating children and teens and their families. Psychologists may help clients manage medications but do not prescribe medication.

## Clinical Social Workers

A licensed clinical social worker (LCSW) has a master's degree, specializes in clinical social work, and is licensed in the state in which he or she practices. An LICSW is also a licensed clinical social worker. A CSW is a certified social worker. Many social workers are trained in psychotherapy, but the credentials vary from state to state. Likewise, the designations (i.e., LCSW, LICSW, CSW) can vary from state to state.

## Different Types of Therapy

There are many types of therapy. Therapists choose the strategies that are most appropriate for a particular problem and for the individual child and family. Therapists will often spend a portion of each session with the parents alone, with the child alone, and with the family together.

Any one therapist may use a variety of strategies, including:

### Cognitive Behavioral Therapy (CBT)

This type of therapy is often helpful with kids and teens who are depressed, anxious, or having problems coping with stress.

Cognitive behavioral therapy restructures negative thoughts into more positive, effective ways of thinking. It can include work on stress management strategies, relaxation training, practicing coping skills, and other forms of treatment.

Psychoanalytic therapy is less commonly used with children but can be used with older kids and teens who may benefit from more in-depth analysis of their problems. This is the quintessential "talk therapy" and does not focus on short-term problem-solving in the same way as CBT and behavioral therapies.

In some cases, kids benefit from individual therapy, one-on-one work with the therapist on issues they need guidance on, such as depression, social difficulties, or worry. In other cases, the right option is group therapy, where kids meet in groups of 6 to 12 to solve problems and learn new skills (such as social skills or anger management).

Family therapy can be helpful in many cases, such as when family members aren't getting along; disagree or argue often; or when a child or teen is having behavior problems. Family therapy involves counseling sessions with some, or all, family members, helping to improve communication skills among them. Treatment focuses on problem-solving techniques and can help parents re-establish their role as authority figures.

## Preparing for the First Visit

You may be concerned that your child will become upset when told of an upcoming visit with a therapist. Although this is sometimes the case, it's essential to be honest about the session and why your child (or family) will be going. The issue will come up during the session, but it's important for you to prepare your child for it.

Explain to young kids that this type of visit to the doctor doesn't involve a physical exam or shots. You may also want to stress that this type of doctor talks and plays with kids and families to help them solve problems and feel better. Kids might feel reassured to learn that the therapist will be helping the parents and other family members too.

Older kids and teens may be reassured to hear that anything they say to the therapist is confidential and cannot be shared with anyone else, including parents or other doctors, without their permission—the exception is if they indicate that they're having thoughts of suicide or otherwise hurting themselves or others.

Giving kids this kind of information before the first appointment can help set the tone, prevent your child from feeling singled out or isolated, and provide reassurance that the family will be working together on the problem.

## Providing Additional Support

While your child copes with emotional issues, be there to listen and care, and offer support without judgment. Patience is critical, too, as many young children are unable to verbalize their fears and emotions.

Try to set aside some time to discuss your child's worries or concerns. To minimize distractions, turn off the TV and let voice mail answer your phone calls. This will let your child know that he or she is your first priority.

Other ways to communicate openly and problem-solve include:

- Talk openly and as frequently with your child as you can.

- Show love and affection to your child, especially during troubled times.

- Set a good example by taking care of your own physical and emotional needs.

- Enlist the support of your partner, immediate family members, your child's doctor, and teachers.

- Improve communication at home by having family meetings that end with a fun activity (e.g., playing a game, making ice-cream sundaes).

- No matter how hard it is, set limits on inappropriate or problematic behaviors. Ask the therapist for some strategies to encourage your child's cooperation.

- Communicate frequently with the therapist.

- Be open to all types of feedback from your child and from the therapist.

- Respect the relationship between your child and the therapist. If you feel threatened by it, discuss this with the therapist (it's nothing to be embarrassed about).

- Enjoy favorite activities or hobbies with your child.

By recognizing problems and seeking help early on, you can help your child and your entire family—move through the tough times toward happier, healthier times ahead.

## Section 28.2

# Helping Children and Teens Cope with Violence and Disaster

Text in this section is excerpted from "Helping Children and Adolescents Cope with Violence and Disasters: What Parents Can Do," National Institute of Mental Health (NIMH), 2013.

## Introduction

Each year, children experience violence and disaster and face other traumas. Young people are injured, they see others harmed by violence, they suffer sexual abuse, and they lose loved ones or witness other tragic and shocking events. Parents and caregivers can help children overcome these experiences and start the process of recovery.

## What Is Trauma?

"Trauma" is often thought of as physical injuries. Psychological trauma is an emotionally painful, shocking, stressful, and sometimes life-threatening experience. It may or may not involve physical injuries, and can result from witnessing distressing events. Examples include a natural disaster, physical or sexual abuse, and terrorism.

Disasters such as hurricanes, earthquakes, and floods can claim lives, destroy homes or whole communities, and cause serious physical and psychological injuries. Trauma can also be caused by acts of violence. The September 11, 2001 terrorist attack is one example. Mass shootings in schools or communities and physical or sexual assault are other examples. Traumatic events threaten our sense of safety.

Reactions (responses) to trauma can be immediate or delayed. Reactions to trauma differ in severity and cover a wide range of behaviors and responses. Children with existing mental health problems, past traumatic experiences, and/or limited family and social supports may be more reactive to trauma. Frequently experienced responses among children after trauma are loss of trust and a fear of the event happening again.

*It's Important to Remember:*

- Children's reactions to trauma are strongly influenced by adults' responses to trauma.
- People from different cultures may have their own ways of reacting to trauma

## Commonly Experienced Responses to Trauma among Children

*Children Age 5 and under May React in a Number of Ways Including:*

- Showing signs of fear
- Clinging to parent or caregiver
- Crying or screaming
- Whimpering or trembling
- Moving aimlessly
- Becoming immobile
- Returning to behaviors common to being younger
- Thumbsucking

- Bedwetting
- Being afraid of the dark.

*Children Age 6 to 11 May React By:*

- Isolating themselves
- Becoming quiet around friends, family, and teachers
- Having nightmares or other sleep problems
- Refusing to go to bed
- Becoming irritable or disruptive
- Having outbursts of anger
- Starting fights
- Being unable to concentrate
- Refusing to go to school
- Complaining of physical problems
- Developing unfounded fears
- Becoming depressed
- Expressing guilt over what happened
- Feeling numb emotionally
- Doing poorly with school and homework
- Losing interest in fun activities.

*Adolescents Age 12 to 17 May React By:*

- Having flashbacks to the event (flashbacks are the mind reliving the event)
- Having nightmares or other sleep problems
- Avoiding reminders of the event
- Using or abusing drugs, alcohol, or tobacco
- Being disruptive, disrespectful, or behaving destructively
- Having physical complaints
- Feeling isolated or confused

- Being depressed
- Being angry
- Losing interest in fun activities
- Having suicidal thoughts.

Adolescents may feel guilty. They may feel guilt for not preventing injury or deaths. They also may have thoughts of revenge.

## What Can Parents Do to Help?

After violence or disaster, parents and family members should identify and address their own feelings—this will allow them to help others. Explain to children what happened and let them know:

- You love them
- The event was not their fault
- You will do your best to take care of them
- It's okay for them to feel upset.

*Do:*

- Allow children to cry
- Allow sadness
- Let children talk about feelings
- Let them write about feelings
- Let them draw pictures about the event or their feelings.

*Don't:*

- Expect children to be brave or tough
- Make children discuss the event before they are ready
- Get angry if children show strong emotions
- Get upset if they begin bedwetting, acting out, or thumbsucking.

*Other Tips:*

- If children have trouble sleeping give them extra attention, let them sleep with a light on, or let them sleep in your room (for a short time).

- Try to keep normal routines, for example, reading bedtime stories, eating dinner together, watching TV together, reading books, exercising, or playing games. If you can't keep normal routines, make new ones together.

- Help children feel in control when possible by letting them choose meals, pick out clothes, or make some decisions for themselves.

## How Can I Help Young Children Who Experienced Trauma?

Helping children can start immediately, even at the scene of the event. Most children recover within a few weeks of a traumatic experience, while some may need help longer. Grief, a deep emotional response to loss, may take months to resolve. Children may experience grief over the loss of a loved one, teacher, friend, or pet. Grief may be re-experienced or worsened by news reports or the event's anniversary.

Some children may need help from a mental health professional. Some people may seek other kinds of help from community leaders. Identify children who need support and help them obtain it.

*Examples of Problematic Behaviors Could Be:*

- Refusing to go to places that remind them of the event

- Emotional numbness

- Behaving dangerously

- Unexplained anger/rage

- Sleep problems including nightmares.

## Adult Helpers Should:

*Pay Attention to Children*

- Listen to them

- Accept/do not argue about their feelings

- Help them cope with the reality of their experiences.

*Reduce Effects of Other Stressors, Such As*

- Frequent moving or changes in place of residence

- Long periods away from family and friends
- Pressures to perform well in school
- Transportation problems
- Fighting within the family
- Being hungry.

*Monitor Healing*

- It takes time
- Do not ignore severe reactions
- Pay attention to sudden changes in behaviors, speech, language use, or strong emotions.

*Remind Children That Adults*

- Love them
- Support them
- Will be with them when possible.

Parents and caregivers should also limit viewing of repetitive news reports about traumatic events. Young children may not understand that news coverage is about one event and not multiple similar events.

## Help for All People in the First Days and Weeks

There are steps adults can take following a disaster that can help them cope, making it easier for them to provide better care for children. These include creating safe conditions, remaining calm and friendly, and connecting with others. Being sensitive to people under stress and respecting their decisions is important.

*When Possible, Help People:*

- Get food
- Get a safe place to live
- Get help from a doctor or nurse if hurt
- Contact loved ones or friends
- Keep children with parents or relatives

- Understand what happened

- Understand what is being done

- Know where to get help.

*Don't:*

- Force people to tell their stories

- Probe for personal details

- Say things like "everything will be OK," or "at least you survived"

- Say what you think people should feel or how people should have acted

- Say people suffered because they deserved it

- Be negative about available help

- Make promises that you can't keep such as "you will go home soon."

## More about Trauma Stress

Some children will have prolonged mental health problems after a traumatic event. These may include grief, depression, anxiety, and posttraumatic stress disorder (PTSD). Some trauma survivors get better with some support. Others may need prolonged care from a mental health professional. If after a month in a safe environment children are not able to perform normal routines or new behavioral or emotional problems develop, then contact a health professional.

Factors influencing how someone may respond include:

- Being directly involved in the trauma, especially as a victim

- Severe and/or prolonged exposure to the event

- Personal history of prior trauma

- Family or personal history of mental illness and severe behavioral problems

- Limited social support; lack of caring family and friends

- Ongoing life stressors such as moving to a new home or new school, divorce, job change, or financial troubles.

Some symptoms may require immediate attention. Contact a mental health professional if these symptoms occur:

- Flashbacks

- Racing heart and sweating

- Being easily startled

- Being emotionally numb

- Being very sad or depressed

- Thoughts or actions to end one's life.

## Section 28.3

# *A Report on Children's Mental Health*

Text in this section is excerpted from "Children's Mental Health—New Report," Centers for Disease Control and Prevention (CDC), November 12, 2015.

## *Children's Mental Health*

The term childhood mental disorder means all mental disorders that can be diagnosed and begin in childhood (for example, attention-deficit/hyperactivity disorder (ADHD), Tourette syndrome, behavior disorders, mood and anxiety disorders, autism spectrum disorders, substance use disorders, etc.). Mental disorders among children are described as serious changes in the ways children typically learn, behave, or handle their emotions. Symptoms usually start in early childhood, although some of the disorders may develop throughout the teenage years. The diagnosis is often made in the school years and sometimes earlier. However, some children with a mental disorder may not be recognized or diagnosed as having one.

Childhood mental disorders can be treated and managed. There are many evidence-based treatment options, so parents and doctors should work closely with everyone involved in the child's treatment—teachers,

379

coaches, therapists, and other family members. Taking advantage of all the resources available will help parents, health professionals and educators guide the child towards success. Early diagnosis and appropriate services for children and their families can make a difference in the lives of children with mental disorders.

## An Important Public Health Issue

Mental health is important to overall health. Mental disorders are chronic health conditions that can continue through the lifespan. Without early diagnosis and treatment, children with mental disorders can have problems at home, in school, and in forming friendships. This can also interfere with their healthy development, and these problems can continue into adulthood.

Children's mental disorders affect many children and families. Boys and girls of all ages, ethnic/racial backgrounds, and regions of the United States experience mental disorders. Based on the National Research Council and Institute of Medicine report (Preventing mental, emotional, and behavioral disorders among young people: progress and possibilities, 2009) that gathered findings from previous studies, it is estimated that 13–20 percent of children living in the United States (up to 1 out of 5 children) experience a mental disorder in a given year and an estimated $247 billion is spent each year on childhood mental disorders. Because of the impact on children, families, and communities, children's mental disorders are an important public health issue in the United States.

## Monitoring Children's Mental Health

Public health surveillance – which is the collection and monitoring of information about health among the public over time – is a first step to better understand childhood mental disorders and promote children's mental health. Ongoing and systematic monitoring of mental health and mental disorders will help

- increase understanding of the mental health needs of children;
- inform research on factors that increase risk and promote prevention;
- find out which programs are effective at preventing mental disorders and promoting children's mental health; and
- monitor if treatment and prevention efforts are effective.

# CDC Issues Comprehensive Report on Children's Mental Health in the United States

A report from the Centers for Disease Control and Prevention (CDC), Mental Health Surveillance Among Children —United States, 2005–2011, describes federal efforts on monitoring mental disorders, and presents estimates of the number of children with specific mental disorders. The report was developed in collaboration with key federal partners, the Substance Abuse and Mental Health Services Administration (SAMHSA), National Institute of Mental Health (NIMH), and Health Resources and Services Administration (HRSA). It is an important step towards better understanding these disorders and the impact they have on children.

This is the first report to describe the number of U.S. children aged 3–17 years who have specific mental disorders, compiling information from different data sources covering the period 2005–2011. It provides information on childhood mental disorders where there is recent or ongoing monitoring. These include ADHD, disruptive behavioral disorders such as oppositional defiant disorder and conduct disorder, autism spectrum disorders, mood and anxiety disorders including depression, substance use disorders, and Tourette syndrome. The report also includes information on a few indicators of mental health, specifically, mentally unhealthy days and suicide.

## Who is Affected?

The following are key findings from this report about mental disorders among children aged 3–17 years:

- Millions of American children live with depression, anxiety, ADHD, autism spectrum disorders, Tourette syndrome or a host of other mental health issues.

- ADHD was the most prevalent current diagnosis among children aged 3–17 years.

- The number of children with a mental disorder increased with age, with the exception of autism spectrum disorders, which was highest among 6 to 11 year old children.

- Boys were more likely than girls to have ADHD, behavioral or conduct problems, autism spectrum disorders, anxiety, Tourette syndrome, and cigarette dependence.

- Adolescent boys aged 12–17 years were more likely than girls to die by suicide.

381

- Adolescent girls were more likely than boys to have depression or an alcohol use disorder.

Data collected from a variety of data sources between the years 2005-2011 show:

Children aged 3–17 years currently had:

- ADHD (6.8%)

- Behavioral or conduct problems (3.5%)

- Anxiety (3.0%)

- Depression (2.1%)

- Autism spectrum disorders (1.1%)

- Tourette syndrome (0.2%) (among children aged 6–17 years)

Adolescents aged 12–17 years had:

- Illicit drug use disorder in the past year (4.7%)

- Alcohol use disorder in the past year (4.2%)

- Cigarette dependence in the past month (2.8%)

The estimates for current diagnosis were lower than estimates for "ever" diagnosis, meaning whether a child had ever received a diagnosis in his or her lifetime. Suicide, which can result from the interaction of mental disorders and other factors, was the second leading cause of death among adolescents aged 12–17 years in 2010.

## Looking to the Future

Public health includes mental health. CDC worked with several agencies to summarize and report this information. The goal is now to build on the strengths of these partnering agencies to develop better ways to document how many children have mental disorders, better understand the impacts of mental disorders, inform needs for treatment and intervention strategies, and promote the mental health of children. This report is an important step on the road to recognizing the impact of childhood mental disorders and developing a public health approach to address children's mental health.

## What You Can Do

**Parents:** You know your child best. Talk to your child's health care professional if you have concerns about the way your child behaves at home, in school, or with friends.

**Youth:** It is just as important to take care of your mental health as it is your physical health. If you are angry, worried or sad, don't be afraid to talk about your feelings and reach out to a trusted friend or adult.

**Health care professionals:** Early diagnosis and appropriate treatment based on updated guidelines is very important. There are resources available to help diagnose and treat children's mental disorders.

**Teachers/School Administrators:** Early identification is important, so that children can get the help they need. Work with families and healthcare professionals if you have concerns about the mental health of a child in your school.

## Section 28.4

# *Treatment of Children with Mental Illness (FAQs)*

Text in this section is excerpted from "Treatment of Children with Mental Illness: Frequently Asked Questions," National Institute of Mental Health (NIMH), 2014.

## *Frequently Asked Questions*

### *What Should I Do If I Am Concerned about Mental, Behavioral, or Emotional Symptoms in My Child?*

Talk to your child's doctor or health care provider. Ask questions and learn everything you can about the behavior or symptoms that worry you. If your child is in school, ask the teacher if your child has been showing worrisome changes in behavior. Keep in mind that every child is different. Even normal development, such as when children obtain language, motor, and social skills, varies from child to child. Ask if your child needs further evaluation by a specialist with experience in child behavioral problems. Specialists may include psychiatrists, psychologists, social workers, psychiatric nurses, and behavioral therapists. Educators also may help evaluate your child.

If you take your child to a specialist, ask, "Do you have experience treating the problems I see in my child?" Don't be afraid to interview more than one specialist to find the right fit. Continue to learn everything you can about the problem or diagnosis. The more you learn, the better you can work with your child's doctor and make decisions that feel right for you, your child, and your family. If you take your child to a specialist, ask, "Do you have experience treating the problems I see in my child?" Don't be afraid to interview more than one specialist to find the right fit. Continue to learn everything you can about the problem or diagnosis. The more you learn, the better you can work with your child's doctor and make decisions that feel right for you, your child, and your family

### How Do I Know If My Child's Problems Need Attention?

Not every problem is serious. In fact, many everyday stresses can cause changes in your child's behavior. For example, the birth of a sibling may cause a child to temporarily act much younger than he or she is. It is important to be able to tell the difference between typical behavior changes and those associated with more serious problems. Pay special attention to behaviors that include:

- Problems across a variety of settings, such as at school, at home, or with peers

- Changes in appetite or sleep

- Social withdrawal or fearful behavior toward things your child normally is not afraid of

- Return to behaviors more common in younger children, such as bedwetting, for a long time

- Signs of being upset, such as sadness or tearfulness

- Signs of self-destructive behavior, such as head-banging or a tendency to get hurt often

- Repeated thoughts of death.

### Can Symptoms Be Caused by a Death in the Family, Illness in a Parent, Family Financial Problems, Divorce, or Other Events?

Yes. Every member of a family is affected by tragedy or extreme stress, even the youngest child. It's normal for stress to cause a child to be upset. Remember this if you see mental, emotional, or behavioral symptoms in your child. If it takes more than 1 month for your child to get used to a situation, or if your child has severe reactions, talk to your child's doctor.

Check your child's response to stress. Take note if he or she gets better with time or if professional care is needed. Stressful events are challenging, but they give you a chance to teach your child important ways to cope.

## How Are Mental Illnesses Diagnosed in Young Children?

Just like adults, children with mental illness are diagnosed after a doctor or mental health specialist carefully observes signs and symptoms. Some primary care physicians can diagnose your child themselves, but many will send you to a specialist who can diagnose and treat children.

Before diagnosing a mental illness, the doctor or specialist tries to rule out other possible causes for your child's behavior. The doctor will:

- Take a history of any important medical problems

- Take a history of the problem—how long you have seen the problem—as well as a history of your child's development

- Take a family history of mental disorders

- Ask if the child has experienced physical or psychological traumas, such as a natural disaster, or situations that may cause stress, such as a death in the family

- Consider reports from parents and other caretakers or teachers.

Very young children often cannot express their thoughts and feelings, so making a diagnosis can be challenging. The signs of a mental illness in a young child may be quite different from those in an older child or adult.

As parents and caregivers know, children are constantly changing and growing. Diagnosis and treatment must be viewed with these changes in mind. While some problems are short lived and don't need treatment, others are ongoing and may be very serious. In either case, more information will help you understand treatment choices and manage the disorder or problem most effectively.

Although diagnosing mental health problems in young children can be challenging, an evaluation by a mental health professional is important. A thorough evaluation can be used to guide treatment and link your child's care to research on children with similar problems.

## Will My Child Get Better with Time?

Some children get better with time. Other children need ongoing professional help. Talk to your child's doctor or specialist about problems that are severe or continuous and affect daily activities. Don't delay seeking help—treatment may produce better results if started early

## Are There Treatment Options for Children?

Yes. Once a diagnosis is made, your child's specialist will recommend a specific treatment. It is important to understand the various treatment choices, which often include psychotherapy or medication. Talk about the options with a health care professional who has experience treating the illness observed in your child. Some treatment choices have been studied experimentally, and other treatments are a part of health care practice. Not every community has every type of service or program.

## What Are Psychotropic Medications?

Psychotropic medications are substances that affect brain chemicals related to mood and behavior. In recent years, research has been conducted to understand the benefits and risks of using psychotropics in children. Still, more needs to be learned about the effects of psychotropics, especially in children under 6 years of age. While researchers are trying to clarify how early treatment affects a growing body, families and doctors should weigh the benefits and risks of medication. Each child has individual needs, and each child needs to be monitored closely while taking medications.

## Are There Treatments Other than Medications?

Yes. Psychosocial therapies can be very effective alone and in combination with medications. Psychosocial therapies also are called "talk therapies" or "behavioral therapies," and they help people with mental illness change behavior. Therapies that teach parents and children coping strategies also can be effective.

Cognitive behavioral therapy (CBT) is a type of psychotherapy that can be used with children. It has been widely studied and is an effective treatment for a number of conditions, such as depression, obsessive-compulsive disorder, and social anxiety. A person in CBT learns to change distorted thinking patterns and unhealthy behavior. Children can receive CBT with or without their parents as well as in a group setting. CBT can be adapted to fit the needs of each child. It is especially useful when treating anxiety disorders.

Additionally, a number of therapies exist for ADHD, oppositional defiant disorder, and conduct disorder and include behavioral parent management training (PMT) and behavioral classroom management.

Some children benefit from a combination of different psychosocial approaches. An example is behavioral PMT in combination with CBT for the child. In other cases, a combination of medication and psychosocial therapies may be most effective. Psychosocial therapies often take time, effort, and patience. Children may learn new skills that may have positive long-term benefits.

## *When Is It a Good Idea to Use Psychotropic Medications in Young Children?*

Some children benefit from a combination of different psychosocial approaches. An example is behavioral PMT in combination with CBT for the child. In other cases, a combination of medication and psychosocial therapies may be most effective. Psychosocial therapies often take time, effort, and patience. Children may learn new skills that may have positive long-term benefits.

Ask your doctor questions about alternatives to medications and about the risks of starting and continuing your child on these medications. Learn everything you can about the medications prescribed for your child. Learn about possible side effects, some of which may be harmful. Know what a particular treatment is supposed to do.

For example, will it change a specific behavior? If you do not see these changes while your child is taking the medication, talk to his or her doctor. Also, discuss the risks of stopping your child's medication with your doctor.

## *Does Medication Affect Young Children Differently than Older Children or Adults?*

Yes. The brains of young children change and develop rapidly. Studies have found that developing brains can be very sensitive to medications. There are also developmental differences in how children metabolize—how their bodies process—medications. Therefore, doctors should carefully consider the dosage or how much medication to give each child. Much more research is needed to determine the effects and benefits of medications in children of all ages. But keep in mind that untreated mental disorders themselves can harm brain development.

Also, it is important to avoid drug interactions. If your child takes medicine for asthma or cold symptoms, talk to your doctor or pharmacist. Drug interactions could cause medications not to work as intended or lead to serious side effects.

### How Should Medication Be Included in an Overall Treatment Plan?

Medication should be used with other treatments. It should not be the only treatment. Consider other services, such as family therapy, family support services, educational classes, and behavior management techniques. If your child's doctor prescribes medication, he or she should evaluate your child regularly to make sure the medication is working. Children need treatment plans tailored to their individual problems and needs.

### What Medications Are Used for Which Kinds of Childhood Mental Disorders?

Medication should be used with other treatments. It should not be the only treatment. Consider other services, such as family therapy, family support services, educational classes, and behavior management techniques. If your child's doctor prescribes medication, he or she should evaluate your child regularly to make sure the medication is working. Children need treatment plans tailored to their individual problems and needs.

### What Does It Mean If a Medication Is Specifically Approved for Use in Children?

When the FDA approves a medication, it means the drug manufacturer provided the agency with information showing that the medication is safe and effective in a particular group of people. Based on this information, the drug's label lists proper dosage, potential side effects, and approved age. Medications approved for children follow these guidelines.

When the FDA approves a medication, it means the drug manufacturer provided the agency with information showing that the medication is safe and effective in a particular group of people. Based on this information, the drug's label lists proper dosage, potential side effects, and approved age. Medications approved for children follow these guidelines.

More studies in children are needed before we can fully know the appropriate dosages, how a medication works in children, and what effects a medication might have on learning and development.

## Why Haven't Many Medications Been Tested in Children?

In the past, medications were seldom studied in children because mental illness was not recognized in childhood. Also, there were ethical concerns about involving children in research. These actions led to a lack of knowledge about the best treatments for children. In clinical settings today, children with mental or behavioral disorders are being prescribed medications at increasingly early ages. The FDA has been urging that medications be appropriately studied in children. Congress passed legislation in 1997 offering incentives to drug manufacturers to carry out such testing. These activities have helped increase research on the effects of medications in children.

There are still ethical concerns about testing medications in children. However, strict rules protect participants in research studies. Each study must go through many types of review before and after it begins.

## How Do I Work with My Child's School?

If your child is having problems in school, or if a teacher raises concerns, you can work with the school to find a solution. You may ask the school to conduct an evaluation to determine whether your child qualifies for special education services. However, not all children diagnosed with a mental illness qualify for these services.

Start by speaking with your child's teacher, school counselor, school nurse, or the school's parent organization. These professionals can help you get an evaluation started. Also, each state has a Parent Training and Information Center and a Protection and Advocacy Agency that can help you request the evaluation. The evaluation must be conducted by a team of professionals who assess all areas related to the suspected disability using a variety of tools and measures.

## What Resources Are Available from the School?

Once your child has been evaluated, there are several options, depending on the specific needs. If special education services are needed, and if your child is eligible under the Individuals With Disabilities Education Act (IDEA), the school district must develop an "individualized education program" specifically for your child within 30 days.

If your child is not eligible for special education services, he or she is still entitled to "free appropriate public education," available to all public school children with disabilities under Section 504 of the Rehabilitation Act of 1973. Your child is entitled to this education regardless of the nature or severity of his or her disability.

## What Special Challenges Can School Present?

Each school year brings a new teacher and new schoolwork. These changes can be difficult for some children. Inform the teachers that your child has a mental illness when he or she starts school or moves to a new class. Additional support will help your child adjust to the change.

## What Else Can I Do to Help My Child?

Children with mental illness need guidance and understanding from their parents and teachers. This support can help your child achieve his or her full potential and succeed in school. Before a child is diagnosed, frustration, blame, and anger may have built up within a family. Parents and children may need special help to undo these unhealthy interaction patterns. Mental health professionals can counsel the child and family to help everyone develop new skills, attitudes, and ways of relating to each other.

Parents can also help by taking part in parenting skills training. These classes help parents learn how to handle difficult situations and behaviors.

Training encourages parents to share a pleasant or relaxing activity with their child, to notice and point out what their child does well, and to praise their child's strengths and abilities. Parents also may learn to arrange family situations in more positive ways. Also, parents may benefit from learning stress management techniques to help them deal with frustration and respond calmly to their child's behavior.

Sometimes the whole family may need counseling. Therapists can help family members find better ways to handle disruptive behaviors and encourage behavior changes. Finally, support groups help parents and families connect with others who have similar problems and concerns. Groups often meet regularly to share frustrations and successes, to exchange information about recommended specialists and strategies, and to talk with experts.

### How Can Families of Children with Mental Illness Get Support?

Taking care of a child with mental illness takes a toll on the parents, family, and other caregivers. Caregivers often must tend to the medical needs of their loved ones before dealing with their own health. The stress that caregivers are under may lead to missed work or lost free time, strained relationships with people who may not understand the situation, and physical and mental exhaustion.

Stress from caregiving can make it hard to cope with your child's symptoms. Research shows that if a caregiver is under enormous stress, his or her loved one has more difficulty sticking to the treatment plan. It is important to look after your own physical and mental health. You may also find it helpful to join a local support group.

### Where Can I Go for Help?

If you are unsure where to go for help, ask your family doctor. Others who can help include:

- Mental health specialists, such as psychiatrists, psychologists, social workers, or mental health counselors
- Health maintenance organizations
- Community mental health centers
- Hospital psychiatry departments and outpatient clinics
- Mental health programs at universities or medical schools
- State hospital outpatient clinics
- Family services, social agencies, or clergy
- School counselors, psychologists, or social workers
- Peer support groups
- Private clinics and facilities
- Employee assistance programs
- Local medical or psychiatric societies.

You also can check the phone book or online under "mental health," "health," "social services," "hotlines," or "physicians" for phone numbers and addresses. An emergency room doctor can also provide temporary help and can tell you where and how to get further help.

391

Chapter 29

# Attention Deficit Hyperactivity Disorder (ADHD)

## What Is Attention Deficit Hyperactivity Disorder (ADHD)?

ADHD is a common mental disorder that begins in childhood and can continue through adolescence and adulthood. It makes it hard for a child to focus and pay attention. Some children may be hyperactive or have trouble being patient. For children with ADHD, levels of inattention, hyperactivity, and impulsive behaviors are greater than for other children in their age group. ADHD can make it hard for a child to do well in school or behave at home or in the community.

ADHD can be treated. Doctors and specialists can help.

## Who Can Develop ADHD?

Children of all backgrounds can have ADHD. Teens and adults can have ADHD too.

This chapter includes excerpts from "Attention Deficit Hyperactivity Disorder," National Institute of Mental Health (NIMH), 2013; and text from "Facts about ADHD," Centers for Disease Control and Prevention (CDC), January 6, 2016.

## What Causes ADHD?

No one knows for sure. ADHD probably stems from interactions between genes and environmental or nongenetic factors.

ADHD often runs in families. Researchers have found that much of the risk of having ADHD has to do with genes. Many genes are linked to ADHD, and each gene plays a small role in the disorder. ADHD is very complex and a genetic test for diagnosing the disorder is not yet available.

Among the non-genetic factors that may increase a child's risk for developing ADHD are:

• Smoking or drinking during pregnancy

• Birth complications or very low birth weight

• Exposure to lead or other toxic substances

• Extreme neglect, abuse, or social deprivation.

Some studies suggest that artificial food additives and dyes may worsen hyperactivity and inattention, but these effects are small and do not account for most cases of ADHD.

## What Are the Symptoms of ADHD?

ADHD has many symptoms. Some symptoms at first may look like normal behaviors for a child, but ADHD makes them much worse and occur more often. Children with ADHD have at least six symptoms that start in the first 12 years of their lives.

Children with ADHD may:

• Get distracted easily and forget things often

• Switch too quickly from one activity to the next

• Have trouble with directions

• Daydream too much

• Have trouble finishing tasks like homework or chores

• Lose toys, books, and school supplies often

• Fidget and squirm a lot

• Talk nonstop and interrupt people

• Run around a lot

- Touch and play with everything they see

- Be very impatient

- Blurt out inappropriate comments

- Have trouble controlling their emotions.

## *How Do I Know If My Child Has ADHD?*

Your child's doctor may make a diagnosis. Or sometimes the doctor may refer you to a mental health specialist who is more experienced with ADHD to make a diagnosis.

There is no single test that can tell if your child has ADHD. To make a diagnosis, the doctor or specialist will examine your child and use several rating scales to track ADHD symptoms. The specialist will also collect information from you, your family, and your child's teachers. Sometimes it can be hard to diagnose a child with ADHD because symptoms may look like other problems. For example, a child may seem quiet and well-behaved, but in fact he or she is having a hard time paying attention and is often distracted. Or, a child may act badly in school, but teachers don't realize that the child has ADHD.

If your child is having trouble at school or at home and has been for a long time, ask his or her doctor about ADHD.

## *How Do Children with ADHD Get Better?*

Children with ADHD can get better with treatment, but there is no cure. There are three basic types of treatment:

1. **Medication.** Several medications can help. The most common types are called stimulants. Medications help children focus, learn, and stay calm. Sometimes medications cause side effects, such as sleep problems or stomachaches. Your child may need to try a few medications to see which one works best. It's important that you and your doctor watch your child closely while he or she is taking medicine.

2. **Therapy.** There are different kinds of therapy. Behavioral therapy can help teach children to control their behavior so they can do better at school and at home.

3. **Medication and therapy combined.** Many children do well with both medication and therapy.

## How Can I Help My Child?

Give your child guidance and understanding. A specialist can show you how to help your child make positive changes. Supporting your child helps everyone in your family. Also, talk to your child's teachers. Some children with ADHD can get special education services.

## How Does ADHD Affect Teens?

Being a teenager isn't always easy. Teens with ADHD can have a tough time. While hyperactivity tends to get better as a child becomes a teen, problems with inattention, disorganization, and poor impulse control often continue through the teen years and into adulthood. School may be a struggle, and some teens take too many risks or break rules. But like children with ADHD, teens can improve with treatment.

## What Can I Do for My Teen with ADHD?

Support your teen. Set clear rules for him or her to follow. Try not to punish your teen every time he or she breaks the rules. Let your teen know you can help.

## Can Adults Have ADHD, Too?

ADHD can continue into adulthood. Like ADHD in children and teens, ADHD in adults can make life challenging. ADHD can make it hard for adults to feel organized, stick with a job, or get to work on time. Adults with ADHD may have trouble in relationships. The disorder can also make adults feel restless.

ADHD in adults can be diagnosed and treated. For some adults, finding out they have ADHD can be a big relief. Being able to connect ADHD to longtime problems helps adults understand that they can get better. If you're an adult and think you may have ADHD symptoms, call your doctor.

## Facts about ADHD

ADHD is one of the most common neurodevelopmental disorders of childhood. It is usually first diagnosed in childhood and often lasts into adulthood. Children with ADHD may have trouble paying attention, controlling impulsive behaviors (may act without thinking about what the result will be), or be overly active.

### Signs and Symptoms

It is normal for children to have trouble focusing and behaving at one time or another. However, children with ADHD do not just grow out of these behaviors. The symptoms continue and can cause difficulty at school, at home, or with friends.

A child with ADHD might:

- daydream a lot

- forget or lose things a lot

- squirm or fidget

- talk too much

- make careless mistakes or take unnecessary risks

- have a hard time resisting temptation

- have trouble taking turns

- have difficulty getting along with others

### Types

There are three different types of ADHD, depending on which types of symptoms are strongest in the individual:

**Predominantly Inattentive Presentation:** It is hard for the individual to organize or finish a task, to pay attention to details, or to follow instructions or conversations. The person is easily distracted or forgets details of daily routines.

**Predominantly Hyperactive-Impulsive Presentation:** The person fidgets and talks a lot. It is hard to sit still for long (e.g., for a meal or while doing homework). Smaller children may run, jump or climb constantly. The individual feels restless and has trouble with impulsivity. Someone who is impulsive may interrupt others a lot, grab things from people, or speak at inappropriate times. It is hard for the person to wait their turn or listen to directions. A person with impulsiveness may have more accidents and injuries than others.

**Combined Presentation:** Symptoms of the above two types are equally present in the person.

Because symptoms can change over time, the presentation may change over time as well.

### Causes of ADHD

Scientists are studying cause(s) and risk factors in an effort to find better ways to manage and reduce the chances of a person having ADHD. The cause(s) and risk factors for ADHD are unknown, but current research shows that genetics plays an important role. Recent studies of twins link genes with ADHD.

In addition to genetics, scientists are studying other possible causes and risk factors including:

- Brain injury

- Environmental exposures (e.g., lead)

- Alcohol and tobacco use during pregnancy

- Premature delivery

- Low birth weight

Research does not support the popularly held views that ADHD is caused by eating too much sugar, watching too much television, parenting, or social and environmental factors such as poverty or family chaos. Of course, many things, including these, might make symptoms worse, especially in certain people. But the evidence is not strong enough to conclude that they are the main causes of ADHD.

### Diagnosis

Deciding if a child has ADHD is a several step process. There is no single test to diagnose ADHD, and many other problems, like anxiety, depression, and certain types of learning disabilities, can have similar symptoms. One step of the process involves having a medical exam, including hearing and vision tests, to rule out other problems with symptoms like ADHD. Another part of the process may include a checklist for rating ADHD symptoms and taking a history of the child from parents, teachers, and sometimes, the child.

### Treatments

In most cases, ADHD is best treated with a combination of behavior therapy and medication. For preschool-aged children (4–5 years of age) with ADHD, behavior therapy is recommended as the first line of treatment. No single treatment is the answer for every child and good treatment plans will include close monitoring, follow-ups and any changes needed along the way.

## Get Help!

If you or your doctor has concerns about ADHD, you can take your child to a specialist such as a child psychologist or developmental pediatrician, or you can contact your local early intervention agency (for children under 3) or public school (for children 3 and older). You can fill out a symptoms checklist and take it to the child's doctor.

# Chapter 30

# *Autism Spectrum Disorder*

## *What Is Autism Spectrum Disorder?*

Autism spectrum disorder (ASD) is a term for a group of developmental disorders described by:

- Lasting problems with social communication and social interaction in different settings

- Repetitive behaviors and/or not wanting any change in daily routines

- Symptoms that begin in early childhood, usually in the first 2 years of life

- Symptoms that cause the person to need help in his or her daily life

The term "spectrum" refers to the wide range of symptoms, strengths, and levels of impairment that people with ASD can have. The diagnosis of ASD now includes these other conditions:

- Autistic disorder

- Asperger's syndrome

- Pervasive developmental disorder not otherwise specified

---

Text in this chapter is excerpted from "Autism Spectrum Disorder," National Institute of Mental Health (NIMH), September 2015.

Although ASD begins in early development, it can last throughout a person's lifetime.

## What Are the Signs and Symptoms of ASD?

Not all people with ASD will show all of these behaviors, but most will show several.

People with ASD may:

- Repeat certain behaviors or have unusual behaviors

- Have overly focused interests, such as with moving objects or parts of objects

- Have a lasting, intense interest in certain topics, such as numbers, details, or facts

- Be upset by a slight change in a routine or being placed in a new or overstimulating setting

- Make little or inconsistent eye contact

- Tend to look and listen less to people in their environment

- Rarely seek to share their enjoyment of objects or activities by pointing or showing things to others

- Respond unusually when others show anger, distress, or affection

- Fail or be slow to respond to their name or other verbal attempts to gain their attention

- Have difficulties with the back and forth of conversations

- Often talk at length about a favorite subject but won't allow anyone else a chance to respond or notice when others react indifferently

- Repeat words or phrases that they hear, a behavior called echolalia

- Use words that seem odd, out of place, or have a special meaning known only to those familiar with that person's way of communicating

- Have facial expressions, movements, and gestures that do not match what they are saying

- Have an unusual tone of voice that may sound sing-song or flat and robot-like

- Have trouble understanding another person's point of view, leaving him or her unable to predict or understand other people's actions

People with ASD may have other difficulties, such as sensory sensitivity (being sensitive to light, noise, textures of clothing, or temperature), sleep problems, digestion problems, and irritability.

People with ASD can also have many strengths and abilities. For instance, people with ASD may:

- Have above-average intelligence

- Be able to learn things in detail and remember information for long periods of time

- Be strong visual and auditory learners

- Excel in math, science, music, and art

## Noticing ASD in Young Children

Some babies with ASD may seem different very early in their development. Others may seem to develop typically until the second or even third year of life, but then parents start to see problems.

## How Is ASD Diagnosed?

Doctors diagnose ASD by looking at a child's behavior and development. Young children with ASD can usually be reliably diagnosed by age 2.

Older children and adolescents should be screened for ASD when a parent or teacher raises concerns based on observations of the child's social, communicative, and play behaviors.

Diagnosing ASD in adults is not easy. In adults, some ASD symptoms can overlap with symptoms of other mental health disorders, such as schizophrenia or attention deficit hyperactivity disorder (ADHD). However, getting a correct diagnosis of ASD as an adult can help a person understand past difficulties, identify his or her strengths, and obtain the right kind of help.

### *Diagnosis in Young Children*

Diagnosis in young children is often a two-stage process:

**General Developmental Screening During Well-Child Checkups**

Every child should receive well-child check-ups with a pediatrician or an early childhood health care provider. Specific ASD screening should be done at the 18- and 24-month visits.

Earlier screening might be needed if a child is at high risk for ASD or developmental problems. Those at high risk include those who:

- Have a sister, brother, or other family member with ASD

- Have some ASD behaviors

- Were born premature, or early, and at a low birth weight

Parents' experiences and concerns are very important in the screening process for young children. Sometimes the doctor will ask parents questions about the child's behaviors and combine this information with his or her observations of the child.

Children who show some developmental problems during this screening process will be referred for another stage of evaluation.

**Additional Evaluation**

This evaluation is with a team of doctors and other health professionals with a wide range of specialties who are experienced in diagnosing ASD. This team may include:

- A developmental pediatrician—a doctor who has special training in child development

- A child psychologist and/or child psychiatrist—a doctor who knows about brain development and behavior

- A speech-language pathologist—a health professional who has special training in communication difficulties

The evaluation may assess:

- Cognitive level or thinking skills

- Language abilities

- Age-appropriate skills needed to complete daily activities independently, such as eating, dressing, and toileting

Because ASD is a complex disorder that sometimes occurs along with other illnesses or learning disorders, the comprehensive evaluation may include:

- Blood tests

- A hearing test

The outcome of the evaluation will result in recommendations to help plan for treatment.

### Diagnosis in Older Children and Adolescents

Older children who begin showing symptoms of ASD after starting school are often first recognized and evaluated by the school's special education team and can be referred to a health care professional. Parents may talk with their child's pediatrician about their child's difficulties with social interaction, including problems with subtle communication, such as understanding tone of voice or facial expressions, body language, and lack of understanding of figures of speech, humor, or sarcasm. Parents may also find that their child has trouble forming friendships with peers. At this point, the pediatrician or a child psychologist or psychiatrist who has expertise in ASD can screen the child and refer the family for further evaluation and treatment.

### Diagnosis in Adults

Adults who notice the signs and symptoms of ASD should talk with a doctor and ask for a referral for an ASD evaluation. While testing for ASD in adults is still being refined, adults can be referred to a psychologist or psychiatrist with ASD expertise. The expert will ask about concerns, such as social interaction and communication challenges, sensory issues, repetitive behaviors, and restricted interests. Information about the adult's developmental history will help in making an accurate diagnosis, so an ASD evaluation may include talking with parents or other family members.

## What Are the Treatments for ASD?

Treating ASD early and getting proper care can reduce a person's difficulties and increase his or her ability to maximize strengths and learn new skills. While there is no single best treatment for ASD, working closely with the doctor is an important part of finding the right treatment program.

## Medications

There are a few classes of medications that doctors may use to treat some difficulties that are common with ASD. With medication, a person with ASD may have fewer problems with:

405

- Irritability

- Aggression

- Repetitive behaviors

- Hyperactivity

- Attention problems

- Anxiety and depression

## Who Is Affected by ASD?

ASD affects many people, and it has become more commonly diagnosed in recent years. More boys than girls receive an ASD diagnosis.

## What Causes ASD?

Scientists don't know the exact causes of ASD, but research suggests that genes and environment play important roles.

- Researchers are starting to identify genes that may increase the risk for ASD.

- ASD occurs more often in people who have certain genetic conditions, such as Fragile X syndrome or tuberous sclerosis.

- Many researchers are focusing on how genes interact with each other and with environmental factors, such as family medical conditions, parental age and other demographic factors, and complications during birth or pregnancy.

- Currently, no scientific studies have linked ASD and vaccines.

# Chapter 31

# *Bipolar Disorder in Children and Teens*

## *Bipolar Disorder in Children and Teens*

**Does your child go through intense mood changes?** Does your child have extreme behavior changes? Does your child get much more excited and active than other kids his or her age? Do other people say your child is too excited or too moody? Do you notice he or she has highs and lows much more often than other children? Do these mood changes affect how your child acts at school or at home?

Some children and teens with these symptoms may have **bipolar disorder**, a serious mental illness.

## *What Is Bipolar Disorder?*

Bipolar disorder is a serious brain illness. It is also called manic-depressive illness or manic depression. Children with bipolar disorder go through unusual mood changes. Sometimes they feel very happy or "up," and are much more energetic and active than usual, or than other kids their age. This is called a manic episode. Sometimes children with bipolar disorder feel very sad and "down," and are much less active than usual. This is called depression or a depressive episode.

---

Text in this chapter is excerpted from "Bipolar Disorder in Children and Teens," National Institute of Mental Health (NIMH), 2015.

Bipolar disorder is not the same as the normal ups and downs every kid goes through. Bipolar symptoms are more powerful than that. The mood swings are more extreme and are accompanied by changes in sleep, energy level, and the ability to think clearly. Bipolar symptoms are so strong, they can make it hard for a child to do well in school or get along with friends and family members. The illness can also be dangerous. Some young people with bipolar disorder try to hurt themselves or attempt suicide.

Children and teens with bipolar disorder should get treatment. With help, they can manage their symptoms and lead successful lives.

## Who Develops Bipolar Disorder?

Anyone can develop bipolar disorder, including children and teens. However, most people with bipolar disorder develop it in their late teen or early adult years. The illness usually lasts a lifetime.

## Why Does Someone Develop Bipolar Disorder?

Doctors do not know what causes bipolar disorder, but several things may contribute to the illness. Family genes may be one factor because bipolar disorder sometimes runs in families. However, it is important to know that just because someone in your family has bipolar disorder, it does not mean other members of the family will have it as well.

Another factor that may lead to bipolar disorder is the brain structure or the brain function of the person with the disorder. Scientists are finding out more about the disorder by studying it. This research may help doctors do a better job of treating people. Also, this research may help doctors to predict whether a person will get bipolar disorder. One day, doctors may be able to prevent the illness in some people.

## What Are the Symptoms of Bipolar Disorder?

Bipolar "mood episodes" include unusual mood changes along with unusual sleep habits, activity levels, thoughts, or behavior. In a child, these mood and activity changes must be very different from their usual behavior and from the behavior of other children. A person with bipolar disorder may have manic episodes, depressive episodes, or "mixed" episodes. A mixed episode has both manic and depressive symptoms. These mood episodes cause symptoms that last a week or two or sometimes longer. During an episode, the symptoms last every day for most of the day.

Children and teens having a manic episode may:

- Feel very happy or act silly in a way that's unusual for them and for other people their age
- Have a very short temper
- Talk really fast about a lot of different things
- Have trouble sleeping but not feel tired
- Have trouble staying focused
- Talk and think about sex more often
- Do risky things

Children and teens having a depressive episode may:

- Feel very sad
- Complain about pain a lot, such as stomachaches and headaches
- Sleep too little or too much
- Feel guilty and worthless
- Eat too little or too much
- Have little energy and no interest in fun activities
- Think about death or suicide

## Can Children and Teens with Bipolar Disorder Have Other Problems?

Young people with bipolar disorder can have several problems at the same time. These include:

- **Substance abuse.** Both adults and kids with bipolar disorder are at risk of drinking or taking drugs.
- **Attention deficit/hyperactivity disorder (ADHD).** Children who have both bipolar disorder and ADHD may have trouble staying focused.
- **Anxiety disorders, like separation anxiety.**

Sometimes behavior problems go along with mood episodes. Young people may take a lot of risks, such as driving too fast or spending too much money. Some young people with bipolar disorder think about suicide. Watch for any signs of suicidal thinking. Take these signs seriously and call your child's doctor.

## How Is Bipolar Disorder Diagnosed?

An experienced doctor will carefully examine your child. There are no blood tests or brain scans that can diagnose bipolar disorder. Instead, the doctor will ask questions about your child's mood and sleeping patterns. The doctor will also ask about your child's energy and behavior. Sometimes doctors need to know about medical problems in your family, such as depression or alcoholism. The doctor may use tests to see if something other than bipolar disorder is causing your child's symptoms.

## How Is Bipolar Disorder Treated?

Right now, there is no cure for bipolar disorder. Doctors often treat children who have the illness in much the same way they treat adults. Treatment can help control symptoms. Steady, dependable treatment works better than treatment that starts and stops. Treatment options include:

- **Medication.** There are several types of medication that can help. Children respond to medications in different ways, so the right type of medication depends on the child. Some children may need more than one type of medication because their symptoms are so complex. Sometimes they need to try different types of medicine to see which are best for them. Children should take the fewest number of medications and the smallest doses possible to help their symptoms. A good way to remember this is "start low, go slow." Medications can cause side effects.

- **Always tell your child's doctor about any problems with side effects.** Do not stop giving your child medication without a doctor's help. Stopping medication suddenly can be dangerous, and it can make bipolar symptoms worse.

- **Therapy.** Different kinds of psychotherapy, or "talk" therapy, can help children with bipolar disorder. Therapy can help children change their behavior and manage their routines. It can also help young people get along better with family and friends. Sometimes therapy includes family members.

## What Can Children and Teens Expect from Treatment?

With treatment, children and teens with bipolar disorder can get better over time. It helps when doctors, parents, and young people work together.

Sometimes a child's bipolar disorder changes. When this happens, treatment needs to change too. For example, your child may need to try a different medication. The doctor may also recommend other treatment changes. Symptoms may come back after a while, and more adjustments may be needed. Treatment can take time, but sticking with it helps many children and teens have fewer bipolar symptoms.

You can help treatment be more effective. Try keeping a chart of your child's moods, behaviors, and sleep patterns. This is called a "daily life chart" or "mood chart." It can help you and your child understand and track the illness. A chart can also help the doctor see whether treatment is working.

## How Can I Help My Child or Teen?

Help begins with the right diagnosis and treatment. If you think your child may have bipolar disorder, make an appointment with your family doctor to talk about the symptoms you notice.

If your child has bipolar disorder, here are some basic things you can do:

- Be patient.
- Encourage your child to talk, and listen to your child carefully.
- Be understanding about mood episodes.
- Help your child have fun.
- Help your child understand that treatment can make life better.

## How Does Bipolar Disorder Affect Parents and Family?

Taking care of a child or teenager with bipolar disorder can be stressful for you, too. You have to cope with the mood swings and other problems, such as short tempers and risky activities. This can challenge any parent. Sometimes the stress can strain your relationships with other people, and you may miss work or lose free time.

If you are taking care of a child with bipolar disorder, take care of yourself too. Find someone you can talk to about your feelings. Talk with the doctor about support groups for caregivers. If you keep your stress level down, you will do a better job. It might help your child get better too.

## Where Do I Go for Help?

If you're not sure where to get help, call your family doctor. You can also check the phone book for mental health professionals. Hospital doctors can help in an emergency. Finally, the Substance Abuse and Mental Health Services Administration (SAMHSA) has an online tool to help you find mental health services in your area.

## I Know Someone Who Is in Crisis. What Do I Do?

If you know someone who might be thinking about hurting himself or herself or someone else, get help quickly.

- Do not leave the person alone.
- Call your doctor.
- Call 911 or go to the emergency room.
- Call National Suicide Prevention Lifeline, toll-free: 1-800-273-TALK (8255). The TTY number is 1-800-799-4TTY (4889).

# Chapter 32

# *Depression in Children and Teens*

If you have been feeling sad, hopeless, or irritable for what seems like a long time, you might have depression.

- Depression is a real, treatable brain illness, or health problem.
- Depression can be caused by big transitions in life, stress, or changes in your body's chemicals that affect your thoughts and moods.
- Even if you feel hopeless, depression gets better with treatment.
- There are lots of people who understand and want to help you.
- Ask for help as early as you can so you can get back to being yourself.

## Regular Sadness and Depression Are Not the Same

### Regular Sadness

Feeling moody, sad, or grouchy? Who doesn't once in a while? It's easy to have a couple of bad days. Your school work, activities, and

This chapter includes excerpts from "Teen Depression," National Institute of Mental Health (NIMH), 2015; and text from "Depression and College Students," National Institute of Mental Health (NIMH), November 2015.

family and friend drama, all mixed with not enough sleep, can leave you feeling overwhelmed. On top of that, teen hormones can be all over the place and also make you moody or cry about the smallest thing. Regular moodiness and sadness usually go away quickly though, within a couple of days.

## *Depression*

Untreated depression is a more intense feeling of sadness, hopelessness, and anger or frustration that lasts much longer, such as for weeks, months, or longer. These feelings make it hard for you to function as you normally would or participate in your usual activities. You may also have trouble focusing and feel like you have little to no motivation or energy. You may not even feel like seeing your best friends. Depression can make you feel like it is hard to enjoy life or even get through the day.

## If You Think You Are Depressed, Ask for Help as Early as You Can.

If you have symptoms of depression for more than 2 weeks, ask for help. Depression can get better with care and treatment. Don't wait for depression to go away by itself. If you don't ask for help, depression may get worse.

1.   Talk to:

    - Your parents or guardian

    - Your teacher or counselor

    - Your doctor

    - A helpline, such as 1-800-273-TALK (8255), free 24-hour help

    - Or call 911 if you are in a crisis or want to hurt yourself

2.   Ask your parent or guardian to make an appointment with your doctor for a checkup. Your doctor can make sure that you do not have another health problem that is causing your depression. If your doctor finds that you do not have another health problem, he or she can treat your depression or refer you to a mental health professional. A mental health professional can give you a thorough evaluation and also treat your depression.

3.  Talk to a mental health professional, such as a psychiatrist, counselor, psychologist, or other therapist. These mental health professionals can diagnose and treat depression and other mental health problems.

## Know the Signs and Symptoms of Depression

Most of the day or nearly every day you may feel one or all of the following:

- Sad
- Empty
- Hopeless
- Angry, cranky, or frustrated, even at minor things

You also may:

- Not care about things or activities you used to enjoy.
- Have weight loss when you are not dieting or wcight gain from eating too much.
- Have trouble falling asleep or staying asleep, or sleep much more than usual.
- Move or talk more slowly.
- Feel restless or have trouble sitting still
- Feel very tired or like you have no energy.
- Feel worthless or very guilty.
- Have trouble concentrating, remembering information, or making decisions.
- Think about dying or suicide or try suicide.

Not everyone experiences depression the same way. And depression can occur at the same time as other mental health problems, such as anxiety, an eating disorder, or substance abuse.

## There Are Ways You Can Feel Better

Effective treatments for depression include talk therapy or a combination of talk therapy and medicine.

*Talk Therapy*

A therapist, such as a psychiatrist, a psychologist, a social worker, or counselor can help you understand and manage your moods and feelings. You can talk out your emotions to someone who understands and supports you. You can also learn how to stop thinking negatively and start to look at the positives in life. This will help you build confidence and feel better about yourself. Research has shown that certain types of talk therapy or psychotherapy can help teens deal with depression. These include cognitive behavioral therapy, which focuses on thoughts, behaviors, and feelings related to depression, and interpersonal psychotherapy, which focuses on working on relationships.

*Medicines*

If your doctor thinks you need medicine to help your depression, he or she can prescribe an antidepressant. There are a few antidepressants that have been widely studied and proven to help teens. If your doctor recommends medicine, it is important to see your doctor regularly and tell your parents or guardian about your feelings, especially if you start feeling worse or have thoughts of hurting yourself.

## Be Good to Yourself

Besides seeing a doctor and a counselor, you can also help your depression by being patient with yourself and good to yourself. Don't expect to get better immediately, but you will feel yourself improving gradually over time.

- Daily exercise, getting enough sleep, spending time outside in nature and in the sun, or eating healthy foods can also help you feel better.

- Your counselor may teach you how to be aware of your feelings and teach you relaxation techniques. Use these when you start feeling down or upset.

- Try to spend time with supportive family members. Talking with your parents, guardian, or other family members who listen and care about you gives you support, and they can make you laugh.

- Try to get out with friends and try fun things that help you express yourself.

## Depression Can Affect Relationships

It's understandable that you don't want to tell other people that you have been struggling with depression. But know that depression can affect your relationships with family and friends, and how you perform at school. Maybe your grades have dropped because you find it hard to concentrate and stay on top of school. Teachers may think that you aren't trying in class. Maybe because you're feeling hopeless, peers think you are too negative and start giving you a hard time.

Know that their misunderstanding won't last forever because you are getting better with treatment. Think about talking with people you trust to help them understand what you are going through.

Depression is not your fault or caused by something you did wrong.

Depression is a real, treatable brain illness, or health problem. Depression can be caused by big transitions in life, stress, or changes in your body's chemicals that affect your thoughts and moods. Depression can run in families. Maybe you haven't realized that you have depression and have been blaming yourself for being negative. Remember that depression is not your fault!

## Answers to College Students' Frequently Asked Questions about Depression

Feeling moody, sad, or grouchy? Who doesn't once in a while? College is an exciting time, but it can also be very challenging. As a college student, you might be leaving home for the first time, learning to live independently, taking tough classes, meeting new people, and getting a lot less sleep. Small or large setbacks can seem like the end of the world, but these feelings usually pass with a little time.

But if you have been feeling sad, hopeless, or irritable for at least 2 weeks, you might have depression. You're not alone. Depression is the most common health problem for college students.1 You should know:

- Depression is a medical illness.

- Depression can be treated.

- Early treatment is best.

- Most colleges offer free or low-cost mental health services to students.

## Q: What Is Depression?

A: Depression is a medical illness with many symptoms, including physical ones. Sadness is only a small part of depression. Some people with depression may not feel sadness at all, but be more irritable, or just lose interest in things they usually like to do. Depression interferes with your daily life and normal function. Don't ignore or try to hide the symptoms. It is not a character flaw, and you can't will it away.

## Q: Are There Different Types of Depression?

A: Yes. The most common depressive disorders include major depression (a discrete episode, clearly different from a person's usual feeling and functioning), persistent depressive disorder (a chronic, low-grade depression that can get better or worse over time), and psychotic depression (the most severe, with delusions or hallucinations). Some people are vulnerable to depression in the winter ("seasonal affective disorder"), and some women report depression in the week or two prior to their menstrual period ("premenstrual dysphoric disorder"). You can learn about these and other types of depression at http://www.nimh.nih.gov/health/topics/depression/index.shtml.

## Q: What Are the Signs and Symptoms of Depression?

A: If you have been experiencing any of the following signs and symptoms nearly every day for at least 2 weeks, you may have major (sometimes called "clinical") depression:

- Persistent sad, anxious, or "empty" mood
- Feelings of hopelessness, pessimism
- Feelings of guilt, worthlessness, helplessness
- Loss of interest or pleasure in hobbies and activities
- Decreased energy, fatigue, being "slowed down"
- Difficulty concentrating, remembering, making decisions
- Difficulty sleeping, early-morning awakening, or oversleeping
- Appetite and/or unwanted weight changes
- Thoughts of death or suicide; suicide attempts
- Restlessness, irritability
- Persistent physical symptoms, such as muscle pain or headaches

Not everyone who is depressed experiences every symptom. Some people experience only a few symptoms. Some people have many. If any of these symptoms is interfering with your functioning—or if you are having thoughts that life is not worth living or ideas of harming yourself—you should seek help immediately; it is not necessary to wait 2 weeks.

## Q: What Are "Co-Occurring" Disorders?

A: Depression can occur at the same time as other health problems, such as anxiety, an eating disorder, or substance abuse. It can also co-occur with other medical conditions, such as diabetes or thyroid imbalance. Certain medications—for example, those for the treatment of severe acne—may cause side effects that contribute to depression; although some women are very sensitive to hormonal changes, modern birth control pills are not associated with depression for most users.

## Q: If I Think I May Have Depression, Where Can I Get Help?

A: If you have symptoms of depression that are getting in the way of your ability to function with your studies and your social life, ask for help. Depression can get better with care and treatment. Don't wait for depression to go away by itself or think you can manage it all on your own, and don't ignore how you're feeling just because you think you can "explain" it. As a college student, you're busy—but you need to make time to get help. If you don't ask for help, depression may get worse and contribute to other health problems, while robbing you of the academic and social enjoyment and success that brought you to college in the first place. It can also lead to "self-medication" with high-risk behaviors with their own serious consequences, such as binge drinking and other substance abuse and having unsafe sex.

Most colleges provide mental health services through counseling centers, student health centers, or both. Check out your college website for information. If you think you might have depression, start by making an appointment with a doctor or health care provider for a checkup. This can be a doctor or health care provider at your college's student health services center, a doctor who is off-campus in your college town, or a doctor in your hometown. Your doctor can make sure that you do not have another health problem that is causing your depression.

If your doctor finds that you do not have another health problem, he or she can discuss treatment options or refer you to a mental health professional, such as a psychiatrist, counselor, or psychologist.

419

A mental health professional can give you a thorough evaluation and also treat your depression.

If you have thoughts of wishing you were dead or of suicide, call a helpline, such as 1-800-273-TALK (8255), for free 24-hour help, call campus security or 911, or go to the nearest emergency room.

## *Q: How Is Depression Treated?*

A: Effective treatments for depression include talk therapy (also called psychotherapy), personalized for your situation, or a combination of talk therapy and medication. Early treatment is best.

## *Q: What Is Talk Therapy?*

A: A therapist, such as a psychiatrist, a psychologist, a social worker, or counselor, can help you understand and manage your moods and feelings. You can talk out your emotions to someone who understands and supports you. You can also learn how to stop thinking negatively and start to look at the positives in life. This will help you build confidence and feel better about yourself as you begin to work with your therapist to find solutions to problems that may have seemed insurmountable when you were feeling depressed and maybe even hopeless. Research has shown that certain types of talk therapy or psychotherapy can help young adults deal with depression.

These include:

- Cognitive behavioral therapy, or CBT, which focuses on thoughts, behaviors, and feelings related to depression

- Interpersonal psychotherapy, or IPT, which focuses on working on relationships

- Dialectical behavior therapy, or DBT, which is especially useful when depression is accompanied by self-destructive or self-harming behavior

All therapies can be adapted to each person's issues, for example, if depression is associated with an anxiety or eating disorder. Your college counseling center may offer both individual and group counseling. Many also offer workshops and outreach programs to support you.

## *Q: What Medications Treat Depression?*

A: If your doctor thinks you need medication to help your depression, he or she may prescribe an antidepressant. There are a number of antidepressants that have been widely studied and proven to help. If your doctor recommends medication, it is important to see your doctor regularly and tell him or her about any side effects and how you are feeling, especially if you start feeling worse or have thoughts of hurting yourself. Although the doctor will attempt to "match" the best medication for your depression, sometimes it takes a little "trial and error" to find the best choice. If you or a close family member has done well on a particular medication in the past, that can be a good predictor of success again.

Always follow the directions of the doctor or health care provider when taking medication. You will need to take one or more regular doses of an antidepressant every day, and it may not take full effect for a few weeks. To avoid having depression return, most people continue taking medication for some months after they are feeling better. If your depression is long-lasting or comes back repeatedly, you may need to take antidepressants longer.

Although all antidepressants can cause side effects, some are more likely to cause certain side effects than others. Tell your doctor if you are often "sensitive" to medication; starting with a low dose and increasing it slowly to a full therapeutic level is the best way to minimize adverse effects. You may need to try more than one antidepressant medicine before finding the one that improves your symptoms without causing side effects that are difficult to live with.

### Q: What Else Can I Do?

A: Besides seeing a doctor and a counselor, you can also help your depression by being patient with yourself and good to yourself. Don't expect to get better immediately, but you will feel yourself improving gradually over time.

- Daily exercise, spending time outside in nature and in the sun, and eating healthy foods can also help you feel better.

- Get enough sleep. Try to have consistent sleep habits and avoid all-night study sessions.

- Your counselor may teach you how to be aware of your feelings and teach you relaxation techniques. Use these when you start feeling down or upset.

- Avoid using drugs and at least minimize, if not totally avoid, alcohol.

- Break up large tasks into small ones, and do what you can as you can; try not to do too many things at once.

- Try to spend time with supportive family members or friends, and take advantage of campus resources, such as student support groups. Talking with your parents, guardian, or other students who listen and care about you gives you support.

- Try to get out with friends and try fun things that help you express yourself. As you recover from depression, you may find that even if you don't feel like going out with friends, if you push yourself to do so, you'll be able to enjoy yourself more than you thought.

Remember that, by treating your depression, you are helping yourself succeed in college and after graduation.

## Q: What Are the Warning Signs for Suicide?

A: Depression is also a major risk factor for suicide. The following are some of the signs you might notice in yourself or a friend that may be reason for concern.

- Talking about wanting to die or to kill oneself

- Looking for a way to kill oneself, such as searching online or buying a gun

- Talking about feeling hopeless or having no reason to live

- Talking about feeling trapped or in unbearable pain

- Talking about being a burden to others and that others would be better off if one was gone

- Increasing the use of alcohol or drugs

- Acting anxious or agitated; behaving recklessly

- Giving away prized possessions

- Sleeping too little or too much

- Withdrawing or feeling isolated

- Showing rage or talking about seeking revenge

- Displaying extreme mood swing

## Q: What Should I Do If I Am Considering Suicide?

A: If you are in crisis and need help, call this toll-free number, available 24 hours a day, every day: 1-800-273-TALK (8255). You will reach the National Suicide Prevention Lifeline, a service available to anyone. You may call for yourself or for someone you care about, and all calls are confidential.

### Q: *What Should I Do If Someone I Know Is Considering Suicide?*

A: If you know someone who is considering suicide, do not leave him or her alone. Try to get your friend or loved one to seek immediate help from his or her doctor, campus security, the student health service, or the nearest hospital emergency room, or call 911. Remove any access he or she may have to firearms or other potential tools for suicide, including medications. You can also call to seek help as soon as possible by calling the Lifeline at 1-800-273-TALK (8255).

### Q: *Where Can I Learn More about Depression and Other Mental Health Issues?*

A: The National Institute of Mental Health (NIMH) website (http://www.nimh.nih.gov) provides information about various mental health disorders and mental health issues. On the website, you can also learn about the latest mental health research and news. The website is mobile-friendly. This means you can access the NIMH website anywhere, anytime, and on any device—from desktop computers to tablets and mobile phones.

# Chapter 33

# *Learning Disabilities*

## *What Are Learning Disabilities?*

Learning disabilities are conditions that affect how a person learns to read, write, speak, and calculate numbers. They are caused by differences in brain structure and affect the way a person's brain processes information.

Learning disabilities are usually discovered after a child begins attending school and has difficulties in one or more subjects that do not improve over time. A person can have more than one learning disability. Learning disabilities can last a person's entire life, but they may be alleviated with the right educational supports.

A learning disability is not an indication of a person's intelligence. Also, learning disabilities are not the same as learning problems due to intellectual and developmental disabilities, or emotional, vision, hearing, or motor skills problems.

Some of the most common learning disabilities include the following:

- **Dyslexia.** This condition causes problems with language skills, particularly reading. People with dyslexia may have difficulty spelling, understanding sentences, and recognizing words they already know.

---

Text in this chapter is excerpted from "Learning Disabilities: Condition Information," National Institute of Child Health and Human Development (NICHD), February 28, 2014.

- **Dysgraphia.** People with dysgraphia have problems with their handwriting. They may have problems forming letters, writing within a defined space, and writing down their thoughts.

- **Dyscalculia.** People with this math learning disability may have difficulty understanding arithmetic concepts and doing such tasks as addition, multiplication, and measuring.

- **Dyspraxia.** This condition, also termed sensory integration disorder, involves problems with motor coordination that lead to poor balance and clumsiness. Poor hand-eye coordination also causes difficulty with fine motor tasks such as putting puzzles together and coloring within the lines.

- **Apraxia of speech.** Sometimes called verbal apraxia, this disorder involves problems with speaking. People with this disorder have trouble saying what they want to say correctly and consistently.

- **Central auditory processing disorder.** People with this condition have trouble understanding and remembering language-related tasks. They have difficulty explaining things, understanding jokes, and following directions. They confuse words and are easily distracted.

- **Nonverbal learning disorders.** People with these conditions have strong verbal skills but great difficulty understanding facial expression and body language. In addition, they are physically clumsy and have trouble generalizing and following multi-step directions.

- **Visual perceptual/visual motor deficit.** People with this condition mix up letters; they might confuse "m" and "w" or "d" and "b," for example. They may also lose their place while reading, copy inaccurately, write messily, and cut paper clumsily. Aphasia, also called dysphasia, is a language disorder. A person with this disorder has difficulty understanding spoken language, poor reading comprehension, trouble with writing, and great difficulty finding words to express thoughts and feelings. Aphasia occurs when the language areas of the brain are damaged. In adults, it often is caused by stroke, but children may get aphasia from a brain tumor, head injury, or brain infection.

## What Are the Indicators of Learning Disabilities?

Many children have difficulty with reading, writing, or other learning-related tasks at some point, but this does not mean they have learning disabilities. A child with a learning disability often has several related signs, and these persist over time. The signs of learning disabilities vary from person to person. Common signs that a person may have learning disabilities include the following:

- Difficulty with reading and/or writing
- Problems with math skills
- Difficulty remembering
- Problems paying attention
- Trouble following directions
- Poor coordination
- Difficulty with concepts related to time
- Problems staying organized

A child with a learning disability also may exhibit one or more of the following:

- Impetuous behavior
- Inappropriate responses in school or social situations
- Difficulty staying on task (easily distracted)
- Difficulty finding the right way to say something
- Inconsistent school performance
- Immature way of speaking
- Difficulty listening well
- Problems dealing with new things in life
- Problems understanding words or concepts

These signs alone are not enough to determine that a person has a learning disability. A professional assessment is necessary to diagnose a learning disability.

Each learning disability has its own signs. Also, not every person with a particular disability will have all of the signs of that disability.

Children being taught in a second language that they are learning sometimes act in ways that are similar to the behaviors of someone with a learning disability. For this reason, learning disability assessment must take into account whether a student is bilingual or a second language learner.

Below are some common learning disabilities and the signs associated with them:

## *Dyslexia*

People with dyslexia usually have trouble making the connections between letters and sounds and with spelling and recognizing words.

People with dyslexia often show other signs of the condition. These may include:

- Failure to fully understand what others are saying
- Difficulty organizing written and spoken language
- Delayed ability to speak
- Poor self-expression (for example, saying "thing" or "stuff" for words not recalled)
- Difficulty learning new vocabulary, either through reading or hearing
- Trouble learning foreign languages
- Slowness in learning songs and rhymes
- Slow reading as well as giving up on longer reading tasks
- Difficulty understanding questions and following directions
- Poor spelling
- Difficulty recalling numbers in sequence (for example, telephone numbers and addresses)
- Trouble distinguishing left from right

## *Dysgraphia*

Dysgraphia is characterized by problems with writing. This disorder may cause a child to be tense and awkward when holding a pen or pencil, even to the extent of contorting his or her body. A child with very poor handwriting that he or she does not outgrow may have dysgraphia.

Other signs of this condition may include :

- A strong dislike of writing and/or drawing
- Problems with grammar
- Trouble writing down ideas

- A quick loss of energy and interest while writing

- Trouble writing down thoughts in a logical sequence

- Saying words out loud while writing

- Leaving words unfinished or omitting them when writing sentences

## Dyscalculia

Signs of this disability include problems understanding basic arithmetic concepts, such as fractions, number lines, and positive and negative numbers.

Other symptoms may include:

- Difficulty with math-related word problems

- Trouble making change in cash transactions

- Messiness in putting math problems on paper

- Trouble recognizing logical information sequences (for example, steps in math problems)

- Trouble with understanding the time sequence of events

- Difficulty with verbally describing math processes

## Dyspraxia

A person with dyspraxia has problems with motor tasks, such as hand-eye coordination, that can interfere with learning.

Some other symptoms of this condition include:

- Problems organizing oneself and one's things

- Breaking things

- Trouble with tasks that require hand-eye coordination, such as coloring within the lines, assembling puzzles, and cutting precisely

- Poor balance

- Sensitivity to loud and/or repetitive noises, such as the ticking of a clock

- Sensitivity to touch, including irritation over bothersome-feeling clothing

## How Many People Are Affected / at Risk for Learning Disabilities?

There is a wide range in estimates of the number of people affected by learning disabilities and disorders. Some of the variation results from differences in requirements for diagnosis in different states.

Some reports estimate that as many as 15% to 20% of Americans are affected by learning disabilities and disorders. In contrast, a major national study found that approximately 5% of children in the United States had learning disabilities. It also found that approximately 4% had both a learning disability and attention deficit/hyperactivity disorder (ADHD). Other research, conducted in 2006, estimated that 4.6 million school-age children in the United States have been diagnosed with learning disabilities.

## What Causes Learning Disabilities?

Researchers do not know exactly what causes learning disabilities, but they appear to be related to differences in brain structure. These differences are present from birth and often are inherited. To improve understanding of learning disabilities, researchers at the NICHD and elsewhere are studying areas of the brain and how they function. Scientists have found that learning disabilities are related to areas of the brain that deal with language and have used imaging studies to show that the brain of a dyslexic person develops and functions differently from a typical brain.

Sometimes, factors that affect a developing fetus, such as alcohol or drug use, can lead to a learning disability. Other factors in an infant's environment may play a role as well. These can include poor nutrition and exposure to toxins such as lead in water or paint. In addition, children who do not receive the support necessary to promote their intellectual development early on may show signs of learning disabilities once they start school.

Sometimes a person may develop a learning disability later in life. Possible causes in such a case include dementia or a traumatic brain injury (TBI).

## How Are Learning Disabilities Diagnosed?

Learning disabilities are often identified when a child begins to attend school. Educators may use a process called "response to intervention" (RTI) to help identify children with learning disabilities. Specialized testing is required to make a clear diagnosis, however.

## Response to Intervention

RTI usually involves the following:

- Monitoring all students progress closely to identify possible learning problems

- Providing a child identified as having problems with help on different levels, or tiers

- Moving this youngster through the tiers as appropriate, increasing educational assistance if the child does not show progress

Students who are struggling in school can also have individual evaluations. An evaluation can:

- Identify whether a child has a learning disability

- Determine a child's eligibility under federal law for special education services

- Help construct an individualized education plan (IEP) that outlines supports for a youngster who qualifies for special education services

- Establish a benchmark for measuring the child's educational progress

A full evaluation for a learning disability includes the following:

- A medical examination, including a neurological exam, to identify or rule out other possible causes of the child's difficulties, including emotional disorders, intellectual and developmental disabilities, and brain diseases

- Exploration of the youngster's developmental, social, and school performance

- A discussion of family history

- Academic achievement testing and psychological assessment

Usually, several specialists work as a team to perform an evaluation. The team may include a psychologist, special education expert, and speech-language pathologist (SLP). Many schools also have reading specialists on staff who can help diagnosis a reading disability.

## Role of School Psychologists

School psychologists are trained in both education and psychology. They can help to identify students with learning disabilities and can diagnose the learning disability. They can also help the student with the disability, parents, and teachers come up with plans that improve learning.

## *Role of SLPs*

All SLPs are trained in diagnosing and treating speech- and language-related disorders. A SLP can provide a complete language evaluation as well as an assessment of the child's ability to organize his or her thoughts and possessions. The SLP may evaluate various age-appropriate learning-related skills in the child, such as understanding directions, manipulating sounds, and reading and writing.

## Is There a Cure for Learning Disabilities?

Learning disabilities have no cure, but early intervention can provide tools and strategies to lessen their effects. People with learning disabilities can be successful in school and work and in their personal lives. More information is available about interventions for learning disabilities.

## What Are the Treatments for Learning Disabilities?

People with learning disabilities and disorders can learn strategies for coping with their disabilities. Getting help earlier increases the likelihood for success in school and later in life. If learning disabilities remain untreated, a child may begin to feel frustrated with schoolwork, which can lead to low self-esteem, depression, and other problems.

Usually, experts work to help a child learn skills by building on the child's strengths and developing ways to compensate for the child's weaknesses. Interventions vary depending on the nature and extent of the disability.

## *Special Education Services*

Children diagnosed with learning and other disabilities can qualify for special educational services. The Individuals with Disabilities Education Improvement Act (IDEA) requires that the public school system provide free special education supports to children with disabilities.

In most states, each child is entitled to these services beginning when he or she is 3 years old and extending through high school or until age 21, whichever comes first.

IDEA states that children must be taught in the least restrictive environments appropriate for them. This means the teaching environment should be designed to meet a child's specific needs and skills and should minimize restrictions on the youngster's access to typical learning experiences.

## Individualized Education Program

A child who qualifies for special education services should receive his or her own Individualized Education Program, or IEP. This personalized and written education plan:

- Lists individualized goals for the child

- Specifies the plan for services the youngster will receive

- Lists the specialists who will work with the child

## Qualifying for Special Education

To qualify for special education services, a child must be evaluated by the school system and meet specific criteria outlined in federal and state guidelines. To learn how to have a child assessed for special services, parents and caregivers can contact a local school principal or special education coordinator.

## Interventions for Specific Learning Disabilities

Below are just a few examples of ways educators help children with specific learning disabilities.

### Dyslexia

- **Special teaching techniques.** These can include helping a child learn through multisensory experiences and by providing immediate feedback to strengthen a child's ability to recognize words.

- **Classroom modifications.** For example, teachers can give students with dyslexia extra time to finish tasks and provide taped tests that allow the child to hear the questions instead of reading them.

- **Use of technology.** Children with dyslexia may benefit from listening to books on tape or using word-processing programs with spell-check features.

## Dysgraphia

- **Special tools.** Teachers can offer oral exams, provide a note-taker, and/or allow the child to videotape reports instead of writing them.

- **Use of technology.** A child with dysgraphia can be taught to use word-processing programs or an audio recorder instead of writing by hand.

- **Other ways of reducing the need for writing.** Teachers can provide notes, outlines, and preprinted study sheets.

## Dyscalculia

- **Visual techniques.** For example, teachers can draw pictures of word problems and show the student how to use colored pencils to differentiate parts of problems.

- **Use of memory aids.** Rhymes and music are among the techniques that can be used to help a child remember math concepts.

- **Use of computers.** A child with dyscalculia can use a computer for drills and practice.

## Dyspraxia

- **Quiet learning environment.** To help a child deal with sensitivity to noise and distractions, educators can provide the youngster with a quiet place for tests, silent reading, and other tasks that require concentration.

- **Alerting the child in advance.** For example, a child who is sensitive to noise may benefit from knowing in advance about such events as fire drills and assemblies.

- **Occupational therapy.** Exercises that focus on the tasks of daily living can help a child with poor coordination.

### *Other Treatments*

A child with a learning disability may struggle with low self-esteem, frustration, and other problems. Mental health professionals can help the youngster understand these feelings, develop coping tools, and build healthy relationships.

Children with learning disabilities sometimes have other conditions such as ADHD. These conditions require their own treatments, which may include therapy and medications.

Chapter 34

# *Pediatric Autoimmune Neuropsychiatric Disorders Associated with Streptococcal Infections (PANDAS)*

## *Overview*

### *What is PANDAS?*

PANDAS is short for Pediatric Autoimmune Neuropsychiatric Disorders Associated with Streptococcal Infections. A child may be diagnosed with PANDAS when:

- Obsessive compulsive disorder (OCD) and/or tic disorders suddenly appear following a strep infection (such as strep throat or scarlet fever); or

- The symptoms of OCD or tic symptoms suddenly become worse following a strep infection.

---

Text in this chapter is excerpted from "PANDAS: Fact Sheet about Pediatric Autoimmune Neuropsychiatric Disorders Associated with Streptococcal Infections," National Institute of Mental Health (NIMH), August 2015.

The symptoms are usually dramatic, happen "overnight and out of the blue," and can include motor and/or vocal tics, obsessions, and/or compulsions. In addition to these symptoms, children may also become moody, irritable, experience anxiety attacks, or show concerns about separating from parents or loved ones.

### What Causes PANDAS?

The strep bacteria is a very ancient organism which survives in its human host by hiding from the immune system as long as possible. It does this by putting molecules on its cell wall that look nearly identical to molecules found on the child's heart, joints, skin, and brain tissues. This is called "molecular mimicry" and allows the strep bacteria to evade detection for a time.

However, the molecules on the strep bacteria are eventually recognized as foreign to the body and the child's immune system reacts to them by producing antibodies. Because of the molecular mimicry, the antibodies react not only with the strep molecules, but also with the human host molecules that were mimicked.

The cross-reactive antibodies then trigger an immune reaction that "attacks" the mimicked molecules in the child's own tissues. Studies at the NIMH and elsewhere showed that some cross-reactive "anti-brain" antibodies target the brain, causing OCD, tics, and the other neuropsychiatric symptoms of PANDAS.

### Could an Adult Develop PANDAS?

PANDAS is considered a pediatric disorder and typically first appears in childhood from age 3 to puberty. Reactions to strep infections are rare after age 12, but the investigators recognize that PANDAS could occur (rarely) among adolescents. It is unlikely that someone would experience these post-strep neuropsychiatric symptoms for the first time as an adult, but it has not been fully studied.

It is possible that adolescents and adults may have immune-mediated OCD, but this is not known. The research studies at the NIMH are restricted to children.

## Symptoms

### How Is PANDAS Diagnosed?

The diagnosis of PANDAS is a clinical diagnosis, which means that there are no lab tests that can diagnose PANDAS. Instead, clinicians use 5 diagnostic criteria for the diagnosis of PANDAS (see below). At the present time the clinical features of the illness are the only means of determining whether or not a child might have PANDAS.

The diagnostic criteria are:

- Presence of obsessive-compulsive disorder and/or a tic disorder

- Pediatric onset of symptoms (age 3 years to puberty)

- Episodic course of symptom severity (see information below)

- Association with group A Beta-hemolytic streptococcal infection (a positive throat culture for strep or history of scarlet fever)

- Association with neurological abnormalities (physical hyperactivity, or unusual, jerky movements that are not in the child's control)

- Very abrupt onset or worsening of symptoms

If the symptoms have been present for more than a week, blood tests (antistreptococcal titers) may be done to document a preceding streptococcal infection.

### Are There Any Other Symptoms Associated with PANDAS Episodes?

Yes. Children with PANDAS often experience one or more of the following symptoms in conjunction with their OCD and/or tics:

- ADHD symptoms (hyperactivity, inattention, fidgety)

- Separation anxiety (child is "clingy" and has difficulty separating from his/her caregivers; for example, the child may not want to be in a different room in the house from his/her parents)

- Mood changes (irritability, sadness, emotional lability)

- Sleep disturbance

- Night-time bed wetting and/or day-time urinary frequency

- Fine/gross motor changes (e.g., changes in handwriting)

- Joint pains.

### What Is an Episodic Course of Symptoms?

Children with PANDAS seem to have dramatic ups and downs in their OCD and/or tic severity. Tics or OCD which are almost always present at a relatively consistent level do not represent an episodic course. Many kids with OCD or tics have good days and bad days, or even good weeks and bad weeks. However, patients with PANDAS have a very sudden onset or worsening of their symptoms, followed by a slow, gradual improvement. If they get another strep infection, their symptoms suddenly worsen again. The increased symptom severity usually persists for at least several weeks, but may last for several months or longer. The tics or OCD then seem to gradually fade away, and the children often enjoy a few weeks or several months without problems. When they have another strep throat infection, the tics or OCD may return just as suddenly and dramatically as they did previously.

### My Child Has Had Strep Throat before, and He Has Tics and / or OCD. Does That Mean He Has PANDAS?

No. Many children have OCD and/or tics, and almost all school aged children get strep throat at some point. In fact, the average grade-school student will have 2–3 strep throat infections each year.

PANDAS is considered as a diagnosis when there is a very close relationship between the abrupt onset or worsening or OCD and/or tics, and a preceding strep infection. If strep is found in conjunction with two or three episodes of OCD/tics, then it may be that the child has PANDAS.

### What Is an Anti-Streptococcal Antibody Titer?

The anti-streptococcal antibody titer determines whether the child has had a previous strep infection. Two different strep tests are commercially available:

- Antistrepolysin O (ASO) titer,* which rises 3–6 weeks after a strep infection, and

- Antistreptococcal DNAase B (AntiDNAse-B) titer, which rises 6-8 weeks after a strep infection.

*Titer refers to the amount of something, in this case biological molecules in blood that indicate a previous infection.*

### What Does an Elevated Anti-Streptococcal Antibody Titer Mean? Is This Bad for My Child?

An elevated anti-strep titer (such as ASO or AntiDNAse-B) means the child has had a strep infection sometime within the past few months, and his body created antibodies to fight the strep bacteria. Some grade-school aged children have chronically "elevated" titers. These may actually be in the normal range for that child, as there is a lot of individual variability in titer values.

Some children create lots of antibodies and have very high titers (up to 2,000), while others have more modest elevations. The height of the titer elevation doesn't matter. Further, elevated titers are not a bad thing. They are measuring a normal, healthy response—the production of antibodies to fight off an infection. The antibodies stay in the body for some time after the infection is gone, but the amount of time that the antibodies persist varies greatly between different individuals. Some children have "positive" antibody titers for many months after a single infection.

### When Is a Strep Titer Considered to Be Abnormal, Or "Elevated"?

The lab at NIH considers strep titers between 0–400 to be normal. Other labs set the upper limit at 150 or 200. Since each lab measures titers in different ways, it is important to know the range used by the laboratory where the test was done—just ask where they draw the line between negative or positive titers.

It is important to note that some grade-school aged children have chronically "elevated" titers. These may actually be in the normal range for that child, as there is a lot of individual variability in titer values. Because of this variability, doctors will often draw a titer when the child is sick, or shortly thereafter, and then draw another titer several weeks later to see if the titer is "rising"—if so, this is strong evidence that the illness was due to strep. (Of course, a less expensive way to make this determination is to take a throat culture at the time that the child is ill.)

### Are There Any Other Symptoms Associated with PANDAS Episodes?

Yes. Children with PANDAS often experience one or more of the following symptoms in conjunction with their OCD and/or tics:

- ADHD symptoms (hyperactivity, inattention, fidgety)

- Separation anxiety (child is "clingy" and has difficulty separating from his/her caregivers; for example, the child may not want to be in a different room in the house from his/her parents)

- Mood changes (irritability, sadness, emotional lability)
- Sleep disturbance
- Night-time bed wetting and/or day- time urinary frequency
- Changes in muscle movements ranging from small muscles (for example handwriting) to large (walking and running)
- Joint pains.

## What If My Child's Doctor Does Not Understand or Does Not Want to Consider PANDAS?

Contact the International OCD Foundation or the PANDAS Network to find a doctor who may be knowledgeable about PANDAS.

## Treatment

### What Are the Treatment Options for Children with PANDAS?

*Treatment with Antibiotics*

The best treatment for acute episodes of PANDAS is to treat the strep infection causing the symptoms (if it is still present) with antibiotics.

- A throat culture should be done to document the presence of strep bacteria in the throat (oropharynx).
- If the throat culture is positive, a single course of antibiotics will usually get rid of the strep infection and allow the PANDAS symptoms to subside.

If a properly obtained throat culture is negative, the clinician should make sure that the child doesn't have an occult strep infection, such as a sinus infection (often caused by strep bacteria) or strep bacteria infecting the anus, vagina, or urethral opening of the penis. Although the latter infections are rare, they have been reported to trigger PANDAS symptoms in some patients and can be particularly problematic because they will linger for longer periods of time and continue to provoke the production of cross-reactive antibodies.

The strep bacteria can be harder to eradicate in the sinuses and other sites, so the course of antibiotic treatment may need to be longer than that used for strep throat.

## Tips for Parents or Caregivers

- Sterilize or replace toothbrushes during/following the antibiotics treatment, to make sure that the child isn't re-infected with strep.

- It might also be helpful to check throat cultures on child's family members to make sure that none are "strep carriers" who could serve as a source of strep bacteria.

## Management of Neuropsychiatric Symptoms

Children with PANDAS-related obsessive-compulsive symptoms will benefit from standard medications and/or behavioral therapies, such as cognitive behavioral therapy (CBT). OCD symptoms are treated best with a combination of CBT and an SSRI medication, and tics respond to a variety of medications.

Children with PANDAS appear to be unusually sensitive to the side-effects of SSRIs and other medications, so it is important to "START LOW AND GO SLOW!!" when using these medications. In other words, clinicians should prescribe a very small starting dose of the medication and increase it slowly enough that the child experiences as few side-effects as possible. If symptoms worsen, the dosage should be decreased promptly. However, SSRIs and other medications should not be stopped abruptly, as that could also cause difficulties.

## What about Treating PANDAS with Plasma Exchange or Immunoglobulin (IVIG)?

Plasma exchange or immunoglobulin (IVIG) may be a consideration for acutely and severely affected children with PANDAS. Research suggests that both active treatments can improve global functioning, depression, emotional ups and downs, and obsessive-compulsive symptoms. However, there were a number of side-effects associated with the treatments, including nausea, vomiting, headaches, and dizziness.

In addition, there is a risk of infection with any invasive procedure, such as these. Thus, the treatments should be reserved for severely ill patients, and administered by a qualified team of health care professionals. Clinicians considering such an intervention are invited to contact the PANDAS research group at the NIMH for consultation.

### *Should an Elevated Strep Titer Be Treated with Antibiotics?*

No. Elevated titers indicate that a patient has had a past strep exposure but the titers can't tell you precisely when the strep infection occurred. Children may have "positive" titers for many months after one infection. Since these elevated titers are merely a marker of a prior infection and not proof of an ongoing infection it is not appropriate to give antibiotics for elevated titers. Antibiotics are recommended only when a child has a positive rapid strep test or positive strep throat culture.

### *Can Penicillin Be Used to Treat PANDAS or Prevent Future PANDAS Symptom Exacerbations?*

Penicillin and other antibiotics kill streptococcus and other types of bacteria. The antibiotics treat the sore throat or pharyngitis caused by the strep by getting rid of the bacteria. However, in PANDAS, it appears that antibodies produced by the body in response to the strep infection are the cause of the problem, not the bacteria themselves. Therefore one could not expect penicillin to treat the symptoms of PANDAS.

Researchers at the NIMH have been investigating the use of antibiotics as a form of prophylaxis or prevention of future problems. At this time, however, there isn't enough evidence to recommend the long-term use of antibiotics.

### *My Child Has PANDAS. Should He Have His Tonsils Removed?*

The NIH does not recommend tonsillectomies for children with PANDAS, as there is no evidence that they are helpful. If a tonsillectomy is recommended because of frequent episodes of tonsillitis, it would be useful to discuss the pros and cons of the procedure with your child's doctor because of the role that the tonsils play in fighting strep infections.

# Part Five

# Other Populations with Distinctive Mental Health Concerns

# Chapter 35

# *Mental Health for Men*

## *Introduction*

Mental health helps us face the challenges in our life, makes us feel comfortable, supports our physical health, and more. But day-to-day stress and difficult times can wear down our mental health. Major changes like losing a job, the death of a loved one, going off to combat, or coming out as gay can be especially hard. And even happy times—like becoming a father—can take a toll on your emotions.

Today, we know a lot more about ways to promote mental health. Try some simple steps, like making sure to get enough sleep, getting social support, exercising, and finding healthy ways to cope when you feel stressed.

If you are struggling with your mental health, you are not alone. In fact, about 1 out of 4 American adults suffers from a mental health condition each year. Experts don't know exactly what causes mental illnesses, but a combination of genes and life events often is involved. **It's important to remember that mental health disorders are real medical illnesses that can't be willed or wished away.**

This section describes some common mental health conditions. These include:

- Alcohol and drug abuse

- Anxiety disorders and PTSD

---

Text in this chapter is excerpted from "Mental Health for Men," Office on Women's Health (OWH), January 10, 2011. Reviewed March 2016.

- Body image and eating disorders

- Depression

Other mental health conditions include bipolar disorder, schizophrenia, and attention deficit hyperactivity disorder (ADHD).

## Alcohol and Drug Abuse

Alcohol and drug use in men often begin early in their lives, during the teen or young adult years. The reasons men begin drinking too much or using drugs vary, and the path from casual, social use to abuse and addiction is complex. What we do know is that abusing alcohol and drugs is very harmful—not only to you, but to the people in your life.

Anything more than moderate drinking can be risky. For a man, moderate drinking is considered two drinks a day.

Years of heavy drinking can lead to heart disease, cancer, and other health problems. Binge drinking, which is drinking five or more drinks at one time, can be especially dangerous.

Consider these risks of drinking too much or using drugs:

- Depression, anxiety, suicide

- Accidents

- Violence, often against loved ones

- Risky sexual behavior, such as unprotected sex or sex with multiple partners

- Employment problems

- Health problems, including cancer and HIV

- Addiction, which is a disease described by uncontrollable cravings and physical dependence

In the moment, it may seem like a good idea to use drugs or alcohol to get high, relax, or escape. But alcohol and drug abuse can soon cause serious problems. Fortunately, substance abuse disorders are also treatable. If you have a problem with drugs or alcohol, seek help from your doctor or a treatment facility. With treatment, it's possible to not only regain your health, but also restore the relationships that matter to you.

## Anxiety Disorders and PTSD

It's natural to feel worried or nervous at times, like before a work presentation or having an operation. But for people with anxiety disorders, everyday situations cause much more worry than most people feel. Often, people with these disorders know their anxiety is extreme, but they can't make the anxious feelings go away.

Types of anxiety disorders include:

- Generalized anxiety disorder

- Obsessive-compulsive disorder (OCD)

- Panic disorder

- Phobias

Posttraumatic stress disorder (PTSD) is one of the more common anxiety disorders. Its symptoms include feeling like you are reliving a dangerous experience. Men who serve in combat may develop PTSD. But it also can come from living through any dangerous experience, like an accident or hurricane. Men who have PTSD may experience it differently from women. For example, women with PTSD may feel very jumpy, but men are more likely to feel angry or have problems with alcohol or drugs.

Social phobia, which makes a person feel very strong fear in social situations, also often affects men. It can come up when you need to speak in a large group, for example, and can cause both emotional and physical symptoms, like feeling sick to your stomach.

## Body Image and Eating Disorders

- Body image issues

- Eating disorders

Did you know that men, like women, can struggle with body image issues or an eating disorder? Men may feel a lot of pressure to have a "perfect," muscular body and may focus too much on exercise and dieting. This focus can wind up hurting a man's body, job, and relationships. But medicines and counseling can help men with eating and body image disorders lead healthy lives.

### Body Image Issues

People with body image issues may feel unhappy with how they look and feel self-conscious about their bodies. If these feelings are extreme, the person may have body dysmorphic disorder (BDD). People with BDD have extreme concern over what they see as flaws. Men and women are affected equally, but may focus on different parts of the

447

body. Men tend to worry more about their skin, hair, nose, muscles, and genitals.

Obsession with food or how you look can be very painful. If you have eating or body image issues, don't let shame or embarrassment keep you from seeking help.

### Eating Disorders

Eating disorders involve extreme emotions, attitudes, and behaviors around weight and food. The most common eating disorder for men is binge eating disorder.

With binge eating disorder, people eat a lot of food even if they feel full. They sometimes may try to make up for their overeating episodes by dieting. Other eating disorders that affect men include anorexia and bulimia.

## Depression

Depression is not the same as a passing blue mood. It is a serious illness that affects the body, mood, and thoughts. People with a depressive illness cannot merely "pull themselves together" and choose to get better. Without treatment, depression can lead to personal, family, and financial problems, and, in some cases, to suicide.

Studies have found that depression is more common in women than men. But we don't know if depression is really less common in men.

It may be that men are just less likely than women to recognize and seek help for depression. Some signs of depression include:

- Ongoing sad, anxious, or "empty" mood
- Feeling hopeless
- Feeling guilty, worthless, or helpless
- Loss of interest or pleasure in activities that were once enjoyable, including sex
- Decreased energy
- Trouble staying focused, remembering, or making decisions
- Trouble sleeping
- Changes in appetite and/or weight
- Restlessness or irritability

- Ongoing physical symptoms like headaches or digestive problems that don't get better with treatment

- Thoughts of death, suicide, or suicide attempts

Men often cope with depression differently than women do. Men may turn to alcohol or drugs, or they may become frustrated, discouraged, angry, irritable, or, sometimes, violent.

If you have symptoms of depression or if emotional problems interfere with your work or family life, see your doctor. Treatment can help most people with depression. Treatment usually involves counseling (talk therapy), medication, or both. If you or someone you care about shows signs of depression, don't wait—seek help now.

Chapter 36

# Mental Health Issues among Women

## Chapter Contents

Section 36.1

# Premenstrual Syndrome and Premenstrual Dysphoric Disorder

Text in this section is excerpted from "Premenstrual
Syndrome (PMS) Fact Sheet," Office on Women's
Health (OWH), December 23, 2014.

## What Is Premenstrual Syndrome (PMS)?

Premenstrual syndrome (PMS) is a group of symptoms linked to the menstrual cycle. PMS symptoms occur 1 to 2 weeks before your period (menstruation or monthly bleeding) starts. The symptoms usually go away after you start bleeding. PMS can affect menstruating women of any age and the effect is different for each woman. For some people, PMS is just a monthly bother. For others, it may be so severe that it makes it hard to even get through the day. PMS goes away when your monthly periods stop, such as when you get pregnant or go through menopause.

## What Causes PMS?

The causes of PMS are not clear, but several factors may be involved. Changes in hormones during the menstrual cycle seem to be an important cause. These changing hormone levels may affect some women more than others. Chemical changes in the brain may also be involved. Stress and emotional problems, such as depression, do not seem to cause PMS, but they may make it worse. Some other possible causes include:

- Low levels of vitamins and minerals

- Eating a lot of salty foods, which may cause you to retain (keep) fluid

- Drinking alcohol and caffeine, which may alter your mood and energy level

452

## What Are the Symptoms of PMS?

PMS often includes both physical and emotional symptoms, such as:

- Acne
- Swollen or tender breasts
- Feeling tired
- Trouble sleeping
- Upset stomach, bloating, constipation, or diarrhea
- Headache or backache
- Appetite changes or food cravings
- Joint or muscle pain .
- Trouble with concentration or memory
- Tension, irritability, mood swings, or crying spells
- Anxiety or depression

Symptoms vary from woman to woman.

## How Do I Know If I Have PMS?

Your doctor may diagnose PMS based on which symptoms you have, when they occur, and how much they affect your life. If you think you have PMS, keep track of which symptoms you have and how severe they are for a few months. Record your symptoms each day on a calendar or PMS symptom tracker. Take this form with you when you see your doctor about your PMS.

Your doctor will also want to make sure you don't have one of the following conditions that shares symptoms with PMS:

- Depression
- Anxiety
- Menopause
- Chronic fatigue syndrome (CFS)
- Irritable bowel syndrome (IBS)
- Problems with the endocrine system, which makes hormones

## How Common Is PMS?

There's a wide range of estimates of how many women suffer from PMS. The American College of Obstetricians and Gynecologists estimates that at least 85 percent of menstruating women have at least 1 PMS symptom as part of their monthly cycle. Most of these women have fairly mild symptoms that don't need treatment. Others (about 3 to 8 percent) have a more severe form of PMS, called premenstrual dysphoric disorder (PMDD).

- Are between their late 20s and early 40s

- Have at least 1 child

- Have a family history of depression

- Have a past medical history of either postpartum depression or a mood disorder

## What Is the Treatment for PMS?

Many things have been tried to ease the symptoms of PMS. No treatment works for every woman. You may need to try different ones to see what works for you. Some treatment options include:

- Lifestyle changes

- Medications

- Alternative therapies

### Lifestyle Changes

If your PMS isn't so bad that you need to see a doctor, some lifestyle changes may help you feel better. Below are some steps you can take that may help ease your symptoms.

- Exercise regularly. Each week, you should get:

  - Two hours and 30 minutes of moderate-intensity physical activity;

  - One hour and 15 minutes of vigorous-intensity aerobic physical activity; or

  - A combination of moderate and vigorous-intensity activity; and

  - Muscle-strengthening activities on 2 or more days.

- Eat healthy foods, such as fruits, vegetables, and whole grains.

- Avoid salt, sugary foods, caffeine, and alcohol, especially when you're having PMS symptoms.

- Get enough sleep. Try to get about 8 hours of sleep each night.

- Find healthy ways to cope with stress. Talk to your friends, exercise, or write in a journal. Some women also find yoga, massage, or relaxation therapy helpful.

- Don't smoke.

## *Medications*

Over-the-counter pain relievers may help ease physical symptoms, such as cramps, headaches, backaches, and breast tenderness. These include:

- Ibuprofen (for instance, Advil, Motrin, Midol Cramp)

- Ketoprofen (for instance, Orudis KT)

- Naproxen (for instance, Aleve)

- Aspirin

In more severe cases of PMS, prescription medicines may be used to ease symptoms. One approach has been to use drugs that stop ovulation, such as birth control pills. Women on the pill report fewer PMS symptoms, such as cramps and headaches, as well as lighter periods.

Researchers continue to search for new ways to treat PMS. Talk to your doctor about whether taking part in a clinical trial might be right for you.

## **Alternative Therapies**

Certain vitamins and minerals have been found to help relieve some PMS symptoms. These include:

- Folic acid (400 micrograms)

- Calcium with vitamin D (see chart below for amounts)

- Magnesium (400 milligrams)

- Vitamin B-6 (50 to 100 mg)

- Vitamin E (400 international units)

**Table 36.1.** Amounts of calcium you need each day

| Ages | Milligrams per day |
|---|---|
| 9–18 | 1300 |
| 19–50 | 1000 |
| 51 and older | 1200 |

Pregnant or nursing women need the same amount of calcium as other women of the same age.

Some women find their PMS symptoms relieved by taking supplements such as:

- Black cohosh

- Chasteberry

- Evening primrose oil

Talk with your doctor before taking any of these products. Many have not been proven to work and they may interact with other medicines you are taking.

## What Is Premenstrual Dysphoric Disorder (PMDD)?

A brain chemical called serotonin may play a role in Premenstrual Dysphoric Disorder (PMDD), a severe form of PMS. The main symptoms, which can be disabling, include:

- Feelings of sadness or despair, or even thoughts of suicide

- Feelings of tension or anxiety

- Panic attacks

- Mood swings or frequent crying

- Lasting irritability or anger that affects other people

- Lack of interest in daily activities and relationships

- Trouble thinking or focusing

- Tiredness or low energy

- Food cravings or binge eating

- Trouble sleeping

- Feeling out of control

- Physical symptoms, such as bloating, breast tenderness, head-aches, and joint or muscle pain

You must have 5 or more of these symptoms to be diagnosed with PMDD. Symptoms occur during the week before your period and go away after bleeding starts.

Making some lifestyle changes may help ease PMDD symptoms. See "What is the treatment for PMS?" above to learn more.

Antidepressants called selective serotonin reuptake inhibitors (SSRIs) have also been shown to help some women with PMDD. These drugs change serotonin levels in the brain. The U.S. Food and Drug Administration (FDA) has approved 3 SSRIs for the treatment of PMDD:

- Sertraline (Zoloft)

- Fluoxetine (Sarafem)

- Paroxetine HCI (Paxil CR)

Yaz (drospirenone and ethinyl estradiol is the only birth control pill approved by the FDA to treat PMDD. Individual counseling, group counseling, and stress management may also help relieve symptoms.

## Section 36.2

# *Women and Depression*

Text in this section is excerpted from "Depression in Women," National Institute of Mental Health (NIMH), 2013.

## *Depression in Women*

### *What Is Depression?*

Everyone sometimes feels sad, but these feelings usually pass after a few days. When a woman has depression, she has trouble with her daily life for weeks at a time. More women than men get depression. It is a serious illness, and most women who have it need treatment to get better.

## What Are the Different Forms of Depression?

The types of depression that affect women include:

• Major depression—severe symptoms that interfere with a woman's ability to work, sleep, study, eat, and enjoy life. An episode of major depression may occur only once in a person's lifetime. But more often, a person can have several episodes.

If the symptoms of depression began either during pregnancy or in the month after giving birth, a woman is said to have postpartum (or peripartum) depression. Women who have had episodes of depression before they became pregnant are at increased risk of postpartum depression.

• Persistent depressive disorder—depressed mood that lasts for at least 2 years. A person diagnosed with persistent depressive disorder may have episodes of major depression along with periods of less severe symptoms, but symptoms must last for 2 years

• Premenstrual dysphoric disorder—symptoms include severe mood swings, depressed mood, and anxiety that appear consistently in the week before a woman's menstrual period and lift within a few days. Symptoms are severe enough to interfere with daily activities and relationships

## What Causes Depression?

Different kinds of factors play a role in the risk of depression. Depression tends to run in families. One of the reasons for this has to do with genes. Some genes increase the risk of depression. Others increase resilience—the ability to recover from hardship—and protect against depression. Experiences such as trauma or abuse during childhood and stress during adulthood can raise risk. However, the same stresses or losses may trigger depression in one person and not another. Factors such as a warm family and healthy social connections can increase resilience.

Research has shown that in people with depression, there can be subtle changes in the brain systems involved in mood, energy, and thinking and how the brain responds to stress. The changes may differ from person to person, so that a treatment that works for one person may not work for another.

During childhood, girls and boys experience depression at about equal rates. By the teen years, however, girls become more likely to experience depression than boys. Researchers continue to explore the reasons for this difference and how changes in hormone levels may be involved in depression risk during a woman's lifetime.

## How Is Depression Treated?

The first step to getting the right treatment is to visit a doctor or mental health professional. He or she can do an exam or lab tests to rule out other conditions that may have the same symptoms as depression. He or she can also tell if certain medications you are taking may be affecting your mood. The doctor should get a complete history of symptoms, including when they started, how long they have lasted, and how bad they are. He or she should also know whether they have occurred before, and if so, how they were treated. He or she should also ask if there is a history of depression in your family.

### Medication

Medications called antidepressants can work well to treat depression. They can take several weeks to work. Antidepressants can have side effects including:

- Headache
- Nausea, feeling sick to your stomach
- Difficulty sleeping and nervousness
- Agitation or restlessness
- Sexual problems

Most side effects lessen over time. Talk to your doctor about any side effects you may have.

It's important to know that although antidepressants can be safe and effective for many people, they may present serious risks to some, especially children, teens, and young adults. A "black box"—the most serious type of warning that a prescription drug can have—has been added to the labels of antidepressant medications. These labels warn people that antidepressants may cause some people, especially those who become agitated when they first start taking the medication and before it begins to work, to have suicidal thoughts or make suicide attempts. Anyone taking antidepressants should be monitored closely, especially when they first start taking them. For most people, though, the risks of untreated depression far outweigh those of antidepressant medications when they are used under a doctor's careful supervision.

*Therapy*

Several types of therapy can help treat depression. Therapy helps by teaching new ways of thinking and behaving, and changing habits that may be contributing to the depression. Therapy can also help women understand and work through difficult relationships that may be causing their depression or making it worse.

Researchers are developing new ways to treat depression more quickly and effectively.

### How Can I Help a Loved One Who Is Depressed?

If you know someone who has depression, first help her see a doctor or mental health professional.

- Offer her support, understanding, patience, and encouragement.
- Talk to her, and listen carefully.
- Never ignore comments about suicide, and report them to her therapist or doctor.
- Invite her out for walks, outings, and other activities. If she says no, keep trying, but don't push her to take on too much too soon.
- Remind her that with time and treatment, the depression will lift.

### How Can I Help Myself If I Am Depressed?

As you continue treatment, gradually you will start to feel better. Remember that if you are taking an antidepressant, it may take several weeks for it to start working. Try to do things that you used to enjoy before you had depression. Go easy on yourself. Other things that may help include:

- Breaking up large tasks into small ones, and doing what you can as you can. Try not to do too many things at once.
- Spending time with other people and talking to a friend or relative about your feelings.
- Postponing important decisions until you feel better. Discuss decisions with others who know you well.

### Where Can I Go for Help?

If you are unsure where to go for help, ask your family doctor. You can also check the phone book for mental health professionals. Hospital doctors can help in an emergency.

Women are more likely than men to attempt suicide. If you or someone you know is in crisis, get help quickly.

- Call your doctor.

- Call 911 for emergency services.

- Go to the nearest hospital emergency room.

- Call the toll-free, 24-hour hotline of the National Suicide Prevention Lifeline at 1-800-273-TALK (1-800-273-8255); TTY: 1-800-799-4TTY (4889).

## Section 36.3

# *Pregnancy and Depression*

Text in this section is excerpted from "Depression during and after Pregnancy–Fact Sheet," Office on Women's Health (OWH), February 12, 2016.

## How Common Is Depression during and after Pregnancy?

Depression is a common problem during and after pregnancy. About 13 percent of pregnant women and new mothers have depression.

## How Do I Know If I Have Depression?

When you are pregnant or after you have a baby, you may be depressed and not know it. Some normal changes during and after pregnancy can cause symptoms similar to those of depression. But if you have any of the following symptoms of depression for more than 2 weeks, call your doctor:

- Feeling restless or moody

- Feeling sad, hopeless, and overwhelmed

- Crying a lot

- Having no energy or motivation

- Eating too little or too much
- Sleeping too little or too much
- Having trouble focusing or making decisions
- Having memory problems
- Feeling worthless and guilty
- Losing interest or pleasure in activities you used to enjoy
- Withdrawing from friends and family
- Having headaches, aches and pains, or stomach problems that don't go away

Your doctor can figure out if your symptoms are caused by depression or something else.

## What Causes Depression? What about Postpartum Depression?

There is no single cause. Rather, depression likely results from a combination of factors:

- Depression is a mental illness that tends to run in families. Women with a family history of depression are more likely to have depression.
- Changes in brain chemistry or structure are believed to play a big role in depression.
- Stressful life events, such as death of a loved one, caring for an aging family member, abuse, and poverty, can trigger depression.
- Hormonal factors unique to women may contribute to depression in some women. We know that hormones directly affect the brain chemistry that controls emotions and mood. We also know that women are at greater risk of depression at certain times in their lives, such as puberty, during and after pregnancy, and during perimenopause. Some women also have depressive symptoms right before their period.

Depression after childbirth is called postpartum depression. Hormonal changes may trigger symptoms of postpartum depression. When you are pregnant, levels of the female hormones estrogen and progesterone increase greatly. In the first 24 hours after childbirth, hormone levels quickly return to normal. Researchers think the big change in hormone levels may lead to depression. This is much like the way smaller hormone changes can affect a woman's moods before she gets her period.

Levels of thyroid hormones may also drop after giving birth. The thyroid is a small gland in the neck that helps regulate how your body uses and stores energy from food. Low levels of thyroid hormones can cause symptoms of depression. A simple blood test can tell if this condition is causing your symptoms. If so, your doctor can prescribe thyroid medicine.

Other factors may play a role in postpartum depression. You may feel:

- Tired after delivery
- Tired from a lack of sleep or broken sleep
- Overwhelmed with a new baby
- Doubts about your ability to be a good mother
- Stress from changes in work and home routines
- An unrealistic need to be a perfect mom
- Loss of who you were before having the baby
- Less attractive
- A lack of free time

## Are Some Women More at Risk for Depression during and after Pregnancy?

Certain factors may increase your risk of depression during and after pregnancy:

- A personal history of depression or another mental illness
- A family history of depression or another mental illness
- A lack of support from family and friends
- Anxiety or negative feelings about the pregnancy
- Problems with a previous pregnancy or birth
- Marriage or money problems
- Stressful life events

- Young age

- Substance abuse

Women who are depressed during pregnancy have a greater risk of depression after giving birth. The U.S. Preventive Services Task Force (USPSTF) recommends screening for depression during and after pregnancy, regardless of a woman's risk factors for depression.

## What Is the Difference between "Baby Blues," Postpartum Depression, and Postpartum Psychosis?

Many women have the baby blues in the days after childbirth. If you have the baby blues, you may:

- Have mood swings

- Feel sad, anxious, or overwhelmed

- Have crying spells

- Lose your appetite

- Have trouble sleeping

The baby blues most often go away within a few days or a week. The symptoms are not severe and do not need treatment.

The symptoms of postpartum depression last longer and are more severe. Postpartum depression can begin anytime within the first year after childbirth. If you have postpartum depression, you may have any of the symptoms of depression listed above. Symptoms may also include:

- Thoughts of hurting the baby

- Thoughts of hurting yourself

- Not having any interest in the baby

Postpartum depression needs to be treated by a doctor.

Postpartum psychosis is rare. It occurs in about 1 to 4 out of every 1,000 births. It usually begins in the first 2 weeks after childbirth. Women who have bipolar disorder or another mental health problem called schizoaffective disorder have a higher risk for postpartum psychosis. Symptoms may include:

- Seeing things that aren't there

- Feeling confused

- Having rapid mood swings
- Trying to hurt yourself or your baby

## What Should I Do If I Have Symptoms of Depression during or after Pregnancy?

Call your doctor if:

- Your baby blues don't go away after 2 weeks
- Symptoms of depression get more and more intense
- Symptoms of depression begin any time after delivery, even many months later
- It is hard for you to perform tasks at work or at home
- You cannot care for yourself or your baby
- You have thoughts of harming yourself or your baby

Your doctor can ask you questions to test for depression. Your doctor can also refer you to a mental health professional who specializes in treating depression.

Some women don't tell anyone about their symptoms. They feel embarrassed, ashamed, or guilty about feeling depressed when they are supposed to be happy. They worry they will be viewed as unfit parents.

Any woman may become depressed during pregnancy or after having a baby. It doesn't mean you are a bad or "not together" mom. You and your baby don't have to suffer. There is help.

Here are some other helpful tips:

- Rest as much as you can. Sleep when the baby is sleeping.
- Don't try to do too much or try to be perfect.
- Ask your partner, family, and friends for help.
- Make time to go out, visit friends, or spend time alone with your partner.
- Discuss your feelings with your partner, family, and friends.
- Talk with other mothers so you can learn from their experiences.
- Join a support group. Ask your doctor about groups in your area.

- Don't make any major life changes during pregnancy or right after giving birth. Major changes can cause unneeded stress. Sometimes big changes can't be avoided. When that happens, try to arrange support and help in your new situation ahead of time.

## How Is Depression Treated?

The two common types of treatment for depression are:

1. **Talk therapy.** This involves talking to a therapist, psychologist, or social worker to learn to change how depression makes you think, feel, and act.

2. **Medicine.** Your doctor can prescribe an antidepressant medicine. These medicines can help relieve symptoms of depression.

These treatment methods can be used alone or together. If you are depressed, your depression can affect your baby. Getting treatment is important for you and your baby. Talk with your doctor about the benefits and risks of taking medicine to treat depression when you are pregnant or breastfeeding.

## What Can Happen If Depression Is Not Treated?

Untreated depression can hurt you and your baby. Some women with depression have a hard time caring for themselves during pregnancy. They may:

- Eat poorly
- Not gain enough weight
- Have trouble sleeping
- Miss prenatal visits
- Not follow medical instructions
- Use harmful substances, like tobacco, alcohol, or illegal drugs

Depression during pregnancy can raise the risk of:

- Problems during pregnancy or delivery
- Having a low-birth-weight baby
- Premature birth

Untreated postpartum depression can affect your ability to parent. You may:

- Lack energy
- Have trouble focusing
- Feel moody
- Not be able to meet your child's needs

As a result, you may feel guilty and lose confidence in yourself as a mother. These feelings can make your depression worse.

Researchers believe postpartum depression in a mother can affect her baby. It can cause the baby to have:

- Delays in language development
- Problems with mother-child bonding
- Behavior problems
- Increased crying

It helps if your partner or another caregiver can help meet the baby's needs while you are depressed.

All children deserve the chance to have a healthy mom. And all moms deserve the chance to enjoy their life and their children. If you are feeling depressed during pregnancy or after having a baby, don't suffer alone. Please tell a loved one and call your doctor right away.

Section 36.4

# *Postpartum Depression and Postpartum Psychosis*

Text in this section is excerpted from "Postpartum Depression Facts,"
National Institute of Mental Health (NIMH), December 13, 2013.

## *What Is Postpartum Depression?*

Postpartum depression is a mood disorder that can affect women after childbirth. Mothers with postpartum depression experience feelings of extreme sadness, anxiety, and exhaustion that may make it difficult for them to complete daily care activities for themselves or for others.

## *What Causes Postpartum Depression?*

Postpartum depression does not have a single cause, but likely results from a combination of physical and emotional factors. Postpartum depression does not occur because of something a mother does or does not do.

After childbirth, the levels of hormones (estrogen and progesterone) in a woman's body quickly drop. This leads to chemical changes in her brain that may trigger mood swings. In addition, many mothers are unable to get the rest they need to fully recover from giving birth. Constant sleep deprivation can lead to physical discomfort and exhaustion, which can contribute to the symptoms of postpartum depression.

## *What Are the Symptoms of Postpartum Depression?*

Some of the more common symptoms a woman may experience include:

- Feeling sad, hopeless, empty, or overwhelmed

- Crying more often than usual or for no apparent reason

- Worrying or feeling overly anxious

- Feeling moody, irritable, or restless

- Oversleeping, or being unable to sleep even when her baby is asleep

- Having trouble concentrating, remembering details, and making decisions

- Experiencing anger or rage

- Losing interest in activities that are usually enjoyable

- Suffering from physical aches and pains, including frequent headaches, stomach problems, and muscle pain

- Eating too little or too much

- Withdrawing from or avoiding friends and family

- Having trouble bonding or forming an emotional attachment with her baby

- Persistently doubting her ability to care for her baby

- Thinking about harming herself or her baby

## How Can a Woman Tell If She Has Postpartum Depression?

Only a health care provider can diagnose a woman with postpartum depression. Because symptoms of this condition are broad and may vary between women, a healthcare provider can help a woman figure out whether the symptoms she is feeling are due to postpartum depression or something else. A woman who experiences any of these symptoms should see a healthcare provider right away.

## How Is Postpartum Depression Different from the "Baby Blues"?

The "baby blues" is a term used to describe the feelings of worry, unhappiness, and fatigue that many women experience after having a baby. Babies require a lot of care, so it's normal for mothers to be worried about, or tired from, providing that care. Baby blues, which affects up to 80 percent of mothers, includes feelings that are somewhat mild, last a week or two, and go away on their own.

With postpartum depression, feelings of sadness and anxiety can be extreme and might interfere with a woman's ability to care for herself or her family. Because of the severity of the symptoms, postpartum depression usually requires treatment. The condition, which occurs in nearly 15 percent of births, may begin shortly before or any time after childbirth, but commonly begins between a week and a month after delivery.

## Are Some Women More Likely to Experience Postpartum Depression?

Some women are at greater risk for developing postpartum depression because they have one or more risk factors, such as:

- Symptoms of depression during or after a previous pregnancy

- Previous experience with depression or bipolar disorder at another time in her life

- A family member who has been diagnosed with depression or other mental illness

- A stressful life event during pregnancy or shortly after giving birth, such as job loss, death of a loved one, domestic violence, or personal illness

- Medical complications during childbirth, including premature delivery or having a baby with medical problems

- Mixed feelings about the pregnancy, whether it was planned or unplanned

- A lack of strong emotional support from her spouse, partner, family, or friends

- Alcohol or other drug abuse problems

Postpartum depression can affect any woman regardless of age, race, ethnicity, or economic status.

## How Is Postpartum Depression Treated?

There are effective treatments for postpartum depression. A woman's health care provider can help her choose the best treatment, which may include:

- **Counseling/Talk Therapy:** This treatment involves talking one-on-one with a mental health professional (a counselor, therapist, psychologist, psychiatrist, or social worker). Two types of counseling shown to be particularly effective in treating postpartum depression are:

- **Cognitive behavioral therapy (CBT),** which helps people recognize and change their negative thoughts and behaviors; and

- **Interpersonal therapy (IPT),** which helps people understand and work through problematic personal relationships.

- **Medication:** Antidepressant medications act on the brain chemicals that are involved in mood regulation. Many antidepressants take a few weeks to be most effective. While these medications are generally considered safe to use during breastfeeding, a woman should talk to her healthcare provider about the risks and benefits to both herself and her baby.

These treatment methods can be used alone or together.

## What Can Happen If Postpartum Depression Is Left Untreated?

Without treatment, postpartum depression can last for months or years. In addition to affecting the mother's health, it can interfere with her ability to connect with and care for her baby and may cause the baby to have problems with sleeping, eating, and behavior as he or she grows.

## How Can Family and Friends Help?

Family members and friends may be the first to recognize symptoms of postpartum depression in a new mother. They can encourage her to talk with a health care provider, offer emotional support, and assist with daily tasks such as caring for the baby or the home.

## Section 36.5

# *Menopause and Mental Health*

This section includes excerpts from "Menopause and Menopause
Treatments—Fact Sheet," Office on Women's Health (OWH), July 16,
2012. Reviewed March 2016; and text from "Menopause and Mental
Health," Office on Women's Health (OWH), September 29, 2010.
Reviewed March 2016.

## What Is Menopause?

Menopause is the point in time when a woman's menstrual periods
stop. Some people call the years leading up to a woman's last period
"menopause," but that time actually is perimenopause.

Periods can stop for a while and then start again, so a woman is
considered to have been through menopause only after a full year
without periods. (There also can't be some other reason for the periods
stopping like being sick or pregnant.) After menopause, a woman no
longer can get pregnant. It is common to experience symptoms such
as hot flashes in the time around menopause.

The average age of menopause is 51, but for some women it happens
in their 40s or later in their 50s. Sometimes called "the change of life,"
menopause is a normal part of life.

## How Can I Manage Symptoms of Menopause?

It is not necessary to get treatment for your symptoms unless they
are bothering you. You can learn about simple lifestyle changes that may
help with symptoms, and some symptoms will go away on their own.
If you're interested in medical treatments like menopausal hormone
therapy (MHT), ask your doctor about the possible risks and benefits.

Here are some ways to deal with symptoms:

### *Hot Flashes*

- Try to avoid things that may trigger hot flashes, like spicy foods,
  alcohol, caffeine, stress, or being in a hot place.
- Dress in layers, and remove some when you feel a flash starting.

- Use a fan in your home or workplace.
- Try taking slow, deep breaths when a hot flash starts.
- If you still get periods, ask your doctor about low-dose oral contraceptives (birth control pills), which may help.
- Some women can take menopausal hormone therapy (MHT), which can be very effective in treating hot flashes and night sweats.
- If MHT is not an option, your doctor may prescribe medications that usually are used for other conditions, like epilepsy, depression, and high blood pressure, but that have been shown to help with hot flashes.

## Vaginal Dryness

- Try to avoid things that may trigger hot flashes, like spicy foods, alcohol, caffeine, stress, or being in a hot place.
- Dress in layers, and remove some when you feel a flash starting.
- Use a fan in your home or workplace.
- Try taking slow, deep breaths when a hot flash starts.
- If you still get periods, ask your doctor about low-dose oral contraceptives (birth control pills), which may help.
- Some women can take menopausal hormone therapy (MHT), which can be very effective in treating hot flashes and night sweats.
- If MHT is not an option, your doctor may prescribe medications that usually are used for other conditions, like epilepsy, depression, and high blood pressure, but that have been shown to help with hot flashes.

## Problems Sleeping

- Be physically active (but not too close to bedtime, since exercise might make you more awake).
- Avoid large meals, smoking, and working right before bed. Avoid caffeine after noon.
- Keep your bedroom dark, quiet, and cool. Use your bedroom only for sleep and sex.

- Avoid napping during the day.
- Try to go to bed and get up at the same times every day.
- If you can't get to sleep, get up and read until you're tired.
- If hot flashes are the cause of sleep problems, treating the hot flashes usually will help.

## Mood Swings

- Try getting enough sleep and staying physically active to feel your best.
- Learn ways to deal with stress. Our fact sheet on "Stress and your health" has helpful tips.
- Talk to your doctor to see if you may have depression, which is a serious illness.
- Consider seeing a therapist or joining a support group.
- If you are using MHT for hot flashes or another menopause symptom, your mood swings may get better too.

## Memory Problems

- Getting enough sleep and keeping physically active may help.
- If forgetfulness or other mental problems are affecting your daily life, see your doctor.

## Urinary Incontinence

- Ask your doctor about treatments, including medicines, behavioral changes, certain devices, and surgery.

## Can Menopausal Hormone Therapy (MHT) Help Treat My Symptoms?

MHT, which used to be called hormone replacement therapy (HRT), involves taking the hormones estrogen and progesterone. (Women who don't have a uterus anymore take just estrogen). MHT can be very good at relieving moderate to severe menopausal symptoms and preventing bone loss. But MHT also has some risks, especially if used for a long time.

MHT can help with menopause by:

- Reducing hot flashes and night sweats, and related problems such as poor sleep and irritability
- Treating vaginal symptoms, such as dryness and discomfort, and related problems, such as pain during sex
- Slowing bone loss
- Possibly easing mood swings and mild depressive mood

For some women, MHT may increase their chance of:

- Blood clots
- Heart attack
- Stroke
- Breast cancer
- Gallbladder disease

Research into the risks and benefits of MHT continues. For example, a recent study suggests that the low-dose patch form of MHT may not have the possible risk of stroke that other forms can have. Talk with your doctor about the positives and negatives of MHT based on your medical history and age. Keep in mind, too, that you may have symptoms when you stop MHT. You can also ask about other treatment options. Lower-dose estrogen products (vaginal creams, rings, and tablets) are a good choice if you are bothered only by vaginal symptoms, for example. And other drugs may help with bone loss.

If you choose MHT, experts recommend that you:

- Use it at the lowest dose that helps
- Use it for the shortest time needed

If you take MHT, call your doctor if you develop any of the following side effects:

- Vaginal bleeding
- Bloating
- Breast tenderness or swelling
- Headaches
- Mood changes
- Nausea

## Who Should Not Take MHT for Menopause?

Women who:

- Think they are pregnant
- Have problems with undiagnosed vaginal bleeding
- Have had certain kinds of cancers (such as breast or uterine cancer)
- Have had a stroke or heart attack
- Have had blood clots
- Have liver disease
- Have heart disease

## Can MHT Prevent Heart Disease or Alzheimer Disease?

A major study called the Women's Health Initiative (WHI) has looked at the effects of MHT on heart disease and other health concerns. It has explored many questions relating to MHT, including whether MHT's effects are different depending on when a woman starts it. Learn more about MHT research results.

Future research may tell experts even more about MHT. For now, MHT should not be used to prevent heart disease, memory loss, dementia, or Alzheimer disease. MHT sometimes is used to treat bone loss and menopausal symptoms. Learn more in Can menopausal hormone therapy (MHT) help my symptoms?

## Are There Natural Treatments for My Symptoms?

Some women try herbs or other products that come from plants to help relieve hot flashes. These include:

- **Soy.** Soy contains phytoestrogens. These are substances from a plant that may act like the estrogen your body makes. There is no clear proof that soy or other sources of phytoestrogens make hot flashes better. And the risks of taking soy products like pills and powders are not known. If you are going to try soy, the best sources are foods such as tofu, tempeh, soymilk, and soy nuts.

- **Other sources of phytoestrogens.** These include herbs such as black cohosh, wild yam, dong quai, and valerian root. There is not enough evidence that these herbs—or pills or creams containing these herbs—help with hot flashes. Also, not enough is known about the risks of using these products.

Make sure to discuss any natural or herbal products with your doctor before taking them. It's also important to tell your doctor about all medicines you are taking. Some plant products or foods can be harmful when combined with certain medications.

## How Much Physical Activity Do I Need as I Approach Menopause?

Physical activity helps many areas of your life, including mood, sleep, and heart health. Aim for:

- At least 2 hours and 30 minutes a week of moderate aerobic physical activity or 1 hour and 15 minutes of vigorous aerobic activity or some combination of the two

- Exercises that build muscle strength on two days each week

If you are not able to follow these guidelines, be as physically active as you can. Your doctor can help you decide what's right for you.

## What If I Have Symptoms of Menopause before Age 40?

Some women have symptoms of menopause and stop having their periods much earlier than expected. This can happen for no clear reason, or it can be caused by:

- Medical treatments, such as surgery to remove the ovaries

- Cancer treatments that damage the ovaries such as chemotherapy or radiation to the pelvic area—although menopause does not always occur

- An immune system problem in which a woman's own body cells attack her ovaries

When menopause comes early on it's own, it sometimes has been called "premature menopause" or "premature ovarian failure." A better term is "primary ovarian insufficiency," which describes the decreased activity in the ovaries. In some cases, women have ovaries that still make hormones from time to time, and their menstrual periods return. Some women can even become pregnant after the diagnosis.

For women who want to have children and can't, early menopause can be a source of great distress. Women who want to become mothers can talk with their doctors about other options, such as donor egg programs or adoption.

Early menopause raises your risk of certain health problems, such as heart disease and osteoporosis. Talk to your doctor about ways to protect your health. You might ask about menopausal hormone therapy (MHT). Some researchers think the risks of MHT for younger women might be smaller and the benefits greater than for women who begin MHT at or after the typical age of menopause.

Let your doctor know if you are younger than 40 and have symptoms of menopause.

## Menopause and Mental Health

### *Problems and Causes*

Midlife is often considered a period of increased risk for depression in women. Some women report mood swings, irritability, tearfulness, anxiety, and feelings of despair in the years leading up to menopause. But the reason for these emotional problems isn't always clear. Research shows that menopausal symptoms such as sleep problems, hot flashes, night sweats, and fatigue can affect mood and well-being. The drop in estrogen levels during perimenopause and menopause might also affect mood. Or it could be a combination of hormone changes and menopausal symptoms.

But changes in mood also can have causes that are unrelated to menopause. If you are having emotional problems that are interfering with your quality of life, it is important to discuss them with your doctor. Talk openly with your doctor about the other things going on in your life that might be adding to your feelings. Other things that could cause feelings of depression and/or anxiety during menopause include:

- Having depression before menopause
- Feeling negative about menopause and getting older
- Increased stress
- Having severe menopausal symptoms
- Smoking
- Not being physically active

- Not being happy in your relationship or not being in a relationship

- Not having a job

- Not having enough money

- Having low self-esteem (how you feel about yourself)

- Not having the social support you need

- Feeling disappointed that you can't have children anymore

## *Ways to Feel Better*

If you need treatment for your symptoms, you and your doctor can work together to find a treatment that is best for you. Depression during the menopausal transition is treated in much the same way as depression that strikes at any other time life. If your mood is affecting your quality of life, here are a few things you can do:

- Try to get enough sleep. Go to bed and wake up at the same times every day. Keep your room cool and dark. Use your bed only for sleeping and sex. Avoid alcohol, caffeine, large meals, or physical activity before bed.

- Engage in physical activity for at least 30 minutes on most days of the week.

- Set limits for yourself, and look for positive ways to unwind and ease daily stress. Try relaxation techniques, reading a book, or spending some quiet time outdoors.

- Talk to your friends or go to a support group for women who are going through the same thing as you. You also can get counseling to talk through your problems and fears.

- Ask your doctor about therapy or medicines. Menopausal hormone therapy can reduce symptoms that might be causing your moodiness. Antidepressants might also help.

Chapter 37

# Mental Health Issues among Older Adults

## Chapter Contents

Section 37.1

# *Depression in Late Life*

This section includes excerpts from "Depression is Not a
Normal Part of Growing Older," Centers for Disease Control and
Prevention (CDC), March 5, 2015; and text from "Depression,"
National Institute on Aging (NIA), August 2013.

## *Depression Is Not a Normal Part of Growing Older*

Depression is a true and treatable medical condition, not a normal
part of aging. However older adults are at an increased risk for experiencing depression. If you are concerned about a loved one, offer to
go with him or her to see a health care provider to be diagnosed and
treated.

Depression is not just having "the blues" or the emotions we feel
when grieving the loss of a loved one. It is a true medical condition
that is treatable, like diabetes or hypertension.

## *How Do I Know If It's Depression?*

Someone who is depressed has feelings of sadness or anxiety that
last for weeks at a time. He or she may also experience

- Feelings of hopelessness and/or pessimism

- Feelings of guilt, worthlessness and/or helplessness

- Irritability, restlessness

- Loss of interest in activities or hobbies once pleasurable

- Fatigue and decreased energy

- Difficulty concentrating, remembering details and making
  decisions

- Insomnia, early-morning wakefulness, or excessive sleeping

- Overeating or appetite loss

- Thoughts of suicide, suicide attempts

- Persistent aches or pains, headaches, cramps, or digestive problems that do not get better, even with treatment

## How Is Depression Different for Older Adults?

Older adults are at increased risk. We know that about 80% of older adults have at least one chronic health condition, and 50% have two or more. Depression is more common in people who also have other illnesses (such as heart disease or cancer) or whose function becomes limited.

Older adults are often misdiagnosed and undertreated. Healthcare providers may mistake an older adult's symptoms of depression as just a natural reaction to illness or the life changes that may occur as we age, and therefore not see the depression as something to be treated. Older adults themselves often share this belief and do not seek help because they don't understand that they could feel better with appropriate treatment.

## How Many Older Adults Are Depressed?

The good news is that the majority of older adults are not depressed. Some estimates of major depression in older people living in the community range from less than 1% to about 5% but rise to 13.5% in those who require home healthcare and to 11.5% in older hospital patients.

## Treating Depression

Your doctor or mental health expert can often treat your depression successfully. Different therapies seem to work for different people. For instance, support groups can provide new coping skills or social support if you are dealing with a major life change. Several kinds of talk therapies are useful as well. One method might help you think in a more positive way. Always focusing on the sad things in your life or what you have lost might contribute to depression. Another method works to improve your relations with others so you will have more hope about your future.

Getting better takes time, but with support from others and with treatment, you can get a little better each day.

Antidepressant drugs (medicine to treat depression) can also help. These medications can improve your mood, sleep, appetite, and concentration. There are several types of antidepressants available. Some of these medicines are effective in a few weeks while you may need to take others for 2 or 3 months before you begin to feel better. Be sure to take your medicine the way it was prescribed for you. Your doctor may want you to continue medications for 6 months or more after your symptoms disappear.

Some antidepressants can cause unwanted side effects, although newer medicines have fewer side effects. Any antidepressant should be used with great care to avoid this problem. Remember:

- The doctor needs to know about all prescribed and over-the-counter medications, vitamins, or herbal supplements you are taking.

- The doctor should also be aware of any other physical problems you have.

- Be sure to take antidepressants in the proper dose and on the right schedule.

If you are still very depressed after trying therapy and/or medication, your doctor can help you choose other treatment options that may work for you.

## Help From Family and Friends

Family and friends can play an important role in treatment. They can encourage someone who is depressed to stay with the treatment plan. Or, they may make appointments or accompany their friend or relative to see the doctor or go to a support group.

Be patient and understanding. Ask your relative or friend to go on outings with you or to go back to an activity that he or she once enjoyed. Encourage the person to be active and busy but not to take on too much at one time.

## Preventing Depression

What can be done to lower the risk of depression? How can people cope? There are a few steps you can take. Try to prepare for major changes in life, such as retirement or moving from your home of many years. Stay in touch with family. Let them know when you feel sad. Friends can help ease loneliness if you lose a spouse. Consider new hobbies that help keep your mind and body active. If you are faced with a lot to do, try to break the task into smaller jobs that are easy to finish.

Regular exercise may also help prevent depression or lift your mood if you are somewhat depressed. Older people who are depressed can gain mental as well as physical benefits from mild forms of exercise like walking outdoors or in shopping malls. Gardening, dancing, and swimming are other good forms of exercise. Pick something you like to do. Begin with 10–15 minutes a day, and increase the time as you are able. Being physically fit and eating a balanced diet may help avoid illnesses that can bring on disability or depression.

Remember, with treatment, most people will begin to feel better. Expect your mood to improve slowly. Feeling better takes time. But, it can happen.

## *What to Look For*

How do you know when you need help? After all, as you age, you may have to face problems that could cause anyone to feel depressed. Perhaps you are dealing with the death of a loved one. Maybe you are having a tough time getting used to retirement and feel lonely, or are losing interest in things that used to bring you pleasure.

After a period of feeling sad, older people usually adjust and regain their emotional balance. But, if you are suffering from clinical depression and don't get help, your depression might last for weeks, months, or even years. If you have several of the following signs of depression and they last for more than 2 weeks, see a doctor.

- An "empty" feeling, ongoing sadness, and anxiety
- Tiredness, lack of energy
- Loss of interest or pleasure in everyday activities, including sex
- Sleep problems, including trouble getting to sleep, very early morning waking, and sleeping too much
- Eating more or less than usual
- Crying too often or too much
- Aches and pains that don't go away when treated
- A hard time focusing, remembering, or making decisions
- Feeling guilty, helpless, worthless, or hopeless
- Being irritable
- Thoughts of death or suicide

If you are a family member, friend, or healthcare provider of an older person, watch for clues. Sometimes depression can hide behind a smiling face. A depressed person who lives alone may appear to feel better when someone stops by to say hello. The symptoms may seem to go away. But, when someone is very depressed, the symptoms usually come back.

Don't ignore the warning signs. If left untreated, serious depression may lead to suicide. Listen carefully if someone of any age complains about being depressed or says people don't care. That person may really be asking for help.

### *How to Find Help?*

Most older adults see an improvement in their symptoms when treated with antidepression drugs, psychotherapy, or a combination of both. If you are concerned about a loved one being depressed, offer to go with him or her to see a health care provider to be diagnosed and treated.

If you or someone you care about is in crisis, please seek help immediately.

- Call 911

- Visit a nearby emergency department or your health care provider's office

- Call the toll-free, 24-hour hotline of the National Suicide Prevention Lifeline at 1-800-273-TALK (1-800-273-8255); TTY: 1-800-799-4TTY (4889) to talk to a trained counselor

## Section 37.2

# *Anxiety and Older Adults*

Text in this section is excerpted from "Anxiety Disorders: About Anxiety Disorders," National Institute on Aging (NIA), January 2016.

## *About Anxiety Disorders*

Occasional anxiety is a normal part of life. You might feel anxious when faced with a problem at work, before taking a test, or making an important decision.

However, anxiety disorders involve more than temporary worry or fear. For a person with an anxiety disorder, the anxiety does not go away and can get worse over time. These feelings can interfere with daily activities such as job performance, school work, and relationships.

## Anxiety Disorders in Older Adults

Studies estimate that anxiety disorders affect up to 15 percent of older adults in a given year. More women than men experience anxiety disorders. They tend to be less common among older adults than younger adults. But developing an anxiety disorder late in life is not a normal part of aging.

Anxiety disorders commonly occur along with other mental or physical illnesses, including alcohol or substance abuse, which may mask anxiety symptoms or make them worse. In older adults, anxiety disorders often occur at the same time as depression, heart disease, diabetes, and other medical problems. In some cases, these other problems need to be treated before a person can respond well to treatment for anxiety.

There are three types of anxiety disorders discussed here.

* generalized anxiety disorder

* social phobia

* panic disorder

### *Generalized Anxiety Disorder (GAD)*

All of us worry about things like health, money, or family problems. But people with generalized anxiety disorder (GAD) are extremely worried about these and many other things, even when there is little or no reason to worry about them. They are very anxious about just getting through the day. They think things will always go badly. At times, worrying keeps people with GAD from doing everyday tasks.

### *Social Phobia*

In social phobia, a person fears being judged by others or of being embarrassed. This fear can get in the way of doing everyday things such as going to work, running errands, or meeting with friends. People who have social phobia often know that they shouldn't be so afraid, but they can't control their fear.

## *Panic Disorder*

In panic disorder, a person has sudden, unexplained attacks of terror, and often feels his or her heart pounding. During a panic attack, a person feels a sense of unreality, a fear of impending doom, or a fear of losing control. Panic attacks can occur at any time.

## *Anxiety Disorders Are Treatable*

In general, anxiety disorders are treated with medication, specific types of psychotherapy, or both. Treatment choices depend on the type of disorder, the person's preference, and the expertise of the doctor. If you think you have an anxiety disorder, talk to your doctor.

# Symptoms of Anxiety Disorders

## *Excessive, Irrational Fear*

Each anxiety disorder has different symptoms, but all the symptoms cluster around excessive, irrational fear and dread. Unlike the relatively mild, brief anxiety caused by a specific event (such as speaking in public or a first date), severe anxiety that lasts at least six months is generally considered to be problem that might benefit from evaluation and treatment.

Anxiety disorders commonly occur along with other mental or physical illnesses, including alcohol or substance abuse, which may mask anxiety symptoms or make them worse. In older adults, anxiety disorders often occur at the same time as depression, heart disease, diabetes, and other medical problems. In some cases, these other problems need to be treated before a person can respond well to treatment for anxiety.

## *Symptoms of Generalized Anxiety Disorder (GAD)*

GAD develops slowly. It often starts during the teen years or young adulthood. Symptoms may get better or worse at different times, and often are worse during times of stress.

People with GAD can't seem to get rid of their concerns, even though they usually realize that their anxiety is more intense than the situation warrants. They can't relax, startle easily, and have difficulty concentrating. Often they have trouble falling asleep or staying asleep.

Physical symptoms that often accompany the anxiety include:

- fatigue

- headaches

- muscle tension
- muscle aches
- difficulty swallowing
- trembling
- twitching
- irritability
- sweating
- nausea
- lightheadedness
- having to go to the bathroom frequently
- feeling out of breath
- hot flashes

When their anxiety level is mild, people with GAD can function socially and hold down a job. Although they don't avoid certain situations as a result of their disorder, people with GAD can have difficulty carrying out the simplest daily activities if their anxiety is severe.

### *Symptoms of Social Phobia*

In social phobia, a person fears being judged by others or of being embarrassed. This fear can get in the way of doing everyday things such as going to work, running errands or meeting with friends. People who have social phobia often know that they shouldn't be so afraid, but they can't control their fear.

People with social phobia tend to:

- be very anxious about being with other people and have a hard time talking to them, even though they wish they could
- be very self-conscious in front of other people and feel embarrassed
- be very afraid that other people will judge them
- worry for days or weeks before an event where other people will be
- stay away from places where there are other people

- have a hard time making friends and keeping friends

- blush, sweat, or tremble around other people

- feel nauseous or sick to their stomach when with other people

### Symptoms of Panic Disorder

In panic disorder, a person has sudden, unexplained attacks of terror, and often feels his or her heart pounding. During a panic attack, a person feels a sense of unreality, a fear of impending doom, or a fear of losing control. Panic attacks can occur at any time.

People with panic disorder may have:

- sudden and repeated attacks of fear

- a feeling of being out of control during a panic attack

- an intense worry about when the next attack will happen

- a fear or avoidance of places where panic attacks have occurred in the past

- physical symptoms during an attack, such as a pounding or racing heart, sweating, breathing problems, weakness or dizziness, feeling hot or a cold chill, tingly or numb hands, chest pain, or stomach pain

### Seeking Treatment

Anxiety disorders are treatable. If you think you have an anxiety disorder, talk to your doctor. If your doctor thinks you may have an anxiety disorder, the next step is usually seeing a mental health professional. It is advisable to seek help from professionals who have particular expertise in diagnosing and treating anxiety. Certain kinds of cognitive and behavioral therapy and certain medications have been found to be especially helpful for anxiety.

## Risk Factors and Diagnosis

Anxiety disorders sometimes run in families, but no one knows for sure why some people have them while others don't. Anxiety disorders are more common among younger adults than older adults, and they typically start in early life. However, anyone can develop an anxiety disorder at any time.

Below are risk factors for these anxiety disorders.

## *Generalized Anxiety Disorder—Risk Factors*

Generalized anxiety disorder (GAD) affects about 6.8 million American adults, including twice as many women as men. The disorder develops gradually and can begin at any point in the life cycle, although the years of highest risk are between childhood and middle age. The average age of onset is 31 years old.

## *Social Phobia—Risk Factors*

Social phobia affects about 15 million American adults. Women and men are equally likely to develop the disorder, which usually begins in childhood or early adolescence. There is some evidence that genetic factors are involved.

## *Panic Disorder—Risk Factors*

Panic disorder affects about 6 million American adults and is twice as common in women as men. Panic attacks often begin in late adolescence or early adulthood, but not everyone who experiences panic attacks will develop panic disorder. Many people have just one attack and never have another. The tendency to develop panic attacks appears to be inherited.

## *Diagnosis Can Be Difficult*

There are a number of reasons why it can be difficult to accurately diagnose an anxiety disorder in older adults.

- Anxiety disorders among older adults frequently occur at the same time as other illnesses such as depression, diabetes, heart disease, or a number of other medical illnesses. Problems with cognition (thinking) and changes in life circumstances can also complicate matters. Sometimes the physical signs of these illnesses can get mixed up with the symptoms of anxiety, making it difficult to determine if a person has a true anxiety disorder. For instance, a person with heart disease sometimes has chest pain, which can also be a symptom of a panic disorder.

- Doctors can have difficulty distinguishing between anxiety caused by adapting to difficult life changes, and a true anxiety disorder. For example, if you fell and broke a hip, you may be

491

justifiably fearful of going out for a while. But that would not mean you have developed an anxiety disorder.

- Sometimes the worrying symptoms of a medical illness can lead to an anxiety disorder. Or, sometimes the side effects of medication can cause anxiety. Also, a disability or a change in lifestyle caused by a medical illness may lead to an anxiety disorder. Muscle tightness, feeling very tense all the time, and difficulty sleeping can also be symptoms of a physical illness or an anxiety disorder, complicating diagnosis.

Here is how these anxiety disorders are diagnosed.

### Generalized Anxiety Disorder (GAD)—Diagnosis

GAD can be diagnosed once a person worries excessively about a variety of everyday problems for at least 6 months.

People with GAD may visit a doctor many times before they find out they have this disorder. They ask their doctors to help them with headaches or trouble falling asleep, which can be symptoms of GAD, but they don't always get the help they need right away. It may take doctors some time to be sure that a person has GAD instead of something else.

### Social Phobia—Diagnosis

A doctor can tell that a person has social phobia if the person has had symptoms for at least 6 months. Social phobia usually starts during youth. Without treatment, it can last for many years or a lifetime.

### Panic Disorder—Diagnosis

People with panic disorder may sometimes go from doctor to doctor for years and visit the emergency room repeatedly before someone correctly diagnoses their condition. This is unfortunate, because panic disorder is one of the most treatable of all the anxiety disorders, responding in most cases to certain kinds of medication or certain kinds of cognitive psychotherapy, which help change thinking patterns that lead to fear and anxiety.

## If You Have Symptoms

Anxiety disorders are treatable. If you think you have an anxiety disorder, talk to your family doctor. Your doctor should do an exam to make sure that another physical problem isn't causing the symptoms. The doctor may refer you to a mental health specialist.

You should feel comfortable talking with the mental health specialist you choose. If you do not, seek help elsewhere. Once you find a mental health specialist you are comfortable with, you should work as a team and make a plan to treat your anxiety disorder together.

### Talk about Past Treatment

People with anxiety disorders who have already received treatment for an anxiety disorder should tell their doctor about that treatment in detail. If they received medication, they should tell their doctor what medication was used, what the dosage was at the beginning of treatment, whether the dosage was increased or decreased while they were under treatment, what side effects may have occurred, and whether the treatment helped them become less anxious. If they received psychotherapy, they should describe the type of therapy, how often they attended sessions, and whether the therapy was useful.

## Medications

Anxiety disorders are treatable, and most disorders can be treated with medication or psychotherapy. For some people, a combination of medication and psychotherapy may be the best treatment approach. Treatment choices depend on the type of disorder, the person's preference, and the expertise of the doctor.

### Who Can Prescribe Medication?

Medication typically must be prescribed by a doctor. A psychiatrist is a doctor who specializes in mental disorders. Many psychiatrists offer psychotherapy themselves or work as a team with psychologists, social workers, or counselors who provide psychotherapy.

### Types of Medications

The main medications used for anxiety disorders are antidepressants, anti-anxiety drugs, and beta-blockers. Medication does not necessarily cure anxiety disorders, but it often reduces the symptoms. Be aware that some medications are effective only if they are taken regularly and that symptoms may recur if the medication is stopped.

## *Choosing Medications*

Choosing the right medication, medication dose, and treatment plan should be based on a person's individual needs and medical situation, and done under an expert's care. Only an expert clinician can help you decide whether the medicine's ability to help is worth the risk of a side effect. Your doctor may try several medicines before finding the right one.

You and your doctor should discuss the following.

- How well medicines are working or might work to improve your symptoms.

- Benefits and side effects of each medicine.

- Risk for a serious side effects based on your medical history.

- How likely the medicines will require lifestyle changes.

- Costs of each medicine.

- Other alternative therapies, medicines, vitamins, and supplements you are taking and how these may affect your treatment.

- How the medication should be stopped. Some drugs can't be stopped abruptly but must be tapered off slowly under a doctor's supervision.

Section 37.3

# *Understanding Memory Loss*

Text in this section is excerpted from "Understanding Memory Loss," National Institute on Aging (NIA), October 2015.

## *Introduction*

We've all forgotten a name, where we put our keys, or if we locked the front door. It's normal to forget things once in a while. However, forgetting how to make change, use the telephone, or find your way home may be signs of a more serious memory problem.

## *Differences between Mild Forgetfulness and More Serious Memory Problems*

### *What Is Mild Forgetfulness?*

It is true that some of us get more forgetful as we age. It may take longer to learn new things, remember certain words, or find our glasses. These changes are often signs of mild forgetfulness, not serious memory problems.

Tell him or her about your concerns. Be sure to make a follow-up appointment to check your memory in the next 6 months to a year. If you think you might forget, ask a family member, friend, or the doctor's office to remind you.

### *What Can I Do about Mild Forgetfulness?*

You can do many things to help keep your memory sharp and stay alert.

### *Here Are Some Ways to Help Your Memory:*

- Learn a new skill.
- Volunteer in your community, at a school, or at your place of worship.

- Spend time with friends and family.
- Use memory tools such as big calendars, to-do lists, and notes to yourself.
- Put your wallet or purse, keys, and glasses in the same place each day.
- Get lots of rest.
- Exercise and eat well.
- Don't drink a lot of alcohol.
- Get help if you feel depressed for weeks at a time.

### What Is a Serious Memory Problem?

Serious memory problems make it hard to do everyday things. For example, you may find it hard to drive, shop, or even talk with a friend. Signs of serious memory problems may include:

- Asking the same questions over and over again
- Getting lost in places you know well
- Not being able to follow directions
- Becoming more confused about time, people, and places
- Not taking care of yourself—eating poorly, not bathing, or being unsafe

### What Can I Do about Serious Memory Problems?

See your doctor if you are having any of the problems listed above. It's important to find out what might be causing a serious memory problem. Once you know the cause, you can get the right treatment.

## Serious Memory Problems—Causes and Treatments

Many things can cause serious memory problems, such as blood clots, depression, and Alzheimer disease. Read below to learn more about causes and treatments of serious memory problems.

### Medical Conditions

Certain medical conditions can cause serious memory problems. These problems should go away once you get treatment. Some medical conditions that may cause memory problems are:

- bad reaction to certain medicines

- depression

- not eating enough healthy foods, or too few vitamins and minerals in your body

- drinking too much alcohol

- blood clots or tumors in the brain

- head injury, such as a concussion from a fall or accident

- thyroid, kidney, or liver problems

*Treatment for medical conditions*

These medical conditions are serious. See your doctor for treatment.

## Emotional Problems

Some emotional problems in older people can cause serious memory problems. Feeling sad, lonely, worried, or bored can cause you to be confused and forgetful.

*Treatment for emotional problems*

- You may need to see a doctor or counselor for treatment. Once you get help, your memory problems should get better.

- Being active, spending more time with family and friends, and learning new skills also can help you feel better and improve your memory.

## Mild Cognitive Impairment

As some people grow older, they have more memory problems than other people their age. This condition is called mild cognitive impairment, or MCI. People with MCI can take care of themselves and do their normal activities.

MCI memory problems may include:

- losing things often

- forgetting to go to events or appointments

- having more trouble coming up with words than other people of the same age

Your doctor can do thinking, memory, and language tests to see if you have MCI. He or she also may suggest that you see a specialist for more tests. Because MCI may be an early sign of Alzheimer disease, it's really important to see your doctor or specialist every 6 to 12 months.

*Treatment for MCI*

- At this time, there is no proven treatment for MCI. Your doctor can check to see if you have any changes in your memory or thinking skills over time.

- You may want to try to keep your memory sharp. The list on page 6 suggests some ways to help your memory.

## Vascular Dementia

Many people have never heard of vascular dementia. Like Alzheimer disease, it is a medical condition that causes serious memory problems. Unlike Alzheimer disease, signs of vascular dementia may appear suddenly. This is because the memory loss and confusion are caused by strokes or changes in the blood supply to the brain. If the strokes stop, you may get better or stay the same for a long time. If you have more strokes, you may get worse.

*Treatment for vascular dementia*

You can take steps to lower your chances of having more strokes. These steps include:

- Control your high blood pressure.
- Treat your high cholesterol.
- Take care of your diabetes.
- Stop smoking.

## Help for Serious Memory Problems

### What Can I Do If I'm Worried about My Memory?

See your doctor. If your doctor thinks your memory problems are serious, you may need to have a complete health check-up. The doctor will review your medicines and may test your blood and urine. You also may need to take tests that check your memory, problem solving, counting, and language skills.

In addition, the doctor may suggest a brain scan. Pictures from the scan can show normal and problem areas in the brain. Once the doctor finds out what is causing your memory problems, ask about the best treatment for you.

### *What Can Family Members Do to Help?*

If your family member or friend has a serious memory problem, you can help the person live as normal a life as possible. You can help the person stay active, go places, and keep up everyday routines. You can remind the person of the time of day, where he or she lives, and what is happening at home and in the world. You also can help the person remember to take medicine or visit the doctor.

Some families use the following things to help with memory problems:

- big calendars to highlight important dates and events

- lists of the plans for each day

- notes about safety in the home

- written directions for using common household items (most people with Alzheimer disease can still read)

## Section 37.4

# *Alzheimer Disease*

Text in this section is excerpted from "Alzheimer's Disease: Fact Sheet," National Institute on Aging (NIA), May 2015.

Alzheimer disease (AD) is an irreversible, progressive brain disorder that slowly destroys memory and thinking skills and, eventually, the ability to carry out the simplest tasks. In most people with AD, symptoms first appear in their mid-60s. Estimates vary, but experts suggest that more than 5 million Americans may have AD.

AD is currently ranked as the sixth leading cause of death in the United States, but recent estimates indicate that the disorder may rank third, just behind heart disease and cancer, as a cause of death for older people.

AD is the most common cause of dementia among older adults. Dementia is the loss of cognitive functioning—thinking, remembering, and reasoning—and behavioral abilities to such an extent that it interferes with a person's daily life and activities. Dementia ranges in severity from the mildest stage, when it is just beginning to affect a person's functioning, to the most severe stage, when the person must depend completely on others for basic activities of daily living.

The causes of dementia can vary, depending on the types of brain changes that may be taking place. Other dementias include Lewy body dementia, frontotemporal disorders, and vascular dementia. It is common for people to have mixed dementia—a combination of two or more disorders, at least one of which is dementia. For example, some people have both AD and vascular dementia.

Alzheimer disease is named after Dr. Alois Alzheimer. In 1906, Dr. Alzheimer noticed changes in the brain tissue of a woman who had died of an unusual mental illness. Her symptoms included memory loss, language problems, and unpredictable behavior. After she died, he examined her brain and found many abnormal clumps (now called amyloid plaques) and tangled bundles of fibers (now called neurofibrillary, or tau, tangles).

These plaques and tangles in the brain are still considered some of the main features of Alzheimer disease. Another feature is the loss of connections between nerve cells (neurons) in the brain. Neurons transmit messages between different parts of the brain, and from the brain to muscles and organs in the body.

## Changes in the Brain

Scientists continue to unravel the complex brain changes involved in the onset and progression of Alzheimer disease. It seems likely that damage to the brain starts a decade or more before memory and other cognitive problems appear. During this preclinical stage of Alzheimer disease, people seem to be symptom-free, but toxic changes are taking place in the brain. Abnormal deposits of proteins form amyloid plaques and tau tangles throughout the brain, and once-healthy neurons stop functioning, lose connections with other neurons, and die.

The damage initially appears to take place in the hippocampus, the part of the brain essential in forming memories. As more neurons die, additional parts of the brain are affected, and they begin to shrink. By the final stage of AD, damage is widespread, and brain volume has shrunk significantly.

### Signs and Symptoms

Memory problems are typically one of the first signs of cognitive impairment related to AD. Some people with memory problems have a condition called mild cognitive impairment (MCI). In MCI, people have more memory problems than normal for their age, but their symptoms do not interfere with their everyday lives. Movement difficulties and problems with the sense of smell have also been linked to MCI. Older people with MCI are at greater risk for developing AD, but not all of them do. Some may even go back to normal cognition.

The first symptoms of AD vary from person to person. For many, decline in non-memory aspects of cognition, such as word-finding, vision/spatial issues, and impaired reasoning or judgment, may signal the very early stages of Alzheimer disease. Researchers are studying biomarkers (biological signs of disease found in brain images, cerebrospinal fluid, and blood) to see if they can detect early changes in the brains of people with MCI and in cognitively normal people who may be at greater risk for Alzheimer disease. Studies indicate that such early detection may be possible, but more research is needed before these techniques can be relied upon to diagnose Alzheimer disease in everyday medical practice.

### Mild Alzheimer Disease

As Alzheimer disease progresses, people experience greater memory loss and other cognitive difficulties. Problems can include wandering and getting lost, trouble handling money and paying bills, repeating questions, taking longer to complete normal daily tasks, and personality and behavior changes. People are often diagnosed at this stage.

### Moderate Alzheimer Disease

In this stage, damage occurs in areas of the brain that control language, reasoning, sensory processing, and conscious thought. Memory loss and confusion grow worse, and people begin to have problems recognizing family and friends. They may be unable to learn new things, carry out multi step tasks such as getting dressed, or cope with new situations. In addition, people at this stage may have hallucinations, delusions, and paranoia and may behave impulsively.

### Severe Alzheimer Disease

Ultimately, plaques and tangles spread throughout the brain, and brain tissue shrinks significantly. People with severe AD cannot communicate and are completely dependent on others for their care. Near the end, the person may be in bed most or all of the time as the body shuts down.

## What Causes Alzheimer Disease?

Scientists don't yet fully understand what causes Alzheimer disease in most people. In people with early-onset Alzheimer, a genetic mutation is usually the cause. Late-onset Alzheimer arises from a complex series of brain changes that occur over decades. The causes probably include a combination of genetic, environmental, and lifestyle factors. The importance of any one of these factors in increasing or decreasing the risk of developing AD may differ from person to person.

### The Basics of Alzheimer Disease

Scientists are conducting studies to learn more about plaques, tangles, and other biological features of Alzheimer disease. Advances in brain imaging techniques allow researchers to see the development and spread of abnormal amyloid and tau proteins in the living brain, as well as changes in brain structure and function. Scientists are also exploring the very earliest steps in the disease process by studying changes in the brain and body fluids that can be detected years before AD symptoms appear. Findings from these studies will help in understanding the causes of AD and make diagnosis easier.

One of the great mysteries of Alzheimer disease is why it largely strikes older adults. Research on normal brain aging is shedding light on this question. For example, scientists are learning how age-related changes in the brain may harm neurons and contribute to AD damage. These age-related changes include atrophy (shrinking) of certain parts of the brain, inflammation, production of unstable molecules called free radicals, and mitochondrial dysfunction (a breakdown of energy production within a cell).

### Genetics

Most people with AD have the late-onset form of the disease, in which symptoms become apparent in their mid-60s. The apolipoprotein E (APOE) gene is involved in late-onset Alzheimer disease. This gene has several forms. One of them, APOE ε4, increases a person's risk of developing the disease and is also associated with an earlier age of disease onset. However, carrying the APOE ε4 form of the gene does not mean that a person will definitely develop Alzheimer disease, and some people with no APOE ε4 may also develop the disease.

Also, scientists have identified a number of regions of interest in the genome (an organism's complete set of DNA) that may increase a person's risk for late-onset Alzheimer to varying degrees.

Early-onset Alzheimer disease occurs in people age 30 to 60 and represents less than 5 percent of all people with AD. Most cases are caused by an inherited change in one of three genes, resulting in a type known as early-onset familial Alzheimer disease, or FAD. For others, the disease appears to develop without any specific, known cause, much as it does for people with late-onset disease.

Most people with Down syndrome develop AD. This may be because people with Down syndrome have an extra copy of chromosome 21, which contains the gene that generates harmful amyloid.

## *Health, Environmental, and Lifestyle Factors*

Research suggests that a host of factors beyond genetics may play a role in the development and course of AD. There is a great deal of interest, for example, in the relationship between cognitive decline and vascular conditions such as heart disease, stroke, and high blood pressure, as well as metabolic conditions such as diabetes and obesity. Ongoing research will help us understand whether and how reducing risk factors for these conditions may also reduce the risk of AD.

A nutritious diet, physical activity, social engagement, and mentally stimulating pursuits have all been associated with helping people stay healthy as they age. These factors might also help reduce the risk of cognitive decline and Alzheimer disease. Clinical trials are testing some of these possibilities.

## *Diagnosis of Alzheimer Disease*

Doctors use several methods and tools to help determine whether a person who is having memory problems has "possible Alzheimer's dementia" (dementia may be due to another cause) or "probable Alzheimer's dementia" (no other cause for dementia can be found).

To diagnose Alzheimer disease, doctors may:

- Ask the person and a family member or friend questions about overall health, past medical problems, ability to carry out daily activities, and changes in behavior and personality
- Conduct tests of memory, problem solving, attention, counting, and language

- Carry out standard medical tests, such as blood and urine tests, to identify other possible causes of the problem

- Perform brain scans, such as computed tomography (CT), magnetic resonance imaging (MRI), or positron emission tomography (PET), to rule out other possible causes for symptoms.

These tests may be repeated to give doctors information about how the person's memory and other cognitive functions are changing over time.

Alzheimer disease can be definitively diagnosed only after death, by linking clinical measures with an examination of brain tissue in an autopsy.

People with memory and thinking concerns should talk to their doctor to find out whether their symptoms are due to AD or another cause, such as stroke, tumor, Parkinson disease, sleep disturbances, side effects of medication, an infection, or a non-Alzheimer's dementia. Some of these conditions may be treatable and possibly reversible.

If the diagnosis is Alzheimer disease, beginning treatment early in the disease process may help preserve daily functioning for some time, even though the underlying disease process cannot be stopped or reversed. An early diagnosis also helps families plan for the future. They can take care of financial and legal matters, address potential safety issues, learn about living arrangements, and develop support networks.

In addition, an early diagnosis gives people greater opportunities to participate in clinical trials that are testing possible new treatments for Alzheimer disease or other research studies.

## Treatment of Alzheimer Disease

Alzheimer disease is complex, and it is unlikely that any one drug or other intervention will successfully treat it. Current approaches focus on helping people maintain mental function, manage behavioral symptoms, and slow or delay the symptoms of disease. Researchers hope to develop therapies targeting specific genetic, molecular, and cellular mechanisms so that the actual underlying cause of the disease can be stopped or prevented.

### Maintaining Mental Function

Several medications are approved by the U.S. Food and Drug Administration (FDA) to treat symptoms of Alzheimer disease.

Donepezil (Aricept®), rivastigmine (Exelon®), and galantamine (Razadyne®) are used to treat mild to moderate Alzheimer (donepezil can be used for severe Alzheimer's as well). Memantine (Namenda®) is used to treat moderate to severe Alzheimer. These drugs work by regulating neurotransmitters, the brain chemicals that transmit messages between neurons. They may help maintain thinking, memory, and communication skills, and help with certain behavioral problems. However, these drugs don't change the underlying disease process. They are effective for some but not all people and may help only for a limited time.

*Managing Behavior*

Common behavioral symptoms of AD include sleeplessness, wandering, agitation, anxiety, and aggression. Scientists are learning why these symptoms occur and are studying new treatments—drug and nondrug—to manage them. Research has shown that treating behavioral symptoms can make people with AD more comfortable and makes things easier for caregivers.

*Looking for New Treatments*

Alzheimer disease research has developed to a point where scientists can look beyond treating symptoms to think about addressing underlying disease processes. In ongoing clinical trials, scientists are developing and testing several possible interventions, including immunization therapy, drug therapies, cognitive training, physical activity, and treatments used for cardiovascular disease and diabetes.

**Support for Families and Caregivers**

Caring for a person with Alzheimer disease can have high physical, emotional, and financial costs. The demands of day-to-day care, changes in family roles, and decisions about placement in a care facility can be difficult. There are several evidence-based approaches and programs that can help, and researchers are continuing to look for new and better ways to support caregivers.

Becoming well-informed about the disease is one important strategy. Programs that teach families about the various stages of AD and about ways to deal with difficult behaviors and other caregiving challenges can help.

Good coping skills, a strong support network, and respite care are other ways that help caregivers handle the stress of caring for a loved one with Alzheimer disease. For example, staying physically active provides physical and emotional benefits.

Some caregivers have found that joining a support group is a critical lifeline. These support groups allow caregivers to find respite, express concerns, share experiences, get tips, and receive emotional comfort. Many organizations sponsor in-person and online support groups, including groups for people with early-stage Alzheimer and their families.

Chapter 38

# Lesbian, Gay, Bisexual, and Transsexual (LGBT) Mental Health Issues

## Chapter Contents

# Section 38.1

# *Mental Health Problems in the LGBT Community*

Text in this section is excerpted from "LGBT Populations: A Dialogue on Advancing Opportunities for Recovery from Addictions and Mental Health Problems," Substance Abuse and Mental Health Services Administration (SAMHSA), 2013.

## *Overview*

Although lesbian, gay, bisexual, and transgender (LGBT) adults in the United States typically are well adjusted and mentally healthy, the Institute of Medicine (IOM) (2011) reports that LGBT populations are at substantially greater risk for substance use and mental health problems.

- LGBT people are more likely to use alcohol and drugs and to continue heavy drinking into later life. In addition, they are more likely to have higher rates of substance use disorders and less likely to abstain from using alcohol and drugs.

- Gay men, lesbians, and male-to-female transgender persons experience methamphetamine use as a significant problem.

Despite limited research on LGBT mental health concerns, studies that compared mental health problems between LGBT populations and the general public reveal similar disparities:

- Gay men are at greater risk for suicide attempts and completions.

- Depression affects gay men at higher rates, often with more severe problems for men who remain "in the closet."

- Women with same-sex partners have higher rates of major depression, simple phobias, and posttraumatic stress disorder.

- Bisexual men and women report consistently higher levels of depression and anxiety; some studies show rates similar to lesbians and gay men, while other studies show higher rates.

- Rates of depression and suicide attempts among both male-to-female and female-to-male transgender persons are higher than for non-transgender populations.

- A multistate study of high school students found a greater likelihood of engagement in "unhealthy risk behaviors such as tobacco use, alcohol and other drug use, sexual risk behaviors, suicidal behaviors, and violence" among LGB students and students who report having sexual contact only with persons of the same or both sexes, than by heterosexual students and students who report having sexual contact only with the opposite sex.

- Adverse, punitive, and traumatic reactions from parents and caregivers in response to the children's LGB identity closely correlate with LGB adolescents' use of illegal drugs, depression, and suicide attempts. Conversely, recent research links accepting family attitudes and behaviors toward their LGBT children—such as advocating for their children when they are mistreated because of their LGBT identity or supporting their gender expression—with significantly decreased risk and better general health in adulthood.

General health studies reveal additional vulnerabilities among LGBT populations:

- Although multiyear U.S. data show relatively stable annual HIV infections, CDC has asserted that an "alarming increase among young, black gay and bisexual men requires urgent action."

- LGBT populations experience higher rates of victimization than the general population.

Importantly, despite some recent advances in understanding and acceptance, LGBT individuals remain subject to the traumas of negative stereotyping, rejection, marginalization, and discrimination—all of which impede help-seeking behaviors. To compound the problem, LGBT individuals with mental health problems, addictions, or both, may experience additional forms of prejudice and discrimination related to each of those conditions. A study of members of sexual minorities with major mental illnesses shows, for example, that a significantly higher percentage of the LGBT group than the control group expressed dissatisfaction with mental health services. The investigators suggest that perceptions of heterosexism and homophobia are likely contributory factors in the subject's dissatisfaction.

## Major Themes

In reflecting upon their personal life experiences, dialogue participants raised a number of core themes related to LGBT individuals' particular vulnerabilities and experiences that affect their behavioral health as well as their overall health and wellness.

### Family Rejection and Family Acceptance

LGBT individuals frequently experience alienation due to lack of acceptance and support from their families of origin. Alienation and isolation often create emotional distress, especially for young people who may lack other sources of support, and in turn can become risk factors for mental health problems (lowered self-esteem and depression, for example) and use of alcohol or drugs to self-soothe or feel part of a peer group.

Rejection of LGBT family members differs from the norm in many cultural groups for which family support is a major source of affirmation and resiliency. Conversely, families that offer acceptance to their LGBT children bestow an important protective factor against suicide, depression, and substance use disorders in early adulthood. Some LGBT individuals make a conscious choice to separate from their family of origin as a positive step to enhance self-determination, personal identity, and self esteem. Others leave home because they perceive themselves to be unsafe among family members who reject LGBT identities in ways that may be psychologically or physically damaging, or both. Giving up family and the support system connected with staying at home may represent the lesser of two evils for some LGBT persons. Still others leave home when their families "kick them out." By contrast, however, many LGBT individuals have redefined what family means to them and have created families of choice: nontraditional families that offer a source of strength and personal affirmation.

### Coming Out

Coming out—the individual process by which a person recognizes, accepts, and shares with others one's sexual and/or gender identity— can be a difficult, emotion-laden undertaking. As noted above, many LGBT individuals struggle with prejudice, discrimination, family disruption, and other traumas as they make decisions to come out, and this process places LGBT individuals at especially high risk for suicide, drug and alcohol use, depression, and physical abuse. LGBT young people who come out also may experience homelessness and increased vulnerability to harassment, bullying, or violence in school. Of course, not all LGBT people come out, but even not coming out can exact an emotional toll in dealing with the dissonance of "passing" as heterosexual and perhaps enduring the consequences of substance use to reduce anxiety. For many LGBT persons, coming out is an ongoing process, not just a single event.

Age, race, ethnicity, education, socioeconomic status, geography, marital status, and parenthood also may affect the pattern or timing of an individual's coming-out process.

Many health providers in practice today learned during their professional training that the sexual orientation of LGB individuals was deviant or pathological. Previous editions of the *Diagnostic and Statistical Manual for Mental Health Disorders* (DSM) (e.g., DMS IV, American Psychiatric Association, 2000) described gender identity disorder as a mental disorder. However, in describing gender-related conditions, the recently released DSM-5 (American Psychiatric Association, 2013) uses the term gender dysphoria to refer to "the distress that may accompany the incongruence between one's experienced or expressed gender and one's assigned gender."

The DSM-5 goes on to explain that, although not all individuals experience distress as a result of such incongruence, many are distressed if they are not able to receive hormones and/or surgery to change their physical appearance to be congruent with their experienced or expressed gender. The current term, gender dysphoria, "is more descriptive than the previous DSM-IV term gender identity disorder and focuses on dysphoria as the clinical problem, not identity per se." Participants reported that some health professionals and organizations marginalize—and some even prefer not to treat—LGBT persons. Keenly aware of this attitude, many LGBT individuals do not disclose their LGBT status to health care providers, and transgender individuals in particular may hesitate to use mainstream health care services. Reluctance to seek health care often results in late diagnosis and suboptimal treatment outcomes for LGBT individuals.

Moreover, seeking professional or legal help for interpersonal violence equates with coming out, a barrier that may impede identification of LGBT victims or perpetrators of interpersonal violence.

### LGBT—Related Stress

A growing body of evidence reveals that stress experienced by LGBT persons negatively affects their mental health and their willingness to seek and access care, and their vulnerability to substance use disorders. The minority stress model developed by Meyer (2003) identifies a constellation of stressors that affect LGBT individuals: identity stress related to concealment and/or disclosure of a stigmatized identity and negative internalized identity, expectations of rejection and discrimination, and the experience of violence and threat of violence, including continuous vigilance. While many use the broader term minority stress, some focus on LGBT-related stress both to emphasize those stressors experienced by LGBT individuals and perhaps to distinguish those stressors from other stressors experienced by ethnic minorities or people with disabilities. The higher prevalence of anxiety, depression, and substance use found among LGB populations results from additive stress related to "nonconformity with prevailing sexual orientation and gender norms."

LGBT health experts agree that discrimination, isolation, and other social pressures increase the risk for LGBT individuals, particularly LGBT youth, to use drugs and alcohol to reduce and cope with stress. Evidence has emerged that racial/ethnic-related minority stressors, both within LGBT communities and in society at large, interact with LGBT-specific minority stressors.

## *Intersection of LGBT with Other Identities*

Individual and group identities are complex. In describing its "intersectional" approach to understanding LGBT health, the IOM (2011) indicates that identities are "shaped not just by race, class, ethnicity, sexuality/sexual orientation, gender, physical disabilities, and national origin, but also by the confluence of all of those characteristics." Other observers have recognized additional intersections, including age and immigrant status, substance abuse and dependence, mental health, HIV/AIDS status, aging, education, criminal justice, homelessness, violence prevention, and social isolation. The IOM (2011) observes that the experiences of LGBT persons within their racial and ethnic communities affect their ultimate health outcomes by mediating such variables as the process of coming out, their use of supports, and the extent to which they affiliate with the LGBT community.

Effects of race, ethnicity, and education are likely to be more significant for low-income than middle-class non-white LGB individuals. Geography, too, may play a role in LGBT health disparities in rural areas or areas with fewer LGBT people, where they "may feel less comfortable coming out, have less support from families and friends, lack access to an LGBT community, and have less access to providers" who can offer culturally competent treatment.

*Trauma*

Trauma negatively affects LGBT individuals in multiple ways. Many young people contend with the emotional wounds inflicted by rejection by family members and schoolmates, and LGBT people of any age may suffer from the effects of prejudice, discrimination, heterosexism, homophobia, and internalized homophobia. Childhood abuse, adult abuse, and interpersonal violence, along with hate crimes, leave both physical and emotional scars. Even just the fear of violence or anti-LGBT harassment can inflict trauma. Invisibility may also represent a form of trauma or may exacerbate it. Research shows that trauma has serious implications for mental health, alcohol and substance use, and related risk-taking behaviors. Research shows also that hate crimes based on sexual orientation bias have more serious and long-lasting psychological effects than other crimes because of the link to core aspects of the victim's identity and community. Because individuals who have been traumatized find it more difficult to focus on their physical well-being, behavioral health problems can exacerbate other health challenges faced by LGBT people, including hepatitis C and HIV/AIDS.

Moreover, anti-LGBT prejudice often impedes survivors of violence, their partners, and their family members from calling on police, prosecutors, courts, or mainstream victim service agencies for help. Domestic violence among gay couples is underreported, but as with all couples, there is a connection between domestic violence and alcohol and drug use. Gay people subjected to physical and sexual abuse in their youth have greatest risk for alcohol and drug use. Transgender individuals are likely to experience some form of discrimination, harassment, violence, or a combination, at some point in their lives.

The first major U.S. study on violence and discrimination against transgender people found that more than 50% have experienced some type of harassment or violence, or both, during their lives, and 25% reported experiencing a physically violent incident.

### Suicide

The Suicide Prevention Resource Center (SPRC) reports that LGB youth are from one and a half to seven times more likely to report having attempted suicide than their non-LGB peers, while transgender youth also likely have higher rates of suicidal behavior. SPRC cautions, however, that it is impossible to know the exact suicide rate of LGBT youth because sexual and gender minorities are often hidden and even unknown, particularly in this age group. According to CDC, suicide is the third leading cause of death among young people 15 to 24 years old in the United States, and more than 4,000 youth die by suicide each year. Many more young people engage in suicidal thoughts, devise plans to kill themselves, or attempt to take their own lives.

Among adults, gay men are at greater risk for suicide attempts and completions, and rates of depression and suicide attempts among transgender persons are higher than for non-transgender populations. In fact, a study of a diverse group of transgender and gender nonconforming participants conducted by the National Gay and Lesbian Task Force and the National Center for Transgender Equality found that a "staggering" 41% of respondents reported attempting suicide, compared to just 1.6% of the general population.

According to SPRC, risk and protective factors play an important role in helping to explain suicidal behavior. SPRC observes that "LGB youth generally have more risk factors, more severe risk factors, and fewer protective factors than heterosexual youth." In many cases "LGB youth lack important protective factors such as family support and safe schools," and many LGB young people "appear to experience depression and substance abuse."

Some risks are unique to LGB youth, for example, self-disclosure of their sexual orientation at an early age. Stigma and discrimination against LGBT individuals directly relate to risk factors for suicide. For example, "discrimination has a strong association with mental illness, and heterosexism may lead to isolation, family rejection, and lack of access to culturally competent care". Additional risk factors for suicide attempts include "previous suicide attempt, depressed mood, eating problems, conduct problems, early sexual debut, number of sexual partners, pubertal timing, self-concept, alcohol and drug use, atypical gender roles, loneliness, peer relations, social support, parental attachment, parental monitoring, and suicidal behavior among family and friends."

## Invisibility of LGBT Individuals and Groups

In contrast with members of other racial and ethnic minorities, social stigma often renders LGBT individuals invisible to their families, to others in the community, to each other, to society in general, and to behavioral healthcare providers and researchers. Some families view LGBT behavior as rebellion against their traditional values and against the family itself, rather than as a part of an individual's identity, and they withdraw their love and support. LGBT young people often proceed invisibly through their schooling, fearful of shunning, bullying, harassment, and violence by their peers. Because openly identifying as LGBT may jeopardize acceptance by both their families and their ethnic communities, many youth of color hide their sexual orientation and thus may appear even less visible than their white LGBT peers.

LGBT people often choose to be invisible in the workplace, where they may fear that self disclosure will trigger expectable social and economic consequences, and in the social realm negative stereotypes and homophobia make it difficult to establish mutual support with other LGBT individuals. This isolation often leads LGBT people to socialize in gay bars and clubs, which in turn may lead many to develop substance use disorders. Mental health providers in both inpatient and outpatient settings who deliver services to both LGBT adults and youth typically fail to recognize the need for treatment plans that reflect their client/consumers' unique needs. This lack of recognition signals, especially to LGBT youth, that "their feelings and self-concepts are invalid and unimportant" and may contribute to their sense of isolation.

Certain institutional practices ignore LGBT populations. Importantly, U.S. census enumerations do not inquire about sexual orientation. Lesbians, gay men, and bisexual adults who do not live together in a same-sex relationship remain invisible in census data, and it is impossible to identify transgender people. In the behavioral health arena, intake forms for residential treatment programs typically ask for marital status—ignoring the existence of same-sex (and other) unmarried couples—and some mental health programs do not consider significant others of the same gender to be family members. Omission of reference to LGBT in such contexts reinforces feelings of invisibility, a sense of isolation, and the belief that "I am the only one in the world who has these feelings."

### LGBT across the Lifespan

The experiences and needs of LGBT people differ across the lifespan, and youth and elders may be particularly vulnerable. Young people may experience harassment and bullying in school because of their actual or perceived sexual orientation or gender identity, or they may be subject to family rejection. They may run away from home and then find themselves homeless and/or involved in drug use or in sex work to support themselves. LGBT youth who remain at home may experience greater difficulty with schoolwork, sexual abuse, and alcohol and drug use than their heterosexual peers. And, because minority LGBT youth are particularly vulnerable to family and peer rejection, many conceal their sexual orientation. Many have no clear role models for how to be gay. Some LGBT youth may "use alcohol and drugs to deal with stigma and shame, deny same-sex feelings, or help them cope with ridicule or anti-gay violence." In addition, LGBT youth face the challenge of learning to manage a stigmatized identity, an "extra burden that makes [them] more vulnerable for substance abuse and unprotected sex, and can intensify psychological distress and risk for suicide". In LGBT culture young adults need not seek relief from negatives in order to be drawn into substance use and abuse. LGBT teens frequently enter "gay society" through bars and clubs, where other patrons may encourage them to drink and use drugs.

Aging LGBT individuals commonly face the dual challenge of actual discrimination and the fear of discrimination, for example, when they contemplate moving into a retirement residence or in their dealings with health and social service networks. Like all elder persons, LGBT individuals who are aging may need to rely more heavily on formal supports, services, and systems for assistance—for example, with housing (providing home-based care required for LGBT individuals to remain in their homes as long as possible), nutrition, health, transportation, socialization, financing, and other important needs. Many aging LGBT people feel they must hide their sexual or gender identity and return to the closet at a time when their needs are significantly increasing and when it is important for service providers to be able to accept the LGBT individual for whom he or she is, as well as to provide culturally competent services.

## Section 38.2

# *LGBT Depression*

Text in this section is excerpted from "Lesbian, Gay, Bisexual, and Transgender Health," Centers for Disease Control and Prevention (CDC), November 12, 2014.

## *LGBT Youth*

Most lesbian, gay, bisexual, transgender, and questioning (LGBTQ) youth are happy and thrive during their adolescent years. Going to a school that creates a safe and supportive learning environment for all students and having caring and accepting parents are especially important. This helps all youth achieve good grades and maintain good mental and physical health. However, some LGBTQ youth are more likely than their heterosexual peers to experience difficulties in their lives and school environments, such as violence.

## Experiences with Violence

Negative attitudes toward lesbian, gay, and bisexual (LGB) people put these youth at increased risk for experiences with violence, compared with other students. Violence can include behaviors such as bullying, teasing, harassment, physical assault, and suicide-related behaviors.

According to data from Youth Risk Behavior Surveys (YRBS) conducted during 2001–2009 in seven states and six large urban school districts, the percentage of LGB students (across the sites) who were threatened or injured with a weapon on school property in the prior year ranged from 12% to 28%. In addition, across the sites?

- 19% to 29% of gay and lesbian students and 18% to 28% of bisexual students experienced dating violence in the prior year.

- 14% to 31% of gay and lesbian students and 17% to 32% of bisexual students had been forced to have sexual intercourse at some point in their lives.

LGBTQ youth are also at increased risk for suicidal thoughts and behaviors, suicide attempts, and suicide. A nationally representative study of adolescents in grades 7–12 found that lesbian, gay, and bisexual youth were more than twice as likely to have attempted suicide as their heterosexual peers. More studies are needed to better understand the risks for suicide among transgender youth. However, one study with 55 transgender youth found that about 25% reported suicide attempts.

Another survey of more than 7,000 seventh- and eighth-grade students from a large Midwestern county examined the effects of school [social] climate and homophobic bullying on lesbian, gay, bisexual, and questioning (LGBTQ) youth and found that

- LGBT youth were more likely than heterosexual youth to report high levels of bullying and substance use;

- Students who were questioning their sexual orientation reported more bullying, homophobic victimization, unexcused absences from school, drug use, feelings of depression, and suicidal behaviors than either heterosexual or LGBT students;

517

- LGB students who did not experience homophobic teasing reported the lowest levels of depression and suicidal feelings of all student groups (heterosexual, LGB, and questioning students); and

- All students, regardless of sexual orientation, reported the lowest levels of depression, suicidal feelings, alcohol and marijuana use, and unexcused absences from school when they were

  - In a positive school climate and

  - Not experiencing homophobic teasing.

## *Effects on Education and Health*

Exposure to violence can have negative effects on the education and health of any young person. However, for LGBT youth, a national study of middle and high school students shows that LGBT students (61.1%) were more likely than their non-LGBT peers to feel unsafe or uncomfortable as a result of their sexual orientation. According to data from CDC's YRBS, the percentage of gay, lesbian, and bisexual students (across sites) who did not go to school at least one day during the 30 days before the survey because of safety concerns ranged from 11% to 30% of gay and lesbian students and 12% to 25% of bisexual students.

The stresses experienced by LGBT youth also put them at greater risk for depression, substance use, and sexual behaviors that place them at risk for HIV and other sexually transmitted diseases (STDs). For example, HIV infection among young men who have sex with men aged 13–24 years increased by 26% over 2008–2011.

## *What Schools Can Do?*

For youth to thrive in their schools and communities, they need to feel socially, emotionally, and physically safe and supported. A positive school climate has been associated with decreased depression, suicidal feelings, substance use, and unexcused school absences among LGBQ students.

Schools can implement clear policies, procedures, and activities designed to promote a healthy environment for all youth. For example, research has shown that in schools with LGB support groups (such as gay-straight alliances), LGB students were less likely to experience threats of violence, miss school because they felt unsafe, or attempt suicide than those students in schools without LGB support groups. A recent study found that LGB students had fewer suicidal thoughts and attempts when schools had gay-straight alliances and policies prohibiting expression of homophobia in place for 3 or more years.

To help promote health and safety among LGBTQ youth, schools can implement the following policies and practices:

- Encourage respect for all students and prohibit bullying, harassment, and violence against all students.

- Identify "safe spaces," such as counselors' offices, designated classrooms, or student organizations, where LGBTQ youth can receive support from administrators, teachers, or other school staff.

- Encourage student-led and student-organized school clubs that promote a safe, welcoming, and accepting school environment (e.g., gay-straight alliances, which are school clubs open to youth of all sexual orientations).

- Ensure that health curricula or educational materials include HIV, other STD, or pregnancy prevention information that is relevant to LGBTQ youth (such as, ensuring that curricula or materials use inclusive language or terminology).

- Encourage school district and school staff to develop and publicize trainings on how to create safe and supportive school environments for all students, regardless of sexual orientation or gender identity, and encourage staff to attend these trainings.

- Facilitate access to community-based providers who have experience providing health services, including HIV/STD testing and counseling, to LGBTQ youth.

- Facilitate access to community-based providers who have experience in providing social and psychological services to LGBTQ youth.

# Section 38.3

# *Parents' Influence on the Mental Health of Lesbian, Gay, and Bisexual Teens*

Text in this section is excerpted from "Parent's Influence
on the Health of Lesbian, Gay, and Bisexual Teens: What
Parents and Families Should Know," Centers for Disease
Control and Prevention (CDC), November 2013.

## *Overview*

The teen years can be a challenging time for young people and
their parents. This fact sheet provides information on how parents can
promote positive health outcomes for their lesbian, gay, or bisexual
(LGB) teen. The information is based on a review of published studies,
which found that parents play an important role in shaping the health
of their LGB teen.

When LGB teens share their sexual orientation (or even if they
choose not to share it), they may feel rejected by important people
in their lives, including their parents. This rejection can negatively
influence an LGB teen's overall well-being.

On the other hand, a positive family environment, with high levels
of parental support and low levels of conflict, is associated with LGB
youth who experience healthy emotional adjustment. These teens
are less likely to engage in sexual risk behaviors and be involved in
violence.

## *How Parents Make a Difference*

Compared to heterosexual youth, LGB teens are more likely to
experience bullying, physical violence, or rejection. As a result, LGB
teens are at an increased risk for suicidal thoughts and behaviors and
report higher rates of sexual risk behavior and substance abuse.

Research suggests that LGB teens experience better health outcomes when their parents support their sexual orientation in positive
and affirming ways. Compared to teens who do not feel valued by their
parents, LGB youth who feel valued by their parents are less likely to

- Experience depression

- Attempt suicide

- Use drugs and alcohol

- Become infected with sexually transmitted diseases

In addition, research among young gay men has shown that having a positive relationship with their parents helped them decide to have safer sex (e.g., using a condom, not having sex with high-risk partners). Many also reported that having a positive parent-teen relationship created a sense of responsibility to avoid HIV infection.

## Specific Actions for Parents

Research on parenting shows how important it is—regardless of their teen's sexual orientation—for parents to

- Have open, honest conversations with their teens about sex

- Know their teen's friends and know what their teen is doing

- Develop common goals with their teen, including being healthy and doing well in school

Although additional research is needed to better understand the associations between parenting and the health of LGB youth, the following are research-based action steps parents can take to support the health and well-being of their LGB teen and decrease the chances that their teen will engage in risky behaviors.

### Talk and Listen

- Parents who talk with and listen to their teen in a way that invites an open discussion about sexual orientation can help their teen feel loved and supported.

- When their teen is ready, parents can brainstorm with him or her how to talk with others about the teen's sexual orientation.

- Parents can talk with their teen about how to avoid risky behavior and unsafe or high-risk situations.

- Parents can talk with their teen about the consequences of bullying. Parents (and their teen) should report any physical or verbal abuse that occurs at school to teachers and the school principal.

## *Provide Support*

- Parents need to understand that teens find it very stressful to share their sexual orientation.

- Parents who take time to come to terms with how they feel about their teen's sexual orientation will be more able to respond calmly and use respectful language.

- Parents should discuss with their teen how to practice safe, healthy behaviors.

## *Stay Involved*

- By continuing to include their teen in family events and activities, parents can help their teen feel supported.

- Parents can help their teen develop a plan for dealing with challenges, staying safe, and reducing risk.

- Parents who make an effort to know their teen's friends and romantic partners and know what their teen is doing can help their teen stay safe and feel cared about.

## *Be Proactive*

- Parents who build positive relationships with their teen's teachers and school personnel can help ensure a safe and welcoming learning environment.

- If parents think their teen is depressed or needs other mental health support, they should speak with a school counselor, social worker, psychologist, or other health professional.

- Parents can access many organizations and online information resources to learn more about how they can support their LGB teen, other family members, and their teen's friends.

- Parents can help their teen find appropriate LGB organizations and go with their teen to events and activities that support LGB youth.

# Chapter 39

# *Victims of Trauma and Disaster*

## *Chapter Contents*

Section 39.1

# *Common Reactions after Trauma*

Text in this section is excerpted from "Common
Reactions after Trauma," U.S. Department of
Veterans Affairs (VA), August 13, 2015.

## *Introduction*

After going through a trauma, survivors often say that their first
feeling is relief to be alive. This may be followed by stress, fear, and
anger. Trauma survivors may also find they are unable to stop thinking about what happened. Many survivors will show a high level of
arousal, which causes them to react strongly to sounds and sights
around them.

Most people have some kind of stress reaction after a trauma. Having such a reaction has nothing to do with personal weakness. Stress
reactions may last for several days or even a few weeks. For most
people, if symptoms occur, they will slowly decrease over time.

### *What Are Common Reactions to Trauma?*

All kinds of trauma survivors commonly experience stress reactions.
This is true for veterans, children, and disaster rescue or relief workers. If you understand what is happening when you or someone you
know reacts to a traumatic event, you may be less fearful and better
able to handle things.

Reactions to a trauma may include:

- Feeling hopeless about the future

- Feeling detached or unconcerned about others

- Having trouble concentrating or making decisions

- Feeling jumpy and getting startled easily at sudden noises

- Feeling on guard and constantly alert

- Having disturbing dreams and memories or flashbacks

- Having work or school problems

You may also experience more physical reactions such as:

- Stomach upset and trouble eating
- Trouble sleeping and feeling very tired
- Pounding heart, rapid breathing, feeling edgy
- Sweating
- Severe headache if thinking of the event
- Failure to engage in exercise, diet, safe sex, regular health care
- Excess smoking, alcohol, drugs, food
- Having your ongoing medical problems get worse

You may have more emotional troubles such as:

- Feeling nervous, helpless, fearful, sad
- Feeling shocked, numb, and not able to feel love or joy
- Avoiding people, places, and things related to the event
- Being irritable or having outbursts of anger
- Becoming easily upset or agitated
- Blaming yourself or having negative views of oneself or the world
- Distrust of others, getting into conflicts, being over-controlling
- Being withdrawn, feeling rejected, or abandoned
- Loss of intimacy or feeling detached

### Recovery from Stress Reactions

Turn to your family and friends when you are ready to talk. They are your personal support system. Recovery is an ongoing gradual process. It doesn't happen through suddenly being "cured" and it doesn't mean that you will forget what happened. Most people will recover from trauma naturally. If your stress reactions are getting in the way of your relationships, work, or other important activities, you may want to talk to a counselor or your doctor. Good treatments are available.

## Common Problems That Can Occur after a Trauma

Posttraumatic Stress Disorder (PTSD). PTSD is a condition that can develop after you have gone through a life-threatening event. If you have PTSD, you may have trouble keeping yourself from thinking over and over about what happened to you. You may try to avoid people and places that remind you of the trauma. You may feel numb. Lastly, if you have PTSD, you might find that you have trouble relaxing. You may startle easily and you may feel on guard most of the time.

Depression. Depression involves feeling down or sad more days than not. If you are depressed, you may lose interest in activities that used to be enjoyable or fun. You may feel low in energy and be overly tired. You may feel hopeless or in despair, and you may think that things will never get better. Depression is more likely when you have had losses such as the death of close friends. If you are depressed, at times you might think about hurting or killing yourself. For this reason, getting help for depression is very important.

Self-blame, guilt and shame. Sometimes in trying to make sense of a traumatic event, you may blame yourself in some way. You may think you are responsible for bad things that happened, or for surviving when others didn't. You may feel guilty for what you did or did not do. Remember, we all tend to be our own worst critics. Most of the time, that guilt, shame, or self-blame is not justified.

Suicidal thoughts. Trauma and personal loss can lead a depressed person to think about hurting or killing themselves. If you think someone you know may be feeling suicidal, you should directly ask them. You will NOT put the idea in their head. If someone is thinking about killing themselves, call the Suicide Prevention Lifeline 1-800-273-TALK (8255) http://www.suicidepreventionlifeline.org. You can also call a counselor, doctor, or 911.

Anger or aggressive behavior. Trauma can be connected with anger in many ways. After a trauma, you might think that what happened to you was unfair or unjust. You might not understand why the event happened and why it happened to you. These thoughts can result in intense anger. Although anger is a natural and healthy emotion, intense feelings of anger and aggressive behavior can cause problems with family, friends, or coworkers. If you become violent when angry, you just make the situation worse. Violence can lead to people being injured, and there may be legal consequences.

Alcohol/Drug abuse. Drinking or "self-medicating" with drugs is a common, and unhealthy, way of coping with upsetting events. You may drink too much or use drugs to numb yourself and to try to deal with difficult thoughts, feelings, and memories related to the trauma. While using alcohol or drugs may offer a quick solution, it can actually lead to more problems. If someone close begins to lose control of drinking or drug use, you should try to get them to see a health care provider about managing their drinking or drug use.

## Summing It All Up

Right after a trauma, almost every survivor will find himself or herself unable to stop thinking about what happened. Stress reactions, such as increased fear, nervousness, jumpiness, upsetting memories, and efforts to avoid reminders, will gradually decrease over time for most people.

Use your personal support systems, family and friends, when you are ready to talk. Recovery is an ongoing gradual process. It doesn't happen through suddenly being "cured" and it doesn't mean that you will forget what happened. Most people will recover from trauma naturally over time. If your emotional reactions are getting in the way of your relationships, work, or other important activities, you may want to talk to a counselor or your doctor. Good treatments are available.

# Section 39.2

# *Coping with Traumatic Events*

Text in this section is excerpted from "Coping with Stress after a Traumatic Event," Centers for Disease Control and Prevention (CDC), 2013.

## Coping with Stress after a Traumatic Event

Traumatic events take different forms—natural disasters (earthquakes, tornados, wildfires), personal loss, school shootings, and community violence—and their effects on us vary. People may feel sad, confused, scared, or worried. Others may feel numb or even happy to be alive and safe. Reactions to traumatic events can be had by those directly impacted as well as by friends and family of victims, first responders, and people learning about the events from the news.

Feeling stressed before or after a traumatic event is normal. But, this stress becomes a problem when we are unable to cope well with it and when the stress gets in the way of taking care of ourselves and family, going to school, or doing our jobs. Coping well with stress begins with recognizing how we are reacting and then by taking steps to manage our reactions in a healthy way.

## Common Stress Reactions to a Traumatic Event

Emotional and physical stress reactions may occur immediately around the time of a traumatic event. For some people, signs of stress may take days or weeks to appear. Some stress reactions are:

- Disbelief and shock
- Feeling sad, frustrated, helpless, and numb
- Fear and anxiety about the future
- Feeling guilty
- Anger, tension, and irritability
- Difficulty concentrating and making decisions
- Crying
- Reduced interest in usual activities
- Wanting to be alone
- No desire for food or loss of appetite
- Sleeping too much or too little
- Nightmares or bad memories
- Reoccurring thoughts of the event
- Headaches, back pains, and stomach problems
- Increased heart rate and difficulty breathing
- Increased smoking or use of alcohol or drugs

## Ways to Cope with Stress after a Traumatic Event

A traumatic event can turn your world upside down. There is no simple fix to feeling better right way. Feeling better will take time. Healthy activities can help you, your family, and community heal.

- Follow a normal routine as much as possible. Wake up and go to sleep at your usual times. Eat meals at regular times. Continue to go to work and school and do activities with friends and family.

- Take care of yourself. Do healthy activities, like eating well-balanced meals, getting plenty of rest, and exercising—even a short walk can clear your head and give you energy. If you are having trouble sleeping, do not drink caffeine or alcohol before going to bed and do not watch TV or use your cell phone or computer in bed. Avoid other things that can hurt you, like smoking, drinking alcohol, or using drugs.

- Talk about your feelings and accept help. Feeling stress after a traumatic event is normal. Talking to someone about how you are doing and receiving support can make you feel better. Others who have shared your experience may also be struggling and giving them support can also help you.

- Turn it off and take a break. Staying up-to-date about a traumatic event can keep you informed, but pictures and stories on television, in newspapers, and on the Internet can increase or bring back your stress. Schedule information breaks. If you are feeling upset when getting the news, turn it off and focus on something you enjoy.

- Get out and help others. Volunteer or contribute to your community in other ways. This community support can be connected to the disaster-related needs or to anything else that you care about. Supporting your community can help you and others heal and see that things are going to get better.

## *Signs that More Help May Be Needed*

Sometimes taking healthy steps on your own to lower stress after a traumatic event is not enough. Getting additional care and support is sometimes needed to feel better and to figure out a way to move forward. This help may come from a licensed mental health professional, doctor, or community or faith-based organization. Signs that more help is needed include:

- Having symptoms of stress, like feeling sad or depressed, for more than two weeks

- Not being able to take care of yourself or family

- Not being able to do your job or go to school

- Alcohol or drug use

- Thinking about suicide

# Section 39.3

# *Disaster Survivors and Mental Health*

Text in this section is excerpted from "Disaster
Mental Health Treatment," U.S. Department of
Veterans Affairs (VA), August 14, 2015.

## *Disaster Mental Health Treatment*

Disasters can cause a wide range of reactions in survivors. Research
has shown that right after a disaster, certain kinds of help can make
things easier for you. Most of those who are affected by disaster will
recover on their own given some time and help. Yet if a survivor is still
having trouble weeks after the disaster, he or she may need further
assistance.

After a disaster, you are likely to do better if you feel-or are helped
to feel-safe, connected to others, and serene or calm. Those who are
hopeful and confident that they can cope with the results of a disaster
also tend to do better.

While group "debriefing" models have been used after disasters,
debriefing is not thought to be as useful as practical help, psychological
first aid, and education.

## *Practical Help*

A key to recovery from disasters is feeling that you have the
resources with which to rebuild your life. The most basic resources
include food, safety, and shelter. Other important resources are family, community, school, and friends. In fact, having resources is so
important that many programs for disaster recovery focus on providing
practical help and building people's resources.

## Psychological First Aid

Survivors in distress may benefit from psychological first aid. The Psychological First Aid Field Operations Guide (PFA) teaches disaster responders and others how to help those recovering from disaster. The guide is based on the most important needs of survivors, such as safety, comfort, calming, and practical help. The guide also includes handouts (PDF) to help survivors, with information on:

• Positive ways of coping

• Connecting with social supports

• Links to needed services

## Education to Build Community Resilience

Resilience means being able to recover or bounce back after a disaster. One way to build resilience is education. Community members need to understand how disasters affect people. They need to know how to cope and use others for support, and how to get further help if needed.

Efforts to reach out and inform the community are sometimes provided by recovery workers, through the media, or on the Internet. Education may focus on:

• Reactions to disaster

• Building resilience and positive coping

• Providing support to each other

• Connecting to health and mental health care providers

Many types of healing practices also go into building community resilience. These practices involve communal, cultural, memorial, spiritual and religious healing practices. Training may be provided to local responders and healers, community leaders, and health providers. These workers are taught to make use of resources that are already in place or that occur naturally after disaster. Workers try to give survivors knowledge, attitudes, and skills that can be used to build the community. Part of the process also involves grieving the community's losses and making meaning of the disaster. Other goals include getting back to the normal rhythms and routines of life, and gaining a positive vision of the future, with renewed hope.

## *Crisis Counseling, Skill-Building, and Other Treatments*

Programs and treatments exist for all levels of need after a disaster. One example is the Crisis Counseling Program (CCP). The Federal Emergency Management Agency (FEMA) supports CCPs for survivors of federally-declared disasters. CCPs focus on both those affected by the disaster and the community as a whole. They provide survivors with practical help in coping with their current issues. They serve a full range of children, teens, parents or caretakers, families, and adults. CCPs also help businesses and neighborhoods. They focus not just on those at highest risk for problems, but also on providing resources to make the whole community stronger.

Skills in Psychological Recovery (SPR) is another model that can often be helpful. SPR works to teach those exposed to all types of trauma skills that will help them be more resilient. SPR is given by trained and supervised crisis counselors. They work with you to help you develop skills, including:

- Problem-solving

- Planning more positive and meaningful activities

- Managing stress and reactions to the disaster

- Engaging in more helpful thinking

- Building healthy social connections

Some survivors may still be in distress after psychological first aid, crisis counseling, or SPR. For those in need of more intensive services, treatment may be needed for problems such as PTSD, anxiety, panic, depression, or guilt. Research supports cognitive behavioral therapy (CBT), a recommended treatment for trauma and PTSD.

Many standard treatments are being revised for use after disaster. An example of a trauma treatment tailored to disaster survivors is Cognitive Behavioral Treatment for Post-disaster Distress (CBT-PD). This is a 12-session program during which survivors are:

- Taught about their symptoms

- Given a breathing technique to manage anxiety

- Directed to engage in pleasant activities

- Taught to change their ways of thinking to be more positive and helpful

This was used after Hurricane Katrina, and people improved even after only a few sessions of the treatment.

## Summing It Up

Recovery programs after disaster span a wide range. The goals of these programs are to help both survivors and the community to recover. No matter where you are on the spectrum of disaster reactions, there should be a program to help you. With support, you can build your resources, resilience, skills, and mental health.

Chapter 40

# *Mental Health Issues among Minority and Immigrant Populations*

## *Racial and Ethnic Minority Populations*

Racial and ethnic minorities currently make up about a third of the population of the nation and are expected to become a majority by 2050. These diverse communities have unique behavioral health needs and experience different rates of mental and/or substance use disorders and treatment access. Communities of color tend to experience greater burden of mental and substance use disorders often due to poorer access to care; inappropriate care; and higher social, environmental, and economic risk factors.

## *Mental Health and African-Americans*

- Poverty level affects mental health status. African-Americans living below the poverty level, as compared to those over twice

This chapter includes excerpts from "Racial and Ethnic Minority Populations," Substance Abuse and Mental Health Services Administration (SAMHSA), February 18, 2016; text from "Mental Health and African Americans," Office of Minority Health (OMH); September 25, 2014; text from "Mental Health and American Indians/Alaska Natives," Office of Minority Health (OMH); September 17, 2013; text from "Mental Health and Asian Americans," Office of Minority Health (OMH); September 18, 2013; and "Mental Health and Hispanics," Office of text from Minority Health (OMH); text from September 20, 2013.

the poverty level, are 3 times more likely to report psychological distress.

- African-Americans are 20% more likely to report having serious psychological distress than Non-Hispanic Whites.

- Non-Hispanic Whites are more than twice as likely to receive antidepressant prescription treatments as are Non-Hispanic Blacks.

- The death rate from suicide for African-American men was almost four times that for African-American women, in 2009.

- However, the suicide rate for African-Americans is 60% lower than that of the Non-Hispanic White population.

- A report from the U.S. Surgeon General found that from 1980 to 1995, the suicide rate among African-Americans ages 10 to 14 increased 233%, as compared to 120% of Non-Hispanic Whites.

## Mental Health Status

**Table 40.1.** Serious Psychological Distress among Adults 18 Years of Age and over, Percent, 2009–2010

| Non-Hispanic Black | Non-Hispanic White | Non-Hispanic Black/ Non-Hispanic White Ratio |
|---|---|---|
| 3.8 | 3.1 | 1.2 |

## Mental Health and American Indians/Alaska Natives

- In 2009, suicide was the second leading cause of death for American Indian/Alaska Natives between the ages of 10 and 34.

- American Indian/Alaska Natives are twice as likely to experience feelings of nervousness or restlessness as compared to non-Hispanic Whites.

- Violent deaths—unintentional injuries, homicide, and suicide—account for 75% of all mortality in the second decade of life for American Indian/Alaska Natives.

- While the overall death rate from suicide for American Indian/ Alaska Natives is comparable to the White population, adolescent American Indian/Alaska Native females have death rates at almost four the rate for White females in the same age groups.

## Mental Health Status

**Table 40.2.** Serious Psychological Distress among Adults 18 Years of Age and over, Percent, 2009–2010

| American Indian/ Alaska Native | Non-Hispanic White | American Indian/Alaska Native/Non-Hispanic White Ratio |
|---|---|---|
| 5.2 | 3.1 | 1.7 |

## Mental Health and Asian Americans

- Suicide was the 10th leading cause of death for Asian Americans, and also was the 10th leading cause of death for White Americans, in 2009.

- Older Asian American women have the highest suicide rate of all women over age 65 in the United States.

- Southeast Asian refugees are at risk for posttraumatic stress disorder (PTSD) associated with trauma experienced before and after immigration to the U.S. One study found that 70% of Southeast Asian refugees receiving mental health care were diagnosed with PTSD.

- For Asian Americans, the rate of serious psychological distress increases with lower levels of income, as it does in most other ethnic populations.

- The overall suicide rate for Asian Americans is half that of the White population.

## Mental Health Status

**Table 40.3.** Serious Psychological Distress among Adults 18 Years of Age and over, Percent, 2009–2010

| Asian American | Non-Hispanic White | Asian American/ Non-Hispanic White Ratio |
|---|---|---|
| 1.6 | 3.1 | 0.5 |

## Mental Health and Hispanics

- Poverty level affects mental health status. Hispanics living below the poverty level, as compared to Hispanics over twice the poverty level, are three times more likely to report psychological distress.

- The death rate from suicide for Hispanic men is almost five times the rate for Hispanic women, in 2009.

- However, the suicide rate for Hispanics is half that of the Non-Hispanic White population.

- Suicide attempts for Hispanic girls, grades 9-12, were 70% higher than for White girls in the same age group, in 2011.

- Non-Hispanic Whites received mental health treatment 2 times more often than Hispanics, in 2008.

## Mental Health Status

**Table 40.4.** Serious Psychological Distress among Adults 18 Years of Age and over, Percent, 2009–2010

| Hispanic | Mexican American | Non-Hispanic White | Mexican/ Non-Hispanic White Ratio | Hispanic/ Non-Hispanic White Ratio |
|---|---|---|---|---|
| 3.6 | 2.8 | 3.1 | 1.2 | 0.9 |

# Chapter 41

# *Link between Mental Health and Poverty*

There is no health without mental health, a growing body of evidence indicates, yet this aspect of care is largely neglected in the developing world. Many live their daily lives amid grinding poverty, ongoing disease outbreaks, political instability and violence—yet there are few, if any, resources available to help them deal with the mental health issues that arise. Depression, anxiety disorders, substance abuse and other crippling conditions pose an enormous burden.

To address this misery, mental health care should be integrated into existing health systems and development programs, according to a landmark series of papers published recently by PLOS Medicine. The five articles are the result of an NIH workshop organized by Fogarty's Center for Global Health Studies and co-sponsored by the National Institute of Mental Health (NIMH), National Heart, Lung and Blood Institute (NHLBI) and National Institute of Child Health and Human Development (NICHD).

"There has been a perception that mental health disorders are problems of wealthy countries and that with so many other competing health priorities in low- and middle-income countries, how could you possibly think about mental disorders?" said Dr. Pamela Y. Collins, Director of NIMH's Office for Research on Disparities and Global

Text in this chapter is excerpted from "Focus: Mental Health Must Be Integrated into Care Delivery," National Institutes of Health (NIH), August 2013.

Mental Health. "Mental disorders are responsible for a substantial burden of illness and disability that must be addressed."

If mental, neurological and substance use disorders remain untreated, global health investments will not efficiently raise the over-all health of targeted populations. Indeed, these conditions account for almost a quarter of all years lived with a disability, according to the Global Burden of Disease Study 2010. This is a huge loss in terms of individuals' well-being and productivity and extends to affecting their family, community and the economy. Mental disorders are associated with many comorbidities and related deaths, including higher HIV infection rates, cirrhosis or cancer tied to alcohol abuse and deaths from suicide.

The WHO estimates that in some low-resource countries, less than 10 percent of people with mental health problems are treated. Even in countries where mental health services are widely available, such as the United States, only about half of potential patients seek and receive attention for their disorders.

In 2011, researchers, clinicians and advocates identified 40 Grand Challenges in Global Mental Health. The recent NIH workshop and resulting papers focus on one of those Challenges: "Redesign health systems to integrate MNS (mental, neurological and substance abuse) disorders with other chronic disease care, and create parity between mental and physical illness in investment into research, training, treatment and prevention."

The meeting focused on how mental health services can be inte-grated into maternal and child health care, HIV treatment and non-communicable disease programs.

Treatment for mental disorders should be part of primary care and other global health priority programs targeted at specific health conditions, according to the papers' authors, led by NIMH's Collins. "The links between HIV and depression, cardiovascular disease and anxiety disorders, diabetes and depression—as well as other conditions—suggest that the best outcomes for these disorders require care that attends to all of them."

# Part Six

# Mental Illness Co-Occurring with Other Disorders

# Chapter 42

# *Cancer and Mental Health*

## *Chapter Contents*

## Section 42.1

## *Psychological Stress and Cancer*

This section includes excerpts from "Adjustment to Cancer: Anxiety and Distress," National Cancer Institute (NCI), January 7, 2015; and text from "Cancer-Related Post-traumatic Stress" National Cancer Institute (NCI), July 7, 2015.

### *Anxiety and Distress Can Affect the Quality of Life of Patients with Cancer and Their Families.*

Patients living with cancer feel many different emotions, including anxiety and distress.

- Anxiety is fear, dread, and uneasiness caused by stress.

- Distress is emotional, mental, social, or spiritual suffering. Patients who are distressed may have a range of feelings from vulnerability and sadness to depression, anxiety, panic, and isolation.

Patients may have feelings of anxiety and distress while being screened for a cancer, waiting for the results of tests, receiving a cancer diagnosis, being treated for cancer, or worrying that cancer will recur (come back).

Anxiety and distress may affect a patient's ability to cope with a cancer diagnosis or treatment. It may cause patients to miss checkups or delay treatment. Anxiety may increase pain, affect sleep, and cause nausea and vomiting. Even mild anxiety can affect the quality of life for cancer patients and their families and may need to be treated.

### *Patients Living with Cancer Can Feel Different Levels of Distress.*

Some patients living with cancer have a low level of distress and others have higher levels of distress. The level of distress ranges from being able to adjust to living with cancer to having a serious mental health problem, such as major depression. However, most patients with cancer do not have signs or symptoms of any specific mental health problem. This summary describes the less severe levels of distress in patients living with cancer, including:

- Normal adjustment—A condition in which a person makes changes in his or her life to manage a stressful event such as a cancer diagnosis. In normal adjustment, a person learns to cope well with emotional distress and solve problems related to cancer.

- Psychological and social distress—A condition in which a person has some trouble making changes in their life to manage a stressful event such as a cancer diagnosis. Help from a professional to learn new coping skills may be needed.

- Adjustment disorder—A condition in which a person has a lot of trouble making changes in his or her life to manage a stressful event such as a cancer diagnosis. Symptoms such as depression, anxiety, or other emotional, social, or behavioral problems occur and worsen the person's quality of life. Medicine and help from a professional to make these changes may be needed.

- Anxiety disorder—A condition in which a person has extreme anxiety. It may be because of a stressful event like a cancer diagnosis or for no known reason. Symptoms of anxiety disorder include worry, fear, and dread. When the symptoms are severe, it affects a person's ability to lead a normal life. There are many types of anxiety disorders:

  - Generalized anxiety disorder.

  - Panic disorder (a condition that causes sudden feelings of panic).

  - Agoraphobia (fear of open places or situations in which it might be hard to get help if needed).

  - Social anxiety disorder (fear of social situations).

  - Specific phobia (fear of a specific object or situation).

  - Obsessive-compulsive disorder.

  - Posttraumatic stress disorder.

There are certain risk factors for serious distress in people with cancer. Nearly half of cancer patients report having a lot of distress. Patients with lung, pancreatic, and brain cancers may be more likely to report distress, but in general, the type of cancer does not make a difference. Factors that increase the risk of anxiety and distress are not always related to the cancer. The following may be risk factors for high levels of distress in patients with cancer:

- Trouble doing the usual activities of daily living.

- Physical symptoms and side effects (such as fatigue, nausea, or pain).

- Problems at home.

- Depression or other mental or emotional problems.

- Being younger, nonwhite, or female.

- Having a lower level of education.

### Cancer-Related Posttraumatic Stress (PTS) Is a Lot Like Posttraumatic Stress Disorder (PTSD) but Not as Severe.

Patients have a range of normal reactions when they hear they have cancer. These include:

- Repeated frightening thoughts.

- Being distracted or overexcited.

- Trouble sleeping.

- Feeling detached from oneself or reality.

Patients may also have feelings of shock, fear, helplessness, or horror. These feelings may lead to cancer-related posttraumatic stress (PTS), which is a lot like posttraumatic stress disorder (PTSD). PTSD is a specific group of symptoms that affect many survivors of stressful events. These events usually involve the threat of death or serious injury to oneself or others. People who have survived military combat, natural disasters, violent personal attack (such as rape), or other life-threatening stress may suffer from PTSD. The symptoms for PTS and PTSD are a lot alike, but most cancer patients are able to cope and don't develop full PTSD. The symptoms of cancer-related PTS are not as severe and don't last as long as PTSD.

### Cancer-Related PTS Can Occur Anytime during or after Treatment.

Patients dealing with cancer may have symptoms of posttraumatic stress at any point from diagnosis through treatment, after treatment is complete, or during possible recurrence of the cancer. Parents of childhood cancer survivors may also have posttraumatic stress.

# Section 42.2

# *Depression in Cancer Patients*

Text in this section is excerpted from "Depression (PDQ®)," National Cancer Institute (NCI), December 3, 2014.

## *Depression*

### *Depression Is Different from Normal Sadness.*

Depression is not simply feeling sad. Depression is a disorder with specific symptoms that can be diagnosed and treated. About one-fourth of cancer patients become depressed. The numbers of men and women affected are about the same.

A person diagnosed with cancer faces many stressful issues. These may include:

- Fear of death.

- Changes in life plans.

- Changes in body image and self-esteem.

- Changes in day to day living.

- Money and legal concerns.

Sadness and grief are normal reactions to a cancer diagnosis. A person with cancer may also have:

- Feelings of disbelief, denial, or despair.

- Trouble sleeping.

- Loss of appetite.

- Anxiety or worry about the future.

Not everyone who is diagnosed with cancer reacts in the same way. Some cancer patients may not have depression or anxiety, while others may have high levels of both.

Signs that you have adjusted to the cancer diagnosis and treatment include being able to stay active in daily life and continue in your roles such as:

- Spouse.

- Parent.

- Employee.

## Some Cancer Patients May Have a Higher Risk of Depression.

There are known risk factors for depression after a cancer diagnosis. Factors that increase the risk of depression are not always related to the cancer.

### Risk Factors Related to Cancer

Risk factors related to cancer that may cause depression include the following:

- Learning you have cancer when you are already depressed for other reasons.

- Having cancer pain that is not well controlled.

- Having advanced cancer.

- Being physically weakened by the cancer.

- Being unmarried (for certain types of cancer).

- Having pancreatic cancer.

- Taking certain medicines, such as:

  - Corticosteroids.

  - Procarbazine.

  - L-asparaginase.

  - Interferon alfa.

  - Interleukin-2.

  - Amphotericin B.

*Risk Factor Not Related to Cancer*

Risk factors not related to cancer that may cause depression include the following:

- A personal or family history of depression or suicide.

- A personal history of alcoholism or drug abuse.

- A personal history of mental problems.

- A weak social support system (not being married, having few family members or friends, having a job where you work alone).

- Stress caused by life events other than the cancer.

- Health problems that are known to cause depression (such as stroke or heart attack).

## There Are Many Medical Conditions That Can Cause Depression

Medical conditions that may cause depression include the following:

- Pain that doesn't go away with treatment.

- Anemia.

- Fever.

- Abnormal levels of calcium, sodium, or potassium in the blood.

- Not enough vitamin B12 or folate in your diet.

- Too much or too little thyroid hormone.

- Too little adrenal hormone.

- Side effects of certain medicines.

## Depression and Anxiety Are Common in Patients Whose Cancer Is Advanced and Can No Longer Be Treated

Patients whose cancer can no longer be treated often feel depressed and anxious. These feelings can lower the quality of life. Terminally ill patients who are depressed report being troubled about:

- Symptoms.

- Relationships.

- Beliefs about life.

Depressed terminally ill patients feel they are "being a burden" even when they don't depend very much on others.

### Family Members Also Have a Risk of Depression

Anxiety and depression are also common in family members caring for loved ones with cancer. Children are affected when a parent with cancer is depressed and may have emotional and behavioral problems themselves.

Good communication helps. Family members who talk about feelings and solve problems are more likely to have lower levels of anxiety and depression.

## Section 42.3

# Cognitive Disorders and Delirium in Advanced Cancer

This section includes excerpts from "Cognitive Effects of Cancer and Cancer Treatment," National Cancer Institute (NCI), October 22, 2013; text from "Cognitive Changes Related to Cancer and Cancer Treatments," National Cancer Institute (NCI), February 20, 2014; and text from "Delirium (PDQ®)," National Cancer Institute (NCI), December 12, 2013.

### Cognitive Disorders and Delirium in Advanced Cancer

Cognitive dysfunction has been demonstrated in cancer patients before, during, and following treatment. It is believed that one-third of patients undergoing chemotherapy experience some degree of cognitive dysfunction during or following treatment, and these deficits can have a significant impact on social and occupational functioning, and overall quality of life. These cognitive difficulties may involve multiple cognitive domains, including working memory, executive function, and processing speed.

Cognitive changes related to cancer and cancer treatments, particularly chemotherapy, have been an important concern for investigators.

Overall, research findings have demonstrated changes in several domains of cognition including working memory, new learning, executive function and spatial abilities. However, the science is not conclusive. There are challenges in the areas of measurement, generalizability of neuropsychological test results to everyday tasks, and interpreting findings across research studies. Moreover, not all cancer patients and survivors experience cognitive late effects. Determining susceptibility and identifying neural pathways remains an important area of exploration. In addition, the number of validated interventions are limited for patients suffering from these symptoms and further work is needed to provide practitioners and patients with empirically sound therapies.

## Cancer and Delirium

Delirium is a confused mental state that can occur in patients who have cancer, especially advanced cancer. Patients with delirium have problems with the following:

- Attention
- Thinking
- Awareness
- Behavior
- Emotions
- Judgement
- Memory
- Muscle control
- Sleeping and waking

There are three types of delirium:

1. **Hypoactive:** The patient is not active and seems sleepy, tired, or depressed.

2. **Hyperactive:** The patient is restless or agitated.

3. **Mixed:** The patient changes back and forth between being hypoactive and hyperactive.

### Delirium May Come and Go during the Day

The symptoms of delirium usually occur suddenly. They often occur within hours or days and may come and go. Delirium is often temporary and can be treated. However, in the last 24 to 48 hours of life, delirium may be permanent because of problems like organ failure. Most advanced cancer patients have delirium that occurs in the last hours to days before death.

## Delirium May Be Caused by Cancer, Cancer Treatment, or Other Medical Conditions

There is often more than one cause of delirium in a cancer patient, especially when the cancer is advanced and the patient has many medical conditions. Causes of delirium include the following:

- Organ failure, such as liver or kidney failure.

- Electrolyte imbalances: Electrolytes are important minerals (including salt, potassium, calcium, and phosphorous) in blood and body fluids. These electrolytes are needed to keep the heart, kidneys, nerves, and muscles working the way they should.

- Infections.

- Paraneoplastic syndromes: Symptoms that occur when cancer-fighting antibodies or white blood cells attack normal cells in the nervous system by mistake.

- Side effects of medicines and treatments: Patients with cancer may take medicines with side effects that include delirium and confusion. The effects usually go away after the medicine is stopped.

- Withdrawal from medicines that depress (slow down) the central nervous system (brain and spinal cord).

### It Is Important to Know the Risk Factors for Delirium

Patients with cancer are likely to have more than one risk factor for delirium. Identifying risk factors early may help prevent delirium or decrease the time it takes to treat it.

Risk factors include the following:

- Serious illness.

- Having more than one disease.

- Older age.

- Dementia.

- Low level of albumin (protein) in the blood, which is often caused by liver problems.

- Infection.

- High level of nitrogen waste products in the blood, which is often caused by kidney problems.

- Taking medicines that affect the mind or behavior.

- Taking high doses of pain medicines, such as opioids.

The risk increases when the patient has more than one risk factor. Older patients with advanced cancer who are hospitalized often have more than one risk factor for delirium.

## *Delirium Causes Changes in the Patient That Can Upset the Family and Caregivers*

Delirium may be dangerous to the patient if his or her judgment is affected. Delirium can cause the patient to behave in unusual ways. Even a quiet or calm patient can have a sudden change in mood or become agitated and need more care.

Delirium can be upsetting to the family and caregivers. When the patient becomes agitated, family members often think the patient is in pain, but this may not be the case. Learning about differences between the symptoms of delirium and pain may help the family and caregivers understand how much pain medicine is needed. Health care providers can help the family and caregivers learn about these differences.

## *Delirium May Affect Physical Health and Communication*

Patients with delirium are:

- More likely to fall.

- Sometimes unable to control bladder and/or bowels.

- More likely to become dehydrated (drink too little water to stay healthy).

They often need a longer hospital stay than patients without delirium.

The confused mental state of these patients may make them:

- Unable to talk with family members and caregivers about their needs and feelings.

- Unable to make decisions about care.

This makes it harder for health care providers to assess the patient's symptoms. The family may need to make decisions for the patient.

## Possible Signs of Delirium Include Sudden Personality Changes, Problems Thinking, and Unusual Anxiety or Depression

When the following symptoms occur suddenly, they may be signs of delirium:

- Agitation.
- Not cooperating.
- Changes in personality or behavior.
- Problems thinking.
- Problems paying attention.
- Unusual anxiety or depression.

## The Symptoms of Delirium Are a Lot Like Symptoms of Depression and Dementia

Early symptoms of delirium are like symptoms of depression and dementia. Delirium that causes the patient to be inactive may appear to be depression. Delirium and dementia both cause problems with memory, thinking, and judgment. Dementia may be caused by a number of medical conditions, including Alzheimer disease. Differences in the symptoms of delirium and dementia include the following:

- Patients with delirium often show changes in how alert or aware they are. Patients who have dementia usually stay alert and aware until the dementia becomes very advanced.

- Delirium occurs suddenly (within hours or days). Dementia appears gradually (over months to years) and gets worse over time.

Older patients with cancer may have both dementia and delirium. This can make it hard for the doctor to diagnose the problem. If treatment for delirium is given and the symptoms continue, then the diagnosis is more likely dementia. Checking the patient's health and symptoms over time can help diagnose delirium and dementia.

## Physical Exams and Other Laboratory Tests Are Used to Diagnose the Causes of Delirium

Doctors will try to find the causes of delirium.

- Physical exam and history An exam of the body to check general signs of health, including checking for signs of disease, such as lumps or anything else that seems unusual. A history of the patient's health habits, past illnesses including depression, and treatments will also be taken. A physical exam can help rule out a physical condition that may be causing symptoms.

- Laboratory tests Medical procedures that test samples of tissue, blood, urine, or other substances in the body. These tests help to diagnose disease, plan and check treatment, or monitor the disease over time.

## Treatment Includes Looking at the Causes and Symptoms of Delirium

Both the causes and the symptoms of delirium may be treated. Treatment depends on the following:

- Where the patient is living, such as home, hospital, or nursing home.
- How advanced the cancer is.
- How the delirium symptoms are affecting the patient.
- The wishes of the patient and family.
- Treating the causes of delirium usually includes the following:
- Stopping or lowering the dose of medicines that cause delirium.
- Giving fluids to treat dehydration.
- Giving drugs to treat hypercalcemia (too much calcium in the blood).
- Giving antibiotics for infections.

In a terminally ill patient with delirium, the doctor may treat just the symptoms. The doctor will continue to watch the patient closely during treatment.

## Treatment without Medicines Can Also Help Relieve Symptoms

Controlling the patient's surroundings may help with mild symptoms of delirium. The following may help:

- Keep the patient's room quiet and well-lit, and put familiar objects in it.
- Put a clock or calendar where the patient can see it.

- Have family members around.

- Keep the same caregivers as much as possible.

Patients who may hurt themselves or others may need to have physical restraints.

### Treatment May Include Medicines

Medicines may be used to treat the symptoms of delirium depending on the patient's condition and heart health. These medicines have serious side effects and the patient will be watched closely by a doctor. These medicines include the following:

- Haloperidol

- Olanzapine

- Risperidone

- Lorazepam

- Midazolam

### Sedation May Be Used for Delirium at the End of Life or When Delirium Does Not Get Better with Treatment

When the symptoms of delirium are not relieved with standard treatments and the patient is near death, in pain, or has trouble breathing, other treatment may be needed. Sometimes medicines that will sedate (calm) the patient will be used. The family and the health care team will make this decision together.

The decision to use sedation for delirium may be guided by the following:

- The patient will have repeated assessments by experts before the delirium is considered to be refractory (doesn't respond to treatment).

- The decision to sedate the patient is reviewed by a team of health care professionals and not made by one doctor.

- Temporary sedation, for short periods of time such as overnight, is considered before continuous sedation is used.

- The team of health care professionals will work with the family to make sure the team understands the family's views and that the family understands palliative sedation.

# Chapter 43

# *Diabetes and Mental Health*

## *Introduction*

People with mental illness, substance use disorders (SUDs), or both are at increased risk for developing diabetes, a chronic metabolic disease with numerous long-term health consequences. Untreated behavioral health disorders can exacerbate diabetes symptoms and complications. In addition, companion features of behavioral health disorders—such as poor self-care, improper nutrition, reduced physical activity, and increased barriers to preventive or primary health care—can adversely affect management of co-occurring diabetes.

## *What Is Diabetes?*

Diabetes is a chronic disease characterized by elevated blood glucose levels. It occurs when glucose digested from food is unable to enter the body's cells to be used for energy. The hormone insulin is necessary for the cells to absorb glucose.

In type 1 diabetes, the pancreas does not make enough insulin or stops making insulin completely; glucose remains in the bloodstream rather than transferring into the cells. A person with type 1 diabetes must be given insulin to live. This form of diabetes most often begins early in life and appears to have both genetic and environmental causes.

---

Text in this chapter is excerpted from "Diabetes Care for Clients in Behavioral Health Treatment," Substance Abuse and Mental Health Services Administration (SAMHSA), 2013.

Type 2 diabetes is far more common than type 1. In the individual with type 2 diabetes, insulin becomes less effective at helping transport blood glucose into cells. If the disease is untreated, over a period of years the cells become progressively more resistant to insulin, even as the pancreas makes increasingly larger amounts of the hormone to compensate. The overworked pancreas can deteriorate to the point where it stops producing insulin altogether.

## How Is Diabetes Linked to Mental Illness?

Diabetes has a complex and reciprocal relationship with mental illness and shares metabolic features with certain mental disorders. For example, insulin resistance and impaired glucose regulation, which are features of diabetes, have been separately observed in patients with mental disorders such as schizophrenia and depression. Mental illness reduces the likelihood that a person with diabetes will be properly treated, just as mental illness is associated with other disparities in care.

Rates of severe psychological distress are twice as high in people with diabetes compared with the rates among those without the disease. In addition, severe psychological distress is negatively associated with processes of diabetes care (e.g., access to prevention services) and outcomes. For young people with type 1 diabetes, previous psychiatric referral is a significant risk factor for death from acute diabetes-related events such as hypoglycemia or coma.

Relationships between diabetes and some specific mental illnesses are discussed below.

### Depression

Diabetes increases risk for depression and depressive symptoms. CDC reports that people with diabetes have roughly a doubled risk of also having depression compared with those who do not have diabetes. Similarly, a person with depression faces a 60-percent increase in risk for type 2 diabetes. A depressive disorder typically precedes a type 1 diagnosis and follows a type 2 diagnosis. Long-term use of antidepressant medications has been implicated in higher risk for type 2 diabetes, although these findings remain controversial.

Among all people with depression, recurrence and longer episodes are more common in people with diabetes than in those without the disease. Even at mild levels, depression can adversely affect glycemic control and a person's ability to perform diabetes self-care.

*Anxiety Disorders*

People with diabetes have an elevated risk for anxiety disorders compared with the general population. Anxieties may be triggered by the burdens of having a chronic disease and by diabetes-specific factors such as having to inject insulin and living with the threat of acute diabetic symptoms and long-term complications. Such stressors may trigger generalized anxiety, obsessive compulsive behavior, or phobic avoidance of activities necessary to managing diabetes such as checking blood glucose levels or injecting insulin.

*Schizophrenia*

People with schizophrenia have higher rates of hyperglycemia and type 2 diabetes than the general population, and diabetes is a leading cause of illness and death for people affected by schizophrenia-related disorders. Antipsychotic medications used to treat schizophrenia and, increasingly, nonpsychotic emotional disorders, are associated with increased risk for type 2 diabetes.

Deficits in learning, attention, memory, and other cognitive functions have been detected in type 1 and type 2 diabetes patients through neurocognitive testing. Deficits may result from a variety of factors, including hypoglycemia, hyperglycemia, and insulin resistance. These cognitive effects can be exacerbated in people who also have schizophrenia, which presents its own risks to cognition.

*Eating Disorders*

Compared with the general public, people with diabetes are more likely to develop eating disorders, which are more likely to occur in young women. Eating disorders increase the risk for poor glycemic control and resulting acute diabetes symptoms.

## How Is Diabetes Linked to Stress?

Stress, which can be experienced without a diagnosis of a mental disorder, increases risk for diabetes symptoms and complications. Hormones that are activated in response to stress (e.g., epinephrine, norepinephrine, cortisol, growth hormone) cause blood glucose levels to increase. Substantial evidence exists that stress can adversely affect the course of diabetes (whether it also can trigger the onset of diabetes is not established). Stress also can interfere with diabetes self-management, although the effects may depend on how the stress is perceived (that is, as positive or negative) and whether psychosocial or psychological support is available.

# Chapter 44

# *Epilepsy and Mental Health*

## *What Are the Epilepsies?*

The epilepsies are chronic neurological disorders in which clusters of nerve cells, or neurons, in the brain sometimes signal abnormally and cause seizures. Neurons normally generate electrical and chemical signals that act on other neurons, glands, and muscles to produce human thoughts, feelings, and actions. During a seizure, many neurons fire (signal) at the same time—as many as 500 times a second, much faster than normal. This surge of excessive electrical activity happening at the same time causes involuntary movements, sensations, emotions, and behaviors and the temporary disturbance of normal neuronal activity may cause a loss of awareness.

Epilepsy can be considered a spectrum disorder because of its different causes, different seizure types, its ability to vary in severity and impact from person to person, and its range of co-existing conditions. Some people may have convulsions (sudden onset of repetitive general contraction of muscles) and lose consciousness. Others may simply stop what they are doing, have a brief lapse of awareness, and stare into space for a short period. Some people have seizures very infrequently, while other people may experience hundreds of seizures

This chapter includes excerpts from "The Epilepsies and Seizures: Hope Through Research," National Institute of Neurological Disorders and Stroke (NINDS), April 2015; and text from "Curing the Epilepsies: The Promise of Research," National Institute of Neurological Disorders and Stroke (NINDS), September 1, 2013.

each day. There also are many different types of epilepsy, resulting from a variety of causes. Recent adoption of the term "the epilepsies" underscores the diversity of types and causes.

In general, a person is not considered to have epilepsy until he or she has had two or more unprovoked seizures separated by at least 24 hours. In contrast, a provoked seizure is one caused by a known precipitating factor such as a high fever, nervous system infections, acute traumatic brain injury, or fluctuations in blood sugar or electrolyte levels.

Anyone can develop epilepsy. About 2.3 million adults and more than 450,000 children and adolescents in the United States currently live with epilepsy. Each year, an estimated 150,000 people are diagnosed with epilepsy. Epilepsy affects both males and females of all races, ethnic backgrounds, and ages. In the United States alone, the annual costs associated with the epilepsies are estimated to be $15.5 billion in direct medical expenses and lost or reduced earnings and productivity.

The majority of those diagnosed with epilepsy have seizures that can be controlled with drug therapies and surgery. However, as much as 30 to 40 percent of people with epilepsy continue to have seizures because available treatments do not completely control their seizures (called intractable or medication resistant epilepsy).

While many forms of epilepsy require lifelong treatment to control the seizures, for some people the seizures eventually go away. The odds of becoming seizure-free are not as good for adults or for children with severe epilepsy syndromes, but it is possible that seizures may decrease or even stop over time. This is more likely if the epilepsy starts in childhood, has been well-controlled by medication, or if the person has had surgery to remove the brain focus of the abnormal cell firing.

Many people with epilepsy lead productive lives, but some will be severely impacted by their epilepsy. Medical and research advances in the past two decades have led to a better understanding of the epilepsies and seizures. More than 20 different medications and a variety of dietary treatments and surgical techniques (including two devices) are now available and may provide good control of seizures. Devices can modulate brain activity to decrease seizure frequency. Advance neuroimaging can identify brain abnormalities that give rise to seizures which can be cured by neurosurgery. Even dietary changes can effectively treat certain types of epilepsy. Research on the underlying causes of the epilepsies, including identification of genes for some forms of epilepsy, has led to a greatly improved understanding of these disorders that may lead to more effective treatments or even to new ways of preventing epilepsy in the future.

## What Is the Impact of the Epilepsies on Daily Life?

The majority of people with epilepsy can do the same things as people without the disorder and have successful and productive lives. In most cases it does not affect job choice or performance. One-third or more of people with epilepsy, however, may have cognitive or neuro-psychiatric co-concurring symptoms that can negatively impact their quality of life. Many people with epilepsy are significantly helped by available therapies, and some may go months or years without having a seizure. However, people with treatment-resistant epilepsy can have as many as hundreds of seizures a day or they can have one seizure a year with sometimes disabling consequences. On average, having treatment-resistant epilepsy is associated with an increased risk of cognitive impairment, particularly if the seizures developed in early childhood. These impairments may be related to the underlying conditions associated with the epilepsy rather than to the epilepsy itself.

## Mental Health and Stigmatization

Depression is common among people with epilepsy. It is estimated that one of every three persons with epilepsy will have depression in the course of his or her lifetime, often with accompanying symptoms of anxiety disorder. In adults, depression and anxiety are the two most frequent mental health-related diagnoses. In adults, a depression screening questionnaire specifically designed for epilepsy helps health-care professionals identify people who need treatment. Depression or anxiety in people with epilepsy can be treated with counseling or most of the same medications used in people who don't have epilepsy. People with epilepsy should not simply accept that depression is part of having epilepsy and should discuss symptoms and feelings with health care professionals.

Children with epilepsy also have a higher risk of developing depression and/or attention deficit hyperactivity disorder compared with their peers. Behavioral problems may precede the onset of seizures in some children.

Children are especially vulnerable to the emotional problems caused by ignorance or the lack of knowledge among others about epilepsy. This often results in stigmatization, bullying, or teasing of a child who has epilepsy. Such experiences can lead to behaviors of avoidance in school and other social settings. Counseling services and support groups can help families cope with epilepsy in a positive manner.

## Psychiatric, Neurodevelopmental, and Sleep Disorders

Co-occurring psychiatric conditions are relatively common in individuals with epilepsy. In adults, depression and anxiety disorders are the two most frequent psychiatric diagnoses. Attention Deficit Hyperactivity Disorder and anxiety frequently affect children with epilepsy.

Therapies commonly used to treat depression in the general population have been shown in randomized controlled trials to be effective in treating depression in people with epilepsy. In those trials, depression medications did not appear to be associated with an increased risk of seizures. However, larger trials with longer follow up would be required to provide reliable estimates of seizure exacerbation risk.

Basic research investigations currently are exploring the possibility that the development of depression, anxiety, and seizures may involve similar causes. In addition, studies of antiseizure drugs have focused on determining whether there may be an increased risk of suicide associated with specific medications.

People with neurodevelopmental disabilities, such as autism spectrum disorder, attention deficit disorder, and learning disabilities are known to be at higher risk for epilepsy. Further investigation is needed to better understand these associations and if there is a shared mechanism between these neurodevelopmental disabilities and the epilepsies. Sleep disorders are common among people with the epilepsies. By one estimate, fully 70 percent of people with epilepsy had some form of disordered breathing during sleep. In another study, researchers found that certain types of seizures were associated with sleeping, while others were more common during times of wakefulness—suggesting that more research is needed on how these patterns might inform medication adjustment.

# Chapter 45

# Human Immunodeficiency Virus (HIV) and Mental Health

## What Is Mental Health?

"Mental health" refers to your emotional, psychological, and social well-being. It is an important part of staying healthy when living with HIV. Your mental health affects how you think, feel, and act. It also helps determine how you handle stress, relate to others, and make choices.

Positive mental health allows you to:

- realize your full potential

- cope with the stresses of life

- work productively

- make meaningful contributions to your community

Positive mental health is important for all individuals at every stage of life, and there are some particular considerations for people living with HIV.

---

Text in this chapter is excerpted from "Staying Healthy with HIV/AIDS: Taking Care of Yourself: Mental Health," U.S. Department of Health and Human Services (HHS), March 7, 2014.

## Why Is Positive Mental Health Important for People Living with HIV?

Your mental health is just as important as your physical health. When you have positive mental health, you generally are able to:

- function better at work, at school, and in relationships.

- cope more effectively with life's difficulties, such as the death of a loved one, ending a relationship, job stress, health issues, and family or financial problems.

- take better care of yourself physically.

- provide better care for your children or other family members.

But mental health problems can affect the way you think, feel, and behave, and can change how well you function at work and at home. If you are living with HIV, mental health problems can affect your physical health by:

- making it harder for you to take all your HIV medicines on time.

- making it harder for you to keep your health appointments or take advantage of your support network.

- interfering with your healthy behaviors, such as getting enough sleep and exercise and avoiding risk behaviors such as having unprotected sex.

- impairing your ability to cope with the stresses of daily life.

Mental health problems are very common among all Americans, not just those living with HIV. In fact, in 2012, about:

- One in five American adults experienced a diagnosable mental illness.

- Nearly 1 in 10 young people experienced a period of major depression.

- Four percent of American adults lived with a serious mental illness, such as schizophrenia, bipolar disorder, or major depression.

As a person living with HIV, it is important for you to be aware that you have an increased risk for developing mood, anxiety, and cognitive disorders. These conditions are treatable. People who experience mental health problems can get better and many recover completely.

You can better manage your overall health and well-being if you know how having HIV can affect your mental health and what resources are available to help you if you need it.

## What Causes Mental Health Problems?

Mental health problems are not caused by "personal weakness." Most are caused by a combination of family history and environmental, biological, and psychosocial factors.

Common factors include:

- a family history of mental health problems and other genetic factors.

- stressful life events or psychosocial reasons, including trauma, sexual and physical abuse, neglect, and illness.

- psychological factors such as unhealthy thinking patterns and trouble managing feelings.

In addition, some forms of stress can contribute to mental health problems for people living with HIV, including:

- having trouble getting the services you need.

- experiencing a loss of social support, resulting in isolation.

- experiencing a loss of employment or worries about whether you will be able to perform your work as you did before.

- having to tell others you are HIV-positive.

- managing your HIV medicines.

- going through changes in your physical appearance or abilities due to HIV/AIDS.

- dealing with loss, including the loss of relationships or even death.

- facing the stigma and discrimination associated with HIV/AIDS.

Starting antiretroviral therapy also can affect your mental health in different ways. Sometimes, it can relieve your anxiety because knowing that you are taking care of yourself can give you a sense of security. However, it can also increase your emotions because coping with the reality of living with HIV can be complicated. In addition, antiretroviral medications may cause a variety of symptoms, including depression, anxiety, and sleep disturbance, and may make some mental health issues worse.

The HIV virus itself also can contribute to mental health problems. Some opportunistic infections (which occur when your immune system is damaged by HIV) can affect your nervous system and lead to changes in your behavior and functioning. Other disorders, such as mild cognitive changes or more severe cognitive conditions, such as dementia, are associated with advanced HIV disease.

For these reasons, it is important to talk to your healthcare provider about your mental health. A conversation about mental health should be part of your complete medical evaluation before starting antiretroviral medications. And you should continue to discuss your mental health with your healthcare team throughout treatment. Be open and honest with your provider about any changes in the way you are thinking, or how you are feeling about yourself and life in general. Also discuss any alcohol or substance use with your provider so that he or she can help connect you to treatment if necessary.

In addition, tell your healthcare provider about any over-the-counter or prescribed medications you may be taking, including any psychiatric medications, because some of these drugs may interact with antiretroviral medications.

## How Do I Know If Something Is Wrong and How Can I Find Help?

Almost everyone faces mental health challenges at some point. This is true for all individuals, not just those living with HIV. It's normal to experience some degree of worrying or fear, particularly after you have been diagnosed with HIV, or when you are experiencing changes in your health, or adjusting to antiretroviral medications. A support network can help you cope during these tough times. But when your mental health symptoms begin to affect your ability to cope and carry out typical functions in your life, it's important to get help.

So how do you know when it's time to get help? Sometimes, you can notice a change in yourself—and, sometimes, the people around you are the ones who notice. Some changes that might be significant include:

- No longer finding enjoyment in activities which usually make you happy
- Withdrawing from social interaction
- Change in memory functioning
- Sleeping too much—or being unable to sleep
- Feeling "sad" or "empty" much of the time

- Feeling guilty

- Feeling tired all the time

- Experiencing sudden and repeated attacks of fear known as "panic attacks"

- Having racing thoughts

- Loss of sexual interest

- Worrying what others are thinking about you

- Hearing voices in your head

- Feelings of wanting to hurt yourself or others

- Intense anger or rage toward others

## Depression

Depression is a serious medical illness. It's more than just a feeling of being "down in the dumps" or "blue" for a few days. Depression is a disorder of the brain. There are a variety of causes, including genetic, environmental, psychological, and biochemical factors. Depression can range from mild to severe, and symptoms can include many of feelings or behaviors listed above.

HIV does not directly cause depression. But depression is one of the most common mental health conditions experienced by people living with HIV, just as it is by the general population. Only a mental health provider can accurately diagnose and treat depression. Recovery from depression takes time but treatments are effective.

## Other Mental Health Conditions

Other mental health conditions include anxiety disorders, mood disorders, and personality disorders. Remember: a mental health disorder may be a pre-existing condition that already was a problem for a person before they had HIV; it may be first seen after an HIV diagnosis; or it may be directly or indirectly caused by the progression of the disease.

## Get Help

If you feel that something might be different or "wrong," it's important to tell your doctor or other healthcare provider—including your nurse, case manager, or social worker—so that he or she can help you. Don't be embarrassed to talk about your feelings. Your feelings are important and valid and the members of your healthcare team should be concerned about you and respect you.

If what you are describing is pattern of behavior and feelings you have experienced over time, your healthcare provider may offer treatment or a referral to a mental health services provider. Mental health providers (psychologists, therapists, psychiatrists, social workers, or nurses) can use many forms of treatment, including medications and/or "talk therapy."

## *Finding Treatment*

One of the hardest parts of having mental health condition is that you may not feel like seeking treatment or going to your appointments once you schedule them. If you are feeling this way, consider asking a friend or family member to help you make and keep your appointments, and share these feelings with your mental health provider. When you follow through, your medical and mental health providers can help you feel better, and can improve your chances of successful HIV treatment. Also you can call 1-800-273-TALK (8255) if you need help in a crisis or are experiencing emotional distress.

To find a mental health treatment provider, use the HIV/AIDS Prevention and Care Services Locator.

Living with HIV can sometimes be overwhelming to deal with, but do not neglect your mental health. The most important thing to remember is that you are not alone; there are support systems in place to help you, including doctors, psychiatrists, family members, friends, support groups, and other services.

Chapter 46

# *Pain, Chronic Illness, and Mental Health*

## *Chapter Contents*

# Section 46.1

# *When Pain Accompanies Depression*

This section includes excerpts from "Chronic Pain
and PTSD: A Guide for Patients," U.S. Department of Veterans
Affairs (VA), August 13, 2015; and text from "Depression and
Chronic Pain," National Institute of Mental
Health (NIMH), April 15, 2009. Reviewed March 2016.

## *Depression and Chronic Pain*

Depression not only affects your brain and behavior— it affects your entire body. Depression has been linked with other health problems, including chronic pain. Dealing with more than one health problem at a time can be difficult, so proper treatment is important.

### *What Is Depression?*

Major depressive disorder, or depression, is a serious mental illness. Depression interferes with your daily life and routine and reduces your quality of life. About 6.7 percent of U.S. adults ages 18 and older have depression.

### *Signs and Symptoms of Depression*

- Ongoing sad, anxious, or empty feelings

- Feeling hopeless feeling guilty, worthless, or helpless

- Feeling irritable or restless

- Loss of interest in activities or hobbies once enjoyable, including sex

- Feeling tired all the time

- Difficulty concentrating, remembering details, or making decisions

- Difficulty falling asleep or staying asleep, a condition called insomnia, or sleeping all the time overeating or loss of appetite

- Thoughts of death and suicide or suicide attempts

- Ongoing aches and pains, headaches, cramps, or digestive problems that do not ease with treatment.

## What Is Chronic Pain?

Chronic pain is pain that lasts for weeks, months, or even years. It often does not ease with regular pain medication. Chronic pain can have a distinct cause, such as a temporary injury or infection or a long-term disease. But some chronic pain has no obvious cause. Like depression, chronic pain can cause problems with sleep and daily activities, reducing your quality of life.

## How Are Depression and Chronic Pain Linked?

Scientists don't yet know how depression and chronic pain are linked, but the illnesses are known to occur together. Chronic pain can worsen depression symptoms and is a risk factor for suicide in people who are depressed.

Bodily aches and pains are a common symptom of depression. Studies show that people with more severe depression feel more intense pain. According to recent research, people with depression have higher than normal levels of proteins called cytokines. Cytokines send messages to cells that affect how the immune system responds to infection and disease, including the strength and length of the response. In this way, cytokines can trigger pain by promoting inflammation, which is the body's response to infection or injury. Inflammation helps protect the body by destroying, removing, or isolating the infected or injured area.

In addition to pain, signs of inflammation include swelling, redness, heat, and sometimes loss of function. Many studies are finding that inflammation may be a link between depression and illnesses that often occur with depression.

Further research may help doctors and scientists better understand this connection and find better ways to diagnose and treat depression and other illnesses.

One disorder that has been shown to occur with depression is fibromyalgia. Fibromyalgia causes chronic, widespread muscle pain, tiredness, and multiple tender points—places on the body that hurt in response to light pressure. People with fibromyalgia are more likely to have depression and other mental illnesses than the general population. Studies have shown that depression and fibromyalgia share risk factors and treatments.

### How Is Depression Treated in People Who Have Chronic Pain?

Depression is diagnosed and treated by a health care provider. Treating depression can help you manage your chronic pain and improve your overall health. Recovery from depression takes time but treatments are effective.

At present, the most common treatments for depression include:

- Cognitive behavioral therapy (CBT), a type of psychotherapy, or talk therapy, that helps people change negative thinking styles and behaviors that may contribute to their depression

- Selective serotonin reuptake inhibitor (SSRI), a type of antidepressant medication that includes citalopram (Celexa), sertraline (Zoloft), and fluoxetine (Prozac)

- Serotonin and norepinephrine reuptake inhibitor (SNRI), a type of antidepressant medication similar to ssri that includes venlafaxine (Effexor) and duloxetine (Cymbalta).

While currently available depression treatments are generally well tolerated and safe, talk with your healthcare provider about side effects, possible drug interactions, and other treatment options.

Not everyone responds to treatment the same way. Medications can take several weeks to work, may need to be combined with ongoing talk therapy, or may need to be changed or adjusted to minimize side effects and achieve the best results.

People living with chronic pain may be able to manage their symptoms through lifestyle changes. For example, regular aerobic exercise may help reduce some symptoms of chronic pain. Exercise may also boost your mood and help treat your depression. Talk therapy may also be helpful in treating your chronic pain.

## Pain and PTSD

### How Common Is Chronic Pain?

Approximately one in three Americans suffer from some kind of chronic pain in their lifetimes, and about one quarter of them are not able to do day to day activities because of their chronic pain. Between 80% and 90% of Americans experience chronic problems in the neck or lower back.

## How Do Health Care Providers Evaluate Pain?

Care providers generally assess chronic pain during a physical exam, but how much pain someone is in is hard to determine. Every person is different and perceives and experiences pain in different ways. There is often very little consistency when different doctors try to measure a patient's pain. Sometimes the care provider may not believe the patient, or might minimize the amount of pain. All of these things can be frustrating for the person in pain. Additionally, this kind of experience often makes patients feel helplessness and hopeless, which in turn increases tension and pain and makes the person more upset. Conversation between the doctor and patient is important, including sharing information about treatment options. If no progress is made, get a second opinion.

## What Is the Experience of Chronic Pain Like Physically?

There are many forms of chronic pain, including pain felt in: the low back (most common); the neck; the mouth, face, and jaw; the pelvis; or the head (e.g., tension and migraine headaches). Of course, each type of condition results in different experiences of pain.

People with chronic pain are less able to function well in daily life than those who do not suffer from chronic pain. They may have trouble with things such as walking, standing, sitting, lifting light objects, doing paperwork, standing in line at a grocery store, going shopping, or working. Many patients with chronic pain cannot work because of their pain or physical limitations.

## What Is the Experience of Chronic Pain Like Psychologically?

Research has shown that many patients who experience chronic pain (up to 100% of these patients) tend to also be diagnosed with depression. Because the pain and disability are always there and that may even become worse over time, many of them think suicide is the only way to end their pain and frustration. They think they have no control over their life. This frustration may also lead the person to use drugs or have unneeded surgery.

## Chronic Pain and PTSD

Some people's chronic pain stems from a traumatic event, such as a physical or sexual assault, a motor vehicle accident, or some type of disaster. Under these circumstances the person may experience both chronic pain and PTSD. The person in pain may not even realize the connection between their pain and a traumatic event. Approximately 15% to 35% of patients with chronic pain also have PTSD. Only 2% of people who do not have chronic pain have PTSD.

One study found that 51% of patients with chronic low back pain had PTSD symptoms. For people with chronic pain, the pain may actually serve as a reminder of the traumatic event, which will tend to make the PTSD even worse. Survivors of physical, psychological, or sexual abuse tend to be more at risk for developing certain types of chronic pain later in their lives.

## Section 46.2

# *Chronic Illness and Depression*

Text in this section is excerpted from "Chronic Illness and Mental Health," National Institute of Mental Health (NIMH), December 18, 2015.

Depression is a real illness. Treatment can help you live to the fullest extent possible, even when you have another illness.

It is common to feel sad or discouraged after a heart attack, a cancer diagnosis, or if you are trying to manage a chronic condition like pain. You may be facing new limits on what you can do and feel anxious about treatment outcomes and the future. It may be hard to adapt to a new reality and to cope with the changes and ongoing treatment that come with the diagnosis. Your favorite activities, like hiking or gardening, may be harder to do.

Temporary feelings of sadness are expected, but if these and other symptoms last longer than a couple of weeks, you may have depression. Depression affects your ability to carry on with daily life and to enjoy work, leisure, friends, and family. The health effects of depression go beyond mood—depression is a serious medical illness with many symptoms, including physical ones. Some symptoms of depression are:

• Feeling sad, irritable, or anxious

- Feeling empty, hopeless, guilty, or worthless

- Loss of pleasure in usually-enjoyed hobbies or activities, including sex

- Fatigue and decreased energy, feeling listless

- Trouble concentrating, remembering details, and making decisions

- Not being able to sleep, or sleeping too much. Waking too early

- Eating too much or not wanting to eat at all, possibly with unplanned weight gain or loss

- Thoughts of death, suicide or suicide attempts

- Aches or pains, headaches, cramps, or digestive problems without a clear physical cause and/or that do not ease even with treatment

## People with Other Chronic Medical Conditions Have a Higher Risk of Depression.

The same factors that increase risk of depression in otherwise healthy people also raise the risk in people with other medical illnesses. These risk factors include a personal or family history of depression or loss of family members to suicide.

However, there are some risk factors directly related to having another illness. For example, conditions such as Parkinson disease and stroke cause changes in the brain. In some cases, these changes may have a direct role in depression. Illness-related anxiety and stress can also trigger symptoms of depression.

Depression is common among people who have chronic illnesses such as the following:

- Cancer

- Coronary heart disease

- Diabetes

- Epilepsy

- Multiple sclerosis

- Stroke

- Alzheimer disease

- HIV/AIDS

- Parkinson disease

- Systemic lupus erythematosus

- Rheumatoid arthritis

Sometimes, symptoms of depression may follow a recent medical diagnosis but lift as you adjust or as the other condition is treated. In other cases, certain medications used to treat the illness may trigger depression. Depression may persist, even as physical health improves.

Research suggests that people who have depression and another medical illness tend to have more severe symptoms of both illnesses. They may have more difficulty adapting to their co-occurring illness and more medical costs than those who do not also have depression.

It is not yet clear whether treatment of depression when another illness is present can improve physical health. However, it is still important to seek treatment. It can make a difference in day-to-day life if you are coping with a chronic or long-term illness.

## People with Depression Are at Higher Risk for Other Medical Conditions.

It may have come as no surprise that people with a medical illness or condition are more likely to suffer from depression. The reverse is also true: the risk of developing some physical illnesses is higher in people with depression.

People with depression have an increased risk of cardiovascular disease, diabetes, stroke, and Alzheimer disease, for example. Research also suggests that people with depression are at higher risk for osteoporosis relative to others. The reasons are not yet clear. One factor with some of these illnesses is that many people with depression may have less access to good medical care. They may have a harder time caring for their health, for example, seeking care, taking prescribed medication, eating well, and exercising.

Ongoing research is also exploring whether physiological changes seen in depression may play a role in increasing the risk of physical illness. In people with depression, scientists have found changes in the way several different systems in the body function, all of which can have an impact on physical health:

- Signs of increased inflammation

- Changes in the control of heart rate and blood circulation

- Abnormalities in stress hormones
- Metabolic changes typical of those seen in people at risk for diabetes

## *Depression Is Treatable Even When Other Illness Is Present.*

Do not dismiss depression as a normal part of having a chronic illness. Effective treatment for depression is available and can help even if you have another medical illness or condition. If you or a loved one think you have depression, it is important to tell your healthcare provider and explore treatment options.

You should also inform the health care provider about all treatments or medications you are already receiving, including treatment for depression (prescribed medications and dietary supplements). Sharing information can help avoid problems with multiple medications interfering with each other. It also helps the provider stay informed about your overall health and treatment issues.

Recovery from depression takes time, but treatment can improve the quality of life even if you have a medical illness. Treatments for depression include:

- Cognitive behavioral therapy (CBT), or talk therapy, that helps people change negative thinking styles and behaviors that may contribute to their depression. Interpersonal and other types of time-limited psychotherapy have also been proven effective, in some cases combined with antidepressant medication.

- Antidepressant medications, including, but not limited to, selective serotonin reuptake inhibitors (SSRIs) and serotonin and norepinephrine reuptake inhibitors (SNRIs).

- While electroconvulsive therapy (ECT) is generally reserved for the most severe cases of depression, newer brain stimulation approaches, including transcranial magnetic stimulation (TMS), can help some people with depression without the need for general anesthesia and with few side effects.

# Chapter 47

# *Parkinson Disease and Depression*

## Introduction

Depression not only affects your brain and behavior—it affects your entire body. Depression has been linked with other health problems, including Parkinson disease. Dealing with more than one health problem at a time can be difficult, so proper treatment is important.

## What Is Depression?

Major depressive disorder, or depression, is a serious mental illness. Depression interferes with your daily life and routine and reduces your quality of life. About 6.7 percent of U.S. adults ages 18 and older have depression.

## Signs and Symptoms of Depression

- Ongoing sad, anxious, or empty feelings
- Feeling hopeless
- Feeling guilty, worthless, or helpless
- Feeling irritable or restless

---

Text in this chapter is excerpted from "Depression and Parkinson's Disease," National Institute of Mental Health (NIMH), 2011. Reviewed March 2016.

- Loss of interest in activities or hobbies once enjoyable, including sex

- Feeling tired all the time

- Difficulty concentrating, remembering details, or making decisions

- Difficulty falling asleep or staying asleep, a condition called insomnia, or sleeping all the time

- Overeating or loss of appetite

- Thoughts of death and suicide or suicide attempts

- Ongoing aches and pains, headaches, cramps, or digestive problems that do not ease with treatment.

## What Is Parkinson Disease?

Parkinson disease is a chronic disorder that worsens over time and results in the loss of brain cells that produce dopamine, a chemical messenger that controls movement. Parkinson disease usually affects people over age 50. The main symptoms of Parkinson disease are:

- Tremor, or shaking, in the hands, arms, legs, jaw, and face

- Rigidity, or stiffness, of the arms, legs, and torso

- Slowness of movement

- Impaired balance and coordination

Parkinson disease can also affect thinking and emotions. At present, there is no way to predict or prevent Parkinson disease.

## How Are Depression and Parkinson Disease Linked?

For people with depression and Parkinson disease, each illness can make symptoms of the other worse. For example, people with both illnesses tend to have more movement problem sand greater levels of anxiety than those who have just depression or Parkinson disease compared with people who are depressed but do not have Parkinson disease, people who have both illnesses may have lower rates of sadness and guilt, but greater problems with concentration. One recent brain imaging study also suggests that people with Parkinson disease may have an unusually high number of reuptake pumps for the brain chemical messenger serotonin. Serotonin helps regulate mood, but overactive pumps reduce serotonin levels, possibly leading to depressive symptoms in some people with Parkinson disease.

## How Is Depression Treated in People Who Have Parkinson Disease?

Depression is diagnosed and treated by a health care providential depression can help you manage your Parkinson treatment and improve your overall health. Recovery from depression takes time but treatments are effective.

At present, the most common treatments for depression include:

- cognitive behavioral therapy (cBt), a type of psycho-therapy, or talk therapy, that helps people change negative thinking styles and behaviors that may contribute to their depression

- Selectiveness behavioral therapy (cBt), a type of psycho-therapy, or talk therapy, that helps people change negative thinking styles and behaviors that may contribute to their depression

- Selective serotonin re uptake inhibitor (ssri), a type of anti-depressant medication that includes citalopram (celexa), sertraline (Zoloft), and fluoxetine (prozac)

- Serotonin and nor epinephrine re uptake inhibitor (snri), a type of antidepressant medication similar to ssri that includes venlafaxine (effexor) and duloxetine (cymbalta)

While currently available depression treatments, particularly ssris, are generally well tolerated and safe for people with Parkinson disease, talk with your health care provider about side effects, possible drug interactions, and other treatment options. Medications can take several weeks to work, may need to be combined with ongoing talk therapy, or may need to be changed or adjusted to minimize side effects and achieve the best results.

A variety of medications can provide dramatic relief from the symptoms of Parkinson disease. However, no current medication can stop the progression of the disease, and in many cases, medications lose their benefit over time. In such cases, the doctor may recommend deep brain stimulation, a surgery that places a battery-operated medical device called a neuro stimulator—similar to a heart pacemaker—to deliver electrical stimulation to areas in the brain that control movement. Some doctors recommend physical therapy or muscle-strengthening exercises to improve movement and balance and make it easier to continue doing daily tasks, such as getting dressed and bathing. Although usually associated with treating severe or treatment-resistant depression, electroconvulsive therapy may improve Parkinson disease symptoms in some people.

# Chapter 48

# Sleep Disorders and Mental Health

## Chapter Contents

# Section 48.1

# *Sleep and Disease*

Text in this section is excerpted from "Brain Basics:
Understanding Sleep," National Institute of Neurological
Disorders and Stroke (NINDS), July 25, 2014.

## *Sleep and Sleep-Related Problems*

Sleep and sleep-related problems play a role in a large number of human disorders and affect almost every field of medicine. For example, problems like stroke and asthma attacks tend to occur more frequently during the night and early morning, perhaps due to changes in hormones, heart rate, and other characteristics associated with sleep. Sleep also affects some kinds of epilepsy in complex ways. REM sleep seems to help prevent seizures that begin in one part of the brain from spreading to other brain regions, while deep sleep may promote the spread of these seizures. Sleep deprivation also triggers seizures in people with some types of epilepsy.

Neurons that control sleep interact closely with the immune system. As anyone who has had the flu knows, infectious diseases tend to make us feel sleepy. This probably happens because cytokines, chemicals our immune systems produce while fighting an infection, are powerful sleep-inducing chemicals. Sleep may help the body conserve energy and other resources that the immune system needs to mount an attack.

Sleeping problems occur in almost all people with mental disorders, including those with depression and schizophrenia. People with depression, for example, often awaken in the early hours of the morning and find themselves unable to get back to sleep. The amount of sleep a person gets also strongly influences the symptoms of mental disorders. Sleep deprivation is an effective therapy for people with certain types of depression, while it can actually cause depression in other people. Extreme sleep deprivation can lead to a seemingly psychotic state of paranoia and hallucinations in otherwise healthy people, and disrupted sleep can trigger episodes of mania (agitation and hyperactivity) in people with manic depression.

Sleeping problems are common in many other disorders as well, including Alzheimer disease, stroke, cancer, and head injury. These sleeping problems may arise from changes in the brain regions and neurotransmitters that control sleep, or from the drugs used to control symptoms of other disorders. In patients who are hospitalized or who receive round-the-clock care, treatment schedules or hospital routines also may disrupt sleep. The old joke about a patient being awakened by a nurse so he could take a sleeping pill contains a grain of truth. Once sleeping problems develop, they can add to a person's impairment and cause confusion, frustration, or depression. Patients who are unable to sleep also notice pain more and may increase their requests for pain medication. Better management of sleeping problems in people who have other disorders could improve these patients' health and quality of life.

## The Future

Sleep research is expanding and attracting more and more attention from scientists. Researchers now know that sleep is an active and dynamic state that greatly influences our waking hours, and they realize that we must understand sleep to fully understand the brain. Innovative techniques, such as brain imaging, can now help researchers understand how different brain regions function during sleep and how different activities and disorders affect sleep. Understanding the factors that affect sleep in health and disease also may lead to revolutionary new therapies for sleep disorders and to ways of overcoming jet lag and the problems associated with shift work. We can expect these and many other benefits from research that will allow us to truly understand sleep's impact on our lives.

## Tips for a Good Night's Sleep

- **Set a schedule:** Go to bed at a set time each night and get up at the same time each morning. Disrupting this schedule may lead to insomnia. "Sleeping in" on weekends also makes it harder to wake up early on Monday morning because it re-sets your sleep cycles for a later awakening.

- **Exercise:** Try to exercise 20 to 30 minutes a day. Daily exercise often helps people sleep, although a workout soon before bedtime may interfere with sleep. For maximum benefit, try to get your exercise about 5 to 6 hours before going to bed.

- **Avoid caffeine, nicotine, and alcohol:** Avoid drinks that contain caffeine, which acts as a stimulant and keeps people awake. Sources of caffeine include coffee, chocolate, soft drinks, non-herbal teas, diet drugs, and some pain relievers. Smokers tend to sleep very lightly and often wake up in the early morning due to nicotine withdrawal. Alcohol robs people of deep sleep and REM sleep and keeps them in the lighter stages of sleep.

- **Relax before bed:** A warm bath, reading, or another relaxing routine can make it easier to fall sleep. You can train yourself to associate certain restful activities with sleep and make them part of your bedtime ritual.

- **Sleep until sunlight:** If possible, wake up with the sun, or use very bright lights in the morning. Sunlight helps the body's internal biological clock reset itself each day. Sleep experts recommend exposure to an hour of morning sunlight for people having problems falling asleep.

- **Don't lie in bed awake:** If you can't get to sleep, don't just lie in bed. Do something else, like reading, watching television, or listening to music, until you feel tired. The anxiety of being unable to fall asleep can actually contribute to insomnia.

- **Control your room temperature:** Maintain a comfortable temperature in the bedroom. Extreme temperatures may disrupt sleep or prevent you from falling asleep.

- **See a doctor if your sleeping problem continues:** If you have trouble falling asleep night after night, or if you always feel tired the next day, then you may have a sleep disorder and should see a physician. Your primary care physician may be able to help you; if not, you can probably find a sleep specialist at a major hospital near you. Most sleep disorders can be treated effectively, so you can finally get that good night's sleep you need.

## Section 48.2

# *Sleep Disorders*

Text in this section is excerpted from "Brain Basics:
Understanding Sleep," National Institute of Neurological
Disorders and Stroke (NINDS), July 25, 2014.

## Common Sleep Disorders

At least 40 million Americans each year suffer from chronic, long-term sleep disorders each year, and an additional 20 million experience occasional sleeping problems. These disorders and the resulting sleep deprivation interfere with work, driving, and social activities. They also account for an estimated $16 billion in medical costs each year, while the indirect costs due to lost productivity and other factors are probably much greater. Doctors have described more than 70 sleep disorders, most of which can be managed effectively once they are correctly diagnosed. The most common sleep disorders include:

- Insomnia

- Sleep apnea

- Restless legs syndrome

- Narcolepsy

### *Insomnia*

Almost everyone occasionally suffers from short-term insomnia. This problem can result from stress, jet lag, diet, or many other factors. Insomnia almost always affects job performance and well-being the next day. About 60 million Americans a year have insomnia frequently or for extended periods of time, which leads to even more serious sleep deficits. Insomnia tends to increase with age and affects about 40 percent of women and 30 percent of men. It is often the major disabling symptom of an underlying medical disorder.

For short-term insomnia, doctors may prescribe sleeping pills. Most sleeping pills stop working after several weeks of nightly use, however, and long-term use can actually interfere with good sleep. Mild insomnia often can be prevented or cured by practicing good sleep habits. For more serious cases of insomnia, researchers are experimenting with light therapy and other ways to alter circadian cycles.

## Sleep Apnea

Sleep apnea is a disorder of interrupted breathing during sleep. It usually occurs in association with fat buildup or loss of muscle tone with aging. These changes allow the windpipe to collapse during breathing when muscles relax during sleep. This problem, called obstructive sleep apnea, is usually associated with loud snoring (though not everyone who snores has this disorder). Sleep apnea also can occur if the neurons that control breathing malfunction during sleep.

During an episode of obstructive apnea, the person's effort to inhale air creates suction that collapses the windpipe. This blocks the air flow for 10 seconds to a minute while the sleeping person struggles to breathe. When the person's blood oxygen level falls, the brain responds by awakening the person enough to tighten the upper airway muscles and open the windpipe. The person may snort or gasp, then resume snoring. This cycle may be repeated hundreds of times a night. The frequent awakenings that sleep apnea patients experience leave them continually sleepy and may lead to personality changes such as irritability or depression. Sleep apnea also deprives the person of oxygen, which can lead to morning headaches, a loss of interest in sex, or a decline in mental functioning. It also is linked to high blood pressure, irregular heartbeats, and an increased risk of heart attacks and stroke. Patients with severe, untreated sleep apnea are two to three times more likely to have automobile accidents than the general population. In some high-risk individuals, sleep apnea may even lead to sudden death from respiratory arrest during sleep.

An estimated 18 million Americans have sleep apnea. However, few of them have had the problem diagnosed. Patients with the typical features of sleep apnea, such as loud snoring, obesity, and excessive daytime sleepiness, should be referred to a specialized sleep center that can perform a test called polysomnography. This test records the patient's brain waves, heartbeat, and breathing during an entire night. If sleep apnea is diagnosed, several treatments are available. Mild sleep apnea frequently can be overcome through weight loss or by preventing the person from sleeping on his or her back. Other people may need special devices or surgery to correct the obstruction. People with sleep apnea should never take sedatives or sleeping pills, which can prevent them from awakening enough to breathe.

## *Restless Legs Syndrome*

Restless legs syndrome (RLS), a familial disorder causing unpleasant crawling, prickling, or tingling sensations in the legs and feet and an urge to move them for relief, is emerging as one of the most common sleep disorders, especially among older people. This disorder, which affects as many as 12 million Americans, leads to constant leg movement during the day and insomnia at night. Severe RLS is most common in elderly people, though symptoms may develop at any age. In some cases, it may be linked to other conditions such as anemia, pregnancy, or diabetes.

Many RLS patients also have a disorder known as periodic limb movement disorder or PLMD, which causes repetitive jerking movements of the limbs, especially the legs. These movements occur every 20 to 40 seconds and cause repeated awakening and severely fragmented sleep. In one study, RLS and PLMD accounted for a third of the insomnia seen in patients older than age 60.

RLS and PLMD often can be relieved by drugs that affect the neurotransmitter dopamine, suggesting that dopamine abnormalities underlie these disorders' symptoms. Learning how these disorders occur may lead to better therapies in the future.

## *Narcolepsy*

Narcolepsy affects an estimated 250,000 Americans. People with narcolepsy have frequent "sleep attacks" at various times of the day, even if they have had a normal amount of night-time sleep. These attacks last from several seconds to more than 30 minutes. People with narcolepsy also may experience cataplexy (loss of muscle control during emotional situations), hallucinations, temporary paralysis when they awaken, and disrupted night-time sleep. These symptoms seem to be features of REM sleep that appear during waking, which suggests that narcolepsy is a disorder of sleep regulation. The symptoms of narcolepsy typically appear during adolescence, though it often takes years to obtain a correct diagnosis. The disorder (or at least a predisposition to it) is usually hereditary, but it occasionally is linked to brain damage from a head injury or neurological disease.

Once narcolepsy is diagnosed, stimulants, antidepressants, or other drugs can help control the symptoms and prevent the embarrassing

*Mental Health Disorders Sourcebook, Sixth Edition*

and dangerous effects of falling asleep at improper times. Naps at certain times of the day also may reduce the excessive daytime sleepiness.

In 1999, a research team working with canine models identified a gene that causes narcolepsy–a breakthrough that brings a cure for this disabling condition within reach. The gene, hypocretin receptor 2, codes for a protein that allows brain cells to receive instructions from other cells. The defective versions of the gene encode proteins that cannot recognize these messages, perhaps cutting the cells off from messages that promote wakefulness. The researchers know that the same gene exists in humans, and they are currently searching for defective versions in people with narcolepsy.

## Section 48.3

# *Sleep and PTSD*

Text in this section is excerpted from "Sleep and PTSD," U.S. Department of Veteran Affairs (VA), June 15, 2007. Reviewed March 2016.

## *Sleep Problems and PTSD*

Many people have trouble sleeping sometimes. This is even more likely, though, if you have PTSD. Trouble sleeping and nightmares are two symptoms of PTSD.

### *Why Do People with PTSD Have Sleep Problems?*

- **They may be "on alert."** Many people with PTSD may feel they need to be on guard or "on the lookout," to protect himself or herself from danger. It is difficult to have restful sleep when you feel the need to be always alert. You might have trouble falling asleep, or you might wake up easily in the night if you hear any noise.

- **They may worry or have negative thoughts.** Your thoughts can make it difficult to fall asleep. People with PTSD often worry about general problems or worry that they are in danger. If you often have trouble getting to sleep, you may start to worry that you won't be able to fall asleep. These thoughts can keep you awake.

- **They may use drugs or alcohol.** Some people with PTSD use drugs or alcohol to help them cope with their symptoms. In fact, using too much alcohol can get in the way of restful sleep. Alcohol changes the quality of your sleep and makes it less refreshing. This is true of many drugs as well.

- **They may have bad dreams or nightmares.** Nightmares are common for people with PTSD. Nightmares can wake you up in the middle of the night, making your sleep less restful. If you have frequent nightmares, you may find it difficult to fall asleep because you are afraid you might have a nightmare.

- **They may have medical problems.** There are medical problems that are commonly found in people with PTSD, such as chronic pain, stomach problems, and pelvic-area problems in women. These physical problems can make going to sleep difficult.

## *What Can You Do If You Have Problems?*

There are a number of things you can do to make it more likely that you will sleep well:

### *Change Your Sleeping Area*

Too much noise, light, or activity in your bedroom can make sleeping harder. Creating a quiet, comfortable sleeping area can help. Here are some things you can do to sleep better:

- Use your bedroom only for sleeping and sex.

- Move the TV and radio out of your bedroom.

- Keep your bedroom quiet, dark, and cool. Use curtains or blinds to block out light. Consider using soothing music or a "white noise" machine to block out noise.

### *Keep a Bedtime Routine and Sleep Schedule*

Having a bedtime routine and a set wake-up time will help your body get used to a sleeping schedule. You may want to ask others in your household to help you with your routine.

- Don't do stressful or energizing things within two hours of going to bed.

- Create a relaxing bedtime routine. You might want to take a warm shower or bath, listen to soothing music, or drink a cup of tea with no caffeine in it.

- Use a sleep mask and earplugs, if light and noise bother you.

- Try to get up at the same time every morning, even if you feel tired. That will help to set your sleep schedule over time, and you will be more likely to fall asleep easily when bedtime comes. On weekends do not to sleep more than an hour past your regular wake-up time.

*Try to Relax If You Can't Sleep*

- Imagine yourself in a peaceful, pleasant scene. Focus on the details and feelings of being in a place that is relaxing.

- Get up and do a quiet activity, such as reading, until you feel sleepy.

*Watch Your Activities during the Day*

Your daytime habits and activities can affect how well you sleep. Here are some tips:

- Exercise during the day. Don't exercise within two hours of going to bed, though, because it may be harder to fall asleep.

- Get outside during daylight hours. Spending time in sunlight helps to reset your body's sleep and wake cycles.

- Cut out or limit what you drink or eat that has caffeine in it, such as coffee, tea, cola, and chocolate.

- Don't drink alcohol before bedtime. Alcohol can cause you to wake up more often during the night.

- Don't smoke or use tobacco, especially in the evening. Nicotine can keep you awake.

- Don't take naps during the day, especially close to bedtime.

- Don't drink any liquids after 6 p.m. if you wake up often because you have to go to the bathroom.

- Don't take medicine that may keep you awake, or make you feel hyper or energized right before bed. Your doctor can tell you if your medicine may do this and if you can take it earlier in the day.

*Talk to Your Doctor*

If you can't sleep because you are in pain or have an injury, you often feel anxious at night, or you often have bad dreams or nightmares, talk to your doctor.

There are a number of medications that are helpful for sleep problems in PTSD. Depending on your sleep symptoms and other factors, your doctor may prescribe some medication for you. There are also other skills you can learn to help improve your sleep.

# Chapter 49

# *Stroke and Mental Health*

## *What Is a Stroke?*

A stroke occurs when the blood supply to part of the brain is suddenly interrupted, such as when a blood vessel bursts or a clot blocks blood flow. Although strokes occur in and damage the brain, they can affect the whole body. Strokes may cause paralysis (the complete or partial loss of the ability to move), speech problems, or the inability to complete daily tasks. Sometimes these effects are temporary and sometimes they are permanent. Stroke survivors often need rehabilitation, therapy that helps people relearn skills or learn new skills. Rehabilitation and recovery are unique for each person.

## *How Are Depression and Stroke Linked?*

Many people require mental health treatment after a stroke to address depression, anxiety, frustration, or anger. Several factors may affect the risk and severity of depression after a stroke, including:

- Area of the brain where stroke damage occurred
- Personal or family history of depression or other mood or
- anxiety disorders
- Level of social isolation before the stroke.

---

This section includes excerpts from "Depression and Stroke," National Institute of Mental Health (NIMH), 2011. Reviewed March 2016; and text from "Personality Changes," U.S. Department of Veteran Affairs (VA), November 22, 2010. Reviewed March 2016.

Stroke survivors who are depressed may be less likely to follow treatment plans and may be more irritable or have changes in personality.

Stroke, heart disease, and depression may also be related. Stroke and heart disease share some risk factors, such as high blood pressure and being overweight. One recent study showed that older people with heart disease who had more severe and frequent depression symptoms were more likely to have a stroke.

## How Is Depression Treated in People Who Have Had a Stroke?

Depression is diagnosed and treated by a health care provider. Treating depression and other mental disorders may help with stroke recovery. After a stroke, treatment with antidepressant medications or problem-solving therapy (a type of psychotherapy, or talk therapy) may prevent serious depression before it begins. Problem-solving therapy helps people identify problems that interfere with daily life and contribute to depressive symptoms and find ways to solve those problems.

Recovery from depression takes time but treatments are effective. At present, the most common treatments for depression include:

- Cognitive behavioral therapy (CBT), a type of psychotherapy, or talk therapy, that helps people change negative thinking styles and behaviors that may contribute to their depression.

- Selective serotonin reuptake inhibitor (SSRI), a type of antidepressant medication that includes citalopram (Celexa), sertraline (Zoloft), and fluoxetine (Prozac).

- Serotonin and norepinephrine reuptake inhibitor (SNRI), a type of antidepressant medication similar to SSRI that includes venlafaxine (Effexor) and duloxetine (Cymbalta).

While currently available depression treatments are generally well tolerated and safe, talk with your health care provider about side effects, possible drug interactions, and other treatment options. For the latest information on medications, visit the U.S. Food and Drug Administration (FDA) website at http://www.fda.gov. Not everyone responds to treatment the same way. Medications can take several weeks to work, may need to be combined with ongoing talk therapy, or may need to be changed or adjusted to minimize side effects and achieve the best results.

If you think you are depressed or know someone who is, don't lose hope. Seek help for depression.

## What Do You Need to Know about Personality Changes After Stroke?

Changes in personality are common after stroke. They are also among the hardest to deal with. Not all changes are permanent. Some may disappear over time. Personality changes to watch for include self-centered attitude, emotional lability, apathy and depression. You may also notice behavior problems. For instance, your loved one may get angry or easily frustrated. They may have impulsive behaviors. Your loved one may even get physically aggressive.

## Why Is It Important to Get Help?

Personality changes are hard for caregivers to handle. Talk with your healthcare team. They can suggest treatments or ways to deal with personality changes. Think about joining a support group. Talking with other caregivers is often helpful.

## What Is Emotional Lability?

Emotional lability is used to describe someone with strong emotions. These emotions are close to the surface and difficult to control. The person becomes upset or cries more easily. Stroke survivors often have intense mood swings. They may be happy and sad in only a few minutes. They may react to everyday events in unexpected ways.

- Be patient. Your loved one cannot help behaving this way. Explain to your loved one that his or her emotions are part of the disease.

- Talk with other family members. Help them understand that stroke survivors have problems controlling their feelings.

- Treat the behavior as a minor problem. Continue what you were doing.

- Change the subject or lead your loved one in a new direction.

## What Is a Self-Centered Attitude?

Many survivors become mainly concerned with their own interests. They may lack empathy, or the ability to understand another's feelings.

- Kindly help your loved one know when they are not being thoughtful.

- Gently remind your loved one to practice polite behavior.

- Praise your loved one for doing thoughtful things for others.

## What Is Apathy?

Apathy is a lack of motivation. Apathy is different than being tired or depressed. A person with apathy shows little emotion or feeling. There is often a loss of interest in the activities.

## What Is Depression?

After a stroke, a person may have negative feelings. They may think that things will never get better. Depression is a common response to the losses that occur from a stroke.

## What Are Behavior Changes?

Stroke survivors often have problems with impulsive behaviors, frustration, anger and aggression. Changes in your loved one's behavior are hard to deal with.

## Helpful Tips

- Personality changes are hard to deal with. Remember, this is part of the stroke injury. Try not to take it personally.

- Avoid comparing your loved one to the way they used to be.

- Seek counseling or join a support group. Talking about your anxieties can help.

- Keep up your own schedule to avoid caregiver burn-out.

## Remember

- Discuss personality changes with your healthcare provider. Ask for an assessment when needed.

- Try to accept the changes you see in your loved one. Avoid comparing your loved one to the way they used to be. Some of the changes may be permanent. Others will disappear over time.

- Be patient and understanding. Your loved one is facing many changes. Your support is important.

# Part Seven

# Living with Mental Health Disorders

Chapter 50

# Caregivers and Mental Health

## Chapter Contents

# Section 50.1

# *Self-Care for Family Caregivers*

Text in this section is excerpted from "Caring for the
Caregiver," National Cancer Institute (NCI), September 2014.

## Who Is a Caregiver?

You may not think of yourself as a caregiver. You may feel you are
doing something natural. You are just caring for someone you love.
Some caregivers are family members. Others are friends.

## What Does "Giving Care" Mean?

Giving care can mean helping with daily needs. These include going
to doctor visits, making meals, and picking up medicines. It can also
mean helping your loved one cope with feelings. Like when he or she
feels sad or angry. Sometimes having someone to talk to is what your
loved one needs most.

While giving care, it's normal to put your own needs and feelings
aside. But putting your needs aside for a long time is not good for
your health. You need to take care of yourself, too. If you don't, you
may not be able to care for others. This is why you need to take good
care of you.

## Your Feelings

It's common to feel stressed and overwhelmed at this time. Like
your loved one, you may feel angry, sad, or worried. Try to share your
feelings with others who can help you. It can help to talk about how
you feel. You could even talk to a counselor or social worker.

## What May Help

Know that you are not alone. Other caregivers share these feelings.
Talk with someone if your feelings get in the way of daily life. Maybe
you have a family member, friend, priest, pastor, or spiritual leader
to talk to. Your doctor may also be able to help.

Here are some other things that may help you:

- Forgive yourself. Know that we all make mistakes whenever we have a lot on our minds. No one is perfect, and chances are that you're doing what you can at this moment.

- Cry or express your feelings. You don't have to pretend to be cheerful. It's okay to show that you are sad or upset.

- Focus on things that are worth your time and energy. Let small things go for now. For example, don't fold clothes if you are tired.

- Don't take your loved one's anger personally. It's very common for people to direct their feelings at those who are closest. Their stress, fears, and worries may come out as anger.

- Be hopeful. What you hope for may change over time. But you can always hope for comfort, joy, acceptance, and peace.

## Asking for Help

Many people who were once caregivers say they did too much on their own. Some wished that they had asked for help sooner.

Accepting help from others isn't always easy. When tough things happen, many people tend to pull away. They think, "We can handle this on our own." But things can get harder as the patient goes through treatment. As a result, many caregivers have said, "There's just too much on my plate."

Take a look at how busy you are now. Be honest with yourself about what you can do. Think about tasks you can give to others. And let go of tasks that aren't as important right now.

### Asking for Help Also Helps Your Loved One.

Don't be afraid to ask for help. Remember, if you get help for yourself:

- You may stay healthier and have more energy.
- Your loved one may feel less guilty about your help.
- Other helpers may offer time and skills that you don't have.

### How Can Others Help You?

People may want to help you but don't know what you need. Here are some things you can ask them to do:

- Help with tasks such as:

- Cooking
- Cleaning
- Shopping
- Yard work
- Childcare
- Eldercare
- Talk with you and share your feelings.
- Help with driving errands such as:
  - Doctor visits
  - Picking up your child
- Find information you need.
- Tell others how your loved one is doing.

### *Know That Some People May Say, "No."*

Some people may not be able to help. There could be one or more reasons such as:

- They may be coping with their own problems.
- They may not have time right now.
- They may not know how to help.
- They may feel uneasy around people who are sick.

## *Caring for Yourself*

### *Make Time for Yourself*

You may feel that your needs aren't important right now. Or that you've spent so much time caring for your loved one, there's no time left for yourself.

Taking time for yourself can help you be a better caregiver. Caring for your own needs and desires is important to give you strength to carry on. This is even more true if you have health problems.

You may want to:

- Find nice things you can do for yourself. Even just a few minutes can help. You could watch TV, call a friend, work on a hobby, or do anything that you enjoy.

- Be active. Even light exercise such as walking, stretching, or dancing can make you less tired. Yard work, playing with kids or pets, or gardening are helpful, too.

- Find ways to connect with friends. Are there places you can meet others who are close to you? Or can you chat or get support by phone or email?

- Give yourself more time off. Ask friends or family members to pitch in. Take time to rest.

Do something for yourself each day. It doesn't matter how small it is. Whatever you do, don't neglect yourself.

### Caring for Your Body

You may feel too busy or worried about your loved one to think about your own health. And yet it's common for caregivers to have sleep problems, headaches, and anxiety, along with other changes. But if you take care of yourself, you can lower your stress. Then you can have the strength to take care of someone else.

Did you have health problems before you became a caregiver? If so, now it's even more important to take care of yourself. Also, adding extra stressors to your life can cause new health problems. Be sure to tell your doctor if you notice any new changes in your body.

Keep up with your own health needs. Try to:

- Go to all your checkups

- Take your medicines

- Eat healthy meals

- Get enough rest

- Exercise

- Make time to relax

These ideas may sound easy. But they can be hard to do for most caregivers. Try to pay attention to how your body and your mind are feeling.

## Going with Your Loved One to Medical Visits

### Before You Go

Your loved one may ask you to come to doctor visits. This may be a key role for you.

Here are some tips for going to the doctor:

- Know how to get there. Give yourself enough time.

- Write down questions you need to ask. Also write down things you want to tell the doctor.

- Keep a folder of your loved one's health information.

- Bring this folder to each visit. Bring all the medicine bottles with you, or keep a list of the names and doses. Bring this list to each visit.

## Talking with the Health Care Provider

Sometimes, people have trouble with medical visits. They don't understand what the doctor says. Or they forget things. Here are some tips for talking with the health care provider:

- If you don't understand an answer, ask the question in a different way.

- If you need to know more, ask.

- Let your doctor or nurse know what your worries are.

- Before you leave the visit, make sure you know what the next steps are for your loved one's care.

- Take notes. Or ask if you can record the visit.

- Let the doctor know if your loved one has had changes or new symptoms.

## Questions to Ask the Doctor or Health Care Team

- What health records should we bring?

- How can we prepare for treatment?

- How long will the treatment take?

- Can he or she go to and from treatment alone?

- How can I help my loved one feel better during treatment?

- Can I be there during treatment?

- What are the side effects of the treatment?

- After treatment, what do we need to watch for? When should we call you?

- How do we file for insurance? Who can help us with insurance?

### *Getting a Second Opinion*

Some people worry that doctors will be offended if they ask for a second opinion. Usually the opposite is true. Most doctors welcome a second opinion. And many health insurance companies will pay for them.

If your loved gets a second opinion, the doctor may agree with the first doctor's treatment plan. Or he or she may suggest a second approach. Either way, you and your loved one have more information and perhaps a greater sense of control. You both can feel better about the choices you make, knowing you looked at all your options.

## Dealing with Help You Don't Need

Sometimes people offer help you don't need. Thank them for their concern. Tell them you'll let them know if you need anything.

Some people may offer unwanted advice. They may do this because they don't know what else to say. It's up to you to decide how to deal with this. You don't have to respond at all. Otherwise, thank them and let it go. Tell them you are taking steps to help your family.

# Section 50.2

# *Dealing with Caregiver Stress*

Text in this section is excerpted from "Caregiver Stress,"
Office on Women's Health (OWH), August 17, 2015.

## Caregiver Stress

A caregiver is anyone who provides care for another person in need, such as a child, an aging parent, a husband or wife, friend, or neighbor. Caregiving can be rewarding, but it can also be challenging. Stress from caregiving is common. Women especially are at risk for the harmful health effects of caregiver stress.

## What Is Caregiver Stress?

Caregiver stress is due to the emotional and physical strain of caregiving. Caregivers report much higher levels of stress than people who are not caregivers. Many caregivers are providing help or are "on call" almost all day. Some caregivers may feel overwhelmed by the amount of care their aging, sick, or disabled family member needs.

## What Are the Signs and Symptoms of Caregiver Stress?

Caregiver stress can take many forms. You may feel frustrated and angry one minute and helpless the next. You may make mistakes when giving medicines. Or you may turn to unhealthy behaviors like smoking or drinking too much alcohol.

Other signs and symptoms include:

- Feeling overwhelmed
- Feeling alone, isolated, or deserted by others
- Sleeping too much or too little
- Gaining or losing a lot of weight
- Feeling tired most of the time
- Losing interest in activities you used to enjoy
- Feeling worried or sad often?
- Having headaches or body aches often
- Memory and focusing

## What Can I Do to Prevent or Relieve Stress?

Here are some tips to help you prevent or manage caregiver stress:

- Take a class that teaches you how to care for someone with an injury or illness. To find these classes, ask your doctor or call your local Area Agency on Aging.
- Find caregiving resources in your community to give you a break. Your community may have adult day care services or respite services.
- Ask for and accept help. Make a list of ways others can help you, such as getting groceries or sitting with the person while you do an errand.

- Make to-do lists, and set a daily routine.

- Stay in touch with family and friends, and do things you enjoy with your loved ones.

- Take care of your health. See your doctor for checkups, find time to be physically active on most days of the week, choose healthy foods, and get enough sleep.

- Ask for and accept help. Make a list of ways others can help you, such as getting groceries or sitting with the person while you do an errand.

# Chapter 51

# For People with Mental Health Problems

## Introduction

If you have, or believe you may have, mental health problem, it can be helpful to talk about these issues with others. It can be scary to reach out for help, but it is often the first step to helping you heal, grow, and recover.

Having a good support system and engaging with trustworthy people are key elements to successfully talking about your own mental health.

### Build Your Support System

Find someone—such as a parent, family member, teacher, faith leader, health care provider or other trusted individual, who:

- Gives good advice when you want and ask for it; assists you in taking action that will help

- Likes, respects, and trusts you and who you like, respect, and trust, too

- Allows you the space to change, grow, make decisions, and even make mistakes

Text in this chapter is excerpted from "For People with Mental Health Problems," U.S. Department of Health and Human Services (HHS), May 31, 2013.

- Listens to you and shares with you, both the good and bad times
- Respects your need for confidentiality so you can tell him or her anything
- Lets you freely express your feelings and emotions without judging, teasing, or criticizing
- Works with you to figure out what to do the next time a difficult situation comes up
- Has your best interest in mind

### Find a Peer Group

Find a group of people with mental health problems similar to yours. Peer support relationships can positively affect individual recovery because:

- People who have common life experiences have a unique ability to help each other based on a shared history and a deep understanding that may go beyond what exists in other relationships
- People offer their experiences, strengths, and hopes to peers, which allows for natural evolution of personal growth, wellness promotion, and recovery
- Peers can be very supportive since they have "been there" and serve as living examples that individuals can and do recover from mental health problems
- Peers also serve as advocates and support others who may experience discrimination and prejudice

You may want to start or join a self-help or peer support group. National organizations across the country have peer support networks and peer advocates. Find an organization that can help you connect with peer groups and other peer support.

### Participate in Your Treatment Decisions

It's also important for you to be educated, informed, and engaged about your own mental health.

- Find out as much as you can about mental health wellness and information specific to your diagnosed mental health problem.
- Play an active role in your own treatment.

Get involved in your treatment through shared decision making. Participate fully with your mental health provider and make informed treatment decisions together. Participating fully in shared decision making includes:

- Recognizing a decision needs to be made

- Identifying partners in the process as equals

- Stating options as equal

- Exploring understanding and expectations

- Identifying preferences

- Negotiating options/concordance

- Sharing decisions

- Arranging follow-up to evaluate decision-making outcomes

## Develop a Recovery Plan

Recovery is a process of change where individuals improve their health and wellness, live a self-directed life, and strive to reach their full potential. Studies show that most people with mental health problems get better, and many recover completely.

You may want to develop a written recovery plan. Recovery plans:

- Enable you to identify goals for achieving wellness

- Specify what you can do to reach those goals

- Can be daily activities as well as longer term goals

- Track your mental health problem

- Identify triggers or other stressful events that can make you feel worse, and help you learn how to manage them

You can develop these plans with family members and other supporters.

# Chapter 52

# *Peer Support and Social Inclusion*

Peer support services are delivered by individuals who have common life experiences with the people they are serving. People with mental and/or substance use disorders have a unique capacity to help each other based on a shared affiliation and a deep understanding of this experience. In self-help and mutual support, people offer this support, strength, and hope to their peers, which allows for personal growth, wellness promotion, and recovery.

Research has shown that peer support facilitates recovery and reduces health care costs. Peers also provide assistance that promotes a sense of belonging within the community. The ability to contribute to and enjoy one's community is key to recovery and well-being. Another critical component that peers provide is the development of self-efficacy through role modeling and assisting peers with ongoing recovery through mastery of experiences and finding meaning, purpose, and social connections in their lives.

SAMHSA's Recovery Community Services Program (RCSP) advances recovery by providing peer recovery support services across the nation. These services help prevent relapse and promote sustained recovery from mental and/or substance use disorders.

---

Text in this chapter is excerpted from "Peer Support and Social Inclusion," Substance Abuse and Mental Health Services Administration (SAMHSA), July 2, 2015.

Through the RCSP, SAMHSA recognizes that social support includes informational, emotional, and intentional support. Examples of peer recovery support services include:

- Peer mentoring or coaching—developing a one-on-one relationship in which a peer leader with recovery experience encourages, motivates, and supports a peer in recovery

- Peer recovery resource connecting—connecting the peer with professional and nonprofessional services and resources available in the community

- Recovery group facilitation—facilitating or leading recovery-oriented group activities, including support groups and educational activities

- Building community—helping peers make new friends and build healthy social networks through emotional, instrumental, informational, and affiliation types of peer support

In 1997, SAMHSA hosted the first in a series of dialogue meetings for mental health peers and representatives from other groups to promote recovery and improve the behavioral health system. The dialogue meetings have led to positive developments, including advances in collaboration, product development, training initiatives, and technical assistance.

Through the Bringing Recovery Supports to Scale Technical Assistance Center Strategy (BRSS TACS), SAMHSA supports peer-run organizations and recovery community organizations in their efforts to promote recovery and improve collaboration. BRSS TACS major activities include:

- Awarding subcontracts on a competitive basis to support peer-run organizations, recovery community organizations, states, territories, and tribes in their efforts to promote recovery and improve collaboration across stakeholders

- Conducting expert panels in key areas of interest to share knowledge, point to gaps in understanding, and develop recommendations for future activities to promote recovery supports

- Providing training and technical assistance through telephone consultations, email resources, peer learning, webcasts, distance learning, and knowledge products

- Developing resources, including webinars, online learning tools, and a Recovery Resource Library

SAMHSA has encouraged the development of several organizations that focus on young people in recovery: Youth M.O.V.E. (Youth Motivating Others through Voices of Experience) was developed by youth and young adults who experienced mental health challenges. This is a nation-wide peer movement with more than 75 chapters across the United States. It includes Young People in Recovery (YPR), which was created and is run by young people who have experienced addictions and substance use issues.

SAMHSA's Recovery to Practice Initiative (RTP) incorporates the vision of recovery into the everyday practice of mental health professionals in several disciplines. RTP trainings include Peer-Delivered Services training to improve the knowledge and skills of peer-providers.

## Community Living and Participation

Recovery for individuals with behavioral health conditions is greatly enhanced by social connection. Yet, many people with mental and/or substance use disorders are not fully engaged in their communities either through personal relationships, social events, or civic activities. Unfortunately, many individuals often remain socially isolated and excluded. Negative perceptions, prejudice, and discrimination contribute to the social exclusion of people living with behavioral health disorders.

People living with mental and/or substance use conditions can increase social connections greatly when they have access to recovery-oriented services and establish positive relationships with family and friends. Greater social connections lead to improved economic, educational, recreational, and cultural opportunities that are generally available.

In a socially inclusive society, people in recovery have the opportunity and necessary supports to contribute to their community as citizens, parents, employees, students, volunteers, and leaders. Prevention activities help create communities in which people have an improved quality of life that includes healthier environments at work and in school, and supportive neighborhoods and work environments. Social connections and understanding also help people in recovery from addictions benefit from alcohol- and tobacco-free activities in the community.

National Recovery Month helps to raise public awareness and understanding that people recover and celebrates those who support individuals in recovery. SAMHSA's Voice Awards also help to build greater public acceptance and understanding of behavioral health issues by helping to educate the entertainment industry.

# Chapter 53

# *Supporting Mental Health Concerns in the Community*

## *Chapter Contents*

## Section 53.1

# *Role of Educators*

Text in this section is excerpted from "For Educators," U.S.
Department of Health and Human Services (HHS), May 31, 2013.

## *Educators*

Educators are often the first to notice mental health problems. Here
are some ways you can help students and their families.

### *What Educators Should Know*

You should know:

- The warning signs for mental health problems.

- Whom to turn to, such as the principal, school nurse, school
  psychiatrist or psychologist, or school social worker, if you have
  questions or concerns about a student's behavior.

- How to access crisis support and other mental health services.

### *What Educators Should Look For in Student Behavior*

Consult with a school counselor, nurse, or administrator and the
student's parents if you observe one or more of the following behaviors:

- Feeling very sad or withdrawn for more than two weeks

- Seriously trying to harm oneself, or making plans to do so

- Sudden overwhelming fear for no reason, sometimes with a racing heart or fast breathing

- Involvement in many fights or desire to badly hurt others

- Severe out-of-control behavior that can hurt oneself or others

- Not eating, throwing up, or using laxatives to make oneself lose
  weight

- Intense worries or fears that get in the way of daily activities

- Extreme difficulty concentrating or staying still that puts the student in physical danger or causes problems in the classroom

- Repeated use of drugs or alcohol

- Severe mood swings that cause problems in relationships

- Drastic changes in the student's behavior or personality

### *What Educators Can Do in Classrooms and Schools*

You can support the mental health of all students in your classroom and school, not just individual students who may exhibit behavioral issues. Consider the following actions:

- Educate staff, parents, and students on symptoms of and help for mental health problems

- Promote social and emotional competency and build resilience

- Help ensure a positive, safe school environment

- Teach and reinforce positive behaviors and decision-making

- Encourage helping others

- Encourage good physical health

- Help ensure access to school-based mental health supports

### *Developing Effective School Mental Health Programs*

Efforts to care for the emotional wellbeing of children and youth can extend beyond the classroom and into the entire school. School-based mental health programs can focus on promoting mental wellness, preventing mental health problems, and providing treatment.

Effective programs:

- Promote the healthy social and emotional development of all children and youth

- Recognize when young people are at risk for or are experiencing mental health problems

- Identify how to intervene early and appropriately when there are problems

Section 53.2

# *Role of Community and Faith Leaders*

Text in this section is excerpted from "For Community
and Faith Leaders," U.S. Department of Health and
Human Services (HHS), October 30, 2014.

## *Creating Community Connections for Mental Health*

Faith and community leaders are often the first point of contact
when individuals and families face mental health problems or traumatic events. In fact, in times of crisis, many will turn to trusted
leaders in their communities before they turn to mental health professionals. When leaders know how to respond, they become significant
assets to the overall health system.

Faith and community leaders can help educate individuals and
families about mental health, increasing awareness of mental health
issues and making it easier for people to seek help. Community connectedness and support, like that found in faith-based and other neighborhood organizations, are also important to the long-term recovery
of people living with mental illnesses.

Faith communities are also in a unique position to reach many of
the millions of Americans who struggle with serious thoughts of suicide each year. Many people having thoughts of suicide feel hopeless,
trapped, or are in such emotional pain or despair, that they struggle
to face another day. Suicidal thoughts are often accompanied by a
spiritual crisis or deep questioning about the purpose of life. If faith
leaders are better able to recognize the signs of suicide and learn how
to respond, they can serve as an expanded safety net for those most
in need.

## *What Community and Faith Leaders Can Do*

**Educate your communities and congregations.** Promote
awareness by educating the members of your communities and congregations about mental health issues through educational forums
and other opportunities.

- Invite local mental health experts–including those who have experienced mental illness–to speak with your congregation or at community gatherings.

- Share facts and common myths about mental health.

- Support the development of a trauma-informed community. Trauma often lies beneath seemingly unrelated problems.

- Organize additional meetings, dinners, or other gatherings for members of your congregation or community to have conversations about mental health.

**Identify opportunities to support people with mental illnesses.** Religious and other community organizations can play an important role in supporting individuals living with mental illnesses and encouraging them to seek help.

- Consider offering your organization's meeting spaces for community conversations and support groups focused on addressing mental health issues.

- Provide space for peer-led groups that give people the chance to tell their stories in their own time and way.

- Include safe shared spaces for people to interact (for example, parks and community centers) that can foster healthy relationships and positive mental health among community members.

- Support community programs (for example. peer mentoring programs or opportunities for volunteering) that encourage social participation and inclusion for all people

- Plan and facilitate a community conversation using SAMHSA's Toolkit for Community Conversations About Mental Health. The toolkit provides information about how to plan a community conversation, how to guide these discussions, and includes information about mental health issues to use during the discussion.

- Share the Toolkit for Community Conversations About Mental Health with your colleagues and leaders in other organizations.

**Connect individuals and families to help.** Strengthen the connections within your community to mental health services and support and enhance linkages between mental health, substance abuse, disability, and other social services.

- Learn the basic signs of mental illnesses and other facts about mental health to encourage those in need to seek help.

- Remind others that people can and do recover from mental health challenges and that help is available and effective.

- Train key community members (such as adults who work with the children, youth, older adults, veterans, and LGBT) to identify the signs of depression and suicide and refer people to resources.

- Develop relationships with local mental health service providers and other family and youth organizations to help to direct individuals and families in need to available services and support in the community.

- Share the SAMHSA treatment locator in your community newsletter or other publications.

**Promote acceptance of those with mental health issues.** The voices of leaders and members of faith-based and other community organizations can greatly influence attitudes about mental health conditions and those who experience them.

- Talk about your own mental health openly.

- Be an example of taking good care of your mental health by making mental wellness a priority in your personal life.

- Be inclusive. Mental health affects all of us.

- Foster opportunities to build connections with individuals and families dealing with mental health challenges through trust and acceptance.

- Foster safe and supportive environments for people to openly talk about mental health, stress, trauma, and related issues.

- Ask, "What happened?" instead of, "What's wrong?" when talking with a friend in need.

- Encourage and express empathy in your family, congregation, and community. Convey a message of nonviolence, acceptance, and compassion.

# Chapter 54

# *Medicare and Mental Health Benefits*

## *Mental Health Care and Medicare*

Mental health conditions like depression or anxiety can happen to anyone at any time. If you think you may have problems that affect your mental health, you can get help. Talk to your doctor or other health care provider if you have:

- Thoughts of ending your life (like a fixation on death or suicidal thoughts or attempts)

- Sad, empty, or hopeless feelings

- Loss of self-worth (like worries about being a burden, feelings of worthlessness, or self-loathing)

- Social withdrawal and isolation (don't want to be with friends, engage in activities, or leave home)

- Little interest in things you used to enjoy

- A lack of energy

Text in this chapter is excerpted from "Medicare and Your Mental Health Benefits," U.S. Department of Health and Human Services (HHS), November 2014; and text from "Health Insurance and Mental Health Services," U.S. Department of Health and Human Services (HHS), December 9, 2014.

- Trouble concentrating

- Trouble sleeping (like difficulty falling asleep or staying asleep, oversleeping, or daytime sleepiness)

- Weight loss or loss of appetite

- Increased use of alcohol or other drugs

Mental health care includes services and programs to help diagnose and treat mental health conditions. These services and programs may be provided in outpatient and inpatient settings. Medicare helps cover outpatient and inpatient mental health care, as well as prescription drugs you may need to treat a mental health condition.

## Medicare Helps Cover Mental Health Services

**Medicare Part A (Hospital Insurance)** helps cover mental health care if you're a hospital inpatient. Part A covers your room, meals, nursing care, and other related services and supplies.

**Medicare Part B (Medical Insurance)** helps cover mental health services that you would get from a doctor and services that you generally would get outside of a hospital, like visits with a psychiatrist or other doctor, visits with a clinical psychologist or clinical social worker, and lab tests ordered by your doctor. Part B may also pay for partial hospitalization services if you need intensive coordinated outpatient care.

**Medicare prescription drug coverage (Part D)** helps cover drugs you may need to treat a mental health condition.

## Outpatient Mental Health Care and Professional Services

### What Original Medicare Covers

**Medicare Part B (Medical Insurance)** helps cover mental health services and visits with these types of health professionals (deductibles and coinsurance may apply):

- Psychiatrist or other doctor

- Clinical psychologist

- Clinical social worker

- Clinical nurse specialist

- Nurse practitioner

- Physician assistant

The health professionals above (except psychiatrists and other doctors) must accept assignment if they participate in Medicare. Ask your healthcare provider if they accept assignment before you schedule an appointment.

Part B covers outpatient mental health services, including services that are usually provided outside a hospital (like in a clinic, doctor's office, or therapist's office) and services provided in a hospital's outpatient department. Part B also covers outpatient mental health services for treatment of inappropriate alcohol and drug use. Part B helps pay for these covered outpatient services (deductibles and coinsurance may apply):

- One depression screening per year. The screening must be done in a primary care doctor's office or primary care clinic that can provide follow-up treatment and referrals. You pay nothing for your yearly depression screening if your doctor or healthcare provider accepts assignment.

- Individual and group psychotherapy with doctors or certain other licensed professionals allowed by the state where you get the services.

- Family counseling, if the main purpose is to help with your treatment.

- Testing to find out if you're getting the services you need and if your current treatment is helping you.

- Psychiatric evaluation.

- Medication management.

- Certain prescription drugs that aren't usually "self administered" (drugs you would normally take on your own), like some injections.

- Diagnostic tests.

- Partial hospitalization.

- A one-time "Welcome to Medicare" preventive visit. This visit includes a review of your potential risk factors for depression. (**Note:** This visit is only covered if you get it within the first 12

629

months you have Part B.) You pay nothing for this visit if your doctor or other health care provider accepts assignment.

- A yearly "Wellness" visit. Medicare covers a yearly "Wellness" visit once every 12 months (if you've had Part B for longer than 12 months). This is a good time to talk to your doctor or other health care provider about changes in your mental health so they can evaluate your changes year to year. You pay nothing for your yearly "Wellness" visit if your doctor or other health care provider accepts assignment.

## *What You Pay*

After you pay your yearly Part B deductible for visits to a doctor or other health care provider to diagnose or treat your condition, you pay 20% of the Medicare-approved amount if your healthcare provider accepts assignment.

If you get your services in a hospital outpatient clinic or hospital outpatient department, you may have to pay an **additional** copayment or coinsurance amount to the hospital. This amount will vary depending on the service provided but will be between 20–40% of the Medicare-approved amount.

**Note:** If you have a Medicare Supplement Insurance (Medigap) policy or other health insurance coverage, tell your doctor or other health care provider so your bills get paid correctly.

## *Medicare May Cover Partial Hospitalization*

Part B covers partial hospitalization in some cases. Partial hospitalization is a structured program of outpatient psychiatric services provided to patients as an alternative to inpatient psychiatric care. It's more intense than the care you get in a doctor's or therapist's office. This type of treatment is provided during the day and doesn't require an overnight stay. Medicare helps cover partial hospitalization services when they're provided through a hospital outpatient department or community mental health center. As part of your partial hospitalization program, Medicare may cover occupational therapy that's part of your mental health treatment and/or individual patient training and education about your condition.

For Medicare to cover a partial hospitalization program, you must meet certain requirements and your doctor must certify that you would otherwise need inpatient treatment. Your doctor and the partial hospitalization program must accept Medicare payment.

In 2014, you pay a percentage of the Medicare-approved amount for each service you get from a doctor or certain other qualified mental health professionals if your health care professional accepts assignment. You also pay coinsurance for each day of partial hospitalization services provided in a hospital outpatient setting or community mental health center.

## What Original Medicare Doesn't Cover

- Meals.

- Transportation to or from mental health care services.

- Support groups that bring people together to talk and socialize. (**Note:** This is different from group psychotherapy, which is covered.)

- Testing or training for job skills that isn't part of your mental health treatment.

# Inpatient Mental Health Care

## What Original Medicare Covers

**Medicare Part A (Hospital Insurance)** helps pay for mental health services you get in a hospital that require you to be admitted as an inpatient. You can get these services either in a general hospital or in a psychiatric hospital that only cares for people with mental health conditions. Regardless of which type of hospital you choose, Part A will help cover mental health services.

If you're in a psychiatric hospital (instead of a general hospital), Part A only pays for up to 190 days of inpatient psychiatric hospital services during your lifetime.

## What You Pay

Medicare measures your use of hospital services (including services you get in a psychiatric hospital) in benefit periods. A benefit period begins the day you're admitted as an inpatient in a hospital (either general or psychiatric). The benefit period ends after you haven't had any inpatient hospital care for 60 days in a row. If you go into a hospital again after 60 days, a new benefit period begins, and you must pay a new deductible for any inpatient hospital services you get.

There's no limit to the number of benefit periods you can have when you get mental health care in a general hospital. You can also have multiple benefit periods when you get care in a psychiatric hospital, but there's a lifetime limit of 190 days.

631

As a hospital inpatient, you pay these amounts in 2014:

- $1,216 deductible for each benefit period

- Days 1–60: $0 coinsurance per day of each benefit period

- Days 61–90: $304 coinsurance per day of each benefit period

- Days 91 and beyond: $608 coinsurance per each "lifetime reserve day" after day 90 for each benefit period (up to 60 days over your lifetime)

- Beyond lifetime reserve days: all costs

Part B also helps cover mental health services provided by doctors and other healthcare professionals if you're admitted as a hospital inpatient. You pay 20% of the Medicare-approved amount for these mental health services while you're a hospital inpatient.

**Note:** If you have a Medicare Supplement Insurance (Medigap) policy or other health insurance coverage, tell your doctor or other health care provider so your bills get paid correctly.

### What Original Medicare Doesn't Cover

- Private duty nursing

- A phone or television in your room

- Personal items (like toothpaste, socks, or razors)

- A private room (unless medically necessary)

## Medicare Prescription Drug Coverage (Part D)

To get Medicare prescription drug coverage, you must join a Medicare Prescription Drug Plan. Medicare drug plans are run by insurance companies and other private companies approved by Medicare. Each Medicare drug plan can vary in cost and in the specific drugs it covers. It's important to know your plan's coverage rules and your rights.

### Medicare Drug Plans Have Special Rules

*Will My Plan Cover the Drugs I Need?*

Most Medicare drug plans have a list of drugs that the plan covers, called a formulary. Medicare drug plans aren't required to cover all drugs, but they're required to cover all (with limited exceptions) antidepressant, anticonvulsant, and antipsychotic medications, which may be necessary to keep you mentally healthy. Medicare reviews each plan's formulary to make sure it contains a wide range of drugs and that it doesn't discriminate against certain groups (like people with disabilities or mental health conditions).

If you take prescription drugs for a mental health condition, it's important to find out whether a plan covers your drugs before you enroll.

## Can My Drug Plan's Formulary Change?

A Medicare drug plan can make some changes to its formulary during the year within guidelines set by Medicare. If the change involves a drug you're currently taking, your plan must do one of these:

- Provide written notice to you at least 60 days prior to the date the change becomes effective.

- At the time you request a refill, provide written notice of the change and a 60-day supply of the drug under the same plan rules as before the change.

## What If My Prescriber Thinks I Need a Certain Drug That My Plan Doesn't Cover?

If you belong to a Medicare drug plan, you have the right to request a coverage determination (including an exception). You can appoint a representative to help you. Your representative can be a family member, friend, advocate, attorney, doctor, or someone else who will act on your behalf. You, your representative, or your doctor or other prescriber must contact your plan to ask for a coverage determination.

## Request a Coverage Determination

You, your representative, or your doctor or other prescriber can request that your plan cover a drug you need. You can request a coverage determination if your pharmacist or plan tells you:

- A drug you believe should be covered isn't covered

- A drug is covered at a higher cost sharing amount than you think you should have to pay

- You have to meet a plan coverage rule (like prior authorization) before you can get the drug you requested

- The plan won't cover a drug because the plan believes you don't need the drug

If you request a coverage determination, your doctor or other prescriber will need to give a supporting statement to your plan explaining why you need the drug you're requesting. You, your representative, or your doctor or other prescriber can request a coverage determination orally or in writing. Your plan may request additional written information from your prescriber.

### Request an Exception

You, your representative, or your doctor or other prescriber can request an exception (a type of coverage determination) if:

- You think your plan should cover a drug that's not on its formulary because the other treatment options on your plan's formulary won't work for you.

- Your doctor or other prescriber believes you can't meet one of your plan's coverage rules (like prior authorization, step therapy, or quantity or dosage limits).

- You think your plan should charge a lower amount for a drug you're taking on the plan's non-preferred drug tier because the other treatment options in your plan's preferred drug tier won't work for you.

If you request an exception, your doctor or other prescriber will need to give a supporting statement to your plan explaining why you need the drug you're requesting. You, your representative, or your doctor or other prescriber can request an exception orally or in writing. Your plan may request additional written information from your prescriber.

### What If I Disagree with My Plan's Coverage Determination or Exception Decision?

Once your plan has gotten your request, in most cases, it has 72 hours (or 24 hours if you request that a fast decision be made) to notify you of its decision. If you disagree with your Medicare drug plan's coverage determination or exception decision, you have the right to appeal the decision. The plan's written decision will explain how to file an appeal. Read this decision carefully.

For more information on your appeal rights, how to file an appeal, and how to appoint a representative to help you:

- Visit Medicare.gov/appeals.

- Call 1-800-MEDICARE (1-800-633-4227). TTY users should call 1-877-486-2048.

## Learn More about Medicare Prescription Drug Coverage

To find out more about Medicare prescription drug coverage :

- Visit Medicare.gov/part-d.

- Visit Medicare.gov/publications to view or print "Your Guide to Medicare's Prescription Drug Coverage."

- Visit Medicare.gov/find-a-plan to find and compare plans in your area. Have your Medicare card, a list of your drugs and their dosages, and the name of the pharmacy you use available. Call 1-800-MEDICARE (1-800-633-4227). TTY users should call 1-877-486-2048.

- Call your State Health Insurance Assistance Program (SHIP) to get personalized help. Visit Medicare.gov/contacts, or call 1-800-MEDICARE to get the phone number.

## Get the Help You Need

Medicare helps you get the information you need.

### Help If You Have Limited Income and Resources

*Extra Help Paying Your Medicare Prescription Drug Costs*

If you meet certain income and resource limits, you may qualify for Extra Help from Medicare to help pay the costs of Medicare prescription drug coverage.

You should apply even if you aren't sure if you qualify.

For more information:

- Visit Medicare.gov, and select "Get help paying costs" under "Your Medicare Costs."

- Visit socialsecurity.gov, and select "Medicare" under "Benefits." To apply for Extra Help online, visit socialsecurity.gov/i1020.

- Call Social Security at 1-800-772-1213. TTY users should call 1-800-325-0778. You can apply for Extra Help by phone or ask for a paper application.

- Contact your State Medical Assistance (Medicaid) office. Visit Medicare.gov/contacts, or call 1-800-MEDICARE (1-800-633-4227) to get the phone number. TTY users should call 1-877-486-2048.

### *State Pharmacy Assistance Programs (SPAPs)*

Many states have SPAPs that help certain people pay for prescription drugs. Each SPAP makes its own rules on how to help its members. To find out if there's an SPAP in your state and how it works:

- Visit Medicare.gov/pharmaceutical-assistance-program/ state-programs.aspx.

- Call your State Health Insurance Assistance Program (SHIP). Visit Medicare.gov/contacts, or call 1-800-MEDICARE (1-800-633-4227) to get the phone number. TTY users should call 1-877-486-2048.

### *Medicare Savings Programs*

If you have limited income and resources, you may be able to get help from your state to pay your Medicare costs (like premiums, deductibles, and coinsurance) if you meet certain conditions.

For more information:

- Visit Medicare.gov, and select "Get help paying costs" under "Your Medicare Costs."

- Contact your State Medical Assistance (Medicaid) office, and ask for information on Medicare Savings Programs. Call if you think you qualify, even if you aren't sure. To get the phone number for your state, visit Medicare.gov/contacts, or call 1-800-MEDICARE.

- Call your State Health Insurance Assistance Program (SHIP). Visit Medicare.gov/contacts, or call 1-800-MEDICARE to get the phone number.

### *Medicaid*

Medicaid is a joint federal and state program that helps with medical costs for some people and families who have limited income and resources. Medicaid also offers some benefits not normally covered by Medicare, like long term nursing home care and personal care services. Each state has different rules about eligibility and applying for Medicaid.

For more information:

- Visit Medicare.gov, and select "Get help paying costs" under "Your Medicare Costs."

- To see if you qualify, call your State Medical Assistance (Medicaid) office. Visit Medicare.gov/contacts, or call 1-800-MEDICARE (1-800-633-4227) to get the phone number. TTY users should call 1-877-486-2048.

### *Your Medicare Rights*

No matter how you get Medicare, you generally have certain rights and protections designed to:

- Protect you when you get health care.

- Make sure you get the health care services that the law says you can get.

- Protect you against unethical practices.

- Protect your privacy.

- To learn more about your Medicare rights:

- Visit Medicare.gov, and select "Your Medicare rights" under "Claims & Appeals."

### *Your Medicare Appeal Rights*

An appeal is an action you can take if you disagree with a coverage or payment decision by Medicare, your Medicare plan, or your Medicare Prescription Drug Plan. If you decide to file an appeal, you can ask your doctor, healthcare provider, or supplier for any information that may help your case. Keep a copy of everything you send to Medicare as part of the appeal. For more information:

- Visit Medicare.gov/appeals.

- Call 1-800-MEDICARE.

## *Health Insurance and Mental Health Services—FAQs*

### *Q: How Does the Affordable Care Act Help People with Mental Health Issues?*

Answer: The Affordable Care Act provides one of the largest expansions of mental health and substance use disorder coverage in a generation, by requiring that most individual and small employer health insurance plans, including all plans offered through the Health Insurance Marketplace cover mental health and substance use disorder services. Also required are rehabilitative and habilitative services that can help support people with behavioral health challenges. These new protections build on the Mental Health Parity and Addiction Equity Act of 2008 (MHPAEA) provisions to expand mental health and substance use disorder benefits and federal parity protections to an estimated 62 million Americans.

Because of the law, most health plans must now cover preventive services, like depression screening for adults and behavioral assessments for children, at no additional cost. And, as of 2014, most plans cannot deny you coverage or charge you more due to pre-existing health conditions, including mental illnesses.

### Q: Does the Affordable Care Act Require Insurance Plans to Cover Mental Health Benefits?

Answer: As of 2014, most individual and small group health insurance plans, including plans sold on the Marketplace are required to cover mental health and substance use disorder services. Medicaid Alternative Benefit Plans also must cover mental health and substance use disorder services. These plans must have coverage of essential health benefits, which include 10 categories of benefits as defined under the health care law. One of those categories is mental health and substance use disorder services. Another is rehabilitative and habilitative services. Additionally, these plans must comply with mental health and substance use parity requirements, as set forth in MHPAEA, meaning coverage for mental health and substance abuse services generally cannot be more restrictive than coverage for medical and surgical services.

### Q: How Do I Find out If My Health Insurance Plan Is Supposed to Be Covering Mental Health or Substance Use Disorder Services in Parity with Medical and Surgical Benefits? What Do I Do If I Think My Plan Is Not Meeting Parity Requirements?

Answer: In general, for those in large employer plans, if mental health or substance use disorder services are offered, they are subject to the parity protections required under MHPAEA. And, as of 2014, for most small employer and individual plans, mental health and substance use disorder services must meet MHPAEA requirements.

If you have questions about your insurance plan, we recommend you first look at your plan's enrollment materials, or any other information you have on the plan, to see what the coverage levels are for all benefits. Because of the Affordable Care Act, health insurers are required to provide you with an easy-to-understand summary about your benefits including mental health benefits, which should make it easier to see what your coverage is. More information also may be available with your state Consumer Assistance Program (CAP).

### Q. What Can I Do If I Think I Need Mental Health or Substance Use Disorder Services for Myself or Family Members?

Here are three steps you can take right now:

- Learn more about how you, your friends, and your family can obtain health insurance coverage provided by Medicaid or CHIP or the Health Insurance Marketplaces by visiting HealthCare. gov.

- Share this infographic with your friends, family, and colleagues so more people know about the mental health benefits accessible under the Affordable Care Act.

### Q: What Is the Health Insurance Marketplace?

The Health Insurance Marketplace is designed to make buying health coverage easier and more affordable. The Marketplace allows individuals to compare health plans, get answers to questions, find out if they are eligible for tax credits to help pay for private insurance or health programs like the Children's Health Insurance Program (CHIP), and enroll in a health plan that meets their needs. The Marketplace Can Help You:

- Look for and compare private health plans.

- Get answers to questions about your health coverage options.

- Get reduced costs, if you're eligible.

- Enroll in a health plan that meets your needs.

# Chapter 55

# *Recovery from Mental Health Problems*

## *Recovery Is Possible*

Most people with mental health problems can get better. Treatment and recovery are ongoing processes that happen over time. The first step is getting help.

## *What Is Recovery?*

- Recovery from mental disorders and/or substance abuse disorders is a process of change through which individuals:
- Improve their health and wellness
- Live a self-directed life
- Strive to achieve their full potential

## *Overview*

The adoption of recovery by behavioral health systems in recent years has signaled a dramatic shift in the expectation for positive

This chapter includes excerpts from "Recovery is Possible," U.S. Department of Health and Human Services (HHS), May 31, 2013; and text from "Recovery and Recovery Support," Substance Abuse and Mental Health Services Administration (SAMHSA), October 5, 2015.

outcomes for individuals who experience mental and/or substance use conditions. Today, when individuals with mental and/or substance use disorders seek help, they are met with the knowledge and belief that anyone can recover and/or manage their conditions successfully. The value of recovery and recovery-oriented behavioral health systems is widely accepted by states, communities, health care providers, peers, families, researchers, and advocates including the U.S. Surgeon General, the Institute of Medicine, and others.

SAMHSA has established a working definition of recovery that defines recovery as a process of change through which individuals improve their health and wellness, live self-directed lives, and strive to reach their full potential. Recovery is built on access to evidence-based clinical treatment and recovery support services for all populations.

Hope, the belief that these challenges and conditions can be overcome, is the foundation of recovery. A person's recovery is built on his or her strengths, talents, coping abilities, resources, and inherent values. It is holistic, addresses the whole person and their community, and is supported by peers, friends, and family members.

The process of recovery is highly personal and occurs via many pathways. It may include clinical treatment, medications, faith-based approaches, peer support, family support, self-care, and other approaches. Recovery is characterized by continual growth and improvement in one's health and wellness that may involve setbacks. Because setbacks are a natural part of life, resilience becomes a key component of recovery.

Resilience refers to an individual's ability to cope with adversity and adapt to challenges or change. Resilience develops over time and gives an individual the capacity not only to cope with life's challenges but also to be better prepared for the next stressful situation. Optimism and the ability to remain hopeful are essential to resilience and the process of recovery. Because recovery is a highly individualized process, recovery services and supports must be flexible to ensure cultural relevancy. What may work for adults in recovery may be very different for youth or older adults in recovery. For example, the promotion of resiliency in young people, and the nature of social supports, peer mentors, and recovery coaching for adolescents and transitional age youth are different than recovery support services for adults and older adults.

The process of recovery is supported through relationships and social networks. This often involves family members who become the champions of their loved one's recovery. They provide essential support to their family member's journey of recovery and similarly experience the moments of positive healing as well as the difficult challenges. Families of people in recovery may experience adversities in their social, occupational, and financial lives, as well as in their overall quality of family life. These experiences can lead to increased family stress, guilt, shame, anger, fear, anxiety, loss, grief, and isolation. The concept of resilience in recovery is also vital for family members who need access to intentional supports that promote their health and well-being. The support of peers and friends is also crucial in engaging and supporting individuals in recovery.

## *Recovery Support*

SAMHSA established the Recovery Support Strategic Initiative to promote partnering with people in recovery from mental and substance use disorders and their family members to guide the behavioral health system and promote individual, program, and system-level approaches that foster health and resilience (including helping individuals with behavioral health needs be well, manage symptoms, and achieve and maintain abstinence); increase housing to support recovery; reduce barriers to employment, education, and other life goals; and secure necessary social supports in their chosen community.

Recovery support is provided through treatment, services, and community-based programs by behavioral health care providers, peer providers, family members, friends and social networks, the faith community, and people with experience in recovery. Recovery support services help people enter into and navigate systems of care, remove barriers to recovery, stay engaged in the recovery process, and live full lives in communities of their choice.

Recovery support services include culturally and linguistically appropriate services that assist individuals and families working toward recovery from mental and/or substance use problems. They incorporate a full range of social, legal, and other services that facilitate recovery, wellness, and linkage to and coordination among service providers, and other supports shown to improve quality of life for people in and seeking recovery and their families.

Recovery support services also include access to evidence-based practices such as supported employment, education, and housing; assertive community treatment; illness management; and peer-operated services. Recovery support services may be provided before, during, or after clinical treatment or may be provided to individuals who are not in treatment but seek support services. These services, provided by professionals and peers, are delivered through a variety of community and faith-based groups, treatment providers, schools, and other specialized services. For example, in the United States there are 22 recovery high schools that help reduce the risk environment for youth with substance use disorders. These schools typically have high retention rates and low relapse rates. The broad range of service delivery options ensures the life experiences of all people are valued and represented.

## Cultural Awareness and Competency

Supporting recovery requires that mental health and addiction services:

- Be responsive and respectful to the health beliefs, practices, and cultural and linguistic needs of diverse people and groups

- Actively address diversity in the delivery of services

- Seek to reduce health disparities in access and outcomes

Cultural competence describes the ability of an individual or organization to interact effectively with people of different cultures. To produce positive change, practitioners must understand the cultural context of the community they serve, and have the willingness and skills to work within this context. This means drawing on community-based values, traditions, and customs, and working with knowledgeable people from the community to plan, implement, and evaluate prevention activities.

Individuals, families, and communities that have experienced social and economic disadvantages are more likely to face greater obstacles to overall health. Characteristics such as race or ethnicity, religion, low socioeconomic status, gender, age, mental health, disability, sexual orientation or gender identity, geographic location, or other characteristics historically linked to exclusion or discrimination are known to influence health status.

SAMHSA is committed to addressing these health disparities by providing culturally and linguistically appropriate prevention, treatment, and recovery support programs. This commitment is reinforced through the agency's disparity impact strategy that monitors programs and activities to ensure that access, use, and outcomes are equitable across racial and ethnic minority groups.

The SAMHSA Office of Behavioral Health Equity (OBHE) works to reduce mental health and substance use disparities among diverse racial and ethnic populations, as well as lesbian, gay, bisexual, and transgender (LGBT) populations. OBHE was established to improve access to quality care and in accordance with section 10334(b) of the Affordable Care Act of 2010, which requires six agencies under the Department of Health and Human Services (HHS) to establish an office of minority affairs.

## Four Dimensions of Recovery

Four major dimensions support a life in recovery:

1. Health: Make informed, healthy choices that support physical and emotional wellbeing.

2. Home: Have a stable and safe place to live.

3. Purpose: Engage in meaningful daily activities, such as a job or school, volunteering, caring for your family, or being creative. Work for independence, income, and resources to participate in society.

4. Community: Build relationships and social networks that provide support.

## Develop a Recovery Plan

If you are struggling with a mental health problem, you may want to develop a written recovery plan.

Recovery plans:

- Enable you to identify goals for achieving wellness

- Specify what you can do to reach those goals

- Include daily activities as well as longer term goals

- Track any changes in your mental health problem

- Identify triggers or other stressful events that can make you feel worse, and help you learn how to manage them

# Part Eight


# Additional Help and Information

# Chapter 56

# Glossary of Terms Related to Mental Health Disorders

**action potential:** Transmission of signal from the cell body to the synaptic terminal at the end of the cell's axon. When the action potential reaches the end of the axon the neuron releases chemical (neurotransmitters) or electrical signals anterior cingulate cortex.

**acupuncture:** A family of procedures involving stimulation of anatomical points on the body by a variety of techniques.

**addiction:** A chronic, relapsing disease characterized by compulsive drug seeking and use, despite serious adverse consequences, and by long-lasting changes in the brain.

**adolescence:** A human life stage that begins at twelve years of age and continues until twenty-one complete years of age, generally marked by the beginning of puberty and lasting to the beginning of adulthood.

**agitation:** A condition in which a person is unable to relax and be still. The person may be very tense and irritable, and become easily annoyed by small things.

**agoraphobia:** An intense fear of being in open places or in situations where it may be hard to escape, or where help may not be available.

---

This glossary contains terms excerpted from documents produced by several sources deemed reliable.

**albumin:** A type of protein found in blood, egg white, milk, and other substances.

**antidepressant:** Medication used to treat depression and other mood and anxiety disorders.

**antipsychotic:** Medication used to treat psychosis.

**appetite:** A desire to satisfy a physical or mental need, such as for food, sex, or adventure.

**axon:** The long, fiber-like part of a neuron by which the cell sends information to receiving neurons.

**benzodiazepine:** A type of CNS depressant prescribed to relieve anxiety and sleep problems. Valium and Xanax are among the most widely prescribed medications.

**beta blockers:** A type of medication that reduces nerve impulses to the heart and blood vessels, which makes the heart beat slower and with less force.

**biofeedback:** A technique that uses simple electronic devices to teach clients how to consciously regulate bodily functions, such as breathing, heart rate, and blood pressure, to improve overall health. Biofeedback is used to reduce stress, eliminate headaches, recondition injured muscles, control asthma attacks, and relieve pain.

**bipolar disorder:** A disorder that causes severe and unusually high and low shifts in mood, energy, and activity levels, as well as unusual shifts in the ability to carry out day-to-day tasks. (Also known as Manic Depression)

**blood clot:** A mass of blood that forms when blood platelets, proteins, and cells stick together. When a blood clot is attached to the wall of a blood vessel, it is called a thrombus.

**cell membrane:** The boundary separating the inside contents of a cell from its surrounding environment.

**central nervous system:** The brain and spinal cord. Also called CNS.

**chronic:** Persisting for a long time or constantly recurring.

**clinical trial:** A scientific study using human volunteers (also called participants) to look at new ways to prevent, detect or treat disease. Treatments might be new drugs or new combinations of drugs, new surgical procedures or devices, or new ways to use existing treatments.

**cognition:** Conscious mental activities (such as thinking, communicating, understanding, solving problems, processing information and remembering) that are associated with gaining knowledge and understanding.

**cognitive behavioral therapy (CBT):** CBT helps people focus on how to solve their current problems. The therapist helps the patient learn how to identify distorted or unhelpful thinking patterns, recognize and change inaccurate beliefs, relate to others in more positive ways, and change behaviors accordingly.

**cognitive impairment:** Experiencing difficulty with cognition. Examples include having trouble paying attention, thinking clearly or remembering new information.

**coinsurance:** An amount you may be required to pay as your share of the cost for services after you pay any deductibles. Coinsurance is usually a percentage.

**comorbidity:** The occurrence of two disorders or illnesses in the same person, also referred to as co-occurring conditions or dual diagnosis. Patients with comorbid illnesses may experience a more severe illness course and require treatment for each or all conditions.

**craving:** A powerful, often uncontrollable desire for drugs.

**cytoplasm:** The substance filling a cell, containing all the chemicals and parts needed for the cell to work properly.

**debilitating:** impairs the vitality and strength of a person.

**deep breathing:** An active process that involves conscious control over breathing in and out. This may involve controlling the way in which air is drawn in (for example, through the mouth or nostrils), the rate (for example, quickly or over a length of time), the depth (for example, shallow or deep), and the control of other body parts (for example, relaxation of the stomach).

**delirium:** A mental state in which a person is confused, disoriented, and not able to think or remember clearly. The person may also be agitated and have hallucinations, and extreme excitement.

**dementia:** Loss of brain function that occurs with certain diseases. It affects memory, thinking, language, judgment and behavior.

**dendrite:** The point of contact for receiving impulses on a neuron, branching off from the cell body.

**DNA:** The "recipe of life," containing inherited genetic information that helps to define physical and some behavioral traits.

**dopamine:** A brain chemical, classified as a neurotransmitter, found in regions that regulate movement, emotion, motivation, and pleasure.

**drowsiness:** A fluctuating intermediate state between alert wakefulness and sleep, that is most often experienced when individuals are struggling to maintain wakefulness at a time appropriate for sleep, as a result of pathologic conditions or sleep deficiency.

**electrolyte:** A substance that breaks up into ions (particles with electrical charges) when it is dissolved in water or body fluids. Some examples of ions are sodium, potassium, calcium, chloride, and phosphate.

**epigenetics:** The study of how environmental factors like diet, stress and post-natal care can change gene expression (when genes turn on or off)-without altering DNA sequence.

**episodic:** Comes and goes.

**fatigue:** Loss of energy or strength.

**formulary:** A list of prescription drugs covered by a prescription drug plan or another insurance plan offering prescription drug benefits. Also called a drug list.

**genes:** A gene is a part of DNA (the genetic instructions in all living things). People inherit one copy of each gene from their mother and one copy from their father.

**glutamate:** The most common neurotransmitter in a person's body, which increases neuronal activity, is involved in early brain development, and may also assist in learning and memory.

**guided imagery:** A practice used for healing or health maintenance that involves a series of relaxation techniques followed by the visualization of detailed images, usually calm and peaceful in nature.

**hippocampus:** A portion of the brain involved in creating and filing new memories.

**hypercalcemia:** Higher than normal levels of calcium in the blood. Some types of cancer increase the risk of hypercalcemia.

**hypersomnia:** A state characterized by subjective report of tiredness and objective evidence of inability to maintain vigilance.

**hypnosis:** An altered state of consciousness characterized by increased responsiveness to suggestion. The procedure is used to effect positive changes and to treat numerous health conditions including ulcers, chronic pain, respiratory ailments, stress, and headaches.

**impulse:** An electrical communication signal sent between neurons by which neurons communicate with each other.

**insomnia:** A chronic or acute sleep disorder characterized by a complaint of difficulty initiating, and/or maintaining sleep, and/or a subjective complaint of poor sleep quality that result in daytime impairment and subjective report of impairment.

**isolation:** State of being separated from others. Isolation is sometimes used to prevent disease from spreading.

**lifetime reserve days:** In original Medicare, these are additional days that Medicare will pay for when you're in a hospital for more than 90 days. You have a total of 60 reserve days that can be used during your lifetime. For each lifetime reserve day, Medicare pays all covered costs except for a daily coinsurance.

**magnetic resonance imaging (MRI):** An imaging technique that uses magnetic fields to take pictures of the brain's structure.

**meditation:** A group of techniques, most of which started in Eastern religious or spiritual traditions. In meditation, individuals learn to focus their attention and suspend the stream of thoughts that normally occupy the mind. This practice is believed to result in a state of greater physical relaxation, mental calmness, and psychological balance. Practicing meditation can change how a person relates to the flow of emotions and thoughts in the mind.

**metabolism:** Metabolism refers to all of the processes in the body that make and use energy, such as digesting food and nutrients and removing waste through urine and feces.

**migraine:** Headaches that are usually pulsing or throbbing and occur on one or both sides of the head. They are moderate to severe in intensity, associated with nausea, vomiting, sensitivity to light and noise, and worsen with routine physical activity.

**mutation:** A change in the code for a gene, which may be harmless or even helpful, but sometimes give rise to disabilities or diseases.

**narcolepsy:** A disorder of sleep and wakefulness characterized by excessive daytime sleepiness, disrupted nighttime sleep, and various combinations of irresistible onset of sleep, cataplexy, hypnagogic hallucinations or sleep paralysis.

**nervous system:** The nervous system controls everything that a person does, such as breathing, moving, and, thinking. This system is made up of the brain, spinal cord, and all the nerves in the body.

**neural circuit:** A network of neurons and their interconnections.

**neuron:** A nerve cell that is the basic, working unit of the brain and nervous system, which processes and transmits information.

**neurotransmitters:** Chemicals in the brain that helps nerve cells communicate with each other.

**norepinephrine:** A neurotransmitter present in the brain and the peripheral (sympathetic) nervous system; and a hormone released by the adrenal glands. Norepinephrine is involved in attention, responses to stress, and it regulates smooth muscle contraction, heart rate, and blood pressure.

**nucleus:** A structure within a cell that contains DNA and information the cell needs for growing, staying alive, and making new neurons.

**opioid:** A compound or drug that binds to receptors in the brain involved in the control of pain and other functions (e.g., morphine, heroin, hydrocodone, oxycodone).

**phobias:** An anxiety disorder in which a person suffers from an unusual amount of fear of a certain activity or situation.

**physical dependence:** An adaptive physiological state that occurs with regular drug use and results in a withdrawal syndrome when drug use is stopped; often occurs with tolerance. Physical dependence can happen with chronic: even appropriate: use of many medications, and by itself does not constitute addiction.

**physical therapy:** Therapy aimed to restore movement, balance and coordination.

**posttraumatic stress disorder (PTSD):** An anxiety disorder that develops in reaction to physical injury or severe mental or emotional distress, such as military combat, violent assault, natural disaster, or other life-threatening events.

**prefrontal cortex:** A highly developed area at the front of the brain that, in humans, plays a role in executive functions such as judgment, decision making and problem solving, as well as emotional control and memory.

**prescription drug abuse:** The use of a medication without a prescription; in a way other than as prescribed; or for the experience or feeling elicited. This term is used interchangeably with "nonmedical" use, a term employed by many of the national surveys.

**psychiatrist:** A doctor (M.D.) who treats mental illness. Psychiatrists must receive additional training and serve a supervised residency in their specialty. They can prescribe medications.

**psychologist:** A clinical psychologist is a professional who treats mental illness, emotional disturbance, and behavior problems. They use talk therapy as treatment, and cannot prescribe medication. A clinical psychologist will have a master's degree (M.A.) or doctorate (Ph.D.) in psychology, and possibly more training in a specific type of therapy.

**puberty:** Time when the body is changing from the body of a child to the body of an adult. This process begins earlier in girls than in boys, usually between ages 8 and 13, and lasts 2 to 4 years.

**purging:** Forcing oneself to vomit.

**recur:** To come back or to return.

**REM sleep:** Rapid eye movement sleep is one of the two major types of sleep. Episodes of REM sleep occur in approximately every 90 to 100 minutes during the night. The REM sleep episodes increase in duration through the night and are characterized by a relatively low voltage, fast frequency EEG, skeletal muscle atonia, rapid eye movements, and dreaming.

**restless legs syndrome (RLS):** Restless legs syndrome is a sensorimotor disorder characterized by a complaint of a strong, nearly irresistible, urge to move the legs that is often made worse by rest and is partially and temporarily relieved by walking or moving the legs. The urge to move the legs worsens in the evening or night with relative relief in the morning.

**schizoaffective disorder:** A mental condition that causes both a loss of contact with reality (psychosis) and mood problems (depression or mania).

**schizophrenia:** A severe mental disorder that appears in late adolescence or early adulthood. People with schizophrenia may have hallucinations, delusions, loss of personality, confusion, agitation, social withdrawal, psychosis and/or extremely odd behavior.

**sedatives:** Drugs that suppress anxiety and promote sleep; the National Survey on Drug Use and Health (NSDUH) classification includes benzodiazepines, barbiturates, and other types of CNS depressants.

**self-esteem:** A feeling of self-worth, self-confidence, and self-respect.

**serotonin:** A neurotransmitter that regulates many functions, including mood, appetite, and sleep.

**sleep disorder:** Sleep disorders are clinical conditions that are a consequence of a disturbance in the ability to initiate or maintain the quantity and quality of sleep needed for optimal health, performance and well being.

**sleep disturbance:** Chronic sleep disruption

**stimulants:** A class of drugs that enhances the activity of monamines (such as dopamine) in the brain, increasing arousal, heart rate, blood pressure, and respiration, and decreasing appetite; includes some medications used to treat attention-deficit hyperactivity disorder (e.g., methylphenidate and amphetamines), as well as cocaine and methamphetamine.

**synapse:** The tiny gap between neurons, where nerve impulses are sent from one neuron to another.

**tai chi:** A mind-body practice that originated in China as a martial art. Individuals doing tai chi move their bodies slowly and gently, while breathing deeply and meditating (tai chi is sometimes called moving meditation).

**thyroid hormone:** A hormone that affects heart rate, blood pressure, body temperature, and weight. Thyroid hormone is made by the thyroid gland and can also be made in the laboratory.

**tolerance:** A condition in which higher doses of a drug are required to produce the same effect achieved during initial use; often associated with physical dependence.

**tumor:** An abnormal mass of tissue that results when cells divide more than they should or do not die when they should. Tumors can be benign or malignant.

**vitamin B12:** A nutrient in the vitamin B complex that the body needs in small amounts to function and stay healthy. Vitamin B12 helps make red blood cells, DNA, RNA, energy, and tissues, and keeps nerve cells healthy.

**white blood cell:** A type of blood cell that is made in the bone marrow and found in the blood and lymph tissue. White blood cells are part of the body's immune system. They help the body fight infection and other diseases.

**yoga:** A combination of breathing exercises, physical postures, and meditation used to calm the nervous system and balance the body, mind, and spirit.

# Chapter 57

# Crisis Hotlines and Helplines Related to Mental Health Disorders

## Important Information about Suicide

*Are you thinking of suicide? If yes, please do the following:*

- Dial: 911
- Dial: 800-273-TALK (8255)
- Check yourself into the emergency room.
- Tell someone who can help you find help right away.
- Stay away from things that might hurt you.

Remember: most people can be treated with a combination of anti-depressant medication and talk therapy. Talk to a health professional for guidance.

## No Insurance

If you don't have insurance:

- Go to the nearest hospital emergency room.

---

Excerpted from "Mental Health: Preventing Suicide," Office on Women's Health (OWH), March 29, 2010; and "Mental Health: Help Hotlines," Office on Women's Health (OWH), October 26, 2015. All contact information was verified and updated in March 2016.

- Look in your local Yellow Pages under Mental Health and/or Suicide Prevention and then call the mental health organizations/crisis phone lines that are listed. There may be clinics or counseling centers in your area operating on a sliding or no-fee scale.

- Some pharmaceutical companies have "Free Medication Programs" for those who qualify. Visit the National Alliance for the Mentally Ill website at http://www.nami.org for more information.

## Helplines and Hotlines

Below is a list of toll-free national helplines and hotlines that provide anonymous, confidential information to callers. They can answer questions and help you in times of need.

*American Foundation for Suicide Prevention*
Toll-Free: 800-821-HELP (800-821-4357)

*Boys Town National Hotline*
(Crisis hotline that helps parents and children cope with stress and anxiety.)
Toll-Free: 800-448-3000

*Center for Substance Abuse Treatment*
Toll-Free: 800-729-6686

*Childhelp National Child Abuse Hotline*
Toll-Free: 800-4-A-CHILD (800-422-4453)

*Covenant House*
(Helping homeless youth in the United States and Canada.)
Toll-Free: 800-999-9999

*Depression and Bipolar Support Alliance*
Toll-Free: 800-826-3632

*Division of Developmental Disabilities (DDD)*
Toll-Free: 1-800-832-9173

*Division of Mental Health Services (DMHS)*
Toll-Free: 1-800-382-6717

*Disaster Mental Health*
Toll-Free: 1-877-294-HELP (1-877-294-4357)

*Hopeline*
Toll-Free: 800-442-HOPE (800-442-4673)

*Kristin Brooks Hope Center*
Toll-Free: 800-442-HOPE (800-442-4673)

*Mental Health America*
(For a referral to specific mental health service or support program in your community.)
Toll-Free: 800-969-NMHA (800-969-6642)

*National Alcoholism and Substance Abuse Information Center*
Toll-Free: 800-662-HELP (800-662-4357)

*National Alliance on Mental Illness (NAMI)*
Toll-Free: 800-950-NAMI (800-950-6264)

*National Domestic Violence Hotline*
Toll-Free: 800-799-SAFE (800-799-7233)

*National Eating Disorders Association Information and Referral Helpline*
Toll-Free: 800-931-2237

*National Organization for Victim Assistance*
Toll-Free: 800-TRY-NOVA (800-879-6682) (Victims/Survivors only)

*National Runaway Switchboard*
Toll-Free: 800-RUNAWAY (800-786-2929)

*National Sexual Assault Hotline*
Toll-Free: 800-656-HOPE (800-656-4673)

*National Suicide Prevention Hotline*
Toll-Free: 800-273-TALK (800-273-8255)

*Postpartum Support International*
Toll-Free: 800-994-4PPD (800-994-4773)

*Postpartum Depression (PPD) Moms*
Toll-Free: 800-PPD-MOMS (800-773-6667)

*S.A.F.E. Alternatives*
Toll-Free: 800-DONTCUT (800-366-8288)

*SAMHSA's National Helpline*
(also known as the Treatment Referral Routing Service)
Toll-Free: 1-800-662-HELP (1-800-662-4357)

*Suicide Prevention Crisis Center*
Toll-Free: 877-7-CRISIS (877-727-4747)

*Trevor Project Suicide*
(A prevention helpline for lesbian, gay, bisexual, transgender, and questioning youth.)
Toll-Free: 866-4U-TREVOR (866-488-7386)

# Chapter 58

# *Mental Health Organizations*

## *Government Organizations*

### *Center for Mental Health Services*
Emergency Services and
Disaster Relief Branch
Phone: 240-276-1310
Fax: 240-276-1320
Website: www.mentalhealth.
samhsa.gov
E-mail: info@mentalhealth.org

### *Center for Substance Abuse Treatment*
1 Choke Cherry Rd.
Rm. 5-1015
Rockville, MD 20857
Phone: 240-276-1660
Toll-Free: 800-662-4357
TDD: 800-487-4889
Website: www.samhsa.
gov/about-us/who-we-are/
offices-centers/csat

### *National Center for Posttraumatic Stress Disorder (NCPTSD)*
U.S. Department of Veterans
Affairs (VA)
810 Vermont Ave., N.W.
Washington, DC 20420
Toll-Free: 800-827-1000
Website: www.va.gov

### *National Institute of Mental Health*
Science Writing, Press, and
Dissemination Branch
6001 Executive Blvd., Rm. 8184,
MSC 9663
Bethesda, MD 20892-9663
Phone: 301-443-4513
Fax: 301-443-4279
Toll-Free: 866-615-6464
TTY: 866-415-8051
Website: www.nimh.nih.gov
E-mail: nimhinfo@nih.gov

Information in this chapter was compiled from various sources deemed reliable.
All contact information was verified and updated in March 2016.

*National Institute of Neurological Disorders and Stroke*
NIH Neurological Institute
P.O. Box 5801
Bethesda, MD 20824
Phone: 301-496-5751
Toll-Free: 800-352-9424
TTY: 301-468-5981
Website: www.ninds.nih.gov

*National Institute on Aging*
Bldg. 31, Rm. 5C27
31 Center Dr., MSC 2292
Bethesda, MD 20892
Phone: 301-496-1752
Toll-Free: 800-222-2225
TTY: 800-222-4225
Website: www.nia.nih.gov
E-mail: niac@nia.nih.gov

*National Institute on Alcohol Abuse and Alcoholism*
5635 Fishers Ln., MSC 9304
Bethesda, MD 20892
Phone: 301-443-3860
Website: www.niaaa.nih.gov
E-mail: niaaaweb-r@exchange.nih.gov

*National Institute on Drug Abuse*
6001 Executive Blvd.
Rm. 5213, MSC 9561
Bethesda, MD 20892-9561
Phone: 301-443-1124
Fax: 301-443-7397
Website: www.drugabuse.gov
E-mail: information@nida.nih.gov

*National Women's Health Information Center (NWHIC)*
Office on Women's Health
200 Independence Ave. SW, Rm. 712E
Washington, DC 20201
Phone: 202-690-7650
Fax: 202-205-2631
Toll-Free: 800-994-9662
TDD: 888-220-5446
Website: www.womenshealth.gov

*Office of Minority Health (OMH)*
Resource Center, P.O. Box 37337
Washington, DC 20013-7337
Phone: 240-453-2882
Fax: 301-251-2160;
240-453-2883
Toll-Free: 800-444-6472
TDD: 301-251-1432
Website: www.minorityhealth.hhs.gov
E-mail: info@minorityhealth.hhs.gov

*Substance Abuse and Mental Health Services Administration (SAMHSA)*
1 Choke Cherry Rd.
5600 Fishers Ln.
Rockville, MD 20857
Fax: 240-221-4295
Toll-Free: 877-726-4727
Website: www.mentalhealth.samhsa.gov

## Private Organizations

### Alzheimer's Association
225 N. Michigan Ave., Fl. 17
Chicago, IL 60601-7633
Phone: 312-335-8700
Fax: 866-699-1246
Toll-Free: 800-272-3900
TDD: 312-335-5886
Website: www.alz.org
E-mail: info@alz.org

### American Academy of Child and Adolescent Psychiatry
3615 Wisconsin Ave., N.W.
Washington, DC 20016-3007
Phone: 202-966-7300
Fax: 202-966-2891
Website: www.aacap.org

### American Art Therapy Association
4875 Eisenhower Ave.
Ste. 240
Alexandria, VA 22304
Phone: 703-548-5860
Fax: 703-783-8468
Toll-Free: 888-290-0878
Website: www.arttherapy.org
E-mail: info@arttherapy.org

### American Association for Geriatric Psychiatry
7910 Woodmont Ave.
Ste. 1050
Bethesda, MD 20814-3004
Phone: 301-654-7850
Fax: 301-654-4137
Website: www.aagponline.org
E-mail: main@aagponline.org

### American Association for Marriage and Family Therapy
112 S. Alfred St.
Alexandria, VA 22314-3061
Phone: 703-838-9808
Fax: 703-838-9805
Website: www.aamft.org
E-mail: central@aamft.org

### American Association of Suicidology
5221 Wisconsin Ave., N.W.
Washington, DC 20015
Phone: 202-237-2280
Fax: 202-237-2282
Website: www.suicidology.org

### American Counseling Association
5999 Stevenson Ave.
Alexandria, VA 22304
Fax: 703-823-0252
Toll-Free: 800-473-2329;
800-347-6647
Website: www.counseling.org
E-mail: webmaster@counseling.org

### American Foundation for Suicide Prevention
120 Wall St., 29th Fl.
New York, NY 10005
Phone: 212-363-3500
Fax: 212-363-6237
Toll-Free: 888-333-2377
Website: www.afsp.org
E-mail: inquiry@afsp.org

*American Psychiatric Association*
1000 Wilson Blvd.
Ste. 1825
Arlington, VA 22209-3901
Phone: 703-907-7300
Toll-Free: 888-357-7924
Website: www.psychiatry.org
E-mail: apa@psych.org

*American Psychological Association*
750 First St., N.E.
Washington, DC 20002-4242
Phone: 202-336-5500
Toll-Free: 800-374-2721
TDD: 202-336-6123
Website: www.apa.org
E-mail: public.affairs@apa.org

*American Psychotherapy Association*
2750 E. Sunshine St.
Springfield, MO 65804
Phone: 417-823-0173
Fax: 417-823-9959
Toll-Free: 800-205-9165
Website: www.
americanpsychotherapy.com

*Anxiety Disorders Association of America*
8701 Georgia Ave.
Silver Spring, MD 20910
Phone: 240-485-1001
Fax: 240-485-1035
Website: www.adaa.org

*Association for Applied Psychophysiology and Biofeedback*
10200 W. 44th Ave.
Ste. 304
Wheat Ridge, CO 80033
Phone: 303-422-8436
Toll-Free: 800-477-8892
Website: www.aapb.org
E-mail: info@aapb.org

*Association for Behavioral and Cognitive Therapies*
305 7th Ave., 16th Fl.
New York, NY 10001
Phone: 212-647-1890
Fax: 212-647-1865
Website: www.abct.org

*Balanced Mind Foundation*
55 E. Jackson Blvd
Ste. 490
Chicago, IL 60604
Fax: 312-642-7243
Toll-Free: 800-826-3632
Website: www.dbsalliance.org
E-mail: info@thebalancedmind.org

*Beyond Blue Ltd.*
Hawthorn W.
P.O. Box 6100
Victoria, AU 3122
Phone: (03) 9-810-6100
Website: www.beyondblue.org.au

*Brain and Behavior Research Foundation*
60 Cutter Mill Rd., Ste. 404
Great Neck, NY 11021
Phone: 516-829-0091
Fax: 516-487-6930
Toll-Free: 800-829-8289
Website: www.bbrfoundation.org
E-mail: info@bbrfoundation.org

*Brain Injury Association of America*
1608 Spring Hill Rd.
Ste. 110
Vienna, VA 22182
Phone: 703-761-0750
Fax: 703-761-0755
Toll-Free: 800-444-6443
Website: www.biausa.org
E-mail: braininjuryinfo@biausa.org

*Canadian Mental Health Association*
Phoenix Professional bldg.
595 Montreal Rd., Ste. 303
Ottawa, ON K1K 4L2
Fax: 613-745-5522
Website: www.cmha.ca

*Canadian Psychological Association*
141 Laurier Ave. W.
Ste. 702
Ottawa, ON K1P 5J3
Phone: 613-237-2144
Fax: 613-237-1674
Toll-Free: 888-472-0657
Website: www.cpa.ca
E-mail: cpa@cpa.ca

*Caring.com*
2600 S. El Camino Real
Ste. 300
San Mateo, CA 94403
Website: www.caring.com

*Depressed Anonymous*
P.O. Box 17414
Louisville, KY 40217
Phone: 502-569-1989
Website: www.depressedanon.com
E-mail: info@depressedanon.com

*Depression and Bipolar Support Alliance*
730 N. Franklin St.
Ste. 501
Chicago, IL 60654-7225
Fax: 312-642-7243
Toll-Free: 800-826-3632
Website: www.dbsalliance.org
E-mail: info@dbsalliance.org

*Families for Depression Awareness*
395 Totten Pond Rd., Ste. 404
Waltham, MA 2451
Phone: 781-890-0220
Fax: 781-890-2411
Website: www.familyaware.org

*Family Caregiver Alliance*
785 Market St., Ste. 750
San Francisco, CA 94103
Phone: 415-434-3388
Toll-Free: 800-445-8106
Website: www.caregiver.org
E-mail: info@caregiver.org

*Geriatric Mental Health Foundation*
7910 Woodmont Ave.
Ste. 1050
Bethesda, MD 20814
Phone: 301-654-7850
Fax: 301-654-4137
Website: www.gmhfonline.org
E-mail: web@GMHFonline.org

*International Foundation for Research and Education on Depression*
P.O. Box 17598
Baltimore, MD 21297-1598
Fax: 443-782-0739
Website: www.ifred.org
E-mail: info@ifred.org

*International OCD Foundation*
P.O. Box 961029
Boston, MA 2196
Phone: 617-973-5801
Fax: 617-973-5803
Website: www.iocdf.org
E-mail: info@ocfoundation.org

*International Society for the Study of Trauma and Dissociation*
8400 Westpark Dr.
Second Fl.
McLean, VA 22102
Phone: 703-610-9037
Fax: 703-610-0234
Website: www.issd.org
E-mail: info@isst-d.org

*International Society for Traumatic Stress Studies*
111 Deer Lake Rd., Ste. 100
Deerfield, IL 60015
Phone: 847-480-9028
Fax: 847-480-9282
Website: www.istss.org
E-mail: istss@istss.org

*Kristin Brooks Hope Center*
1250 24th St., N.W., Ste. 300
Washington, DC 20037
Phone: 202-536-3200
Fax: 202-536-3206
Toll-Free: 800-784-2433
TDD: 877-838-2838
Website: www.hopeline.com

*Mautner Project*
1300 19th St. N.W., Ste. 700
Washington, DC 20036
Phone: 202-332-5536
Fax: 202-332-0662
Toll-Free: 866-628-8637
Website: www.whitman-walker.org/service/community-health/mautner-project
E-mail: info@mautnerproject.org

*Mental Health America*
(formerly National Mental Health Association)
2000 N. Beauregard St., 6th Fl.,
Alexandria, VA 22311
Phone: 703-684-7722
Fax: 703-684-5968
Toll-Free: 800-969-6642
Website: www.nmha.org
E-mail: webmaster@mentalhealthamerica.net

*Mental Health Association of Westchester*
580 White Plains Rd.
Tarrytown, NY 10591
Website: www.mhawestchester.org

*Mind*
15-19 Broadway
Stratford
London, E15 4BQ
Phone: +44-208-519-2122
Fax: +44-208-522-1725
Website: www.mind.org.uk
E-mail: contact@mind.org.uk

*National Alliance on Mental Illness (NAMI)*
3803 N. Fairfax Dr.
Ste. 100
Arlington, VA 22203
Phone: 703-524-7600
Fax: 703-524-9094
Toll-Free: 800-950-NAMI
(800-950-6264 Helpline)
Website: www.nami.org
E-mail: info@nami.org

*National Association of Anorexia Nervosa and Associated Disorders (ANAD)*
750 E. Diehl Rd., #127
Naperville, IL 60563
Phone: 630-577-1333;
630-577-1330 (Helpline)
Fax: 630-577-1323
Website: www.anad.org
E-mail: anadhelp@anad.org

*National Association of School Psychologists*
4340 E.W. Hwy
Ste. 402
Bethesda, MD 20814
Phone: 301-657-0270
Fax: 301-657-0275
Toll-Free: 866-331-6277
TTY: 301-657-4155
Website: www.nasponline.org
E-mail: center@naspweb.org

*National Center for Child Traumatic Stress*
Duke University
411 W. Chapel Hill St., Ste. 200,
Durham, NC 27707
Phone: 919-682-1552
Fax: 919-613-9898
Website: www.nctsn.org
E-mail: info@nctsn.org

*National Center for Victims of Crime*
2000 M St. N.W., Ste. 480
Washington, DC 20036
Phone: 202-467-8700
Fax: 202-467-8701
Website: www.victimsofcrime.org
E-mail: webmaster@ncvc.org

*National Council on Problem Gambling*
730 11th St. N.W.
Ste. 601
Washington, DC 20001
Phone 202-547-9204
Fax 202-547-9206
Toll-Free: 800-522-4700
Website: www.ncpgambling.org
E-mail: ncpg@ncpgambling.org

*National Eating Disorders Association*
165 W. 46th St.
New York, NY 10036
Phone: 212-575-6200
Fax: 212-575-1650
Toll-Free: 800-931-2237
Website: www.
nationaleatingdisorders.org
E-mail: info@
NationalEatingDisorders.org

*National Federation of Families for Children's Mental Health*
9605 Medical Center Dr.
Ste. 280
Rockville, MD 20850
Phone: 240-403-1901
Fax: 240-403-1909
Website: www.ffcmh.org
E-mail: ffcmh@ffcmh.org

*Postpartum Support International*
6706 S.W. 54th Ave.
Portland, OR 97219
Phone: 503-894-9453
Fax: 503-894-9452
Toll-Free: 800-944-4773
Website: www.postpartum.net
E-mail: support@postpartum.net

*Psych Central*
55 Pleasant St., Ste. 207
Newburyport, MA 1950
Phone: 978-992-0008
Website: www.psychcentral.com
E-mail: talkback@psychcentral.
com

*Psychology Today*
115 E. 23rd St., 9th Fl.
New York, NY 10010
Phone: 212-260-7210
Toll-Free: 888-875-3570
Website: www.psychologytoday.
com

*Royal College of Psychiatrists*
17 Belgrave Sq.
London, SW1X 8PG
Phone: 020-7235-2351
Fax: 207-245-1231
Website: www.mentalhealthuk.
org

*Suicide Awareness Voices of Education (SAVE)*
8120 Penn Ave. S., Ste. 470
Bloomington, MN 55431
Phone: 952-946-7998
Website: www.save.org

*Suicide Prevention Resource Center (SPRC)*
Education Development Center, Inc.
43 Foundry Ave.
Waltham, MA 02453-8313
Fax: 617-969-9186
Toll-Free: 877-438-7772
Website: www.sprc.org
E-mail: info@sprc.org

# *Index*

# *Index*

# O

obesity
  Alzheimer disease 503
  binge eating disorder 214
  bipolar disorder 126
  mental illness 82
  polycystic ovary syndrome 129
  prevention 69
  sleep apnea 590
obsessions
  anorexia nervosa 210
  body dysmorphic disorder 218
  obsessive-compulsive disorder 152
  PANDAS 436
obsessive-compulsive disorder (OCD)
  brain stimulation 333
  compulsive hoarding 155
  overview 152–5
  PANDAS 436
  psychosocial therapies 387
  Tourette syndrome 260
"Obsessive-Compulsive Disorder:
  When Unwanted Thoughts Take
  Over" (NIH) 152n
occupational therapy
  defined 434
  depression 629
OCD *see* obsessive-compulsive
  disorder
Office of Minority Health (OMH)
  contact 664
  publications
    mental health and African
      Americans 535n
    mental health and American
      Indians/Alaska Natives 535n
    mental health and Asian
      Americans 535n
    mental health and Hispanics
      535n
Office of Personnel Management
  publication
    persistent depressive disorder
      114n
Office on Women's Health (OWH)
  publications
    addictive behavior 226n
    caregiver stress 609n

Office on Women's Health (OWH)
  publications, *continued*
    depression and anxiety 38n
    depression and pregnancy 461n
    menopause 472n
    menopause treatments 472n
    mental health for men 445n
    premenstrual syndrome 452n
olanzapine
  atypical antipsychotics 129
  delirium 555
older adults
  Alzheimer disease 499
  depression 93
  mental health 263
omega-3 fatty acids, described 338
OMH *see* Office of Minority Health
opioid, defined 654
oppositional defiant disorder
  childhood mental disorders 381
  described 245
OWH *see* Office on Women's Health
oxcarbazepine
  anticonvulsant medications 318
  mood stabilizers 318
oxycodone, opioid use disorder 235

# P

palliative sedation, delirium 556
paliperidone, antipsychotics 316
PANDAS *see* Pediatric Autoimmune
  Neuropsychiatric Disorders
  Associated with Streptococcal
  Infections
"PANDAS: Fact Sheet about Pediatric
  Autoimmune Neuropsychiatric
  Disorders Associated with
  Streptococcal Infections" (NIMH)
  435n
panic attacks
  antidepressants 309
  described 150
  premenstrual dysphoric disorder
    456
panic disorder
  overview 149–51
  treatment 275
  *see also* anxiety disorders

688